CW00794027

THE CONSTITUTION OF EQU

The Constitution of Equality

Democratic Authority and Its Limits

THOMAS CHRISTIANO

OXFORD
UNIVERSITY PRESS

*This book has been printed digitally and produced in a standard specification
in order to ensure its continuing availability*

OXFORD
UNIVERSITY PRESS

Great Clarendon Street, Oxford OX2 6DP
United Kingdom

Oxford University Press is a department of the University of Oxford.
It furthers the University's objective of excellence in research, scholarship,
and education by publishing worldwide. Oxford is a registered trade mark of
Oxford University Press in the UK and in certain other countries

© Thomas Christiano 2008

British Library Cataloguing in Publication Data
Data available

Library of Congress Cataloging in Publication Data
Data available

ISBN 978-0-19-954903-0

For Aline and Joseph

Acknowledgments

This book has taken me over ten years to write so the list of acknowledgments is long. For enormously helpful discussion on all or nearly all the ideas of this book I thank my lifelong friends and philosophical companions John Christman, Houston Smit, and Andrew Williams. I thank Jerry Gaus, David Estlund, Clark Wolf, Andrew Altman, Kit Wellman, Andrew Cohen, Peter Lindsay, and Bill Edmundson for commenting on the whole manuscript at a wonderful conference on the manuscript at Georgia State University put on by Kit Wellman and Andrew Altman in February 2005. I also thank Matthew Clayton for very helpful comments on the whole manuscript. For discussions and comments on individual chapters that helped make this a better book, I thank Allen Buchanan, Jerry Cohen, Serena Olsaretti, Paul abu Habib, Julian Lamont, Joseph Chan, Charles Beitz, Jeff McMahan, Mark Philp, Sam Kerstein, Eleonore Stump, David Miller, Mark Fleurbaey, Dave Schmidtz, Will Braynen, Stefan Sciaraffa, Nicole Hassoun, Leif Wenar, Alyssa Bernstein, Mark Lebar, Gideon Yaffe, Mark Schroeder, Andrei Marmor, Geoff Brennan, Joseph Tolliver, Keith Lehrer, Josh Cohen, Michael Otsuka, Terry Price, Chandran Kukathas, Steven Wall, Jerry Postema, Joe Levine, David Golove, Paula Casal, Craig Duncan, Suzanne Dovi, and Susan Hurley.

I wrote this book with the assistance of a visiting fellowship at Oriel College, Oxford, in the Fall of 1997, a National Humanities Center fellowship in 1999– 2000, and a visiting fellowship at All Souls College, Oxford, in the Fall of 2004. The University of Arizona supported all this time off with sabbatical and other support. Chris Maloney, head of my philosophy department, has been unfailing in enthusiastically giving support in various forms. I also thank my editor at Oxford University Press, Dominic Byatt, for his patient and encouraging help in preparing the manuscript.

Contents

Introduction   1

1. The Basis of Equality   12

2. Social Justice and Public Equality   46

3. Democracy as the Public Realization of Equality   75

4. An Egalitarian Conception of Liberal Rights   131

5. Equality and Public Deliberation   190

6. The Authority of Democracy   231

7. The Limits to Democratic Authority   260

Index   301

Introduction

What are the moral foundations of democracy and liberal rights? Why is it important to make collective decisions democratically? And when the democratic decisions conflict with our own sense of what is just, what reasons do we have for setting aside our own views and going along with the democratic decisions? And what are the limits to this authority that democratic decisions have over us? These are the basic questions I attempt to answer in what follows.

Though democracy is a highly valued method for making collective decisions, there is little clarity regarding the grounds of the value of democracy. Most discussions of democracy either proceed as if there were no question of importance here or proceed on the basis of vague and unsystematic accounts of the grounds of democracy. The usual idea is that democracy is a good thing and that it should be a part of a just society. But the sense of its value is so strong that it seems to preclude reflection on the basis of this value.

And yet an examination of the grounds of democracy is essential if we are to understand the exact implications of our adherence to democratic principles. For instance, we need to know what the proper relationships between democratic and liberal rights are in order to have a solid foundation for the construction of a constitutional order. But it is unclear how we can have any such knowledge without a grasp of the values that underpin these rights. An appreciation for the normative grounds of democracy and for the basis of its authority can help us grasp the proper role of institutions of judicial review of democratic legislation in a democracy. Without a conception of the grounds of democracy we have very little but unsystematic intuitions to go on to settle these questions. And recent debates about the democratic deficit of international and transnational institutions often proceed without much in the way of systematic accounts of the nature and basis of democracy. Even if we are skeptical about the prospects for democracy in transnational institutions for the near term future, a proper grasp of the fundamental principles may guide our evaluation and design of these institutions.

Furthermore, an account of the grounds of democracy may help us respond to many who do not have allegiance to democratic principles. Opponents of democracy can be found among laissez-faire liberals who argue that nearly all major social decision-making ought to be left to market forces. And many argue that democracy has no intrinsic value and that institutions of collective decision-making ought to be shaped to bring about the best outcomes according to some particular account of what those best outcomes are. Obviously, if one accepts one of these major political views, one is likely to have a very different conception of what institutions a society ought to have than if we have a robustly democratic political theory.

It does not help the cause of democracy, nor does it advance our understanding of how to resolve disputes among these various political theories, simply to insist on the value of democracy. The only way to adjudicate these debates is to offer systematic accounts of the grounds of democracy and see how these accounts fare in comparison with the opposing views.[1]

The central animating contention of this book is the idea that democracy realizes public equality in collective decision-making. I argue that public equality, or the idea that the institutions of society must be structured so that all can see that they are being treated as equals, is the core principle of social justice. I will show that it is the moral foundation of democracy and the basis of liberal rights. Since it is at the basis of both democratic rights and liberal rights, I contend, the principle of public equality can ground the authority of democratic decision-making in a political society and it can show us where the limits of democratic authority can be found. So the principle of public equality both grounds the moral value of democratic decision-making and provides a just basis for constitutional limits on democracy. The idea of public equality, I argue throughout this book, provides the key to answering the central worries about the moral foundations and limits of democratic decision-making. These are the propositions I defend in this book.

For one thing, an account of the grounds of democracy can help us see how to respond to certain well-known objections to democracy. For example, many have objected to democracy on the grounds that it allows for the tyranny of the majority. But I will show in what follows that a proper appreciation of the foundations of democracy in public equality can lead us to understand the proper role of majority rule and the limits of majority rule in decision-making. In particular I will argue that the very same principle of public equality that underwrites democracy also underwrites basic liberal rights. And this fact, I claim, can help us see both the basis of the authority of democracy and the limits of that authority.

---

[1] An important exception to my claims above is the work of deliberative democrats inspired by the works of John Rawls and Jurgen Habermas. The most illustrious of attempts to find a systematic grounding for democracy is the work of Joshua Cohen, which I discuss in some detail in Chapter 5.

Others have argued that democracy is rule by the ignorant and ought to be replaced by elite rule. But I argue that the principle of public equality that grounds democracy can help us see why equality of citizenship is important. Public equality can also show how there can be a fruitful division of labor in society between ordinary citizens and expertise that preserves what is important in equality of citizenship while legitimating an important role for expertise in the making of law and policy.

In this book, I will offer a theory of the moral foundations of democracy. I will argue that democratic institutions have intrinsic moral value. They are essential to the public realization of equality in a political society. The main idea I want to defend is that democratic and liberal rights are grounded in the same fundamental principle of public equality. One cannot justify the one without the other. This parallelism of justification also implies a parallelism of structure. Liberal rights guarantee each person rights that give them the freedom with which they can act rightly or wrongly but which people have duties not to interfere with. In the same way, democratic assemblies have rights to make decisions, which are sometimes just and unjust but which citizens must nevertheless obey. Democracy has real authority over many issues that arise in a democratic society and this authority is grounded in the preeminent importance of the principle of public equality in evaluating political societies. So though the citizen attempts to advance justice and the common good according to her lights, she rightly accepts the decision of the democratic assembly as authoritative even if it goes against her sense of what ought to be done. I will argue, however, that there are certain standards of justice that not even fully democratic decision-making may violate. These standards constitute the limits to democratic authority. And the ground of these standards is the very same principle of public equality that provides the moral justification of democracy in the first place. All of these ideas, I contend, are grounded in the fundamental moral principle of public equality that animates social justice. Hence, I claim to give a moral vindication of the authority of democracy and the limits of that authority.

THE BASIC IDEAS

I begin by defending and explaining the basic principle of public equality. My starting point is a defense of the principle of equality as one of the basic principles of justice. Justice is grounded in the dignity of persons and it thereby demands that each person's well-being be advanced but that no person be sacrificed for the sake of the greater good of others. The proper response to the equal dignity of persons is to advance the interests or well-being of persons equally. Justice demands that the well-being of each person be advanced equally or at least that all persons have available to them equal basic conditions for advancing their well-being. And these principles give the most fundamental aim of social and political institutions: to advance the common good and to make sure that each person's well-being is advanced equally.

When we attempt to realize equality among persons in a political society regulated by laws that guide the actions and deeply affect the welfare of every person in society, we are required to do so in accordance with a public conception of equality. Political society establishes social justice among its members through its system of rights and duties and its distribution of burdens and benefits. It does this primarily by setting up institutions regulated by law. But it must do so in a way that each person can see that he or she is being treated as an equal in the process. Hence, the members of society must be treated in a publicly clear way as persons whose well-being matters and whose well-being matters equally.

But how can a society achieve this publicly clear realization of equality? The most pervasive facts of our experience in any moderately complex society are the facts of diversity in the conditions of each person's well-being and disagreement about our interests, the nature of justice, and what will promote the common good and justice. Our experience has shown us that we are all deeply fallible in our efforts to come to an understanding of our own interests as well as those of others and the common good. Moreover, we know that our conceptions of the interests of the members of society and how the common good is to be conceived tend to reflect the limited conditions of life that we have experienced and thus tend to be cognitively biased toward our own well-being. How, amid all this disagreement, diversity, fallibility, and cognitive bias can we hope to structure a society in such a way that each citizen can see that he or she is being treated as an equal?

Democracy and basic liberal rights along with a guarantee of a decent minimum of economic resources, I contend, are the most fundamental and indispensable principles for achieving this public realization of the equal advancement of the well-being of citizens. They treat persons as equals in a way that each person can see, precisely because they acknowledge the multitude of differences between persons and respect those differences. Democracy and liberal rights do this by giving each person a say in the shaping of the world he or she shares in common with others and giving each person a say in shaping the conditions for the realization of his or her own individual interests. Though the moral foundation of my account of democracy and liberal rights as grounded in public equality is individualistic, the implications of the account are not exclusively individualistic. I argue that the principle of public equality that grounds liberal rights can provide some grounds under certain circumstances for protecting the interests of persons as members of certain marginalized groups in society.

The fact that democracy and liberal rights both are necessary to the realization of public equality is what underwrites the thesis that democracy has authority over issues over which there is substantial disagreement and the thesis that democracy's authority is limited by the necessity of maintaining public equality. The account of the authority of democracy and its limits grounds some basic guidelines for the design of a constitutional order that realizes public equality. Hence, the idea of public equality provides the foundations for democracy and some instances of judicial review over democratically made legislation. Public equality can also help us understand the claims of certain highly politically marginalized groups in political society such as indigenous peoples in the Americas. I argue that the existence of a persistent minority in collective decision-making implies that the democratic assembly fails to satisfy public equality fully. This too suggests a limit to the authority of the democratic assembly and thereby implies that steps must be taken to afford the minority greater political autonomy or greater say in collective decision-making, depending on the particular situation.

HOW THE ARGUMENT WORKS

The arguments I offer in this work are of a variety of sorts. On the one hand, the argument of this book is a partly foundationalist one. In part, the argument relies on the intuitive strength of the initial starting premises concerning the dignity of persons and the importance of well-being in the argument for equality. Also, the accounts of the fundamental interests of persons are meant to be intuitively compelling starting points in the arguments for publicity, democracy, and liberal rights. These elements are meant to provide relatively uncontentious starting points for my arguments for equality, publicity, democracy, and liberal rights as well as the accounts of the authority of democracy and its limits.[2]

---

[2] It is important to note that the relation of ground to consequent is not necessarily a relation of premise to conclusion. The latter relation, in order to be legitimate, must start from premises that are more evident to the audience than the conclusion and this relation will depend on the audience. The relation of ground to consequent is not based on the idea that the ground is more evident to some particular group of persons. It is an account of the objective relations that exist among values. Sometimes one principle is grounded in another less evident principle as is the case between democratic and liberal principles and the principle of equality. In my argument for equality, the relation of ground to consequent corresponds to the relation of

But the argument has strong coherentist elements as well. The elucidation of the grounds of a principle can help us understand that principle better than we had previously understood it even if the ground is less evident. And I try to show this in the case of the grounds of democracy. For I show that democracy's grounds are the same as those of liberal rights. And this has important implications for how we are to conceive of the relations between these two systems of rights. In my view, the grounding of democracy and liberal rights in the principle of public equality provides a satisfying solution to many long-standing problems of political theory. Furthermore, I take it as an important desideratum that a basic moral and political theory has a unified core of grounding principles that illuminate all the parts of the view. While I do not agree with Sidgwick that this is a sine qua non of moral theory, I do think that it is a good thing if you can get it. And I claim in this book to have achieved this in some measure by showing that democracy and liberal rights are grounded in public equality.

In addition, my conception of the grounds of democratic and liberal rights is meant to provide a good explanation of what I take to be the complexity and fine-grained nuance of the phenomena that I am trying to account for. The history of liberal and political institutions should provide some abstract guidance to the theorist in determining how a normative theory about these institutions should be constructed. So I take it as an important desideratum of a political theory that the principles that it supports can account for the complexity and nuance that we see in the actual institutions and practices that we have experienced. This guidance is very abstract; it need not be conservative in the sense that the institutions that exist are the right ones. But the theory must be able to explain for instance why liberal rights have the complex structure they have.

The accommodation of the fine-grained texture of liberal rights and democratic rights is a result of the central importance of the requirement to advance the well-being of persons in the main social and political institutions. In this respect, my view shares something with classical utilitarianism. It shares a respect for the empirically discernable and multifaceted conditions under which well-being can be advanced. Many political theories fail to do this because there is little room in their approaches for anything other than a priori argument. They tend to produce inflexible and crude principles that simply are not capable of dealing with the rich diversity of empirical conditions that we face in political life.

premise to conclusion. The dignity of persons and the corresponding principle of well-being are both grounds of, and premises in an argument for, the principle of equality. The principle of equality is ground of democracy and liberal rights but most would not accept that it is a more evident principle than the principles of democracy (although some would).

At the same time, I claim to capture the idea that there are certain limits founded in justice to what one may do to persons in a political society. Thus my approach attempts to avoid the excessive flexibility of a consequentialism that justifies sacrificing some individuals for the sake of others. The principle of equality when combined with the importance of the well-being of persons simultaneously accommodates the rich empirically graspable diversity of moral and political life while setting strong constraints on how one may treat persons. Thus I claim, in part, to reconcile considerations that have seemed to many to support consequentialism with considerations that have seemed to support a more deontological approach. This reconciliation will be most evident in Chapter 4.

This empirical aspect of the arguments I make in this book implies that they depend fairly heavily on ideas that require empirical testing to be fully defensible. I invoke ideas about cognitive bias in persons, the fruitfulness of debating opposite points of view in the democratic forum as well as the idea that people can see that they are being treated publicly as equals in a democratic society. These ideas are essential to the argument but I cannot provide a full validation of them here. They require extensive empirical research. Unfortunately, the research on these hypotheses has been thin in many cases and is still in the process of being developed. I invoke some of the research where I can and I invoke historical evidence at other points. At times the argument simply relies on commonsense ideas. Good political theory is necessarily a mix of empirical and purely moral components. What political philosophy must do is provide the underlying ideas of justice and the good and it must provide a map that gives us pointers as to what kinds of empirical research needs to be done to fill out the overall political theory. This is the most we can expect from philosophy in political theory. It is only one part of an overall division of labor in the construction of an adequate political theory. This makes the conclusions somewhat tentative and revisable in the light of new empirical evidence. It also makes the basic approach highly receptive to new and surprising empirical research.

So the arguments I offer in this book are meant to have a multifaceted methodological base. Considerations of foundational principle mesh with considerations of rational unity and considerations of respect for the long experience societies have had with political institutions. And all of these considerations are meant in the end to hang together in a coherent whole.

Finally, this book does not pretend to provide a complete theory of justice or the good society. What it does claim to do is to provide the most important principles of a complete theory of social justice. Many issues remain undiscussed. For instance, I do not discuss the relative merits of different desert conceptions of justice. Nor do I discuss the many important debates about multiculturalism though I do attempt to show what space there is for this in the theory of democracy. This is because the principal focus of the theory is on the foundations of the authority of democracy and the limits of the authority of democracy. In my view, many of the substantive issues of justice are ones that must be debated within the democratic forum. The theory defended here does have implications for these debates. It states that these debates must be framed within a fundamentally egalitarian theory. And it states that for the most part different theoretical contributions on these issues ought to be offered in the democratic forum where they can be discussed among equals. And in the last chapter, I argue that the kinds of cultural, social, and political cleavages in society that produce persistent minorities in democracies are serious moral challenges to the authority of democracy and thereby provide some important space for the claims of marginalized minorities.

OUTLINE OF THE CHAPTERS OF THIS BOOK

In the first chapter, I provide a fundamental argument for the principle of equality of advancement of interests that underwrites the principle of public equality and thereby the whole theory of democracy, liberal rights, and the basis of the authority of democracy and its limits. The animating idea behind this principle is the conception of the person as a being that has a special worth not to be sacrificed for the sake of other persons. My conception of the person provides the basis for an account of the well-being of the person and of the importance of advancing the well-being of each person. This conception of the person also provides the basis of what I call the generic principle of justice and the principle of well-being. I add support for the principle of equality by defeating what is probably its most serious challenge: the leveling down objection. Though I do not fully examine the principle that each should receive in accordance with his or her deserts, I do argue that such a principle must be subordinate to the principle of equality and that the principle of equality should be seen as the fundamental framing principle of justice.

In Chapter 2, I take this highly abstract and impersonal principle of equality and show how it must be used to guide the establishment of justice in society. The task of the chapter is to defend the basic principle that must constrain any kind of effort to realize justice in a society. The principle of publicity, which has ancestors in a variety of basic principles of law, constrains the realization of principles of justice by requiring that those principles be ones that people can see to be in effect. Thus the maxim, justice must not only be done, it must be seen to be done. I show how this principle can be defended with the help of the principle of equality and with the help of a conception of the function of principles of social justice as well as an account of the basic facts and fundamental interests that are brought into play when justice is to be realized in a particular society. From these arguments, I defend a principle of public equality or the public realization of the equal advancement of interests.

The principle of public equality is the central principle in all the arguments that follow. It is on the basis of the principle of public equality that the arguments for the justice of democracy and liberal rights are grounded. It is also on the basis of the importance of publicity to social justice that I ground the authority of democracy and the limits of the authority of democracy in Chapters 6 and 7.

In Chapter 3, the main purpose is to show that democracy is one of the necessary conditions of the public realization of equality in any moderately complex society. Here I call on the basic facts of social life and some of the fundamental interests that are peculiarly salient in this context. First, the basic facts I call on are the facts of diversity, disagreement, fallibility, and cognitive bias. These facts about persons in societies color everything that we must think about how to structure the society. Any theory, I contend, that does not attempt to accommodate these facts in its conception of how to establish justice in society is fundamentally flawed. Furthermore, there are fundamental interests that stand out when these facts are taken into account. First, the interest each person has in correcting for the cognitive biases of others is essential. Second, the interests that each person has in making the world he or she lives in a home are fundamental to the advancement of the well-being of that person. Third, each person has interests in being able to learn the truth as far as possible about their interests and about the common good and justice. Finally, each person has a fundamental interest in being recognized and affirmed as an equal among other persons. These facts and interests and the basic principle of public equality, I contend, support the most important thesis of this book: that social justice requires that there be a collective decision-making process for the whole society and that each person has by right an equal say in the collective decisions of their society.

I also consider a number of minor and two major objections to my account. The first major objection I consider is the view that laissez-faire property rights are the best way to distribute power equally against the background of basic facts and interests that I have elaborated. This view states that the best way to treat persons as equals is to disaggregate power and allow only a minimal state. I argue that this approach is incompatible with the underlying principle of equality. Next, I consider the objection that political power is best distributed in proportion to the knowledge citizens have. This is the most plausible competitor principle to democracy as it ties in to the importance of knowledge in decision-making and it suggests a possible role of desert in collective decision-making. Knowledge seems to be a relevant desert basis when it comes to distributing political power. I show that the principle that power must be apportioned to knowledge cannot be justified given the underlying principles I have defended.

In Chapter 4, I defend an account of basic liberal rights on the foundations of the principle of public equality and an account of the facts of social life and the basic interests people have in liberal rights. It defends an account of the nature and basis of the fundamental liberal rights of freedom of conscience, freedom of private pursuits, freedom of association, and freedom of speech. One of the main results of the chapter is to show that liberal rights can be grounded in a way that is parallel to the democratic rights. Liberal rights are best understood as partly realizing public equality once the basic facts of diversity, disagreement, fallibility, and cognitive bias are taken into account and the interests that people have against the background of these facts are laid out. My account of liberal rights simultaneously explains the complexity and peculiar structure of liberal rights and the fact that liberal rights are trumps against many other interests people have in social life. My account also attempts to show how important liberal rights are while taking due account of the costs the exercises of liberal rights impose on people in society. I also attempt to respond to some natural objections that will occur to the reader. And I try to show that there is some space within my conception of liberal rights for accommodating the concerns of marginalized groups.

In Chapter 5, I attempt to understand and ground the place of deliberation in a just liberal democratic society. Up till now I have argued that the principle of public equality requires that citizens have democratic and liberal rights in society. I give an account of the role of deliberation in democracy and defend a view of how public deliberation can be justly undertaken. In the chapter, I deal with one of the principal rivals to my account of democracy. Many proponents of deliberative democracy have argued that in addition to the equalities I have defended, citizens ought to act in accord with what is called the principle of reasonableness, which says roughly that a reasonable person only proposes terms of association to his fellow citizens on a shared basis of justification. Citizens, this account asserts, must defend proposals for social organization only on grounds that other citizens can reasonably accept. This principle has been defended in a variety of ways. I argue that all the various arguments are deeply problematic and I argue that the considerations adduced in a number of the arguments actually end up opposing the principle of reasonableness once they are properly understood.

In Chapter 6, I argue that not only is democracy a highly desirable method of making decisions, it is a method that has authority over a wide range of issues. Once again, the principle of public equality is the key to appreciating this thesis. My account of democracy says that democratic decision-making has intrinsic value. But it also allows that the results of democratic decision-making can be assessed independently of the process of decision that produced them. This sets up a possible conflict between the intrinsic value of democracy and the values of the outcomes. What are we to do when we grant that the decision was made democratically but we disagree with the outcome and believe it to be unjust? My argument here shows that the democratic values should win out in these circumstances and that democracy therefore has authority. The democratic assembly has the right to make decisions and even mistaken decisions. Each person has a duty, grounded in public equality and owed to the democratic assembly, to go along with the decision even when he or she disagrees with it.

In Chapter 7, I discuss the limits and principal failures of democratic authority. Here I give an account of the nature of the limits to democratic authority. I show that there are certain things that the democratic legislature may try to do that undercut its claim to authority in those instances altogether. Here my accounts of the grounding of democratic and liberal rights in public equality and the parallelism of these grounds play a crucial role. I show that when a democratic assembly attempts to violate the basic democratic rights or liberal rights of its citizens, it no longer realizes public equality. As a consequence, I argue, it no longer has authority in that instance. It forfeits its right to rule in that instance. These are the negative limits of democratic authority. I also argue, however, that the democratic assembly weakens its authority by failing to ensure that each citizen has a decent minimum of economic resources with which to live a good life and that the democratic assembly weakens its authority when permanent minorities are formed in the society that never get their way in the democratic assembly. The failure to provide a basic minimum can be seen by all to be a violation of public equality and so is the existence of a persistent minority, or so I shall argue. All of these limits and principal failures are grounded in the principle of public equality that underwrites the authority of democracy in the first place. Hence we have a highly unified and nuanced account of the nature and basis of democratic authority and of the limits of democratic authority.

1

The Basis of Equality

The basic institutions of society are charged with the task of advancing the interests of all members of society equally. A just society advances the interests of all persons in it and it advances the interests of persons equally. This basic principle of justice is the moral foundation of democracy and liberal rights. A person's right to participate in the shaping of the world she shares in common with others, which characterizes a well-functioning democracy, is grounded in her fundamental interests as a member of political society. Most importantly, equality in political rights is grounded in the principle of equality in the advancement of the interests of it members. No political society can rightly claim to advance the interests of its members without giving them a say in how it is organized. And no political society can justly claim to advance the interests of its citizens equally without giving each citizen an equal say in the shaping of its institutions. In a parallel way, a person's rights to the freedoms of conscience, expression, and association and to the protections afforded by the rule of law are also grounded in his fundamental interests. And the equal rights to these freedoms are founded on the equal importance of each person's fundamental interests. The principle of equality of advancement of interests is the basis of democratic and liberal rights. Without the principle of equality and a conception of the fundamental interests of persons in society, no secure defense of the intrinsic worth of democracy and liberal rights is possible.[1] And a correct understanding of the interests of persons in society and the principle of equality is sufficient for understanding the basis of democracy and liberal rights. The rest of this book is devoted to demonstrating that the principle of equality and the fundamental interests of persons in society are the grounds of democracy and liberal rights.

But what is there to be said in favor of equality and how are the main objections to this principle to be overcome? It is essential to provide an argument for the idea that equality in the advancement of interests is the principle of distributive justice because many have rejected this principle

---

[1] I have argued that the principle of equality is necessary to ground the intrinsic worth of democracy in my *The Rule of the Many* (Boulder, CO: Westview, 1996), chapters 1 and 2.

and because it is so important to the evaluation of political societies. Such an argument can also help us see how one main objection to equality—the leveling down objection—can be met. Some have objected to the principle of equality of advancement of interests on the grounds that it implies that everyone should be made worse off if that is the only way that equality can be achieved. In this chapter, I sketch a defense of the principle of equality of advancement of interests. The argument proceeds by showing that justice is grounded in the dignity of persons. The dignity of persons, properly understood, grounds some main principles at the root of justice and these main principles ground the principle of equality in the distribution of well-being. Then I will undermine one objection to the principle of equality. Once we see how the principle of equality is grounded we will see that it is a common good principle: it does not permit leveling down for the sake of feasible equality.

Another objection has led some to resist the idea of equality: the disruptive interference objection. Some have argued that equality must be rejected because it seems to justify continual and disruptive interference in the lives of persons in order to maintain equality. I respond in part to this objection, first, by defining more clearly the role of the principle of equality and its relations with the rights and duties that characterize the relationships of family, friends, and colleagues. Second, in the rest of the book I will show that once equality is properly understood it can be shown to be the basis of a constitutional order in which each person has an equal say over the world she shares with others and which respects fundamental freedoms and the rule of law. Far from sanctioning continual and disruptive interference with people's lives, the principle of equality provides the grounds on which the security and freedom of the person can be guaranteed.

In what follows, first, I lay out the concept of the person that grounds the main principles of justice on which equality is based. Second, on the basis of this conception of the person, I defend each of the main principles: the principle of equal status, the principle of well-being, and the generic principle of justice. Then I defend the thesis that there are no relevant differences among persons under certain circumstances. Third, these principles are then shown to ground the principle of equality. Fourth, I address the objection that a principle of sufficiency is superior to a principle of equality. Fifth, I elaborate on the role of the principle of equality in relation to other special moral roles. Sixth, I address the leveling down objection. I show why this objection matters and why it fails. Finally, I show how certain basic conceptions of distributive justice relate to the principle of equality defended here.

PERSONS

The importance of justice, of giving each person her due, is grounded in the dignity of persons. This value cannot be fully grasped if we attend only to the values of pleasure or other forms of utility, as utilitarians do. In addition to the values of pleasure, happiness, beauty, and others that can be promoted, we must acknowledge another kind of value that is not primarily to be promoted and that is the value of *humanity*. The fact of humanity confers a special status on most human beings, a dignity which ought to be honored.[2]

The humanity of a person is that person's capacity to recognize, appreciate, engage with, harmonize with, and produce intrinsic goods.[3] It is in virtue of this feature of human beings that they bring something unique and distinctive to the world. They are capable of seeing the value in the world. They see the values of life, beauty, natural order, and pleasure among other things. They are also capable of appreciating these values. They enjoy them; they celebrate and affirm these values. And, the appreciation, enjoyment, and love of valuable things are in themselves of great value. Human beings are also capable of engaging with these values and harmonizing with these values. They can make their lives be in harmony with the values of life and beauty and they do this because they appreciate and love these values and want to be part of a world that includes them. They are also capable of producing valuable things. They produce justice, beauty, culture, and happiness in others. They do this once again because they appreciate and love these values.

The relation of persons to value is distinctive. There are objects in the world that have value independent of persons and these objects are appreciated and enjoyed by persons. So there are person-independent values. But many objects of value are created through the self-conscious activity of persons. Social justice, knowledge, art, friendship as well as the appreciation and enjoyment of valuable things are products of self-conscious activity. These are person-dependent values. Persons do not merely cause these things to come about as say a river causes the conditions of life to come about; they realize these things self-consciously and through their own activity because they appreciate them. And it is the fact that they bring them about self-consciously, and as a result

---

[2] See Philip Pettit, "Consequentialism," in *A Companion to Ethics* for the helpful distinction between promoting and honoring.

[3] The notion of humanity I sketch here owes much to Immanuel Kant's conception of humanity in his *Groundwork of the Metaphysics of Morals* [(Cambridge: Cambridge University Press, 1990) trans. Mary Gregor with introduction by Christine Korsgaard]. It is also quite different in that the value of humanity, in my view, connects human beings with the realm of value in the world and is not the ground of all value, as many Kantians would have it. I have critiqued what I take to be the Kantian conception of the dignity of persons in my paper "Two Conceptions of the Dignity of Persons" in *Annual Review of Law and Ethics* (forthcoming, 2008).

of their appreciation, which gives the values their special quality. Consider the difference between looking at a particular formation of stone as merely a natural object and looking at that same formation as the product of a self-conscious attempt to realize beauty and express something about the values of life by a human being. We can appreciate the beauty of the natural rock formation, but when we look at it as the product of self-conscious human activity and as displaying an appreciation of value, it takes on a whole new dimension of value.

This new dimension of value derives from the fact that we are thinking of the human being as a kind of authority in the realm of value. They are authorities in the realm of value in two ways: one, they are uniquely capable of recognizing and appreciating value as well as self-consciously producing it and two, their exercise of this authority is itself intrinsically valuable. This authority is analogous to the authority of a judge, who has the capacity of determining what the law is or what qualifies for an award or prize and is able to bring about changes in the world in accordance with that determination. But the authority of persons also has intrinsic value when it is exercised. For, there is intrinsic value in the recognition and appreciation of intrinsic value as well as in the self-conscious production or creation of value.

The idea that persons have dignity because they are authorities in the realm of value introduces a distinctive kind of value insofar as the person has value in addition to the various exercises of her capacities and her mental states. By analogy, we value the love that someone has for us because it derives from an independent being who loves self-consciously and authoritatively. And we value the work of art because it comes from the artist. In the same way, the value that human beings bring to the world in their appreciation of the world is partly constituted by the fact that it comes from independent beings that are authorities in the realm of value.

It is the fact that human beings have this highly significant authority in the realm of value that gives them a special status in the world. We can see this from the following two observations. To fail to acknowledge the special authority of human beings in the realm of value is to cut oneself off from all the values that are realized in this way. Think again of the stone sculpture. If we were to think of this as merely the product of natural forces, we would recognize and appreciate beauty but we would fail to see something fundamental about its value. It is only once we see it as the product of a human being and we think of this human as not merely being a set of causal forces but in addition being a kind of authority in the realm of value that we come to see the full value of it.

This conception of persons as authorities in the realm of value implies that to treat persons as mere means for bringing about more of the goods they produce (such as appreciation of intrinsic good, creation of intrinsic good) is to fail to acknowledge their special status. And to sacrifice them for the sake of other intrinsic values is also to fail to acknowledge their status. It is a status that may not be sacrificed or used merely for the sake of these goods because it is more important than they are. It is more important than they are because it is the main ground of their value. Again, the analogy with the lover may be helpful. To use the lover as a means to acquiring love is to miss a fundamental dimension of what love is all about. It is because the appreciation of the values in the world comes from a being with the kind of authority human beings have that the appreciation is so important. Indeed, the appreciation, harmonization with, and production of value by human beings derives its distinctive character and value from the fact that it is an activity engaged in by a being that has the kind of authority human beings have.

There are two different aspects of this value that are worth repeating. One is that human beings have a special worth as existing things. Hence, their worth goes beyond the mere valuing of events and states of affairs that is characteristic of consequentialist reasoning. It is in virtue of certain essential properties of these substances that they are due a certain kind of treatment. This idea of what is due or owed to something does not work with events or states of affairs. We do not owe states of affairs or events anything; these are not the sorts of things to which something can be owed or due.

The second feature that is important is that the nature of the worth of persons is not primarily expressed by talk of the promotion of this value. The primary form of valuation of these kinds of beings is honoring or respecting or acknowledging the dignity of these kinds of beings. Of course, this is consistent with saying that it is important that human beings continue to inhabit the earth and that their survival be promoted.

The only way to acknowledge the special status of human beings as authorities in the realm of value is to make sure that what happens to them and what we do to them be responsive to their special worth when we deal with them. In other words, it is the status in virtue of which we must make sure that we give each his or her due. And what is due to this kind of being is that it be enabled to exercise its enormously valuable authority, or so I shall argue.[4]

---

[4] The notion of the status of humanity that I have sketched here bears some resemblance to the idea of the status of inviolability that has been discussed by Francis Kamm in "Non-Consequentialism, the Person as an End-in-Itself, and the Significance of Status," *Philosophy and Public Affairs* (Autumn 1992), pp. 354–399 and 385. It is also similar to that discussed by Thomas Nagel in "Personal Rights and Public Space," *Philosophy and Public Affairs* (Spring 1995), pp. 83–107 and 91. The status of humanity, in my view, supports a distributive principle. Whether it supports constraints on how we may treat persons in particular cases cannot be addressed here. It may be that the status of humanity constrains what we may do to bring about justice. In that

EQUAL STATUS

Human persons have *equal moral status*. Since the status of humanity derives from the fact that humanity is a kind of authority in the realm of values, equal status is based on the fact that human beings all have essentially the same basic capacities to be authorities in the realm of value.

This does not mean that they appreciate the same values. The realm of value is an extremely pluralistic world. No one can experience and appreciate more than a small proportion of that realm of values. Indeed, to be able to appreciate many of the values of the world requires the kind of discipline and focus that rules out appreciating many other values.

The question of how to establish the truth of the equal moral status of persons is one of the most profound problems of moral philosophy and, to my knowledge, has not been answered completely. In the context of the view that I am defending here, the problem is made difficult by the fact that people are obviously differently capable of appreciating intrinsic values. Some, it would seem, are more capable than others in this respect. One might ask, since the status of persons is based on the possession of the distinctive capacity to appreciate value, why cannot difference in status be based on difference in capacities?[5]

I cannot say that I have more than a few remarks that might help build an answer to this question. The first observation is that the worth of persons far outstrips in importance any of the values that any particular person can produce, hence it cannot be gauged merely in terms of the amount and quality of the values a person is capable of producing. This is implied by the idea that persons have dignity. If this is true, then though some may be more capable of appreciating and producing more value than others each person's possession of dignity is itself of such great significance that differences in how much they can appreciate are of marginal significance. The second observation is that the world of value is so pluralistic that it is hard to compare the values of the products of different people or at least the capacities to produce value. This, of course, is primarily an epistemic and practical difficulty but the difficulty may be so deep for us human beings that we cannot do better than fall back on equality of status.

---

case, it would play a role in the process of establishing justice among persons in actions practices and institutions. I discuss the establishment of justice in detail in chap. 2.

[5] See Richard Arneson, "What, If Anything, Renders All Humans Equal?" in *Singer and His Critics* ed. Dale Jamieson (Oxford: Blackwell Publishers, 1999), pp. 103–28, and see Jeremy Waldron, *God, Locke and Equality* (Cambridge: Cambridge University Press, 2002) for incisive discussions of this issue.

The third observation is that the inequalities in abilities we see in the world around us are almost entirely the result not of difference in capacity but in external circumstances. The development of these capacities can be suppressed in particular persons as a result of poor education and other highly adverse circumstances, but this speaks not to the worth of the capacity but of the external circumstances.

These remarks do no more than gesture at a possible argument and they are unsatisfactory as they stand, but I will have to leave the issue and proceed as if the idea that persons have equal moral status is a well-established premise.

PERSONS AND WELL-BEING

That well-being is a fundamental good can be seen from the fact that societies are devoted to realizing the common good and that the common good is to be understood in terms of well-being. Well-being can also be seen to be a fundamental good once I say a bit about what I take to be well-being. I understand by well-being that quality of a person's life that involves an appreciative and active engagement with intrinsic goods. In addition, well-being requires that a person enjoys or takes pleasure in or is happy with the appreciation and active engagement with intrinsic good. Hence a person's well-being is enhanced when that person is enjoying the experience of a work of art. Or a person's well-being is enhanced when that person happily acts morally. The account of well-being presupposed here is neither entirely subjectivist nor objectivist strictly speaking. It includes an objective factor and the subjective appreciation of the objective good as it is realized in the person.[6]

In terms of the conception of humanity I have just sketched, the well-being of a person is, broadly speaking, the happy exercise of the distinctive authority of persons. We can see why well-being ought to be promoted. It is an intrinsic good that contributes to the good of the world.

This idea of well-being brings together two quite distinct aspects of our thought about the good of a person. On the one hand, it captures the fact that well-being is a good that is good for a person. In this respect to say that a person's life is a good life is not sufficient for saying that that person has well-being. For it may be that the person does many good things and does so self-consciously but is miserable in doing so. So, the man on the rack may be doing what he knows to be the right thing but to the extent that he suffers in

---

[6] For an account of well-being that is very similar to the one here, see Stephen Darwall, *Welfare and Rational Care* (Princeton: Princeton University Press, 2002), chapter 5.

doing so and does not enjoy the doing of the right, he does not thereby have well-being. This is because though his life may be good, it is not good for him. This goodness for him can only be had if that person enjoys the good.

This account of well-being, though it is grounded in intrinsic good, can explain the conceptual distinction between acting well and acting for one's self-interest. A person may sacrifice his well-being on this account for the sake of a greater good.[7]

The second thought this idea of well-being is meant to bring out is that well-being is a special kind of intrinsic value. First, to the extent that there are intrinsic goods, the appreciation of intrinsic goods is itself valuable. Second, to the extent that enjoyment of intrinsic goods is a fuller way in which we, as embodied human beings, can appreciate intrinsic goods, the enjoyment of intrinsic goods is not only intrinsically good in itself, it constitutes an essential part of the fullest realization of our natures as authorities in the realm of value. It gives us an account of the flourishing of persons.

So the account of well-being on offer, then, brings together two central thoughts about well-being: the fact that it is good for the person and the fact that it constitutes the flourishing of the person.

In addition, this account of well-being explains why well-being is important to justice. To honor the distinctive authority of the person is to ensure that it happily exercises that authority in its life. Ensuring the happy exercise of its distinctive authority is a fitting response to the fact that a person has that distinctive authority. To the extent that well-being consists in the happy exercise of the distinctive authority of human beings and each person is due the exercise of that distinctive authority, well-being is due each person.

The more a person has well-being, in general, the better. Each person has an overall good that is an unattainable maximum at least for practical purposes. But how much well-being ought we to try to ensure that a person has? This is not immediately determined by the fact that more well-being is better than less for each person. That is why well-being is an indeterminate principle. The nature of well-being does imply that a person ought to have his or her well-being advanced. But the principle of well-being does not specify exactly how much for most circumstances. We need other principles to determine this.

---

[7] The same cannot be said, I think, for Joseph Raz's account which asserts that a person's well-being consists in the successful and wholehearted pursuit of rational aims. Raz's account seems to me to suggest the paradoxical assertion that the man on the rack has well-being (on the rack). See Raz's *The Morality of Freedom* (Oxford: Oxford University Press, 1986). Raz does include a notion of enjoyment in the idea of a person's self-interest, so this idea is close to the notion of well-being I am defending here. See also Robert Adams, *Finite and Infinite Goods* (Oxford: Oxford University Press, 1999), chapter 3, for another similar conception of well-being.

TWO BASIC IDEAS OF JUSTICE

Two fundamental ideas about justice play key roles in my argument. The first is that justice consists in each person receiving his or her due. I will call this the *principle of propriety*. The idea behind this is that justice is concerned with ensuring that each person has what is due him or what it is fitting that that person have. What is due a person is grounded in some quality of the person that gives the person a certain status or merit. The idea is that inasmuch as the person possesses a certain status or merit, it is fitting that the person have a certain thing. This is what the person is due. The idea is close to the ideas of rights and desert, though it is more abstract and more fundamental than either of these notions. On the one hand, the idea of what a person is due establishes something like a claim that person has on the things that are due him. On the other hand, the ideas of rights and desert are notions that flesh out and articulate what a person is due in particular moral theories. But the basic idea is that justice is concerned with persons having those things that it is fitting that they should have. There is a kind of bond, a bond of fittingness, between the features of the person and the treatment justice requires, which is characterized as what the person is due.

For example, many have thought that it is fitting that a virtuous person be happy or that a vicious person not be happy. Here the idea is that happiness is the virtuous person's due and unhappiness is the vicious person's due. Virtue and vice are relevant qualities of persons, many have thought, because of which a person ought to be happy or unhappy. Happiness has been thought by many to be a fitting response to virtue and unhappiness a fitting response to viciousness, on these accounts.

I have argued above that the fundamental characteristic of human beings in virtue of which justice is owed them is their dignity. And this dignity is grounded in their humanity or the fact that they are authorities in the realm of value. And I have argued that the fitting response to this dignity is to enable persons to exercise their distinctive authority and to enjoy that exercise. So what is due to a person is that that person's well-being be advanced. This leaves it unclear as to how much the well-being of a person ought to be advanced when we take the well-being of others into account. This is where the principle of generic justice comes in.

The second principle is the commonly accepted principle that one ought to treat relevantly like cases alike and relevantly unlike cases unlike. This principle, called the *generic principle of justice*, is sometimes taken as directly supporting a principle of egalitarian justice. Many authors infer a principle of egalitarian justice once they have shown that there are no relevant differences between persons. I want to show that this inference, in the form that it usually takes, is mistaken but that there is a good version of the inference.

The generic principle regulates those reasons that accord specifically with the principle of propriety. First, as a regulator of reasons, it requires that one act in accordance with the relevant reasons relating to a particular situation and it requires that one's treatments of different situations be consistent with the same set of reasons. It requires that one's treatment of situations be in accord with the reasons that apply and not with irrelevant considerations. And since the reasons are general, when two situations are relevantly alike, the reasons that apply are the same.

Second, the generic principle of justice concerns reasons that are given by the principle of propriety. So it tells us to treat persons who are relevantly similar alike. And it requires that the relevant similarities and distinctions among persons that justify similar or different treatment be ones that are connected with what is due to a person. The properties of persons in virtue of which they are to be treated similarly or differently from others may not be incidental or merely relational properties of those persons. They must be qualities or features that display a distinctive worth or status in the persons. What is due to a person is what ought to be done or ought to be had by a person by virtue of meritorious features or features that display the worth or status of the person that are relevant to the ownership. What the person is due is a fitting response to the worth of the person in question.

The reason this principle is a generic principle is because it is a schema into which any consideration of justice can fit. But it is a principle of justice because it requires that the features that determine relevant likeness and unlikeness among persons in virtue of which the same or differential treatment of them is justified are features that ground what is due to a person. So it is not a mere principle of consistency. One way in which it is different from a mere principle of consistency is that it requires us to ensure that the actions which are due to people are the same or different, depending on the sameness or difference of the relevant qualities of the person. One may think that it is perfectly consistent to love one person and not another person, even though they are the same in the relevant respects. One has only so much love to go around. There would be nothing irrational in this. But considerations of justice are not like this. This is because considerations of justice are grounded in qualities of persons that make certain treatments due to those persons. It is not a relevant reason, as far as justice is concerned, for treating one person one way and another a different way that one does not care about the other person, or that one does not have any more time. The reasons that justice deals with have their sources in the persons who are being dealt with. So the reasons are grounded in the persons and, as a consequence, the relevant likeness and unlikeness must be qualities of the persons who are the subjects of justice. As a consequence, the generic principle of justice (including the principle of propriety) is grounded in the special status of persons. To fail to act in accordance with the generic principle is to treat some person in a way that is not fitting to that person given how one is treating everyone else.

Let me illustrate the way relevant meritorious qualities function in reasoning about justice by way of a contrast with utilitarian reasoning. Utilitarianism at least logically permits that one do something harmful to one person in order to advance the interests of others. One might suppose that there are circumstances where harm to one person will benefit others while the very same harm to another, who is similar in other respects, will not benefit others. E. F. Carritt's example of a utilitarian judge who convicts an innocent person of a crime in order to stop some great evil comes to mind here.[8] On a utilitarian principle, this could be quite consistent with insisting on not convicting an innocent person under other less dangerous circumstances. Now the mere principle of reason that says treat like cases alike, with no restriction on the nature of the likeness, would not rule out that one harm the one and not the other.

But this action would not be just, whatever else one might think of its justification. And the reason it would not be just is that it predicates the difference in treatment between the two people on the basis of something that is not a difference of merit or status between the two. It predicates the treatment of the one on the basis of something that somehow does not have to do with his distinctive worth. Justice, in contrast, requires that what we do to people should depend on morally relevant facts about their status or merit. And the generic principle, to the extent that it includes the principle of propriety, requires that the differences and similarities among people that ground different or similar treatments ought to be a fitting response to the worth or status of those people.

Of course, utilitarianism requires that one take each person into account or into consideration. Each person is to count for one and no more than one. The utilitarian takes each person's well-being into account when deciding what to do. But the decision itself does not require that one suit the action or the event to the person. The result of the utilitarian calculus is such that the action or event that is decided on for a particular person may be justified because of its effects on another person. So even if a person's well-being has been taken into account, the utilitarian decision may be to sacrifice that person for the sake of another's well-being or for the sake of many other persons' well-being. The actual treatment of that person is not suited to that person. And it is

---

[8]   See E. F. Carritt, *Ethical and Political Thinking* (Oxford: Clarendon Press, 1947), p. 65.

precisely this that the principle of propriety forbids. It says that the treatment of a person or the event that occurs to a person must be somehow fitting for that person.

We can see that prioritarianism does not satisfy the generic principle either. It allows for the sacrifice of some for the sake of the overall good, where goodness is understood as a decreasing function of well-being. As a consequence, prioritarianism countenances inequalities even if they are not based on considerations connected to the merit or status of the person. This does not show that there is no room for prioritarian considerations in thinking about what to do, it just says that prioritarianism is not a possible conception of justice and that it may often recommend what is unjust. To the extent that justice is a fundamental moral concern, this shows that prioritarianism is at variance with a fundamental moral principle. It also shows that the principle of equality that I defend below is not a version of prioritarianism.

It is also worth contrasting the generic principle of justice with Rawls's difference principle. Rawls argues that social and economic inequalities can be justified to the extent that they work to the benefit of the worst off. Some will be justifiably better off than others if this is necessary to make the others better off. As I see it, this cannot be a principle of justice, since it predicates the greater advantages to some on the basis of factors that are not grounded in differences of merit between persons. It does not ground the just differences of treatment of persons in differences between those persons. Hence it does not accord with the generic principle of justice. That said, it may well be that Rawls's difference principle is a principle of justified injustice.

The generic principle is a *second-order principle*. That is, it is a principle that regulates the operation of other principles. And in some cases the principle merely requires a second-order equality. It functions in a merely second-order way when *determinate* normative considerations already apply to the cases at hand. Determinate normative considerations are ones that yield determinate requirements on action in a way on their own. An example of a determinate normative consideration is the consideration that one ought to comply with one's contractual obligations. Here, what one is required to do is specified exactly by the contract. And this requirement is dependent only on the conditions for a valid promise and not otherwise on the context in which it is found. Of course, determinate normative considerations are only *pro tanto* considerations so they may be overridden by other considerations.[9]

---

[9] The generic principle of justice does have some bite even in the case of determinate normative considerations. For in the case of considerations of justice, the principle imposes a constraint of *generalization* over what is due to persons on the agent's reasoning. For example, if one believes that each person is owed the complete product of the things that he or she helps produce, then one will not be able to satisfy everyone's claim and the principle is self-defeating. Or a principle

But, as we have seen above, the principle of well-being is an indeterminate principle; it does not specify exactly how much well-being each person ought to receive. It only says that more well-being is better than less.[10] In the case of the principle of well-being, the generic principle has a substantive effect on determining the correct principle of justice. Instead of implying that each person ought to receive the same treatment where the treatment is defined prior to the operation of the generic principle, when the principle is applied to well-being, it requires a distribution of well-being in proportion to the relevant differences in merit or status of persons.

NO RELEVANT DIFFERENCES

We have seen that persons are fundamentally equal in that they have equal moral status. What kinds of differences are relevant reasons for treating people differently in particular with respect to their well-being? The usual relevant reasons are connected with considerations of desert, reciprocity, productivity, and need. A relevant difference between two persons with regard to how they ought to be treated will include whether one person deserves more than another or one person is more productive than another or one person is needier than another. These are the traditional bases of differential treatment.

In order to establish no relevant differences uncontroversially, I propose an initial narrowing of the scope of the argument. The argument is to be applied to people before the age of adulthood. At this stage in life, it is normally thought that individuals are not deserving of greater fundamental goods than others nor are people's relative productivities thought to be such that they entitle them to greater shares of fundamental goods.[11]

---

of justice that required that each person have unlimited liberty would also be self-defeating. So the generic principle of justice imposes a constraint of generalization on determinate normative considerations, which may, in effect, defeat certain such considerations.

[10] In this sense, the principle of well-being might be thought to be determinate to the extent that it recommends maximizing a person's well-being, taking nothing else into account. But when we consider what to do concerning the well-being of others, the generic principle would initially recommend the principle that one maximize each person's well-being. But this is impossible and so the generic principle must select levels of well-being for each person that are consistent with the generic principle. Another way of trying to make the principle of well-being a determinate principle is to introduce a principle of sufficiency. I will argue against this possible strategy below.

[11] One relevant difference that merits discussion but that I discuss elsewhere is inheritance. For those who regard private property as a basic component of justice and who assert that that right includes a full right of bequest, one child might have a right to greater resources

To determine the exact age at which we think that a person becomes capable of deserving more than others or not is not essential here as long as the persons beneath the age of maturity are still capable of appreciating intrinsic value. My inclination is to say that the ages of 16–18 are the right ones for this transition but it is compatible with this argument that the ages are 12 or 14. Furthermore, that I am defending equality beneath one of these ages should not be taken to imply that I think we should accept a principle of desert or a principle of productivity above these ages. I have grave doubts about either of these principles at any age. And, in any case, my suspicion is that once the egalitarian argument I am making has been accepted, the only principles of desert or productivity that can be accepted are ones that are very close to a principle of equality for whole lives. I will have more to say about this later. People beneath these ages are nevertheless capable of well-being to a significant extent and this is the quality that is relevantly similar among them when the other considerations do not differentiate them.

Now we can see that the conception of the equal dignity of persons grounds the fundamental value of well-being and the generic principle of justice (which includes the principle of propriety). Once we add the principle that there are no relevant differences among persons, we can see the argument for equality.

EQUALITY

The principle to be defended is the principle that well-being ought to be distributed equally by the institutions of the society. The generic principle of justice coupled with the equal status of persons and the no relevant difference thesis and the principle of well-being give us all the necessary premises for defending this principle. They are the grounds of equality.

The key idea is in two parts. One, we ought to advance the well-being of persons and two, if there is a reason for any person to be brought to a certain level of well-being, then the same reason holds for every person to be brought

than another because someone has given those greater resources to him. See Robert Nozick, *Anarchy, State and Utopia* (New York: Basic Books, 1974) for a view of this sort. See also John Christman, *The Myth of Property* (Oxford: Oxford University Press, 1994) and G. A. Cohen, *Self-Ownership, Freedom and Equality* (Cambridge: Cambridge University Press, 1995) for some quite persuasive criticism of this whole approach. I critique this approach in my "A Foundation for Egalitarianism," in *Egalitarianism: New Essays on the Nature and Value of Equality* eds. Kasper Lippert-Rasmussen and Nils Holtug (Oxford: Oxford University Press, 2007).

to that level of well-being. Once we have ruled out relevant differences, only equal status comes in to determine how much well-being each person ought to have. The generic principle rules out maximization of well-being over all because this does not ground what is given to each in what is due to each. And it rules out maximization of each person's well-being separately because this kind of maximization cannot be generalized. And the principle of well-being rules out sufficiency, as we will see in the next section, at least for the cases that arise in the world as we know it. The question is, does the generic principle determine the level we ought to bring about when we are dealing with the principle of well-being?

Since we are concerned with advancing well-being, we need to select levels of well-being for each person until we come to the point that is consistent with the generic principle of justice and the absence of relevant differences and equality of status. The only such point is equality of well-being. Hence, there is a reason for a person to be made as well off as possible consistent with everyone else being that well off. Any other distribution of well-being would violate either the generic principle of justice or the fundamental value of well-being or the equal status of persons coupled with the no relevant differences thesis.

Therefore, only equality of well-being is compatible with the fundamental value of well-being, the generic principle of justice, the equality of persons, and the absence of relevant differences between persons. Notice that without equality of status the generic principle coupled with the no relevant differences thesis does not imply equality. This is because the absence of relevant differences is not a sufficient basis for saying that the cases are alike. If there were no remaining equality when the relevant differences are ruled out, the implication of the application of the generic principle would simply be indeterminate. Furthermore, it is essential that for each person, more well-being is better than less, otherwise the concern with equality of well-being would be without point.

Here is a way of making this argument intuitive. If there are two people and we believe that one person ought to be better off than the other, it follows that we think that there is a reason for the better off person to be better off than the other and justice requires that this reason be a relevant difference between them. But, by hypothesis, there are no relevant differences and the persons have equal status, so it follows that the same reasons hold for each to be that well off. So, if the other person is not as well off, then that person is being treated in violation of the generic principle of justice or of his equal status. Hence, either the better off person does not have reason to be treated that way or there is a relevant difference or the generic principle is false. By hypothesis, there is no relevant difference between these persons of equal status, and the generic principle of justice is true. Therefore, the better off person does not have reason to be treated better than the worse off person. There is only one level of well-being that can satisfy the generic principle of justice, the fundamental value of well-being, and the fact of no relevant differences among equals and that is the level at which there is equality of well-being.

Here we have derived the principle of equality of condition from the generic principle of justice, equality of status, no relevant differences, and the fundamental value of well-being.

SUFFICIENCY

Many have objected to equality on the grounds that distributive justice requires only that each person have what is described as a sufficient amount of good. We might think that there is a level of well-being that we can bring about for people, which is enough or adequate for each person. And we might think that this principle can be made consistent with the generic principle at least under certain circumstances. There may be circumstances in which everyone has enough and then the generic principle conjoined with the principle of sufficiency can yield a determinate and plausible answer.[12]

Let us distinguish between two different levels of sufficiency that might be thought to fit the bill here. The first notion of sufficiency is the level of a *decent minimum*. This is the share of goods a person needs to live a decent life. It is generally thought to be above the level of mere subsistence but it is also thought to be beneath the level that would make a person as well off as possible.[13] A second level of sufficiency is a kind of *maximal sufficiency*. At this level a person has so much that one cannot make any further substantial contribution to that person's well-being.

The currency of sufficiency in my discussion is well-being. At the decent minimum a person is living a reasonably good life with what he has. People can have very different levels of well-being above this threshold. And the maximal notion is that level of well-being at which a person's life cannot be substantially improved. If we are dealing with a subjectivist standard, it is the level at which a fully informed person no longer cares if he has more than what he has. If it is

---

[12] See Harry Frankfurt, "Equality as a Moral Ideal," in *Equality* ed. Louis Pojman (Oxford: Oxford University Press, 1997), pp. 261–73, for this kind of view.

[13] See David Miller, *The Principles of Social Justice* (Cambridge: Harvard University Press, 1999) for a defense of this kind of principle.

an objective level of well-being, then it is a level beyond which improvements cannot be made except perhaps trivial improvements.[14]

There are some clear problems with the decency standard of sufficiency. If we accept the importance of sufficiency as part of a conception of justice, does justice have nothing to say when there are conflicts of interests above the level of sufficiency? Surely this cannot be right. An example of this might be the division of office space in an academic building. Suppose that each person thinks that a single office is quite enough for performing the tasks of doing research, receiving students, relaxing by listening to music, or reading a novel, and so on. Surely no one will quarrel with this. Now suppose that there are four separable and similar rooms to be divided between two people. The chairman gives one to one of them and gives three to another. He does not ground this difference on differential need or on greater merit. He reasons that one is sufficient for the one and three is more than sufficient for the other and there is no reason to be concerned about the inequality. The person with three offices will now have separate offices in which to receive students, work, and relax or read. Let us suppose that both can get along with only one office but that they both also like the idea of having separate rooms for separate activities. Is there no injustice here? Surely there is and one of these people will complain loudly about the unequal treatment over and above the adequate. Indeed, short of arguments connected with the common good or perhaps of greater need or merit, the idea is that a less than equal division is unjust.

Furthermore, since the decent level of sufficiency is greater than the level of biological need satisfaction, it is important to know what one must do when there are conflicts of interests among those who do not reach this level of sufficiency. The solutions to such conflicts require that one invoke a principle in addition to that of sufficiency. And this is, at least for most of human history, a large set of cases.[15]

Now if we take the maximal notion of sufficiency, then I think the sufficiency theorist has a powerful idea with which to criticize my argument. If there were a maximal level of well-being at which nearly everyone could be, then there would be no further reason to be concerned with equality or any kind of distribution above the level. So even if people were differently well off, there would be no reason to complain if everyone were at his or her maximal sufficiency level. Such a state of the world may be described as

---

[14] See Raz, *The Morality of Freedom*, for this kind of account.

[15] I do not want to imply that the notion of a decent minimum has no work to do. It may be that it identifies a threshold beneath which there is greater urgency in increasing a person's well-being. I am not sure about this because I am not sure that a nonarbitrary decent minimum can be defined. My point is only that this principle is not a suitable alternative to equality.

beyond the circumstances of egalitarian justice. The circumstances of egalitarian justice, I claim, are the circumstances in which people can be made substantially better off than they are. The aspiration to equality relies on the thought that the things we want to equalize are such that more of them are better than less. If some thing, of which the just distribution was in question, were not such that more is better than less, then who would care about equality? Justice may still be possible in such a world, because we might at least want to be sure that everyone does actually have the maximally sufficient amount, but equality would no longer matter once we were talking about the distribution of good over and above the level of sufficiency. So this notion of sufficiency does offer a substantial challenge to the argument for equality.

The relevant part of my argument that is inconsistent with the maximal sufficiency notion is the premise that asserts that persons are capable of an unlimited amount of well-being at least when we consider the circumstances of human life as we know them and as they are likely to be for the long-term future. The trouble with the maximal notion is that it does not seem that for now or ever in the past or for the long-term future, this level will be reached by many people, if any. Perhaps some can reach this level, but the vast majority of people will always be able to improve their well-being in substantial and important ways. There are always new ways in which we can improve our well-being. We know this because we have conceptions of worlds in which our well-being is vastly greater than it presently is. The idea of heaven in the world's monotheistic religions and the idea of enlightenment in other religions point to our capacity to grasp greatly improved states of well-being. Furthermore, we find that with every new technological invention and every new medical advance as well as with every new advance in our understanding of the sources of and forms of treatment of mental illness, we can see new ways of improving our well-being. And this is a very large set of cases. Human beings tend to have capacities for well-being that far outstretch what they have available to them. It is hard to see how, for most people, the maximal level of sufficiency can be met.

As a consequence, though the maximal level of sufficiency would imply a serious criticism of the argument for equality if it could be met for most people, that maximal level simply cannot be met at least in the world as we know it.

In general, then, the idea that there is an attainable level of sufficiency above which moral concern does not extend is implausible. So the idea that distributive concerns ought actually to be limited to a principle of sufficiency is also quite implausible since, on the decency standard, there are important questions of how to distribute good above and beneath the level of sufficiency.

And since no one or nearly no one can satisfy the maximal standard, the distributive question of how to distribute below that level is always the live issue.[16]

THE ROLE OF THE PRINCIPLE OF EQUALITY

It is important here to pause and reflect on the role of the principle of equality I have defended and to allay some worries that might arise in the reader. The principle of equality stands out as a fundamental principle when we take the impersonal point of view toward persons. When we step back from our particular interests, roles, and special relationships and we take a perspective on persons and their lives generally, we see that it is important that their well-being is advanced and that that well-being be advanced in a way that accords with justice.

But we might worry that this principle seems to eliminate any room for the rights and duties of special relationships or any space for the individual to cultivate her own life as she sees fit. The principle seems to permit or even require each person to ignore the special demands imposed on him in the special relationships he enjoys and it seems to license continual interference with the lives and relations of each person in the name of equality. I want to respond to these objections by defining the role of the principle of equality and its relations to our special roles and relationships. In the rest of this book, I try to show how the principle of equality grounds basic liberal and democratic rights.

The impersonal standpoint is particularly suited to the justification and evaluation of institutions, though it can have bearing more widely than that.[17] When we ask, for example, whether markets or democratic institutions are defensible institutions, we do not generally look merely from our own perspective or even from the perspective of ourselves as duty holders within the system. We ask whether the scheme as a whole is justified in terms of its overall impacts on the lives of persons. And we evaluate the system of duties and rights from that perspective. And the same holds for all the major institutions of society and the combinations of these institutions.

---

[16] See Paula Casal, "Why Sufficiency Is Not Enough," (*Ethics*, January 2007) for a lucid and much more detailed criticism of the principle of sufficiency. I provide a qualified defense of a kind of sufficiency principle in Chapter 7 where I argue that provision of an economic minimum is necessary to the public realization of equality and is a condition on the authority of democracy.

[17] Indeed, I think that the principle of equality extends beyond the evaluation of institutions. But I do not pursue this issue in this book.

The notion of treatment in the generic principle is a partly metaphorical notion because justice as I have described it does not normally impose requirements directly on each individual person. The principle I defend is an abstract and impersonal principle that allows us to evaluate what happens to people as a consequence of the overall institutional framework they live under. It says that there is something unjust in one person's life going worse than another's when there is no relevant reason for that difference. For example, we see it as clearly unjust when a child raised in a poor family and neighborhood faces far less opportunity for self-development and social advancement than children in wealthier circumstances. There may be little anyone can do about this in the short term, but there is still injustice there.

Moreover, as Thomas Nagel says, "Institutions, unlike individuals, don't have their own lives to lead."[18] So we rightly impose impersonal standards on institutions that we do not fully impose on ourselves as individuals. Hence, the impersonal standpoint is the right standpoint from which to elaborate principles for the assessment of institutions. But the impersonal standpoint, as I have argued, does not imply a fully consequentialist account of the standards we grasp from this standpoint. In particular, the key value of the dignity of persons can be apprehended from the impersonal standpoint and it implies limitations on what one can do to persons for the sake of the greater good.

The principle plays a large role in our lives not primarily by getting each person to try to ensure equality among all persons but by regulating the institutions that people live in. The principle does not require that each person abandon her roles and special relationships within society. Nor does it replace the special duties one owes to family, friends, and colleagues. So a father is not required to treat his son and the children of others equally. The principle invites us to think about how all the rights, duties, roles, and special relationships fit together in an overall institutional scheme so that people's interests are advanced and in such a way that they are advanced equally. It may require us to rethink our relationships and modify them, as has happened to all the elements of the institution of the family in the last two centuries. But in general it will not require us to abandon wholesale relationships so important to the well-being of each person.

---

[18] See Thomas Nagel, *Equality and Partiality* (New York: Oxford University Press, 1991), chapter 6, esp. p. 59, for the idea of a moral division of labor between institutions and individuals, where institutions are charged with the task of ensuring equality. I do not think that the division of labor can be quite as hard and fast as Nagel supposes for reasons given by G. A. Cohen in his "Where the Action Is: On the Site of Distributive Justice," *Philosophy and Public Affairs*, vol. 26, no. 1 (Winter, 1997), pp. 3–30.

While a parent cannot rightly be expected to treat the interests of her child and those of others as on a par in the normal course of her life, she is able to rise to a more impersonal perspective when asked to look at the arrangements in society overall. She can then see all parents and children as equals. People commonly do this as democratic citizens and sometimes even as participants in the making of constitutions. And when we find ourselves constrained by the operation of rules we see as just, we sometimes evaluate matters from this impersonal perspective and accept the outcomes even when our interests or those of our children are not as well advanced as they would be under less just institutions. Each person, on this view, does have a duty to play a role in trying to make the overall institutional arrangement in which they live just as well as to comply with just rules.

In the rest of the chapters of this book, I will attempt to show how the principle of equality I have defended along with a conception of fundamental human interests requires that individuals have a secure set of basic liberties with which to live out their lives and shape their relationships as they see fit. It also underpins the right to democracy within a constitutional order.

THE LEVELING DOWN OBJECTION

It has been said by some that the principle of egalitarian justice is subject to a fatal intuitive objection. The objection is that the principle of equality defended has an extremely implausible implication. Suppose two alternative states S1 and S2 are such that in S1 everyone is equally well off and in S2 everyone is better off than in S1 but some are better off than others. To some, the principle of equality appears to say that S2 is worse than S1 at least in the respect relevant to the principle of equality. This is because S1 is egalitarian while S2 is not. So S2 represents a departure from equality while S1 does not (Table 1.1). Thus the principle of equality appears to imply that, at least as far as equality is concerned, we ought to make everyone worse off. Of course, other principles may contend with equality and override its recommendation in this case. But the worry is that to the extent that the principle of egalitarian justice makes the recommendation that everyone be made worse off, that is a strike against the principle.[19]

---

[19] See Derek Parfit, "Equality or Priority?" *The Lindley Lecture* (Lawrence, KS: University of Kansas, 1991), p. 23, for an account of the objection. See also Jan Narveson, "On Dworkinian Equality," *Social Philosophy and Policy*, vol. 1, no. 1, pp. 1–22, and Harry Frankfurt, "Equality as a Moral Ideal," p. 266, for other sympathetic accounts of this objection.

Table 1.1.

	S1	S2	S3
A	2	7	5
B	2	3	5

WHY THE LEVELING DOWN OBJECTION MATTERS

This would be a real problem for the principle of equality, were it correct.[20] For most egalitarians seem to hold both to the idea that equality is important and to the idea that well-being is important (or at least opportunity for well-being or capacities for functioning). And these two judgments seem to come together in their egalitarianisms. For one thing, many egalitarians think that the promotion of well-being or at least the opportunities or access to well-being is important. This suggests that these egalitarians cannot be indifferent between two egalitarian states S1 and S3, which are such that everyone is better off (or has more opportunities or access to being better off) in S3 than in S1. Egalitarians must prefer the Pareto superior equality to the Pareto inferior equality, and that preference derives from the correct understanding of the principle of equality that I have defended, or so I shall argue. (See Table 1.1.)

Here is the argument for this thesis. There is an internal connection between the rationale for equality and the value of the relevant fundamental good that is equalized. If it were not true that more well-being is better than less, then there would be no point to equality. There would be no reason to care about equality. Since the importance of well-being or opportunity for well-being seems to be built in to the principle of equality—it is the reason for the principle taking the shape that it does—they cannot be indifferent between these two states.

To take an example, suppose that we are concerned with distributing bread among persons and we have much more than is needed. In this context there is a definite level at which each person has enough and beyond which more does not matter. In this context we would only be concerned that each receive enough of the bread and beyond that we would not care how much each gets.

---

[20] Not everyone agrees that this is a strike against the principle of egalitarian justice. Larry Temkin argues that there are other principles that may have strongly Pareto inefficient implications. Temkin cites principles of retributive desert that imply in some circumstances that everyone ought to be worse off than they could because they deserve to be worse off. He argues that many accept such a view despite its welfare diminishing character. See Larry Temkin, "Equality, Priority and the Leveling Down Objection," in *The Ideal of Equality* eds. Mathew Clayton and Andrew Williams (New York: St. Martin's Press, 2000), pp. 126–161, esp. p. 138.

Whether we distribute equal amounts of bread or not would be, in and of itself, a matter of indifference.

Of course, if we did not have enough for everyone, we might be concerned with equal distribution. So if we had enough for everyone to survive but not enough to satisfy everyone we would be concerned with the correct distribution of bread. But in this case, it is precisely because the amount of bread we have is such that more is better than less for everyone that we concern ourselves with its distribution.

Another example is a concern over how many letters people have in their last names. For the most part people are indifferent to how many letters they have in their names. As a consequence, they will be indifferent to quantitative distribution of letters in each person's name. Equality could not be important in this context.

So a necessary condition for equality mattering is that the thing being equalized is such that more is better than less. I want to argue that since the truth of the proposition that more substantial good is better than less substantial good is a necessary condition for the principle of equality in the substantial good having a point, the right account of the principle of equality must somehow include the idea that equalities in which everyone is better off are better than equalities in which everyone is worse off.

Clearly this proposition is not a conceptual one. One can imagine a principle of equality of shares in substantial good that does not concern itself with whether people have more of that substantial good. But the question is, does such a principle make sense? The things of which we care about egalitarian distribution are things that we want more of rather than less for everyone. And it is because we want more of rather than less of these things for everyone that we think that egalitarian distribution of these things matters.

Moreover, the principle of equality does not have any component that justifies lowering the welfare of a person (or the opportunity for welfare). It makes sense for some noncomparative desert principles to favor a Pareto inefficient outcome in those circumstances where everyone deserves to be badly off. But this is part of the value theory of these conceptions of desert. If every person in a society turned out to be vicious, then each might deserve to be badly off. And the introduction of a new set of resources that could make everyone better off would not be an improvement; indeed, on the desert theory if everyone were to be made better off than they deserved to be, that would be worse. On these views, it is better that a person who deserves it be worse off. We may reject this value theory, but it makes some sense. But there is no analogous feature in egalitarian principles.[21] The egalitarian theorists are not in the position of

---

[21] There may be some question about whether leveling down applies to comparative desert theories. Suppose that two people produce two things. One of these things is very valuable and

the noncomparative desert theorist. There is nothing in the value theory that says that it is better for a person to be worse off.

Because there is an internal connection between the importance of equality and the idea that it is better to have more rather than less of the thing being equalized, the leveling down objection is an objection that ought to be taken seriously by egalitarians, if it works. But I do not think that it works. And the fact that it does not work can be seen in a number of ways.

A GAP IN THE LEVELING DOWN OBJECTION

The leveling down objection derives its apparent strength from the claim that an egalitarian must think that something is lost when there is some inequality. This claim follows from the central egalitarian claim that all inequalities are unjust. And from this it is inferred that any egalitarian state must be better than any nonegalitarian state, at least in one respect. And from this it is inferred that there is one important respect in which an egalitarian state is better than a strongly Pareto superior state (one in which everyone is better off).

But, from the fact that there is loss from inequality it does not follow that any egalitarian state is better in respect of equality than any nonegalitarian state. What the egalitarian does need to say is that every nonegalitarian state is unjust because it is not equal. There is some (Pareto noncomparable) egalitarian state that is superior to the nonegalitarian state (even if it does not maximize utility or total good.)

Consider the three states: S1, S2, and S3 in Table 1.1. S1 and S3 are egalitarian and S2 is nonegalitarian. Both S3 and S2 are strongly Pareto superior to S1. S2 and S3 are Pareto noncomparable. But S3 is egalitarian and S2 is not. The difference is that in S2 at least one person is better off and another is worse off than in S3. All the egalitarian is committed to asserting is that there is something lost in S2 because all the people in S2 are not equally well off.

the other is only a little bit and the things cannot be divided up. Now we must distribute these things between the two of them. Now suppose that one of them is a bit more deserving than the other but the two objects are very different in value so that their distribution cannot fit the differential merits. Indeed, the only way to fit the merits would be to give the small object to the more deserving person and destroy the large object. This is because the more deserving person is only a little more deserving and the smaller object has only a little value. Would such a desert theory require the destruction of the larger, more valuable object?

Here we can see pressures in the direction of distributing the more valuable object as well as pressures in the direction of destroying the more valuable object. After all, some will say, the less deserving person deserves something. And if we distribute in accordance with the exact merits, the less deserving will not get anything. But if we make sure the less deserving gets something, the less deserving will get much less than he deserves at least by comparison with the more deserving.

This may merely imply that S3 is better or more just than S2. It is compatible with this to say that S2 is better or more just than S1 just as S3 is. And this set of claims is sufficient to ground the claim that for every inequality, there is something lost with respect to equality.

Of course, S3 may not be feasible but this is not a reason to think that failure to be S3 is not the defect in S2.[22] All that is needed for the egalitarian is to say that relative to some nearby possible equality that is set at a level of well-being in between that of the persons in the unequal state (perhaps at the average of the well-being of the two persons), the unequal state is missing something or is unjust because it is not equal. Justice does not obey the "ought implies can" principle entirely. In part it serves as an ideal to be approximated.

We can see this in a variety of contexts. We know that even the best penal system is likely to convict some innocent persons and let some guilty persons go free and we are inclined to think that these are injustices even though we cannot improve the system that makes these errors beyond a certain point. I think we can see it in a distributive case as well. If we have two persons who have contributed equally to the production of a pair of unequal but indivisible substantial goods, we may think that there is some injustice in giving the better good to one and the lesser good to the other. Each person in the circumstance will feel some regret at the imperfect justice of the distribution, even if they used a lottery to determine who gets what.

This is an egalitarian theory but it does not say that any equality is better in some respect to any inequality. It says merely that every inequality is unjust because it is not equal.

What my argument so far has shown is that there is a significant gap in the leveling down objection against equality. It has shown that a crucial inference is unsupported by the objector and that alternatives to that inference are logically possible. What I want to show in the next section is that the logically possible alternative missed by the proponents of the leveling down objection is in fact the one that the argument for equality I have provided supports.

What I argue for in the following is not a complete principle but a strategy for constructing such a principle. We do not have the time to construct a complete principle and I am not sure I can do it at the moment anyway. But it is a defensible strategy, which implies that there is some principle that satisfies the strategy, which is the correct principle of equality. It is sufficient to defeat the leveling down objection that this is a legitimate strategy.

---

[22] As I see it, a state of affairs can be unjust even if there is no way to improve it and we can have a conception of what is just under the circumstances even if we cannot bring about that justice. Justice does not obey the "ought implies can" principle entirely. In part it serves as an ideal to be approximated.

AN ARGUMENT FOR EQUALITY WITHOUT LEVELING DOWN

The first important extension of the argument for equality of condition generates an account of justice in the cases of unequal Pareto improvements
over feasible equality. I have in mind *strong* Pareto improvements, in which
everyone is better off, and *weak* Pareto improvements, in which someone is
better off under inequality than under feasible equality and no one is worse
off. There are a number of cases of this sort. In one sort of case, some goods are
lumpy, so we cannot achieve a completely egalitarian distribution. The second
case involves production. In such cases, the complexities and uncertainties of
production require that incentives be offered to those who are most suited to
the tasks to be performed. In this kind of case, inequalities arise as a kind of
by-product of the process of production.[23] My thesis is that if all persons can
be made better off than under the best feasible equality, then the principle of
equality I have defended implies that normally we should choose that state in
which some are better off and none are worse off than under the best feasible
equality.

First, I shall consider whether it is just to bring about a strong Pareto
improvement over feasible equality given the argument I have made above. So
I will compare just two states and I shall just consider this for two persons: A
and B. This is a narrow idealization but it is hard enough to grasp it properly.
The argument proceeds by comparing two states: S1 in which A and B are
equally well off and S2 in which both are better off than in S1 but A is better
off than B.

The strong Pareto improvement in S2 pushes us in a direction that does not
allow us fully to satisfy the constraint on reasons stated by generic equality.
There is a failure of justice in cases of unequal distribution. In our example,
either A is being treated better than the reasons allow in his case or B is being
treated worse than the reasons allow in his case or both of these claims are
true.

If we compare S1 (feasible equality) and S2 (strong Pareto improvement),
the generic principle of justice says that there is something wrong in S2
because it is not equal. But I want to say that there is something even worse in
S1 with regard to justice. And so we have reason to prefer S2 to S1, from the
point of view of justice. What is my reason for this?

The fundamental reason for this is that the principle of equality is partly
grounded in a concern for the well-being of each person. The argument I
gave in the first half of this chapter for the principle of equality requires the

---

[23] See my "Cohen on Incentives and Inequality," in *Ethics and Economics* eds. Christi Favor,
Gerald Gaus, and Julian Lamont (Buffalo: Humanities Press, 2000).

principle of well-being as an essential premise. And we have seen that equality seems to lack any point when the thing to be equalized is not such that more is better than less.

This idea can be captured in a conception of a plausible strategy for constructing a principle of equality that gives us a plausible account of greater and smaller departures from equality. The way I am thinking of this example is that both S1 and S2 may be unjust and thus departures from justice, but the question is, which one is a greater departure from justice? I will propose a strategy for constructing a principle that gives us a schematic account of how to assess the size of the departure from ideal equality.

The strategy for constructing the principle comes in two stages: first, the strategy calls for a rule identifying the ideal equality point in a given circumstance. Second, the strategy calls for a way of assessing departures from the ideal equality point.

THE IDEAL EQUALITY POINT

My proposal is that the rule identifying the ideal equality point in a given circumstance sets the equality point as a potential Pareto optimal point. That point is better than the worst off position in the best Pareto optimal inequality but not as good as the better position in the inequality. Since it may not be feasible, it is only potentially Pareto optimal. In the example we are discussing, we identify some ideal equality point called S3 in which B is better off than in S2 but A is worse off than in S2. And in S3 A and B are better off than in S1.

The circumstance in which we determine the ideal equality point is defined in terms of the best Pareto optimal state or that Pareto optimal state that has the highest average utility among all feasible states. The ideal equality point or complete justice is to be understood as an equal and Pareto optimal distribution of the goods that are present in the best Pareto optimal state.

The average point of well-being between A and B in S2 is the ideal equality point. This seems like a natural equality point for the circumstance because it equalizes all the welfare gains from the best Pareto optimal inequality. It is suited to the circumstance since it equalizes only those goods that are available in the circumstance. Hence it is not a purely utopian standard since it is suited to the circumstances in which the persons find themselves. At the same time, the ideal equality point has real bite as a principle of equality since it says that A's superior possession of good is unjust and should be redistributed to B. Still, the ideal equality point, though suited to the circumstance, need not be itself feasible though sometimes it will be. We can see that justice is not always feasible such as when two equally deserving persons create goods that are unequal in value and that cannot be divided up. They will both, if they are just, regard the unequal distribution as regrettable and in some sense wrong even if they both think that they should not waste the goods. So at the first stage, we identify the ideal equality point as the one at which both A and B are at the mean level of well-being of the Pareto optimal outcome.[24]

Just to be clear, the ideal equality point is not a mere ideal, it is the standard in the circumstance against which all states that fail to satisfy it are judged unjust. It could be called alternatively complete or full justice. States that do not satisfy it in the circumstances are unjust.

APPROXIMATIONS TO IDEAL EQUALITY

The second stage is to determine which departures from the ideal equality point are greater departures from justice and which departures are smaller ones. The smaller departures from justice are more just than the greater departures from justice. One can imagine many approximation rules here. One proposal is consistent with the requirement of leveling down that many people have worried about. It says, among other things, that all equalities are more just than all inequalities. This is an approximation rule. But it fails to register the importance of well-being (or any kind of substantial good) that is essential to the principle of equality. And so, it must be rejected as a rule of approximating the ideal equality point.

Instead of describing a rule here, I will describe what I take to be some plausible constraints on the construction of such a rule. These constraints mostly are implied by the argument I have given above for the principle of equality. The first and clearest constraint on the construction of such a rule is that the most just state of affairs in the circumstances must be the ideal equality point. So the rule will recommend the ideal equality point whenever it is feasible. This aspect of the rule follows from the fact that the ideal equality point is the fullest realization of equality in the circumstances at hand.

The second constraint on the approximation rule is that the rule must never favor Pareto inferior states over Pareto superior states. This aspect of the rule

[24] One way that I would argue we should not specify the principle is to say that the principle asserts that equality at the highest level of well-being is the only fully just arrangement. The reason for this rejection is that such a principle would not be distinctively egalitarian. This is because it would say what nonegalitarians could readily agree to, which is that Pareto improvements are to be pursued. I doubt if many want to disagree with that. What makes the principle of equality distinctive is that it recommends making some people worse off if that will make others better off and it recommends this up to the point of equality.

follows from the importance of the well-being of all persons that is essential to the principle of equality. And this aspect of the rule is what ensures that the principle of equality never implies leveling down.

The third constraint on the rule of approximation is that the rule does not track average or total utility. There will be cases in which some states are closer approximations to the ideal equality point than others even though the others have a greater amount of average utility. This aspect of the rule of approximation follows from the fact that the principle at issue is not a principle of average utility or total utility and so will prefer many egalitarian states that have lower average utility. But remember this condition is to be combined with the second condition that says that the rule never selects Pareto inferior states as more just than Pareto superior states. Thus the rule will select some states that have less average utility than others on condition that they are all Pareto noncomparable.

The fourth and final constraint on the rule of approximation tells us that the rule must not depart too much from the difference principle. This does not follow directly from any of the aspects of the principle of equality that I have defended. It is an intuitive idea about approximating equality. But it requires some explanation. One, I say that the rule must not depart too far from the difference principle because I think that some realizations of the difference principle get very close to leveling down and are what I call quasi-leveling down. For example, if we image two states of affairs such that in one each is equally well off and in the other one person is much better off while another is only a tiny bit worse off than in the equal state, the difference principle will favor the equal distribution. And we can make it so that the difference between worst off persons in the unequal state of affairs and those in the equal state of affairs is arbitrarily small though still significant. The difference principle will always prefer the equal state even if the advantage to the worst off is extremely small while the advantage to the better in the unequal state is must greater. This seems to me to suggest that the difference principle involves something like leveling down in some circumstances, what I call quasi-leveling down. Still, the difference principle in many circumstances does seem to give an intuitively plausible answer to the question of what the best approximation to equality is and so I say that the approximation rule should not be the same as the difference principle but it should not depart too far from it. Admittedly, this is a vague constraint, but my intention here is just to give a sense of what a rule of approximation to ideal equality is that does not imply leveling down. It is worthwhile noting here that this explains two features of the difference principle. One, it is not a principle of justice in the sense that it defines ideal justice in a circumstance. Hence, this approach departs from Rawls's conception of the difference principle as a principle of justice. Nevertheless, the difference principle does stand out in many circumstances as the best way to approximate full justice and so it can be thought of as a principle of justified injustice or even as a principle of the least unjust outcome (with the caveat noted above that it does not always pick out the least unjust state).[25]

I think it is intuitively clear that we can construct a rule that satisfies these four constraints. And when we do have such a rule we can be said to show that a plausible principle of equality does not imply leveling down.[26]

Notice that the principle of equality articulated in the above way will give us some practical guidance even in those circumstances where the ideal equality point is infeasible. It does this by telling us what feasible states are the most just approximations of the ideal equality point and thereby telling us what the least unjust outcome is in the circumstances. So the principle of equality I have elaborated does give us practical guidance even when the ideal cannot be achieved.

The strategy accords with the principle of equality I defended in this chapter because the ideal equality point is the product of the principle of well-being and the generic principle. The generic principle ensures that only equality is the ideal point; the principle of well-being ensures that the Pareto superior equality is more just than the Pareto inferior equality. And the method of assessing departures from equality in terms of total distance of well-being from the ideal equality point seems highly intuitive.[27]

This seems to me to give exactly the right result. The idea is that there *is* injustice in an unequal condition when there are no relevant differences between the persons between whom the inequality holds. But, there is *less* injustice in such an unequal condition than in an equal condition that is strongly or even weakly Pareto inferior.

But this shows how one can think that there is something lost and problematic in efficient inequality, and also think that it does not follow that egalitarians are committed to the proposition attributed to them in the leveling down objection. For that objection to work against an egalitarian principle of justice, it is not enough that the egalitarian is committed to the injustice of inequality. The leveling down objection applies to equality only if the egalitarian is also committed to the claim that inequality is worse from the point of view of the

---

[25] It should be noted here that prioritarianism in one form or another may deliver many of the same verdicts as the rule of approximation to equality I have constructed here. What is important to note, however, is that the prioritarian principle has no way to describe the unequal outcomes as unjust, which they are.

[26] Indeed, in a paper I am coauthoring with Will Braynen, we are constructing just such a mathematical rule of approximation. See Thomas Christiano and Will Braynen, "Inequality, Injustice and the Leveling Down Objection," *Ratio* (forthcoming, 2008).

[27] I thank Gideon Yaffe, Andrei Marmor, and Mark Schroeder for pressing me to clarify this argument.

principle of equality than a Pareto inferior equality. But it is this last claim that the egalitarian need not and indeed ought not be committed to, as I have argued.

Have I simply changed the question? I have responded to the leveling down objection by defending a principle that seems to avoid it. But is this really what egalitarians are after? Or is it a new principle? I want to defend the claim that it is the right principle of equality. Remember that an essential part of the rationale for the principle of equality involves the claim that more substantial good is better than less. The argument I have given for equality involves this essential premise. What would be the point of equality if this were not so? Given the internal connection between equality and the idea that more is better than less when it comes to the thing equalized and given the argument for equality that I have given, it seems reasonable to hold that this is the proper conception of equality.

EQUALITY, PRODUCTIVITY, AND DESERT

Does this principle extend beyond youth? It would appear that at least it extends to the point where considerations of desert and productivity arise. But does it extend to them as well? Here is a way in which it might. Each person's well-being matters equally and so conditions for well-being ought to be equal. Productivity and desert, if they are legitimate concerns of justice, are principles that imply relative increases or decreases of the well-being of each person. Therefore, each ought to have equal conditions for being productive and deserving *if* differential rewards to productivity and desert are legitimate principles by which the society is to be organized.

Is this an arbitrary claim about productivity and desert? I do not think so. Each of these principles requires that prior conditions be in place in order for them to be legitimate. In order for a person to be productive, a person must have those things that are necessary tools for productivity. The right to these tools cannot itself be given by the principle of productivity itself. The right must be given by a prior principle. To the extent that we have argued for the great and universal importance of equality of well-being, a right in each person to the conditions of productivity is implied by the principle of equal conditions for well-being. Should the right to the conditions of well-being also determine the shape of the principle of productivity as well? It is hard to see why not in the light of the previous considerations.

The same kind of consideration goes for comparative positive desert claims but for different reasons. Comparative positive desert claims can only be justified when there is a prior baseline that specifies that each person had some chance to engage in the deserving action. One person cannot deserve more in the comparative sense than another for an action he performed and the other did not, if the other person did not have the opportunity to engage in the action. That itself is not sufficient to show that equality is the necessary baseline. But desert does require a baseline and the principle of egalitarian justice determines justice in the absence of considerations of differential desert. It would appear that complete justice would require that at least at the start each have a chance to engage in deserving actions that is consistent with equal conditions for well-being.

What these remarks imply is that to the extent that the principle of equal advancement of well-being applies to youth, it also applies at least to the initial conditions for the operation of the principles of desert and productivity. If the principles of desert or productivity are legitimate principles, and I am not arguing here that they are, they must be constructed in such a way that each person has an equal opportunity to become more deserving of greater well-being or productive of greater well-being. Suppose that at the moment at which desert can begin to play a role in determining how well a person's life goes, some persons have greater chances than others to become deserving of more well-being than others. That seems to imply that the well-being of those favored persons is in some sense more favored than the well-being of the less favored persons. But, by hypothesis, there is no relevant difference between them such that one ought to be more favored with respect to well-being than the others. This is because we are considering them, as it were, at the moment at which desert will start to come into play. That moment is not one in which it has come into play and so it is regulated by the same principle as regulated distribution of well-being in youth.

It stands to reason that a theory that asserts that through youth well-being must be distributed equally among persons because there are no relevant differences between them will also assert that justice requires that the conditions under which desert of unequal shares can occur must also be distributed equally. Suppose that one person has had a thriving life as a consequence of having received a good education and a decent set of resources in youth with which to realize his talents while another has had a miserable life as a consequence of having received no education and little or no resources in youth with which to realize her talents. Their differing fortunes are due in significant part to differences in conditions in youth that favored one person's thriving and disfavored another's. Again, by hypothesis, there is no relevant difference between them that could justify these differing conditions for the achievement of well-being. And so this must be considered an injustice.

So the principle of equal advancement of well-being, even if it is to be supplemented by some principle of desert, has a reach that goes beyond youth. It is what we might call a fundamental principle because it places constraints on all other principles that might come into play. It sets initial conditions on the operation of the other principles.

But equality also constrains the other principles. For, the other principles cannot generate inequalities that are inconsistent with the demand that the inequalities be ones that anyone could have benefited from. My sense is that this constrains principles of desert to remain close to effort-based principles, because principles of desert that favored persons with a lot of natural talent are ones that do not seem to provide people with equal initial conditions with which to lead thriving lives. They seem to favor some right from youth over others even though there is no relevant difference between them.

Of course, differential abilities and circumstances that arise from effort and that subsequently benefit a person might be compatible with this constraint. And so significant differences in well-being that result from differential deserts are still compatible with the constraints the principle of equality places on other principles, should those other principles ever be defensible.

The other main aspect of this principle that I want to emphasize is its function as a kind of default principle of justice. That is to say, when other principles such as desert are not in play to help justify inequalities, justice requires equality. This proposition is a necessary consequence of the argument that I have given since when other principles do not come into play, there are no relevant differences that can justify inequalities. And since there is always the fundamental equality of status that requires equality when there are no relevant differences, equality is the fallback position.

This idea that equality is the fundamental principle that serves as initial condition, constraint, and default for other principles will loom large in what follows when we move from the impersonal and abstract principle of equality to the public principles that must regulate the establishment of justice in actual societies. For when we look to the establishment of justice in society as a whole, we will be first concerned to make sure that the institutions of society are structured fundamentally to advance the well-being of all persons equally. For the institutions of society frame the different possible life courses for persons. They frame the opportunities people face as well as the contours of the lives people can live. Even if we accept some inequality generating principles such as desert principles, the institutions must in some fundamental way give each person equal opportunities for success. Hence the institutions must be set up in such a way that the well-being of each person can be equally advanced.

CONCLUSION

So far I have argued that egalitarianism is the principle of justice that ought to regulate the distributions of goods during the preadult phase of life. I have also argued that equality of well-being is the basis for a kind of equality of opportunity for well-being at the onset of adulthood. And equality of well-being can only be suspended if there are defensible principles of desert or productivity that can justify inequalities. I have also argued that equality can be abridged (in a way that is consistent with its underlying rationale) when all can be made better off as a consequence. So we avoid the leveling down objection.

This chapter has only defended a very abstract principle of justice. I do not claim that this principle is all there is to be said about justice. I think that justice is something that must be established in the world through social practices and institutions as well as the actions of persons. But for this to be, justice must not only be done, it must be seen to be done. So justice requires publicity as well as fair distribution. It is when we combine the idea that individuals' interests ought to be equally advanced with the idea of publicity that we get a defense of democracy and liberal rights. It is to these topics that I turn now.

2

Social Justice and Public Equality

Democracy and liberal rights are the most important realizations of the principle of equality that lies at the foundation of justice. It will be the task of the next three chapters to show how the highly abstract and impersonal principle of equality grounds these fundamental social and political institutions. The idea that democracy and liberal rights are grounded in the principle of equality illuminates the consequences of the principle of equality and helps us understand the normative basis of democracy and liberalism as well as the complexity and subtlety of our normative thinking about these institutions. In addition, it will give us insight into the nature and basis of the political authority of democracy and the limits of that authority that are grounded in liberal rights.

   In order to show how democracy and liberal rights are grounded in equality I need to explain the ideas of social justice and public equality and show how they are grounded in the principle of equality and how they ground democracy and liberal rights in turn. By "social justice" I mean the justice of institutions and interactions among persons. Social justice is the attempt to realize the highly impersonal and abstract conception of justice as equality in the institutions and interactions among persons. My thesis in this chapter is that social justice requires that equality be publicly realized. That is, social justice requires that justice must not only be done, it must be seen to be done. In the case of justice as equality, it must not only be the case that people are treated as equals, they must be able to see that they are treated as equals. Hence, social justice requires what I call public equality. I argue that public equality is grounded on the principle of equality defended in the last chapter and the circumstances of disagreement, diversity, fallibility, and cognitive bias that attend efforts to implement the principle of equality in any moderately complex society as well as the interests that accompany these facts. That is the first stage of the argument for grounding of democracy on equality. In Chapter 3, I argue that democracy is one of the basic institutions that realize public equality. In other words, in a democracy people can see that they are treated as equals. That is the second stage of the argument. In Chapter 4, I will ground the liberal rights in public equality in a way that is parallel to the democratic rights. In Chapters 6 and 7, I will show how the principle of public equality can tell us when democratic decision-making has authority and what the limits to democratic authority are.

In what follows, I will explain what I mean by "social justice" and "publicity." I will show how the idea of publicity that I defend has deep roots in the legal traditions of constitutional democracies. I will then offer an account of the context in which the publicity of justice becomes especially important. Then I will provide a number of arguments for saying that publicity is grounded in the principle of equal advancement of interests. And I will respond to some objections along the way. I will conclude by articulating an account of how one shows that a particular principle is grounded in public equality.

SOCIAL JUSTICE AS A WEAKLY PUBLIC PRINCIPLE

The principle of equality I defend in Chapter 1 is a highly abstract principle of justice. It applies across the board to all human beings and other rational beings that have interests like the ones humans have. The main subject of this essay is *social justice*, by which I mean the justice of social institutions and relationships among persons. Social justice comes into play when persons attempt to establish justice among themselves in various forms of treatment including social rules, norms, institutions, and more informal interactions. Under these circumstances, persons set up rules so that they can make claims against one another to be treated in ways that display the equal importance of each person and his interests. Social justice is concerned with realizing the abstract principle of equality among persons in social relations.

Since social justice concerns the kinds of *claims* people can make against each other in determining the appropriate balance of benefits and burdens, social justice is essentially *a weakly public principle*. It is not enough that justice is done; it must be seen to be done. So the principle that requires that the basic institutions of society equally advance the interests of the members of the society must do so in a way that is compatible with this requirement. It must be given an interpretation that satisfies publicity. Before moving on to the argument for democracy, I will explain the idea that social justice must be public and the circumstances under which it is important and I will provide a defense of the necessity of publicity to social justice.

The weak notion of publicity demands that the principles of social justice be ones that people can in principle see to be in effect or not. The notion of "in principle possibility" here is to be specified relative to facts about the limitations on human cognitive abilities. To be sure, publicity does not require that each person actually see that he or she is being treated justly. It requires only that each person can see that he or she is being treated justly once the basic facts about our cognitive limitations are taken into account and given a reasonable informed effort on his part. So a principle that requires that we go beyond our ordinary cognitive limitations to determine whether it has been realized or not is not a public principle of justice. But a principle that a person can, given normal cognitive faculties, see to be realized if he makes a reasonable effort is a public principle even if the person does not in fact see it to be realized on account of not having made a reasonable effort or on account of ignoring the basic facts of cognitive limitation. In this respect the principle of weak publicity is like the legal principle that law must be publicly promulgated.[1] This principle does not require that everyone actually know what the law is; it merely requires that each person can know what the law is given reasonable effort.

PUBLICITY IN LEGAL SYSTEMS AND MORAL INTERACTIONS

The idea of publicity defended here is similar to, though not identical with, the ideas of publicity in the legal traditions of liberal democracies. First, the paradigm case of the need for publicity can be seen in the case of criminal justice. Here the most flagrant cases of injustice are the various ways in which criminal prosecutions and trials are held in secret. When a person has no opportunity to hear the charges or the evidence that the government has against him, the legal principle of publicity is violated in a fundamental way. It is unjust when the trial of a person takes place in secret, as in the case of a "star chamber" trial. Here a high premium is put on the idea that the charges and proceedings ought to be open to view to all who wish to take the trouble to view them. Most particularly, the charges, evidence, and proceedings ought to be open to the accused and the accusers as well as to independent judges

[1] Let us contrast this notion of publicity with John Rawls' notion. Rawls states that a society satisfies a public conception of justice when, "everyone accepts and knows that the others accept the same principles of justice, and the basic institutions satisfy and are known to satisfy these principles." This notion of publicity includes four separable conditions: (*a*) that everyone accepts the same principles; (*b*) that everyone knows that the others accept the same principles; (*c*) the basic institutions satisfy the principles; and (*d*) the basic institutions are known to satisfy the principles. In contrast to Rawls's conception of publicity, the idea I defend is a weak notion since it does not require agreement on basic principles of justice within a community. Nor does it require that the basic institutions be known to be just by everyone.

and juries. Each must be given full access to all the materials relating to the charges and the proceedings of the trial.

Another case in which the importance of publicity can be seen is the promulgation of the law. That the law must be publicly promulgated is one of the most fundamental principles of law. Each must be able to know what the law is and in order for that to be the case, the legislature must take certain steps to make the law public so that all persons who have the desire to know it can find it out for themselves.[2] This principle requires not only that the law be made available to people, it also requires that the law be clear and understandable to reasonable persons. Vague, ambiguous, and confusing law fails to meet this standard and most liberal democracies do not accept that such law can be fully authoritative.

It has also been a basic principle of modern societies that legislation must be made in a public way, that is, it must be made in a way that anyone who wishes to take the trouble can see how the legislation was made. They can sit in chamber while the legislation is made or they can read the proceedings for making legislation afterwards.

Conflict of interest laws also illustrate the importance given to publicity in modern societies. For conflict of interest laws and ethical standards not only attempt to avoid actual conflicts of interest, they also attempt to stave off the appearances of impropriety. The appearance of impropriety, when it could be reasonably suspected of government officials that they have violated some norm of government practice, is often sufficient grounds for the dismissal of government officials or rejection of their actions. Here the idea is that the activities of government officials must not only be open to inspection, they must be publicly above suspicion.[3]

Let us take an intuitive example. Imagine the case of a person who has borrowed money from another. When the agreed upon due date arises, the other person asks for her money. The debtor then truthfully says that he has paid the creditor already. But the creditor has no recollection of this. Now the debtor explains that he has put the money somehow directly in the creditor's

---

[2] This principle is explicitly formulated for trials and legislation in John Bouvier, *Bouvier's Law Dictionary* new edition by Francis Rawle (London: Sweet and Maxwell, 1898), vol. 2, pp. 793–4. See also William Blackstone, *Commentaries on the Laws of England* (Chicago: University of Chicago Press, [1765] 1979), book I, p. 46. The demand for the publication of the law was made in the early Roman Republic by the plebs against the patrician magistrates, who initially wanted to keep them secret. See Barry Nicholas, *An Introduction to Roman Law* (Oxford: Oxford University Press, 1962), p. 15.

[3] In modern law, references to the principle that justice must be seen to be done, cite Lord Hewart, in Rex *v.* Sussex Justices *ex parte* McCarthy, November 9, 1923, who states that "a long line of cases shows that" this principle is "of fundamental importance." See *Law Reports King's Bench Division*, vol. 1 (1924), p. 259.

bank account. The creditor, let us say, cannot determine this because there are too many transactions going in and out of her account. She simply cannot verify the deposit. And the debtor was quite aware of this when he deposited the money. Contrast this case with one in which the debtor pays the creditor back by giving her the money personally. Here everything is out in the open. The first case is a case of justice done but not seen to be done while the second case is one of justice being done and being seen to be done. What I want to say is that the first case is defective with regard to justice while the second is not. The first pay back is not worthless nor is it completely unjust, but there is a defect in its justice compared to the second case.[4]

What these examples do is serve to illustrate a number of features of publicity that are relevant to my principle of weak publicity. First, they each make the transparency of a procedure an ideal. Individuals are supposed to be able to see how the procedure works and how it has worked in each instance of its operation. They must be able to see all the main crucial considerations people use in employing the procedure. Trials must be conducted in a way that is transparent to those who are accused and the accusers as well as those who must judge of the guilt or innocence or liability of the accused. Legislation must be transparent in the sense that it must be possible to know that there is the legislation and what the content of the legislation is.

In addition the fairness of the procedures must be transparent. This is most clearly in view in the case of conflict of interest laws. Here, it is crucial that the fairness of the procedure be "above suspicion." If there is any reason to think that a public function is exercised in a way that raises suspicion concerning its fairness, it is thought that this is a reason for thinking the public function has been improperly exercised. Presumably, this is part of the rationale behind the publicity of trials and legislative decision-making. Making these functions transparent in the first sense gives people confidence that the functions are fairly performed. When legislation is made in a way that is impossible for many interested parties to see, there is suspicion that it is made in a questionable way. When trials are held in secret, the accused have reason to worry that they are being unfairly treated.

Finally, the standards of publicity listed above also imply the fundamental importance of ordinary, reasonable persons being able to grasp the law and the procedures for using the law as well as the fairness of the process. Laws and

---

[4] Of course, there are times when I do not care whether I can tell whether someone has paid me back. These examples do not undermine the idea that there is a failure of respect when actions done in satisfaction of my claim are knowingly performed in a way that in principle I cannot know about. And there are times when the person who is owed a certain treatment cannot know that the claim is being satisfied, such as posthumous promise keeping. But others who are trustees can find out and that should be sufficient.

procedures for using the laws are to be laid out in ways that are unambiguous, reasonably precise, and clear to ordinary citizens. Furthermore, conflict of interest laws are set up to avoid the appearance of impropriety to ordinary citizens. The public standard of evaluation of laws and government activities is whether intelligent and reasonable citizens can grasp what they are and whether reasonable citizens would suspect unfairness in the activity.

PUBLICITY IN SOCIAL JUSTICE

Unlike the legal and legislative examples above, the publicity I will argue for here relates to basic principles of *social justice*. The idea of weak publicity that I defend here is more abstract than the principles I have just discussed. It states that principles of social justice must be public. This means that the principles are such that institutions that realize these principles must be transparently in accord with the principles. It must be transparent to the persons involved that the institutions are treating them in accordance with social justice. This imposes constraints on the principles. They must be ones that people can see to be in effect in political or legal institutions. Another way of putting this is that the institutions that satisfy the principles of social justice must be able to display the fact of their justice to ordinary persons.

To the extent then that the fundamental principle of justice is equality, it must be the case that the institutions people live in can be seen by those citizens to be treating them as equals. And for this to be the case, the principle of equality must be given a public form, so that when it is realized, people can see it to be in play and can see it as a form of equality.

Publicity is not itself an independent good or requirement. Indifferent actions that are done publicly do not thereby become just. Nor do injustices become more just if they are public. Publicity is a dimension of those requirements associated with social justice. It is not a separable component of social justice. Publicity is a dimension on which one can do better or worse. There is justice in actions that have little publicity. In our example of the debtor who has paid back the creditor in a way that she cannot see, there is justice in his action, it is simply a defective justice. A lesser publicity makes a just action less just or defective with regard to justice. A greater publicity makes a just action more just or more complete with regard to justice. And the polarity reverses with reversals in justice. So a more public injustice is a greater injustice than a less public injustice. For example, if an injustice is in fact perpetrated on someone but those who have perpetrated it do not agree that it is an injustice (as long as their beliefs are held conscientiously and they fall within a certain range) the injustice is less than if all, including the perpetrators, rightly believe that it is an injustice. In these respects, publicity for societies is a bit like voluntariness for individuals. Just as the voluntariness makes a wrong action worse than an involuntary wrong action and a voluntary right action is better than an involuntary right action, so the action of a society that publicly does right is better than one that does right in a way that is not public. And a public injustice is worse than an injustice that is not public.

Finally, weak publicity requires only that people be able to see that they are treated in accordance with what are *in fact* the correct principles of justice. It does not require that her views about the basic principles of justice are correct. In our examples above, the creditor may, for some reason, believe that she is entitled to more than the agreed amount of money. So even if she is fully aware that the debtor paid his debt to her as their agreement specified, she may think that he has not acted justly because she has a (let us say) false conception of justice that requires debtors to pay back even more than what the agreement specified. In this case, the principle of weak publicity is still satisfied under the assumption that what the debtor did was in fact just and what he did was publicly accessible to the creditor.

Here it is important to lay aside a potentially misleading feature of the idea of publicity of social justice. To say that social justice must be public does not imply that all the activities of the state must be transparent. All that it implies is that reasonable citizens can see that the basic institutions of the society are treating them justly. There may be defensible kinds of secrecy in a just society, which are compatible with public equality. Most obviously those kinds of secrecy that are necessary for the proper fulfillment of the state's activities as for example in the case of some aspects of diplomacy. Some kinds of secrecy may be necessary to equality such as in the case of the secrecy of jury deliberations. And some kinds of secrecy may be properly approved of by a democratic assembly. I do not wish to take a stand here on what kinds of secrecy are defensible. I only wish to distinguish publicity from transparency in the usual sense. That said, there is a sense in which the publicity of social justice involves transparency. Principles of social justice are public when it can be transparent to reasonably well-informed and conscientious persons that those principles are implemented by the basic institutions of the society.[5]

In sum, social justice is concerned with the principles that govern the activities of a society or a group of persons when they attempt to bring about

---

[5] To be sure, duplicitous injustice is worse than open injustice other things being equal. But this is not directly germane to the claim about publicity of principles of social justice I am making here. The latter merely requires that the principles be such that people can see that they are realized in institutions or actions. The former can occur with institutions regulated by public principles; the facts are simply obscured in a particular case.

justice for themselves. It states that in a society attempting to establish justice among its people, the principles underlying its institutions must realize justice in a public way or in a way that reasonable and properly informed people can see to be realized. So in a society attempting to realize egalitarian justice, it must be the case that equality is realized in a way that the members of society can see that they are being treated as equals once they are properly informed and make a reasonable effort.

THE CONTEXT IN WHICH PUBLICITY ASSUMES IMPORTANCE

Publicity acquires special importance for justice when people are attempting to implement justice among themselves. The state is the most important case of the attempt to establish justice. One of the main functions of the state is to establish justice among persons. What does it mean to say that the state and its legal system establish justice? It means that the legal system of a reasonably just society determines how one is to treat others justly if one is to treat them justly at all. What the state does, if it is reasonably just, is settle for practical purposes what justice consists in by promulgating public rules for the guidance of individual behavior. The state makes and executes laws that determine what is each person's by right and what are each person's duties toward others as well as toward the whole society. The state also sets up courts for the resolution of conflicts between persons that are intended to resolve the conflicts justly. The state makes a claim to act in the name of justice. Of course, it often fails to do so. Often it merely claims to act in the name of justice while in fact advancing only the interests or concerns of a particular class or group of people. But it does make the claim and that is one thing that identifies the establishment of justice as one of the basic functions of the state.

The state is only one way in which individuals attempt to establish justice among themselves. Individuals also attempt to treat each other justly. In doing this, they attempt to establish justice in their actions and in the norms that arise in their interactions. They may do this by setting up norms, trade agreements, or simply coordinating among themselves. The state is not a logically necessary condition for people to interact with each other justly. But it is, as I will show below, socially necessary for justice to be established when the full complexity and richness of human societies are at issue.

Why are public rules for the guidance of behavior so important to justice? First, in Joseph Raz's words, justice underdetermines what system of rules we must adopt.[6] Many different systems of rules can realize the same principles of justice. To be sure, we may have a general sense that human beings have conditional rights to own property, but, in general, we do not know whether *this* person has a right to *this* particular property and what the particular implications are until we know what the rules for the society are. To act justly it is essential for us to be on the same page with others, to coordinate with them on the same rules. Otherwise, though two people may be perfectly conscientious and even believe in the same basic principles, they will end up violating each other's rights if they follow different sets of rules that implement the same principles. To suppose otherwise is to suppose that there are clear natural rights and duties accessible to all (or a set of highly salient conventional rules) concerning how we should act even in the most detailed circumstances.[7] Since, in order to treat others justly, we must be acting on the basis of the same rules, in a complex society we need an authority for promulgating those rules in a publicly clear way and we must expect individuals to comply with the rules the authority lays down.

Since the rules are likely to be quite complex, individuals must take the rule maker to be authoritative in order to successfully act on the basis of the same rules. Why are they likely to be complex? One reason is that the constraints we must abide by in dealing with other people justly are quite complex and subject to a number of different realizations. Rules defining property rights, such as when they are acquired, when a voluntary exchange occurs, when exchange is not exploitative, when one person's use of his property imposes too much of an externality on others, when a person loses his property as a result of lack of use, and so forth, are all very complex on their own and require that there be public rules. A second reason is that justice is at least in some significant part concerned with ensuring the common good and certain kinds of distributions of power, opportunities, education, and income. Rules defining property and its limits as well as taxation are necessarily quite complex because they must satisfy both the concern that certain constraints

---

[6] As Raz puts it, morality underdetermines the law, in his "On the Authority and Interpretation of Constitutions," in *Constitutionalism: Philosophical Foundations* ed. Larry Alexander (Cambridge: Cambridge University Press, 1998).

[7] Locke thinks that the relatively simple principles of justice that he defends must be publicly promulgated in settled and known law. He does not go as far I do in saying that the state is a socially necessary institution for the establishment of justice. See John Locke, *Second Treatise on Civil Government* (Indianapolis, IN: Hackett Publishers, 1990), chapter 7. Kant thinks that there is an a priori connection between the state and justice that is made through the connection between justice and the general will and the connection between the general will and a unified coercive apparatus. In a sense, my view is in between Kant's a priori connection between state and justice and Locke's idea that the connection is one of convenience.

be respected and that certain overall distributional properties be maintained in the society.

The complexity of the rules and the variety of realizations of justice make it such that I cannot determine for myself what to do; I must comply with the rules because they are made by the public rule maker. There are two connected reasons for this. One, if I rely on my own judgment, I will often be mistaken about what a useful public rule will do. Others will not be able to rely on me if I follow my own judgment alone and I will not be able to rely on them. Thus a public rule maker satisfies a coordinating function. Two, I will also not be able to rely on my fellow citizens to treat me in accordance with the same rules by which I deal with them if they or all of us follow the rules each of us thinks are best. So the public rule maker enables us to treat each other in accord with a basic principle of equality. Equality in this case is partly realized by the rule of law. These particular rules determine what are just interactions among persons, only because there is an artificially created public set of rules that defines property, fair contribution to political society, and other matters in social life.[8]

To avoid misunderstanding, to say that the legal system establishes justice among persons is not the same as to say that the legal system defines or constitutes justice among persons. To say that the legal system establishes justice is to say that what the legal system does will, for practical purposes, determine what justice demands among persons. We live in societies where there is a lot of disagreement about justice but we must live in accordance with common rules. The common rules the legal system lays down are usually compromises among different ideas of justice that the persons in society have. Sometimes particular groups of rules embody one group's conception of justice and not another's. We know that we must live with compromise on justice in pluralistic societies and so we are willing to treat the rules of the legal system as the rules of justice for practical purposes even when we disagree with them. So to say that the legal rules establish justice does not imply that we cannot think that they are unjust. Indeed, much discussion and debate in democratic societies concerns this very question.

The big questions for the establishment of justice are whether the rules were arrived at in a reasonably just way and whether the rules themselves are at least within some range of tolerability. These questions are answered in this book by means of conceptions of the authority of democracy and the limits to that authority.

My thesis is that when individuals come together to establish justice among themselves whether by means of the state or some other system of norms and

---

[8] To be sure, not all coordination problems require public rule makers for their solution. But the complexity of the coordination in the case of justice does require a public rule maker.

rules, it is essential that the system of rules be publicly just. It is essential, in other words, that justice not only be done but that it can be seen to be done.

THE ARGUMENTS FOR THE PRINCIPLE OF PUBLICITY

There are two types of arguments for the principle of weak publicity: the formal argument and the substantive arguments. First, social justice concerns the kinds of claims people can make against each other in determining the appropriate balance of benefits and burdens. Principles of social justice must spell out ideals that people can appeal to in criticizing their relations with each other and social justice must be able to provide, at least in principle, concrete guidance as to how to legitimate their relations. A principle that cannot be seen by individuals to be implemented or one that does not permit individuals to be able to see that it is not implemented is not able to provide the guidance social justice provides. It is not enough that justice is done; it must be seen to be done.

Now I shall provide a substantive argument for publicity. Here is the intuitive idea behind the argument to come. Social justice requires that individuals be treated as equals. In order for the system of rules, norms, and laws by which justice is established among persons to treat people as equals it must be that they evince an equal respect for the judgment of all of those on whom the rules have a major impact. The system of rules and laws realize that equal respect when they are made in a way that they can be seen by all to be treating them as equals.

Here is the more detailed argument. I argue that each citizen has fundamental interests in being able to see that he is being treated as an equal in a society where there is significant diversity among persons in the conditions of well-being, and where there is disagreement about justice and wherein each citizen can acknowledge fallibility and cognitive bias in their capacities for thinking about their interests and about justice.

The background conditions of these fundamental interests are the facts of diversity, pervasive disagreement, cognitive bias, and fallibility. By diversity of persons, I mean that the interests of persons are quite different. One basis of diversity of persons is diversity in natural talents and handicaps. Individuals with sensitive ears are likely to get a lot more out of music than others do. Individuals with strong constitutions are likely to get a lot more out of physically demanding activities than others do. Individuals who are intellectually talented are likely to find more rewards in intellectual activities than others do. These are just a few crude ways in which individuals differ from one another that affect their capacities for well-being. People differ from each other in myriad ways aside from these and the combination of these differences guarantees that the well-being of different people is likely to be quite different.

The diversity of persons in any moderately complex society is also assured by the fact that persons are raised in families that live in very different sectors of societies. The division of labor in society guarantees that individuals have very different experiences. They also learn very different things from those with whom they interact. Different sectors of society tend to develop distinct cultures and even worldviews. They also equip individuals with distinctive abilities and sensibilities, which condition their capacities for well-being.

Of course, the dynamism of normal societies ensures that because individuals move between sectors of societies, they are likely to have a real mix of traits from different sectors of the society. Furthermore, societies are dynamic in others ways that condition the interests of their members. People move from society to society thus mixing different cultural traditions and experiences and sensibilities. The net result of all these conditions of diversity and their mixture with other conditions is to guarantee that individuals' capacities for well-being are extremely diverse.

Notice, that these conditions of diversity with respect to well-being do not in any way presuppose a subjectivist account of well-being. This diversity of conditions implies that people's capacities to achieve objectively valuable states are quite diverse and clearly their abilities to appreciate and enjoy these states are likely to be extremely diverse. Of course, to the extent that there is a subjective element to well-being, which consists in the appreciation and enjoyment of intrinsic goods, there will be a great deal of diversity in capacities for well-being.

The fallibility of moral judgment is pervasive, even when confined to the parameters set by a principle of equality. And the sources of fallibility listed below are also sources of disagreement. The principle of equality requires one to compare and weigh the interests of persons who are quite different from oneself and who have lived their lives in parts of the society that are quite different from one's own. The trouble is that one is likely to be quite often mistaken about what those interests are and how to compare them to one's own. Indeed, individuals are rarely able to give as much as rough sketches of their own interests in social life and most often individuals find themselves in the process of continually adjusting their conceptions of what is good for themselves and others. People's understandings of other people's interests are likely to be far more fallible and subject to arbitrary influences. In many cases, people simply do not have the knowledge or understanding to come to anything more than an extremely crude and faulty grasp of other people's interests.

Furthermore, the principles by which to bring together all these varied, complex, and obscure interests are likely to be quite often very difficult to discern and assess. Most obviously, comparisons between interests are likely to be at best extremely crude and highly defective. Moreover, discerning whether another person's interests are authentic or autonomous or overblown is likely to be a highly hazardous enterprise. Determining whether another's interests are genuinely her own is also highly problematic.

Different conceptions of equality and their appropriate applications are also likely to lead to serious disagreement. If we think of the different options for the interpretation of equality under discussion recently, such as equality of welfare, equality of opportunity for welfare, equality of resources, equality of capacities, equality in the distribution of primary goods, and equality of access to advantage to name just a few, we can see how differing interpretations of the ideal of equality are also likely to attract serious disagreement. Just to name a few disagreements, theorists disagree on the extent and significance of voluntariness in the generation of people's interests. Theorists also disagree on the importance of a person's judgment in defining the interests and equal shares of each person. Theorists disagree on the extent to which some kind of freedom (the correct understanding of which is itself highly controversial) is necessary to the characterization of equality. The issues that lead to disagreements about the above conceptions of equality also lead to disagreements regarding whether some form of equality of outcome ought to be accepted over some form of equality of starting points, such as equality of opportunity, either of the formal variety or of the more positive variety that demands equal starting points in life.

The correct application of any one of these principles is also likely to be an extremely fallible process fraught with controversy. In many cases, it is unquestionably best for people not even to try to apply the principles. And in many of these cases it is highly likely that it is best not even to try to figure out whether these principles are satisfied or not.[9] For example, to argue that a person's interests ought not to be as much advanced as another's because they are somehow illegitimately expensive interests to satisfy is highly likely to be an extremely hazardous and fallible process. In addition, merely attempting to determine when expensive interests are to be satisfied and when they are not is a difficult matter on which people disagree. Common sense and the ubiquity of controversy among intelligent persons on these matters are sufficient to underscore these points.

Against this background of diversity, universal fallibility, and disagreement, citizens' judgments are usually cognitively biased toward their interests and

---

[9] See G. A. Cohen, "Expensive Taste Rides Again," in *Dworkin and His Critics* ed. Justine Burley (Oxford: Blackwell Publishers, 2004), pp. 3–29, esp. 18.

backgrounds in various ways, and as a consequence, controversy over principle often reflects conflict of interests. Obviously citizens' judgments reflect the various conditions that affect their well-being. Their judgments reflect their experiences, sensibilities, and abilities and those of the people they most interact with. Individuals' judgments of what is just or unjust are in two main ways more sensitive to their own interests than those of others. One, persons understand their own interests better than the interests of others. And so they tend quite reasonably to interpret the interests of others in the light of their understanding of their own interests. So each person's conception of the common good or of equality of interests will tend to be grounded in conceptions of other people's interests that assimilate them to their own, and assume that others' interests are qualitatively similar to their own. But this implies that conceptions of equality and the common good will reflect the interests of the persons who advance them. Since in complex societies individuals' interests are likely to be qualitatively quite diverse, failing to take account of a particular group's conception of the common good may well imply ignoring their qualitatively distinctive interests. Two, individuals are more sensitive to the harms they undergo than to those of others, so they may inadvertently unduly downplay harms to others. This holds especially when they do not fully understand those harms. The harms of others are assigned lesser weight. Both the tendency qualitatively to assimilate the interests of others to one's own and to assign a lesser weight to the clearly distinctive interests of others distort one's judgments about the proper distribution of benefits and burdens to the detriment of others. And more generally, the conceptions one has of other people's interests are likely to reflect the conditions that ensure one's own capacities for well-being.

This fact of cognitive bias is also likely to play a role in the creation of disagreements regarding conceptions of equality and their applications. The principles by which one compares and balances the interests of different persons are highly likely to be affected by cognitive bias. How much significance one places on voluntariness in determining claims of justice, how much importance one places on one's own judgment in deciding what is good for one, and how one compares one's interests to those of others are all likely to be deeply affected by cognitive bias. These kinds of things receive different weights and significances in the activities characteristic of different sectors of society and each person is most likely to reflect that fact in his or her own judgment on these matters. The variety of valuations of freedom, voluntariness, self-determination, personal integrity, and preference satisfaction as well as intrinsic goods are likely to reflect the conditions in which people develop their views. These views are likely to be cognitively biased toward the conditions that determine the capacity for well-being of a person and thus are likely to reflect the interests of the different persons in the debates.

None of this is meant to suggest that individuals generally intentionally mold principles to their own advantage or use such principles as a mask for their own interests. Though they often do that, individuals also simply have natural cognitive biases toward their own interests. The more pluralistic a society is the more there will be disagreement, fallibility and the more the cognitive biases will distort their understanding of other people's interests.[10]

Obviously, all of these facts are likely to produce an enormous amount of conscientious disagreement on how equality is to be realized among persons. My point here is not to argue that there is no truth of the matter regarding what human interests really are or what the correct conception of equality really is. I think that there are truths of the matter here. My point is that our understandings of these principles and their application are likely to lead to serious conscientious disagreement and are likely to be highly fallible in a way that is important to how we structure our political institutions. To see why these disagreements and fallibility are important, we need to enumerate the interests that are engaged when these facts are present.

So far I have described the background facts about judgment in societies. Now I will describe the fundamental interests that are put into play when these background facts about judgment obtain. The first fundamental interest is the interest in correcting for cognitive bias. Given natural cognitive biases, and the prevalence of disagreement about justice, each citizen has a fundamental interest in correcting the cognitive biases of others. To be treated in accordance with someone else's conceptions of equality, of my interests, and of how to compare my interests with hers is likely to lead to a serious setback to my interests given the facts of cognitive bias. No citizen wants merely to be treated in accordance with someone else's conception of equality. Each has an interest in being treated as an equal, in at least some fundamental respects, in a way that he can agree that he is being treated as an equal. If all citizens have this perception then there is at least to that extent a bulwark against the biases working against anyone's interests.

To be required to live in a world that is shaped entirely by another's judgments, in the light of the facts laid out above, is to have one's interests set back and it is to have the other's interests advanced if the fact of cognitive bias is present. This implies that being required to submit entirely to the judgment of another, no matter how conscientious that other is, is to have one's interests

---

[10] Is there inequality in the distribution of cognitive bias? Surely there could be, but I will argue in Chapter 3 that the different views concerning inequality of capacity for knowledge ought not to be taken into account in the basic institutions of society, though individuals are encouraged to form their own opinions on this matter.

subordinated to the other's interests. This phenomenon of subordination of interests is deepened to the extent that we are talking about groups of persons determining the society in accordance with their shared judgments and other groups not having the opportunity to make the society conform to their judgments.

The subordination of interests does not always imply that those who do the subordinating are better off than those who are subordinated. We may not be able to determine that one way or the other. The normal case will probably be one in which those whose views of how society ought to be organized prevail are the ones who are better off. But this need not be the case in every instance. What it does seem to imply is that, given the facts of disagreement and cognitive bias, the interests of those who are being subordinated are being given less significance than those of the others. They are being treated as unequals or inferiors in the sense that their interests seem to matter less than those of the others. Hence, we have an important kind of inequality that arises from the lack of publicity in a society. And we can see how publicity advances a kind of equality among the members of the society. Publicity provides essential protection to every member against the inevitable and pervasive tendencies of imperfectly constituted cognitive agents to judge in a way that is biased toward their own interests.

A second fundamental interest in publicity emerges when we see that individuals' judgments often reflect modes of life to which they are accustomed and in which they feel at home. To live in a world governed by the principles one adheres to as opposed to someone else's is often, in Michael Walzer's apt simile, like living in one's own home furnished by one's own familiar things and not in someone else's or in a hotel.[11]

The interest in being at home in the world is fundamental because it is at the heart of the well-being of each person. Being at home in the world one lives in implies that one can appreciate that world and enjoy its many valuable qualities. Being at home in the world one lives in is one of the socially necessary conditions for one to have well-being. For it is the condition in which one has a sense of fit, connection, and meaning in the world one lives in and it is therefore the condition in which one can experience the value of the things

[11] See Michael Walzer, "Interpretation and Social Criticism," *Tanner Lectures on Human Values VIII* (Salt Lake City: University of Utah Press, 1988), p. 14. Walzer overplays the significance of this consideration by turning it into the central idea of his political theory and he seems to thereby allow deeply unjust societies to be just. A theory that takes the interests of individuals seriously can give it a modest significance for justice. The ultimate source of this idea is G. W. F. Hegel's, *The Philosophy of Right* trans. T. M. Knox (Oxford: Oxford University Press, 1952), p. 24. See Michael Hardimon, *Hegel's Social Philosophy: The Project of Reconciliation* (Cambridge: Cambridge University Press, 1994), for a full discussion of this idea.

around one. It gives one an orientation among the things in one's world that enables one to appreciate them.

To the extent that there are interests related to this sense of at-homeness, and their judgments about justice reflect this sense, individuals have interests in the world they live in conforming to their judgments. Each citizen has a fundamental interest in having a sense of being properly at home in the society in which he lives. To the extent that a person sees himself as being treated as an equal, he has that sense of being properly at home in an egalitarian world.

Living in a world that corresponds in no way to one's own judgment of how the world ought to be arranged is to live in a world that is opaque and perhaps even hostile to one's interests. It is to live in a world where one does not see how legitimately to make it responsive to one's interests. It is like playing a game whose rules do not make any sense to one. One is at a loss. Of course, such an experience can be an adventure if it is had for brief periods and if one experiences it against the background of a place from which to secure sustenance and to which one may return. But living in a world where one is permanently barred from feeling at home is a serious setback to one's interests.

Those who live in this world, which does make sense to them, by comparison, do have their interests advanced. Here again, we can see that those who are required to live in a world that is shaped to accord with the judgments of others have their interests subordinated to those of the others. We can see then another way in which lack of publicity implies a serious inequality when we consider the facts of disagreement and cognitive bias. Publicity, or the ability to see that one is treated justly and as an equal, is itself a kind of bulwark of equality.

Again, since we do not have clear comparisons of well-being, it will not always be clear that those who dominate the society are better off than those who do not, though we have reason to believe that in the normal case they will be. What is fairly clear is that the interests of those for whom the society is opaque are being set back for the sake of the interests of those whose judgments do correspond to the society in some significant way. And it is also clear that this setback is not for the sake of equality; it is not for the sake of redressing an inequality between them. So a society that fails publicly to embody justice at least from the informed and conscientious points of view of one of the groups is one that is treating that group as an inferior.

It is important that there be some significant fit between one's own conception of the way the world ought to be organized and the way it is organized. But there are limits to this requirement of at-homeness. That limit is set by the principle of equality itself. That is, the interest in being at home in one's world may not sacrifice equality itself. The interest may only be satisfied by being at home in an egalitarian world. Hence the principle of publicity that is defended by this interest in at-homeness is a principle of public equality. Someone who judges that others ought to be subordinated to him because they are inferior does not generate a claim to be able to have the world correspond to this particular judgment. He does have some claim, namely to be able to see the world conform to equality given his cognitive limitations and given the facts I have listed above, but he cannot have a claim to see the world conform to his judgment against equality.

The reason for this is twofold. One, the principle of equality of advancement of interests is the fundamental principle of justice. It is the principle that conditions our concerns for the interests of persons. So, we cannot invoke interests that are incompatible with that principle of equality when we are trying to lay out its implications. Two, since equality is the fundamental principle of justice and well-being consists in the appreciation of and enjoyment of intrinsic goods, being at home in an unjust world cannot, at least in that respect, be a contribution to one's well-being.

The third fundamental interest is in being treated as a person with equal moral standing among one's fellow citizens. To be treated in a way that entirely ignores one's way of perceiving how one is treated constitutes a serious loss of status for a person in a society. A person whose judgment about that society is never taken seriously by others is treated in effect like a child or a madman. Such a person is denied recognition of his or her moral personality, indeed of those capacities in virtue of which he has the special status of person. The society is expressing its indifference to the capacity of this person to appreciate justice and thus is expressing its indifference to his special moral status of humanity. This already is a serious setback to his interests as a person with humanity.

Moreover, if the facts of cognitive bias, at-homeness, and standing are taken into account by citizens, it should be clear that those adult persons who are denied the right of being able to see that they are being treated as equals are having their interests set back for the sake of the interests of the dominant group. They are being treated as inferiors and being told that their interests are not worthy of equal or perhaps any consideration of justice. This is a disastrous loss of moral standing. Since there is a deep interest in having one's moral standing among one's fellows clearly recognized and affirmed, such a denial of the right to publicity must be a serious setback of interests.

WHY THE INTERESTS IN PUBLICITY ARE FUNDAMENTAL

Now that we have described the interests that ground the importance of publicity, it is important to emphasize how fundamental these interests are.

This is necessary because if publicity is to be an important dimension of social justice, it must be shown that the interests that ground it are fundamental. First, I want to bring out the political nature of these interests. Second, I want to show why these interests are central human interests and among the most important human interests. Third, I want to stave off worries about the universality of these interests.

The interests in correcting for cognitive bias, in being at home in the world, and in being recognized and affirmed are peculiarly political interests. This means that they emerge as salient human interests in circumstances of pluralism and in which there are competing efforts to shape the world around one. The interest in correcting for cognitive bias emerges in these circumstances because the fact of cognitive bias threatens to make efforts to shape the world by a particular group highly oppressive to the other groups in society. One group's efforts to shape the social world threaten to turn that world into one that reflects their interests and that is hostile to the interests of other quite different groups. So each group has a distinctively political interest in correcting for those cognitive biases.

The interest in being at home in the world also emerges as a salient interest in a pluralistic world where each is trying to shape the world in accordance with her best understanding. One does not usually think of one's activities as making a home for oneself in the sense of organizing the world so that it makes sense and so that one can find an orientation in that world in order to pursue one's interests. One thinks of one's activities as the right ones or as the appropriate ones. The idea of being at home in the world emerges when one sees oneself as one among many persons who are quite diverse, who have disagreements and in whom there is cognitive bias and each of whom wish to shape the world in accordance with her conception of what is good and right. It is at this point that one comes to insist on being able to shape one's world according to one's own understanding. It is at this point that one insists on making the world make sense to one because one sees that if it makes sense only to others, one will not be able to find one's way in that world and one will not be able to advance one's interests in that world. It is only at this point that one can see that one's interests depend on this. And, of course, one comes to see that others' interests depend on this as well.

The interest in being recognized and affirmed as an equal is a straightforward political interest in that one must demand recognition and affirmation of others as a result of the fact that one makes a claim on others to be treated in accordance with social justice.

The fundamental importance of the interests in correcting for cognitive bias and in being at home in the world derives from the basic fact that they are conditions for the realization of all one's other interests in a pluralistic social world. The first interest protects one from having one's life dominated by considerations that serve only another's interests. The second interest gives one the ability to pursue one's own well-being by ensuring that the world around one makes sense to one. They are both general interests without which one would have a very hard time pursuing any of one's other interests, particularly in a pluralistic world in which different persons assert competing claims to shape it.

The interest in being recognized and affirmed as an equal is fundamental because it is connected with the interest each person has in being treated in accordance with social justice and in knowing that she is treated in accordance with social justice.

I will also argue in what follows that these fundamental interests are compatible with all the other main fundamental interests persons have. In particular, I will argue that the requirement of publicity supports a robust set of democratic and liberal rights as well as rights to an economic minimum. So the interests that support publicity are not defeated by considerations of other fundamental interests in liberty and material goods.

These three interests are universal human interests in pluralistic societies in the sense that all rational persons have these interests in pluralistic societies. The first two are universal because they are general conditions for the advancement of well-being under conditions of pluralism. The third is universal because it is tied to the fundamental principle of justice as equality.

Here I want to stave off a worry about the universality of the interest in being at home in the world. The metaphor of being at home in the world is apt to mislead the reader in an important set of cases to which it applies. I have argued that when one is at home in the world one is able to make sense of the world one lives in and have a sense of how one fits in with it and is connected with it. But the metaphor suggests also a level of comfort with the world one lives in. And though many persons who are at home in the world they live in will have a sense of comfort with that world, this is not a necessary condition of being at home in the world. So the idea of being at home in the world does not entail that one is happy in that world. Though it is a condition of the pursuit of one's well-being, it does not entail that one can achieve happiness but only that one can make certain kinds of improvements to one's life.

For example, those who believe that the world is inalterably fallen and sinful and those who believe, as Buddhists do, that all of life is impermanent and full of suffering are not likely to think that the world is a place in which one will feel comfortable or even that one ought to feel comfortable in that world. Nevertheless, these people must still think it is important to be at home in the world in the sense in which I have defined it. For they still have distinctive ways of understanding the world and distinctive ways of ordering the world in which they live that are connected to their worldviews. And they might still experience a sense of disorientation in a world that is dominated by a very different worldview. And this sense may undermine their efforts to achieve any kind of improvement in their lives in accordance with the views they hold.

In sum the interests in correcting for cognitive bias, in being at home in the world, and in being recognized and affirmed as an equal are universal and fundamental interests of persons in pluralistic political societies. And as we shall see, they are compatible with other fundamental interests in liberty and material goods. Therefore, we can see that the requirement of publicity that is grounded in these interests is a fundamental requirement of social justice.

AN EGALITARIAN OBJECTION TO PUBLICITY

Against all of these arguments for publicity, someone might object that in trying unilaterally to impose his conception of equality and violating publicity, he is merely trying to implement the correct conception of equality among him and his fellow citizens. He might object that he cannot be properly accused of subordinating the interests of others to his own if this is what he is trying to do. He is merely trying to bring about equality. To this objection we can respond that given knowledge of the facts of judgment, he is in fact subordinating the interests of others to his own at least with respect to the interests in judgment enumerated above.

But there is a second nearby objection that is more telling. The objector might agree that he is subordinating the interests in judgment of the others to his own, but he could attempt to sustain the objection by saying that he is doing so for the sake of greater equality overall. He claims to have the correct conception of equality and claims thereby that if he implements it, people will be in a just state of affairs that advances their interests equally. He admits that there is a loss to those who are unilaterally imposed upon but he thinks that the loss is worth it for the sake of imposing the conception of equality that he claims to be the correct one. How can anyone object on the basis of equality?

This is an important objection because it calls for an application of my statements about the character of the facts and interests at stake in judgment. The proposed objection supposes that the facts and interests that I have outlined only pertain to the exercise of judgment and are separable from the interests at stake in the disagreement about policy. It gives the impression that those whose interests in judgment are being set back are merely complaining that their voices are not taken seriously and that they could make this complaint despite their belief that the unilateral imposer may be right about the substance of the matter. They seem to be displaying the vice of willfulness and asserting that the unilateral imposer is failing to placate their self-regard by ignoring their judgment. Just having your judgment ignored by another, even if the other person is right, is a kind of insult on this interpretation. But this particular setback to interests is entirely separable from the issues at stake in the disagreement in the first place. Or so the objection might go.

The response to this objection is that the facts about cognitive bias and the interests in correcting for it, the interests in being at home in the world, and the interests in being affirmed as an equal are more fundamental than the objection supposes. These facts and interests do not merely pertain to the exercise of judgment in the sense that one can set back those interests without setting back the interests that the unilaterally imposed regime is supposed to advance. The above propositions about the facts and interests in judgment imply that the unilaterally imposed form of equality will, in all likelihood, set back the interests of those who are imposed upon. The facts and interests connected with judgment are not separable from the interests that are at issue in the disagreements about policy. If the facts and interests in judgment are set back then the interests at stake in the issues that are disagreed on are highly likely to be set back. If the interest in judgment that involves correcting for cognitive bias is set back then the policies that are implemented without regard for what others think are likely to advance the interests of the unilateral imposer. And if the interest in judgment that is connected to being at home in the world is set back, then the person in question is likely to have her interests set back when the unilaterally imposed policy is brought about. Even the interest in being recognized and affirmed as an equal is likely to be set back by the unilaterally imposed policy because its setback is connected to the setback of the two interests just described. So the thesis is that when the interests in judgment are set back, this implies that the interests at stake in the policy being judged will be set back.

So what must be said in response to this objection is that if the person in question is apprised of all the facts about judgment and the connected interests we have laid out in this section, then he can properly be accused of an indefensible hubris. Given the facts about judgment and the interests in judgment, this person is guilty of a kind of self-assertion that is incompatible with treating his fellows as equals.

Here we can see the respect in which the three interests I have described are fundamental. These interests are fundamental in the sense that they are deep conditions of well-being in social life and they are compatible with all the other fundamental interests in social life. For, as we will see in what follows, these interests cannot be satisfied if one's basic material well-being is not satisfied and one's basic capacities for pursuing one's good are not realized.

PUBLICITY AND FURTHER DISAGREEMENT

Two remarks are worth making here. One, it is not necessary that there be consensus on the principles that are publicly embodied. So it is not necessary that there is agreement on the principle of equality itself. All that is required is that people can see that they are being treated as equals. This is because a requirement of consensus would impose an impossible burden on principles of justice. Theories simply cannot get off the ground if they require agreement on principles themselves as a condition of justice. They push the respect for judgment to a point that undermines justice and eventually defeats itself. A theory of justice must rely on the truth or legitimacy of its central claims as well as the strength of its arguments. A theory of justice of the sort that I am defending here is able to do this while avoiding self-defeat because it states that the respect for judgment displayed by a concern for publicity is itself based on equal advancement of interests; respect for judgment is not something that is of rock bottom significance. Its significance is explained by a deeper concern for well-being.

Two, it is clear that no society can fully publicly embody justice. This is because citizens are bound, as a consequence of the facts of diversity, disagreement, fallibility, and cognitive bias, to disagree about what justice requires in a society. Hence, the requirement of publicity will need to take into account the impossibility of full publicity. The only way it can do this is publicly to embody equality in a way that is compatible with and respects the wide range of disagreements about what justice requires. This, in my view, is where democracy and liberal rights come in.

So the requirement of publicity does not assert that all of social justice must be public but only that there must be a fundamental respect in which the social justice of a society be realized in a public way. This is another respect in which the present conception of publicity is distinct from the Rawlsian one. While Rawls requires that principles of social justice generally be public principles, the present conception recognizes the impossibility of all principles of social justice being public. It recognizes that within the framework provided by public realizations of equality, such as democracy and liberal rights, citizens will reasonably disagree about how to realize equality in many matters of substantive law and policy. This just follows from the facts of judgment we have been discussing. And even though the principles of social justice that are to regulate substantive law and policy are the subjects of conscientious disagreement and thus are not likely to be fully public principles, they can nevertheless be objectively true or false.

So while the public realization of equality is a necessary condition on the justice of the society, publicity is not a requirement on all principles that are realized in a society. As we will see, the way to make the requirement of publicity compatible with the inevitable plurality of opinion and interest in society is to require that people be publicly treated as equals in the processes in which decisions must be made despite the presence of undiminished disagreements.

PUBLICITY: THE EGALITARIAN STANDPOINT FOR ESTABLISHING JUSTICE AMONG PERSONS

The import of these arguments is that when people try to establish justice among themselves, they must do so in a public way. Attempts to establish justice among persons are actions we engage in on the basis of our judgments of justice. Our interests in judgment and the principle of equality ground the requirement that principles of social justice must be public. Everyone must be able to see that they are treated as equals. This means that principles of social justice must be justified in a way that the points of view of everyone are taken into account. This is the only way to deal with the imperfections and distortions that inevitably accompany our efforts to establish justice that is compatible with treating all the members as equals.

The requirement of publicity on principles of social justice amounts to the requirement that every person with ordinary cognitive abilities, who understands the cognitive limitations on persons and the fundamental interests in judgment and who makes a conscientious effort can see that they are being treated as equals when the principles of social justice are realized. One way to appreciate the requirement of publicity on principles of social justice is to see that it implies that we must evaluate principles of social justice from the *egalitarian standpoint*. It is the one standpoint that genuinely treats each one of us as equals that *we* have as a society on the issues that come before a society. The egalitarian standpoint is to be distinguished from each person's standpoint taken separately. Recall that according to the arguments above, if one attempts to establish equality or justice from one's own individual standpoint alone and without regard for the points of view of others, one engages in a deeply oppressive and inegalitarian project. What publicity does is require that the principles of social justice be accessible to the points of view of everyone taken together. In order to filter out cognitive biases and alienating differences in each person's standpoint, we now ask what everyone would agree to when they are properly informed and conscientiously trying to figure out what equality implies for society. This is the egalitarian standpoint from which principles of social justice are evaluated. The egalitarian standpoint is characterized by three distinct elements. First, equality itself is constitutive of the standpoint because each person's interests are taken equally into account in the standpoint. Second, from the standpoint we attempt to figure out what equality demands. Third, individuals decide what equality demands when informed by the background facts of disagreement, diversity, fallibility, and cognitive bias and the fundamental interests people have under the circumstances where they are trying to establish justice among themselves. Because the object is to find a principle of equality everyone can agree to, the egalitarian standpoint filters out the cognitive biases of persons as well as other alienating differences and arrives at principles of social justice that all can see to be ways of treating each as an equal. So the question to be asked of the egalitarian standpoint is, what principles of equality are such that everyone can agree that they are treated as equals by the realization of those principles when they take into account the facts of judgment and the interests in judgment? The principles that are justified from this public standpoint are the principles of *public equality*. And the just institutions and states of affairs that satisfy these principles are called the *public realization of equality*.

Of course within the bounds provided by public equality we can still attempt to realize more particular, less fully public conceptions of justice. We can appeal to considerations that are not fully public to advance justice among our fellows as long as this is within the bounds established by public equality.

The egalitarian standpoint provided by publicity is not like Rawls's original position. One, it is essential to the egalitarian standpoint that individuals can actually occupy the standpoint in their own society. The standpoint is hypothetical to the extent that not everyone does occupy it and yet it still provides a standard of assessment that applies to them. In this respect, it is like the standard of the reasonable person in the law. In the law, one asks, what would a reasonable person think in this context, and that is a standard by which one evaluates everyone's mental state. In the same way, one can ask, would an ordinary but conscientious person properly informed about the facts of judgment and the associated interests agree that the institutions that realize this principle actually treat him as an equal? If we can expect everyone who satisfies the above description to agree to this description of a particular principle then that principle is a public principle. And the principle applies to everyone, even those who, for want of conscientiousness or proper information do not accept it.

Two, unlike the original position argument, it starts from a principle of justice that has been defended prior to the argument. It is grounded on the conception of justice provided by the principle of equality of advancement of interests, which has been defended in Chapter 1. And the function of the standpoint is only to provide a justification of a particular realization of the principle of equality of advancement of interests among persons. So it is not the ground of justification of the principles of justice. It is the condition under which arguments for a particular version of the principle of equality are to be made. Three, a related contrast is that in the original position, each party thinks in terms of how best to advance her interests or those she represents. Within the egalitarian standpoint, in contrast, each party is to think about what equality demands in the light of the facts and interests in judgment.

Four, the principles that are justified from the egalitarian standpoint do not exhaust the principles of social justice for the regulation of society. Once public equality is established in society, individuals may make further arguments for other realizations of equality. In what follows I will argue that democracy and liberal rights are public realizations of equality. But within the democratic forum citizens will argue for more controversial ideas about justice to be embodied in law and policy. These controversial ideas are not fully public since there is reasonable disagreement on them. But since they are argued for in the context of democratic and liberal institutions, they are not oppressive impositions even though they are not fully public. In this case, public equality provides the framework and foundation in which further more controversial ideas about justice are hashed out.

JUSTIFICATION FROM THE EGALITARIAN STANDPOINT

Here I want to discuss a complexity about the nature of the justification from the egalitarian standpoint. My aim here is to argue that the public realization of equality is intrinsically just. And I will go on to argue that democracy is one essential component of the public realization of equality. All of this is meant to show that democracy is intrinsically just. But the arguments for the use of the egalitarian standpoint are in part instrumental. Publicity is a kind of guarantee against the subordination of interests of one person or group by others when we are trying to establish justice among persons. Furthermore, as we will see, the arguments individuals make from the egalitarian standpoint in support of a particular conception of public equality are often instrumental arguments. That is, it appears that we are pursuing public equality not for its own sake but only as a guarantee against bias and the subordination of interest.

In a sense, from a god's eye point of view, public equality does not have intrinsic value. And by implication democracy and liberal rights do not have intrinsic value since they are public realizations of equality. The idea here is that a god can determine without error exactly what equal advancement of interests really requires in every instance. Perfect knowledge and power, at least according to the arguments presented above, can sidestep the requirement of publicity in trying to implement equality. This is because none of the imperfections of fallibility, disagreement, and cognitive bias are attributable to such a god, by hypothesis.

But we face the problem of what we must do once we acknowledge the fact that we do not occupy the divine standpoint. We must attempt to argue for and defend standards for social justice, which make sense to us and in a way that treats each person as an equal. The arguments above show that the standpoint from which we must make these arguments, if we are to embody equality in that very standpoint, is the egalitarian standpoint. The public standpoint from which we attempt to argue for and against principles of social justice is the deepest standpoint we can occupy as equals.

To say that a particular standard is *instrumentally justified* implies that there is some end state that the pursuit of the standard helps bring about. So, to say that the standard is instrumentally justified implies that we are in the possession of a standard that we can show to be independently defensible and that can be promoted by the instrumentally defended standard. Either this independently defended end state is one that we can see from the egalitarian standpoint to be justified or it is justified from another point of view than the egalitarian standpoint, say from the divine point of view. In the latter case, we must have access to the divine point of view for the justification of the independently justified standard. In the former case, we must agree that some particular standard is defensible as a realization of equality.

But we do not have access to the divine standpoint from which the argument for the independent standard can be made; we only have our own standpoint. So the only way that an instrumental argument for a particular political standard can work is if we have agreement from the egalitarian standpoint on the value of the end state that it is supposed to produce. That would make that end state standard a principle of public equality. And it will be intrinsically valuable. And those standards that are justifiable as a consequence of their bringing about the end state are merely instrumentally justified.

Here we can see that intrinsic justification is relative to the standpoint from which the arguments are made. So those principles that can be justified in the egalitarian standpoint without reference to further end states are intrinsically justified, even though the very same principles may not be intrinsically justified from the standpoint of perfect knowledge and power to which those in the first standpoint have no access. But this does not undermine the intrinsic justification of the standards from the first standpoint.

What I am going to argue is that the only standards on which we can achieve agreement in the egalitarian standpoint are the principles of democracy, liberal rights, and an economic minimum. There are no other states whose value we can agree on that can serve as end states that justify democracy or liberal rights. In particular we disagree on the justice of the outcomes of democratic decision-making and the goodness of the results of our exercises of liberal rights. Pervasive disagreement is the norm on these other states. Therefore, if we look at the matter only from our own public standpoint, we will see that democracy and liberal rights are intrinsically justified.

To be sure, since (as I will argue) democracy and liberal rights and an economic minimum are ones that can be agreed upon in the egalitarian standpoint, it follows that democratic institutions are partly evaluated by whether they manage to protect democracy, liberal rights, and the economic minimum. But beyond these there is no agreement on justice in law and policy in terms of which we can evaluate democracy from the egalitarian standpoint. Therefore, with the exception of these, democracy will be entirely intrinsically justified from the egalitarian standpoint.

We cannot do any better in attempting to realize equality than to do it publicly. It may not be the best we can do if we rank states of affairs according to a god's eye point of view. It is by its nature the best we can do from our own point of view if we are to understand our point of view as an egalitarian point of view or that point of view that inherently treats the interests of each as equally important in the structure of the standpoint as well as in its content. There are no deeper or more fundamental standards in terms of which we can see that considerations of public equality are defeated. There are no further considerations that we can appeal to in justifying the dismissal of the points of view of fellow members of society except, of course, public equality itself. Hence, what may appear to be only a second best from a god's eye point of view is intrinsically justified from the point of view of us imperfect human beings.

As we will see in what follows, social justice cannot be fully public. What can be done at most is to show that certain basic institutions can be justified as embodying public equality. In particular the institutions of democratic rights, liberal rights, and the guarantee of a basic minimum can be shown to be required by the idea of public equality. But within the context of these institutions, individual citizens will argue for more particular realizations of equality. They will, of course, attempt to make them as publicly defensible as possible but the standards they defend in the public forum will normally fail to satisfy the requirements of publicity. As long as the attempts to implement these only partially public principles are made within the setting provided by the democratic and liberal rights, the principles will be legitimate candidates for implementation by the society.

It is clear from the forgoing that public equality is not the whole of justice. It has a special role in the establishment of justice among persons but there are issues of justice that are outside the purview of public equality. First of all, there are the issues that arise in democratic societies that concern the conflicting and competing conceptions of justice that citizens bring to the democratic forum. These are not fully public notions of justice; that is why there is considerable disagreement on them. Yet citizens do not act wrongly in trying to implement these through the democratic process. Second, the issues of global justice will invariably involve only very partially public ideas. As we set our sights more and more on attempting to establish institutions of social justice for the global sphere we will attempt to set up institutions for deliberating about and adjudicating ideas about global justice that realize public equality. Presumably, if the arguments below are right, these institutions will have a very strongly democratic and liberal cast. For the moment however, we can still use the principle of equality to evaluate the global order and propose solutions for it.

More generally, the requirement of publicity does not rule out the kinds of theoretical discussions of the nature of equality that have yielded so much fruit in the past 30 years. What the requirement implies, assuming the arguments for democracy and liberal rights to come are correct, is that to the extent that these ideas of equality are not fully public ideas, they must be offered as proposals for establishing social justice in a democratic and liberal society.

CONCLUSION

When we try to implement equality in our social relations and institutions, we must implement public equality. That is the conclusion of this chapter. In Chapters 3 and 4, I argue that democracy and liberal rights are grounded in public equality. This will help us see not only what the normative basis for democracy and liberalism is. It will also help us grasp the complexity, subtlety, and nuance of our normative thinking about democracy and liberalism. Furthermore, it will help us see how democracy has authority and how liberal rights constitute limits to the authority of democracy.

3

Democracy as the Public Realization of Equality

Many think that democracy is an inherently just method for making collective decisions against the background of disagreement in society. But it is not easy to make clear sense of this idea or the grounds of the intrinsic justice of democracy. For one thing, citizens use the democratic method to promote what they take to be good outcomes for themselves and from the point of view of justice. So why should not we generally evaluate democracy on the basis of its outcomes alone? Why should not democracy be evaluated, as Hobbes and Mill assumed, entirely on the basis of its ability to bring about social peace and justice? Another question is, if democracy is somehow intrinsically just, what are the relations between the justice of democracy and the justice or goodness of the outcomes of democratic decision-making? Are democratic decisions authoritative when looked at from a moral point of view? What are the limits to this authoritativeness? Another fundamental question is, if people are different in their abilities to discern justice and interests, why do they get an equal say in the process of decision-making, as democracy seems to require? These questions must be answered if we are to have a proper understanding of the normative basis of democracy and the foundations of constitutionalism.

In this chapter, I will show that democracy is grounded in the principle of public equality that has been defended in the last two chapters. Thinking of the grounds of democracy in this way will help us understand the sense in which democracy is intrinsically just while preserving the idea that democracy serves important purposes that are independent of it and it will help us understand the reasons for equality of citizenship. It will also set the stage for the later chapters on the authority of democracy and its limits.

The basic idea is that when there are pervasive disagreements about justice and the common good and about the desirability of substantive laws and policies, there is a way in which decisions can be made that treats each citizen publicly as an equal that nevertheless respects these disagreements. Democratic decision-making is the unique way to publicly embody equality in collective decision-making under the circumstances of pervasive conscientious disagreement in which we find ourselves. Democratic decision-making enables us all to see that we are being treated as equals despite disagreements as long as we take into account the facts of judgment and the interests that accompany them. Because democratic decision-making realizes public equality in this way, and there is pervasive disagreement on its outcomes, it is intrinsically just. This is the argument I develop in this chapter.

In what follows, I will start with a description of the problem of disagreement over how to shape the common world in which we find ourselves. Then I will proceed to the argument that democracy is the unique realization of public equality in collective decision-making about this common world. This will require an account of the fundamental interests that are advanced equally in a publicly clear way by democracy. I will also show how this gives us an account of the intrinsic justice of democracy. Then I will clarify some important features of the nature of the equality that democracy embodies. Finally, I will deal with two fundamental objections to the idea that democracy has intrinsic worth. Again the idea of public equality will be essential to my responses to these worries. In Chapter 4, I will show that liberal rights are also grounded in the principle of public equality. In Chapters 6 and 7, I will argue for an account of the authority of democracy and its limits on the basis of the idea that democracy is the public realization of equality in collective decision-making.

THE PROBLEM OF DISAGREEMENT

The argument so far has supported the idea that the establishment of justice in society requires that justice be publicly embodied in the institutions of society. I have claimed that one main function of the state is to establish justice in its laws and policies among the members of the society. I have argued that because states establish justice they must embody the equal advancement of interests in a way that can be publicly clear in principle to its members. The problem is that there are numerous good faith disagreements about what justice actually requires even if we confine ourselves to accounts of justice that are meant to realize equality. The list of disagreements I described in Chapter 2 is only a start to a comprehensive list. In addition to the various forms of equality of outcome and resources and starting points, there are also good faith disagreements about the roles of desert, self-ownership, and property more generally in an account of justice that is devoted to treating individuals as equals. Furthermore, there are disagreements about the natures of the interests that people have. In addition to the obvious impact on a conception of justice these disagreements have, some of the disagreements have a particular relationship to collective decision-making. These debates include disagreements about the proper roles of culture, community, and identity in our understanding of a person's well-being. It seems clear to me that all of these kinds of disputes can easily be understood as disputes about the proper interpretation and application of the principle of equal advancement of interests. All of them can be seen as attempting to establish equality among citizens.

These different types of principles can all be seen in the debates that take place in modern political societies. An account of how publicly to treat people as equals, I maintain, must include an account of how best to treat people as equals in the light of the pervasive types of conscientious disagreement that we can expect to see in political societies.

Oddly enough there is a dynamic in modern democracies that seems to militate against seeing the importance of equality in politics. In ordinary political life we are often inclined to see those who advance opposing positions on justice in politics as enemies, criminals, or merely as promoting disguised versions of their interests or the interests of their patrons. Of course, people do promote their interests in politics and sometimes they do so in disguised and sinister ways. And even those who conscientiously advance distinctive points of view in politics are likely to be promoting views that reflect their interests in various ways. The inclination in politics to see those who have different views as enemies, traitors, lackeys, criminals, or just plain advancers of sinister aims is natural enough. Much of it is merely the result of the intensity of debates in politics, the need for frequent preaching to the choir, and the desire to encourage and organize the faithful coupled with the inability of people to understand each other's arguments. No one who participates in the politics of contemporary modern democracies can escape the inclination to strong partisanship. But this inclination should not blind us to the fact that people do have sincere disagreements and they do have genuine arguments for their opposing views. And these debates are rarely concluded in a way that gives decisive victory to any one of the participants. Furthermore, the fact that people often present positions in political debates that reflect their own interests in varying degrees ought not to blind us to the fact that all persons' views (including our own) reflect their interests, backgrounds, and other sources of distorting bias in some degree or other. This is not something anyone can escape. In a genuinely egalitarian society, these disagreements and the attendant passions are likely to arise but they must never allow us to forget that the public realization of equality requires that each person be given a say in how the society he or she lives in is organized, or so I shall argue.

The problem of disagreement is particularly important when we consider that in order for a society to establish justice among its members, it must do so in a way that imposes a single unitary system of law on the whole of the society. When a system of law establishes justice, it draws everyone into the arrangement whether they agree with it or not. And this means that individuals are quite often enlisted in respecting and supporting laws and policies that they disagree with. The question for a conception of equality is how can a society acknowledge and respect the disagreements that exist among its members and attempt to establish justice among them in a way that embodies public equality?

THE GROUNDS OF DEMOCRACY

Here I shall give an argument to the effect that democratic decision-making is uniquely suited for satisfying the principle of public equality against the background of disagreement, diversity, fallibility, and cognitive bias when it comes to determining features of our common world. Given these facts of judgment, deep conflicts of interest arise from the fact that people have conflicting aspirations to shape the common world they live in. When we consider that there are deep conflicts of opinion and interests in how we ought to organize our common world, over the shared properties of society, we see that justice ought naturally to apply to these conflicts of interest. The basic idea then is that the equality involved in democratic decision-making is a uniquely public realization of the equal advancement of interests when the background facts of judgment and the interests in judgment are taken into account. This is the argument I will develop in what follows.

THE COMMON WORLD

The idea of a common world plays a key role in understanding the normative basis of democracy. I will start with what I take to be intuitive features of a common world and then elaborate a definition of the common world. All the disagreements and the attendant conflicts of interest involve conflicting conceptions of how to shape the common world we live in. These conflicts concern, first of all, the establishment of justice. Since we must set up a unitary system of law, we cannot but set up a system of law that is imposed on all. The system of property, contract, and torts, the systems of collective provision of goods financed through taxation, and the systems of regulation (to name just a few elements of the legal system) are all shared arrangements. Such a system affects the interests of all the members of the society because it establishes duties that each person must fulfill and it thereby imposes burdens on each person. It also sets up a system of the rights of each person and other legal advantages from which each person benefits. And it distributes the advantages and disadvantages of social life. Such a system also engages the moral interests of each person by enlisting him or her into a common project of establishing justice among them. Each person must not only act in ways that respect the rights and other advantages conferred on others, each person is also required to support the legislative, executive, and judicial apparatuses that are set up to carry out the laws and policies. And each person is required to do what justice demands for the common good and distributive justice, which require the redistribution of income and wealth. In this way the establishment of justice creates a common world shared by all the members of the society and in which the interests of all members are deeply intertwined.

Furthermore, the creation of a common society usually requires that at least some public goods be created by the state or at least regulated by the legal system. For one thing, creation of a common society requires at least some devotion to a common system of education. How much the system should be in common is likely to be a matter of controversy but that there must be at least common standards of education as well as a devotion to the education of all members cannot be doubted. These are necessary to the maintenance of a thriving society, which advances the common good and justice. What these common standards are and how they are to be realized are matters that the members of society must decide in common and on which there is much disagreement.

The creation of a common society requires also that collective goods such as pollution control and the regulation of environmental damage be at least monitored and often controlled by common institutions. The creation and regulation of public systems of roads, parks, sewers, and waste management are all things about which the society must make at least some very important common decisions. There are numerous other public goods that must be at least monitored and often created and regulated by the society as a whole in order for the society to thrive. How much the society ought to provide as a whole, who should pay the costs, and how it should do so will be matters of a great deal of controversy that will also determine key aspects of the common world we share. Furthermore, all these decisions have important and differing impacts on each individual. They establish a distribution of benefits and burdens for everyone and they enlist the participation of each person in morally loaded activities.

Here, I will articulate the notion of a *common world*. A common world is a set of circumstances among a group of persons in which the fundamental interests of each person are implicated in how that world is structured in a multitude of ways. It is a world in which the fulfillment of all or nearly all of the fundamental interests of each person are connected with the fulfillment of all or nearly all of the fundamental interests of every other person. This world is marked by a deep interdependence of interests among the members.

Modern political societies are characterized by comprehensive systems of provision and regulation of the basic needs of all the citizens. They regulate the systems of education, basic health care, provision of public goods, taxation and redistribution of income and wealth, criminal law, and punishment as well as the system of tort law. They define the system of property rights and contracts. They provide comprehensive systems of law enforcement. They create highly unified and integrated internal markets that are regulated in unified and systematic ways. They provide a unified system of defense against external attacks. They provide essential infrastructure for all the necessary utilities of everyday life as well as commerce and sanitation. And they provide essential sources of information on matters of expert knowledge. All of these activities and more, which implicate the fundamental interests of their citizens, are done in a highly unified way that looks to the overall interests of all citizens and attends to the basic fairness of the system as a whole. It is this unified system of regulation and the societal and economic effects of this system that make a common world among citizens.

There are three facts about the idea of a common world that I want to bring out. First, there are many ways in which people's interests conflict and overlap with each other. This is important because in a common world, compromise is possible since one can have one's own way on one contentious issue in return for others having their way on other issues. And given the multiplicity of connections, there is a great deal of room for compromise and accommodation. Second, given the many ways in which people's interests are connected with the interests of others, there is an opportunity to have a sense of overall justice in the relations among persons. Even if one group's interests are advanced by some features of that common world, there is a chance that overall the interests of each are advanced equally. Third, in a common world the members of that world have, roughly speaking, equal stakes in how that world is structured. Since all or nearly all of the fundamental interests of each person are at stake, there is a kind of fundamental equality of stake in that world.

For democracy in political societies to be intrinsically important it must apply to what I have called a common world. The common world condition is distinct from what is sometimes called the "all affected" condition according to which every person who is affected by an action ought to have a say in it.[1] And it is different from the condition some have defended which asserts that when the actions of persons in one part of the world engage and direct the actions of persons elsewhere, they all ought to have a say. It is also distinct from the condition that asserts that when actions of persons in one part of the world affect at least some of the fundamental interests of those in other parts of the world, each ought to have a say in these actions.[2] The common world condition is different from these other conditions in that in the common world, all or nearly all the fundamental interests of each person are implicated and so each person has roughly equal stakes in the shape of the common world.

I do not object to these other principles as principles that give others a say in what affects them or directs them or affects their fundamental interests. What I object to is the idea that these other principles are adequate to grounding the intrinsic value of democracy. As I see it the idea of a common world is important because of its connection to the underlying principle of equality. The main idea behind the importance of a common world is the idea that in a common world individuals have roughly equal stakes in the world they live in. Their interests are roughly equally at stake in such a world as a result of the idea that all or nearly all of their fundamental interests are at stake for each person. This is what makes a common world peculiarly suited to democratic decision-making, which as we will see is grounded in equality.

These facts distinguish the world of modern political societies from more partial associations. In clubs, economic enterprises, commercial ventures, and trade unions, the interests that people have are partial. As a consequence, the interests that people have in them are likely to be quite varied. There is no reason to think in general that people's interests are equally served by any one of these associations. That is, for any association, there is no reason to think that the interests of the members are equally at stake in that association. This follows from the diversity of interests among persons. As a consequence there is reason to think that people do not have equal stakes in these partial associations. And it is reasonable to think that the interests that people have in such arrangements in the case of transnational associations are also likely to be varied and partial and consequently their stakes in these arrangements are not likely to be equal. In contrast, the world created and sustained by political

[1] See Carol Gould, *Globalizing Democracy and Human Rights* (Cambridge: Cambridge University Press, 2004), p. 175, for this principle.
[2] See Carol Gould, *Globalizing Democracy and Human Rights*, pp. 176–80, for a review and critique of some different approaches and a defense of the approach that makes human rights central to determination of who ought to have a say in collective decisions. See also Thomas Pogge, *World Poverty and Human Rights* (Cambridge: Polity Press, 2002), p. 184.

societies touches on so many of the basic interests of persons that it is far less likely to touch on more of the basic interests of some people than on others.

To say that people inhabit a common world in most modern political societies is not to deny the many ways in which societies have become interconnected in the last half century through the process of globalization. There are many and increasing numbers of interdependencies of interests of persons across borders. But the extent of interdependencies of interests within political societies is far greater on the whole. One recent commentator has said with regard to global economic integration: "The best estimates of multinationalized production indicate that such activity comprises less than 10 percent of output even in the world's most integrated economies."[3] Though globalization in economic activity is an important phenomenon, this does not undercut the claim that interdependency is far greater within political societies than between them.

To say that people share a common world conceptually does not require that they share a culture or even nationality. One may live in a world in which one's interests are deeply connected with the interests of others but where there is little shared culture. Multinational states and multiethnic states can all be cases of culturally heterogeneous but common worlds. To be sure, the lack of shared culture or nationality in multicultural or multinational states has sometimes made such common worlds fragile and filled with strife. But it is because the interests of persons in these states are intertwined that they experience such strife. So some common worlds may prove unstable as a result of the particular diversity of groups in those societies and as a consequence some cultural commonalities may be socially necessary conditions for stability in those societies. But there is still an important conceptual distinction between the idea that a society is a common world and the idea that the society is culturally or ethnically or nationally homogeneous.

To be sure, the common worlds that most states include are products of highly contingent and morally arbitrary causes. They are the results of the long-term formations of common legal, political, and educational institutions as well as regulatory, welfare, and taxation regimes within certain territorial confines. These activities over the last number of centuries have forged common worlds for their citizens. And in many cases, these common worlds were forged by the use of force and fraud. But however one thinks

---

[3] See Geoffrey Garret, "Global Markets and National Politics: Collision Course or Virtuous Circle?" *International Organization*, vol. 54, no. 4 (Autumn 1998), pp. 787–824, esp. p. 791. Garret goes on to remark that the level of global economic integration is about as high as it was at the end of the nineteenth century and that the reason for our current sense of increasing globalization is the massive contraction of global trade that took place in the mid twentieth century.

of how these common worlds are formed, the fact of a common world is a morally relevant fact now. Arbitrariness of origins does not imply the moral unimportance of the phenomenon that has been formed. To see why this common world is morally important we must continue the argument for democracy.

Many have argued that democratic institutions ought to expand to global or at least transnational levels because clearly people are affected by what happens beyond their borders. But I would enter a cautionary note on this move on the grounds that mere mutual impacts among persons is not sufficient to ground democratic institutions. It must be the case that the individuals have roughly equal stakes in the things that connect them in order to justify giving each an equal say in these relationships. And though people are affected by what happens in societies beyond their borders, the normal case is such that the impacts on interests are not equal. It seems to me that for the time being, the principal community in which people clearly have equal stakes is the modern state. The reason for this is that in the modern state people share a common world. I will have more to say about this claim and exceptions to this claim in Chapter 7 of this book.

EQUALITY AND THE COMMON WORLD

But we cannot divide up this world into privately held pieces and then distribute them so that each person lives on her own island, so to speak. Our common social world in many ways constitutes an indissoluble unity. This much follows from the facts that we are establishing justice for the society and that we need to bring about collective goods for the society. The very effort to divide things up into privately held parcels in a fair way requires a common scheme of justice for those among whom the fair division is taking place. And the collective goods are goods that are shared by the persons in society. And this indissoluble unity is central to the interests of each person. So a fully resource egalitarian principle cannot help us solve the problem of how justly to shape the common world we live in.[4] There must be an egalitarian principle that applies to the common world we live in that does not involve the division of that world into privately held parcels but that applies to that common world as a whole.

[4] On this, see Ronald Dworkin, *Sovereign Virtue: The Theory and Practice of Equality* (Cambridge, MA: Harvard University Press, 2000), chapter 2. Dworkin asserts that equality of resources is a principle suited to the division of privately held goods and does not concern public or collective goods.

Now, of course, we could try to do this by trying to make everyone equally well off or giving each person equal opportunity for well-being. And given the principle of equality of advancement of interests, these could be legitimate aims to pursue. The trouble is that we have no clear and public ways to measure our own or others' happiness. And we have no clear and public way to compare our own well-being with that of others except in crude ways. Nor do we have any clear or public ways to measure and compare the opportunities that people have for well-being. The attempts to unilaterally realize any of these or related principles would be mired in controversy in innumerable ways. Indeed, from the egalitarian standpoint, any such attempt would quickly draw the criticism that the society was in fact being organized to advance the interests of some over others. These points follow from the facts of diversity, disagreement, fallibility, and cognitive bias, which I have called the facts of judgment, and from the interests in judgment. No effort at somehow equalizing well-being or the opportunity for it among participants with regard to these common features of society is publicly defensible even to those who accept equal advancement of interests.

It should be noted that these criticisms apply to an equality of resources scheme as well as the welfarist versions of equal distribution I discussed above. An equal resources scheme cannot serve as the foundation of public justice in part because it too invokes notions that cannot be fully publicly defended. It must have a way of determining who has more or less talent and who has greater handicaps. And it must do this in ways that answer to the preferences of each person since talents and handicaps are ultimately defined in terms of the preferences of those who have them. Furthermore, how much a person is to be taxed for having greater than normal talents also requires a conception of that person's preferences over the talents and the activities the talents permit. And how much a person is to be compensated for handicaps is also to be determined in terms of that person's preferences as well as the preferences that most people have over these things. Though these principles do not require the direct comparison of the well-being of one person against another's, they do require a huge amount of information about each person's preferences and their relationships to other persons' preferences. And this information is either largely absent or likely to be extremely controversial.

So these commonly advanced egalitarian principles fail to provide a publicly clear measure of equality. But they also are likely to fail to provide a publicly acceptable account of equality. This is because they rely on highly controversial accounts of the idea of equality such as that opportunity for welfare or access to welfare or resources or capacities ought to be the main objects to be equally distributed. These accounts rely on highly controversial ideas of how the voluntary choices and judgments of individuals or the good of individuals should enter into the judgment of equality. So even if we could, *per impossibile*, provide clear measures of welfare or opportunity or talent, we would still be left with highly controversial accounts of how these things should be distributed.

What this implies is that these kinds of principles cannot serve as the foundations of public equality in a society. The implementation of these principles cannot be seen as realizations of equality from the egalitarian standpoint. It may be legitimate for people to offer these principles for the regulation of society once the public realization of equality is already in place. But they cannot serve as the foundation of the public realization of equality because they cannot pass the test set up by the egalitarian standpoint of publicity. A person who lived in a society where one of these principles was unilaterally imposed and applied, even if he agreed to it, would likely have reason to think that the society at its base is favoring the interests of some particular group at the expense of others' interests since it is highly likely that the principle and its application would be highly controversial.

DEMOCRACY, PUBLIC EQUALITY, AND THE COMMON WORLD

If we think of the common world as essentially a nondivisible good, we cannot divide it into resources and then distribute them in a publicly egalitarian way. We can, however, distribute resources for participating in the collective decision-making that shapes this common world. We can distribute votes, resources for bargaining, coalition building, and deliberation in reasonably clearly equal ways. This would be a democratic way of resolving the problem; is it justified? The first step in the argument here is to defeat the argument that democracy must be evaluated solely on the basis of its outcomes. The second step is to show that democracy is grounded in public equality. In order to do this, I will describe the fundamental interests that ground the democratic rights and show how democracy constitutes a genuine form of equal advancement of interests when taking account of the facts of judgment and the interests in judgment. Finally, I will sketch an argument for why making decisions democratically makes those decisions legitimate even if they are unjust. This argument will be developed in more detail in Chapter 6 on the authority of democracy.

INTERESTS, JUDGMENT, AND CHOICE INSENSITIVITY

I have spoken of conflicts of interests being resolved by democratic means. Democracy does not, however, directly constitute a solution to conflicts of interest. In a democracy, conflicts are resolved via processes of discussion, negotiation, and voting. And citizens carry out these activities on the bases of their judgments. Citizens advance their interests by talking and voting on the basis of what they judge to be their interests just as citizens advance the common good and justice by talking and voting on the basis of what they judge justice and the common good to be. The system of rights to property, rights of association, and rights to expression and privacy plays a large role in defining our common world. But we would not say that disagreements about the contours of these rights are per se conflicts of interests. In this way, Ronald Dworkin is right to say that these matters are for the most part, choice insensitive matters.[5] The right decision in these cases is not a matter of what choices people make or what interests people have in deciding the outcomes. These are matters of justice where we have the sense that there is a right answer to the questions at issue. And citizens attempt to discern the right answers to these questions when they engage in much of the deliberations distinctive of democratic societies. It would be completely false to the way democratic citizens conduct themselves in the processes of discussion to characterize them as attempting merely to advance their interests. Of course, they are looking out for their interests and they often give their own interests too much weight in determining what the common good requires and what justice demands. Indeed, the conclusions they arrive at often reflect their interests in this context. But they are usually not primarily trying to advance their own interests in the process. They desire that the society they live in be just and the interests of each be advanced in the context of the advance of the interests of all.

We might think, with Dworkin, that we ought to infer from these observations about the point of view of the citizen that we ought not to concern ourselves with how a political process can be intrinsically fair or just to the citizens. We might think that if the correct aspiration of citizens is to arrive at and implement the best conception of justice and the common good, then we ought to judge political processes entirely by how good the outcomes of the decision-making processes are.[6] We might be tempted by an *instrumentalist* approach to collective decision-making processes that

---

[5] See Ronald Dworkin, *Sovereign Virtue: The Theory and Practice of Equality*, p. 204.
[6] See Dworkin, *Sovereign Virtue*, pp. 184–210, esp. for this argument pp. 204–5.

sees these processes as evaluable entirely in terms of their outcomes. I want to focus on the inference from the judgmental orientation of citizens to arrive at the best conception of justice and the common good to the claim that political processes must be evaluated entirely in terms of their outcomes.

How, if justice is a matter of public realization of equal advancement of interests, can we show that democracy offers such a public equality? Do we have reason to offer a democratic solution to conflicts of interests and conflicts of judgment regarding what is right in matters that pertain to civil and economic justice?

Though Dworkin is right in insisting on the choice insensitivity of most if not all of the issues that arise in the democratic forum, it would be a mistake to infer from this that the principle of public realization of equality in advancement of interests has nothing to say about how fairly to make decisions in this context. Though democratic citizens do attempt to arrive at the best judgments of how to understand the common good and justice and strive to implement these in law and policy, it is still the case that public equality demands that the interests of each person be publicly advanced equally in the process of decision-making. We can make a case for the intrinsic fairness or justice of the process of decision-making on the basis of a principle of the publicly equal advancement of interests. Let us see why.

First let us defeat the inference from choice insensitivity to instrumentalism. We can see that the inference does not hold in other contexts in which issues have choice insensitive answers. With regard to individual choice, we can see that the issues that individuals make choices about are often choice insensitive. There is often a right answer to the question of what a person ought to do in some circumstance because one course of action would lead to an uninteresting and not very worthwhile life even from that person's point of view while the other would lead to a very worthwhile life for that person (and no other moral issues are at stake). But, it would be consistent with this observation to say that we owe a duty of respect to that person not to interfere with that person's actions. In Jeremy Waldron's felicitous phrase, that person has a "right to do wrong."[7] I do not mean to endorse that claim here; all I mean to do here is to show that from the existence of a choice insensitive answer to the question of what a person ought to do, it does not follow that there is no intrinsic reason for not interfering with that person's action.

---

[7] See Jeremy Waldron's, "A Right to Do Wrong," in *Liberal Rights* (Oxford: Oxford University Press, 1990).

THE INTRINSIC FAIRNESS OF DEMOCRACY

Now I want to provide the reason for why there is an intrinsic fairness or justice to the democratic process despite the fact that the issues to which the process applies are for the most part choice insensitive. The facts of diversity, fallibility, disagreement, and cognitive bias and the interests we have along with the principle of public equality provide the keys to the final stretch of the argument for democracy. Justice requires that we be publicly treated as equals. But what is the best way to do this? Democratic decision-making on the issues in contention is one necessary part of the uniquely public way of realizing equality among citizens.

THE FUNDAMENTAL INTERESTS THAT GROUND DEMOCRACY

We can, with the tools I have been developing, say why democracy is one of the main ways in which the equality of citizens is expressed in society. Once we occupy the egalitarian standpoint of publicity we can see that the facts of diversity, disagreement, fallibility, and cognitive bias and the interests in being able to correct for others' cognitive biases, being at home in society and in having one's equal moral standing publicly recognized and affirmed ground the principle that each should have an equal say in a collective decision-making process concerning the organization of society. Moreover, each has an interest in learning about his interests as well as justice, which is best realized in a process of discussion with others wherein others take one's views seriously and respond to one's views about justice and interests. Given these facts of judgment and interests in judgment, each person's judgment about how society ought to be organized must be taken seriously. If someone's judgment is not permitted a say in society, then the interests described above will be set back. Anyone who is excluded from participation in discussion and decision-making can see that his or her interests are not being taken seriously and may legitimately infer that his or her moral standing is being treated as less than that of others. So justice, which requires public equality, demands an equal say for each. Let us look at each of the elements of this argument.

From the egalitarian standpoint, the facts of diversity, disagreement, fallibility, and cognitive bias loom large. The reason for this is that on the issues that divide people concerning the justice of society, there is likely to be a great deal of disagreement. The first interest that is deeply implicated in this context is the interest in correcting for cognitive bias. Given that each person's judgment has cognitive biases toward her own interests built into the judgments and given the diversity of persons, each person can see that any attempt to impose a particular view of justice unilaterally in law and policy by a group of persons is likely to fail to take into account and properly reflect the interests of those who are imposed upon. Her interests are likely to be neglected because they are ill understood and because they are likely not to be given due weight by others who do not share those interests. And the principles by which her interests are accommodated to the others' interests are likely to fail fully to find the proper place for those interests. As a consequence, a decision procedure that accorded no weight to a person's judgment or significantly less weight to that judgment than to those of others, and more worryingly to the judgments of all the members of whole groups of persons, can be expected, given the normal functioning of human cognitive systems, to give short shrift to the interests of those persons.

It is not as if this has not been tried. Many thinkers and legal traditions have expressed the view that a person could be virtually represented by others even if those others' places in society, background experiences, and distinctive conditions of flourishing were very different. This was the theory behind the denial of the rights to vote of working-class persons, African-Americans, women and the American colonists before the American War of Independence. It was also the theory behind the Leninist conception of a vanguard party. The results have always been the same. The interests of the members of these groups were not adequately taken into account. Is this because those who did hold power were selfish and grasping, merely claiming to be concerned with the welfares of the others? It seems to me to be highly unlikely that this is generally true. Surely men did not think that they merely wanted to advance their own interests at the expense of women. We have good reason to think that people in fact have been sincerely concerned with the well-being of others. The problem is that the well-being of others is not so easy to understand. They must be there to speak for those interests and to stand up for them. They must be there to make sure that those interests get an adequate hearing and that they are properly accommodated in the scheme of justice that is chosen. Otherwise, the even well-meaning efforts of those who need not listen to them are likely to miss their marks.

Perhaps it is the case that this fact was not always well understood. It is a contingent fact. But we now know that it is an extraordinarily deeply rooted contingent fact that can be explained with some fairly simple ideas. And the implication of our knowledge of this simple fact is that virtually everyone in a society that fails to accord an equal voice to a group of people when matters of public law and policy are at stake knows that the interests of those people are going to be neglected in important if not entirely predictable ways. What this implies is that a society that withholds the vote from some groups of people, or diminishes their political power in some clear way, is publicly expressing a lack of concern for those people. And, given this knowledge, it is clear that the public withholding will be done for the sake of advancing the interests of those who do hold power. From an egalitarian standpoint, a society that fails to give all of its sane adult members the vote or that significantly diminishes the power of some group is publicly treating some of its members as inferiors because the ruling group is setting back the interests of those members for the sake of advancing its own interests.

Recall that the egalitarian standpoint from which this judgment is made must be properly informed, which means that the judgments people make from that standpoint must be informed by the facts of diversity, disagreement, and cognitive bias and the interests that I have described. In this context, if people judge the justice of an arrangement where a minority or even a majority assumes for itself the right to rule others, they will judge that it advances the interests of the ruling class at the expense of the others. Hence, they will judge that it is profoundly unjust from an egalitarian standpoint. It cannot but fail to implement public equality.

Notice how this argument makes the aspiration of each citizen to achieve justice in her society compatible with the need to ensure that each person has a say in the process of deciding on how the society is best organized. Each citizen will, within the context regulated by a principle of democracy, try to arrive at a correct assessment of, and bring about, justice as much as possible. But they will insist that democracy regulate the collective decision-making process because they know that otherwise their interests or the interests of whoever is excluded are likely to be neglected by a process that excludes them. As a consequence, they also know that those who are excluded or whose political power is significantly less than others are being publicly treated as inferiors. They need not think that their aims in the democratic process must be to pursue their own interests in order for them to think that the process must publicly ensure the equal advancement of interests.

The very same conclusion is supported when we invoke the interest each person has in being at home in the world she lives in. I have already defended the claim that this is a fundamental interest of persons. Each person has a fundamental need to have a sense of fit with the world around him, a sense of connection with that world, a sense that this world makes some sense to him.

What are some of the elements of being at home in the world? First, as Will Kymlicka has pointed out, it is important for a person to face an array of meaningful choices in life, ones that offer a sense of fulfillment and intrinsic reward.[8] For this she needs an understanding of the rules of the game in society and a sense that these rules make sense so that she can pursue her interests in such a world. Second, it is important that a person be able to affirm the institutions of which he is a part and which play a large role in directing his life. For that he needs to understand them and he needs to think of them as making sense. Third, it is important that the ways in which the institutions affirm or discourage activities he might engage in make sense to him for the most part. Fourth, it is important that a person have the sense of being connected with other people in the sense that she can appreciate what they are doing and can experience some sense of identification with their actions and achievements. In this respect it matters that the person can identify with the larger projects of the society as a whole as well as the particular projects of parts of society. Fifth, it also matters that that person's projects are ones that others can identify with and affirm, so that the person does not have a sense of anomie. Sixth, it also matters that each person have a sense that his or her more intimate self is protected and in some cases provided for in a way that makes sense to him or her and in a way that does not disgust or humiliate him or her. And seventh, his intimate self must be provided for in a way that she knows will not generate the disgust in others or their humiliation and therefore alienation from others.

Of course, this sense of fit and connection are partly fulfilled by the voluntary associations of which he is a part such as family, friendships, professional or work associations, clubs, and perhaps religious or moral associations. And this will be part of the basis for a right to freedom of association we will discuss in Chapter 4. Here the idea is that one basic way in which this interest of a person will be satisfied is when that person has a sense of fit, connection, and meaningfulness in the larger society. In some part this interest will be satisfied if the person and all the persons in the groups to which the person belongs have some say in how the legal system and policies they must obey are arranged. They also must have some say in the choice of public provision of collective goods as well as the character of the collective goods the society is to bring about. These institutions and policies frame the lives they are to lead and frame all the activities and associations they are members of. And so they have a deep interest in having the sense that they fit in with these institutions.

In addition, though each person is a member of smaller groups that play a large role in making the world they live in a home, given the dynamism of societies and the likelihood that people will change memberships and identifications on occasion, it is essential that the person be at home in the larger

---

[8] See Will Kymlicka, *Liberalism, Community and Culture* (Oxford: Oxford University Press, 1989), for an insightful discussion of this.

world. And finally, if the person is not to be alienated from the larger project of justice the society is engaged in it is important that he have a sense of being at home in that legal and political framework.

Given this fundamental interest in being at home in the world, if a person or a group of persons has no say in the world they live in, it is highly likely that their interests will be set back and this will be for the sake of the interests of those who rule. The ruling class will be able to form a world in which they experience a sense of fit, connection and meaningfulness. They deprive those who have no say of such a sense of being at home in the world. The disenfranchised will be enlisted in a larger societal project that makes little sense to them and that provides little reward for them. This situation occurs, of course, because the facts of diversity, cognitive bias and disagreement obtain in the world they live. So, from an egalitarian standpoint, the disenfranchisement of a group cannot but be seen as a public treatment of that group as inferiors. Hence it must be rejected as unjust.

The same reasoning applies to cases in which persons or groups of persons have systematically less political power than other groups. These people will have significantly less impact on the world in which they live and will be less able to make the world they live in a home than others are. As a consequence, they will live in a world that is primarily dominated by others' sense of how the world ought to be shaped.[9]

Another interest that is promoted by each person's democratic right is the interest in learning the truth about matters of social importance. The reason this interest is promoted by the democratic right and set back by disenfranchisement and other lesser forms of disempowerment is that one of the main ways in which a person learns about matters of social importance is when others respond to the views that they have on these issues. This process of trial and error is promoted by the democratic right. The basic idea here is that each person learns on matters of political and moral importance primarily through trial and error and the main process of trial and error a person learns from is debate and discussion with others. But others will not respond to a person whose judgment is not accorded respect and in particular they will not respond to people who have little or no power. The reason for this is that in a society where one must deal with a lot of different people with different interests and views, there will be barely enough time just to deal with those who have power. As a consequence, those who have no power will not receive a hearing and thus will not have the opportunities that others have to learn from the trial and error process. And those who have significantly

---

[9] Recall that I have argued in Chapter 2 that the interest in being at home in the world is conditional on that world being egalitarian in a minimal sense.

less power will rarely receive a hearing and the benefits of a trial and error process.

Finally, we come to the last interest advanced by the democratic rights. The interest in having one's equal standing among one's fellow citizens recognized and affirmed is, given the interests and facts described above, greatly set back by disenfranchisement and any other significant form of disempowerment. The reason for this is each person has an interest in having her moral personality acknowledged and respected by her fellow citizens. Each person, qua person, has the capacity of understanding and appreciating what is valuable. This is what gives a person the special status that she has among the things in the world. To exclude a person from participating in the processes by which the choice of how the society is to be regulated is to fail to acknowledge that person's capacity for moral judgment and to treat her like a child or an animal. This is a serious loss of status. And if the political power of a particular group is systematically less than that of others, this implies a lesser regard for their capacities of judgment.

In addition, given the arguments above, if a person is disenfranchised in a society that suggests a failure to acknowledge that person's interests in correcting for cognitive bias, being at home in the world, and learning. And if a person or group of persons have systematically less power than other groups then that group's interests can be expected to be correspondingly less well advanced. From the egalitarian standpoint, given the facts of disagreement, diversity, and cognitive bias, that suggests that the person's interests count for little if anything. In other words, disenfranchisement or systematic political disadvantage implies the claim that the person's interests are less worthy of advancement and that the person is not owed the same considerations of justice as others are. This is a terrible loss of status and therefore a serious setback to the interests of a person. It is a public way of treating the person as an inferior.[10]

---

[10] It is important to note an interesting detail here. The interest in being recognized and affirmed as an equal is not set back by every inequality. This can be seen when we recall the discussion of the leveling down objection in Chapter 1. There I argued that leveling down was not an implication of the principle of equality properly understood. I argued that while all inequalities are unjust, a Pareto superior inequality is more just than a Pareto inferior equality. This has implications for our understanding of when the interest in being recognized and affirmed as an equal is set back. For it seems clear that if the inequality in power is Pareto superior to any feasible equality in power and this is a publicly clear fact, then the inequality does not seem to be a setback to anyone's interests. For each person's interests have been advanced publicly as much as possible consistent with the principle of equality. Hence there is no implication of inferior status here. Of course, as I argued in Chapter 1, there is still injustice here because some people's interests are not being as well advanced and others' are. But the injustice is not a consequence of a setback to the interest in equal standing. I will discuss an example of this later in this chapter. I thank David Estlund and George Rainbolt for discussion on this point.

The interests in correcting for cognitive bias, in being at home in the world, and in being recognized and affirmed as an equal as well as the interest in truth are preeminent interests because they are fundamental to our well-being as limited rational beings in political environments. They are political interests because they are interests that arise when people make competing claims to shape the common world they live in. They are fundamental political interests because they are the conditions for the realization of all or nearly all other interests in a person's life. Each person's interest in correcting for cognitive bias is fundamental in a world where persons make competing claims to shape the world they live in in accordance with their conceptions of how it ought to be shaped. In such a world, if one suffers significant disadvantage in one's ability to correct for the cognitive biases of others, one's interests generally will be set back in favor of the interests of others. And each person's interest in being at home in the world is fundamental because being at home in the world is essential to our pursuit of our interests and projects. Our ability to pursue our projects and interests is deeply dependent on our world making sense to us so that we can navigate through that world. And in a world where people make competing claims to shape that world on the basis of different conceptions of how it ought to be shaped, these interests stand out and are threatened. And the interest in being recognized and affirmed as an equal is essential to us as rational beings who seek to establish justice. Finally, the interest in truth is essential because we seek to establish justice on the basis of our judgments.

These interests are also publicly preeminent interests in political environments because everyone can see that all have these interests even when people cannot understand the more particular interests that people have. Though I may not be able to understand why a person thinks the way she does about justice, I do understand that she has an interest in making her judgments approximate as much as possible to the truth. Though I do not understand a person's conception of her well-being, I do understand that her ability to elaborate that conception ought not to be usurped by others. I know that each person faces severe limitations in understanding another's interests. And though I may not understand what another person needs in her environment to advance her interests, I do know what it is like to be in an environment which is unfamiliar to me and makes little sense to me.

The argument implies that there ought to be an institutionalized way in which the particular judgments of a person are accorded the respect that is embodied in the right to an equal say in the process of collective decision-making. This requirement of equal respect for judgment is primarily a principle for regulating the political institutions of society. It also requires each citizen to take some account of the views of other citizens. But it requires no more than that. Otherwise the principle would be inconsistent. One way in which we extend respect to each individual is by allowing each individual to formulate his or her own judgments about the worth of other people's judgments. People may choose for themselves whom to believe and whom to ally with or whose arguments are most reliable. What is essential for political institutions is that they give each person an equal right to participate in this process of debate and adjudication. And each citizen accords respect to other citizens by taking account of their views, keeping an open mind, and being willing to submit to the force of the better argument. This is how all citizens must respect each person's capacity for judgment.

DEMOCRACY AND EQUALITY

So let us put the pieces together for this main stretch of argument. The idea is that we share a common world in which we wish to establish justice and advance the common good. Since we have roughly equal stakes in this common world justice demands that our interests be advanced equally within it. And social justice demands that we realize equality in accordance with a publicly clear measure so that justice may be seen to be done. But we must do this in the context of pervasive disagreement among persons over how to establish justice and the common good and the facts of diversity, cognitive bias, and fallibility of persons. And each has fundamental interests in advancing his or her judgment in this context. When these facts and interests are acknowledged we see that the only way to advance the interests of persons equally in a way that each can plausibly see to be treating him or her as an equal is to give each an equal say (within a limited scope) over how the common world is to be shaped. So democracy is a realization of public equality in collective decision-making.

Let us look at the three main planks of this final stretch of argument. First, democracy itself realizes a kind of equal advancement of interests. Each person is given instruments by which his or her fundamental interests are advanced. Each person's fundamental interests are advanced through the exercise of democratic rights. This much follows from the facts and interests in judgment. And democracy ensures that they be given instruments so that they have equal abilities to advance their interests. So we are justified in thinking that there is some important kind of equality of advancement of interests, since each person has equal abilities to exercise the democratic rights by which the fundamental interests are advanced.

Second, there is good reason to think that democracy is a publicly clear way of realizing a kind of equality. It involves equality in voting power, equality of opportunities to run for office, and ideally equality of opportunities to participate in the processes of negotiation and discussion that lead up to voting. It is a form of equality that has most often been taken as a sine qua non of treating persons as equals. Historically, it has been, aside from basic civil rights, the main way in which members of society have recognized and affirmed the equality of their fellow citizens. And it has been one of the main expressions of the demand for equal treatment in society along with the demand for civil rights. Furthermore, many of the main features of democracy provide reasonably clear public measures of equality. One person, one vote, equal rights to stand for office, rights connected with equal representation, and basic rights of participation are widely recognized standards of equality that are easy to determine and verify. Hence, we have good reason to think that it is a publicly clear way of recognizing and affirming the equality of citizens. And, democracy realizes equality publicly in a way that is uniquely tailored to the problem of pervasive disagreement.

This equality in decision-making cannot be justified by reference to any further substantive equality in law and policy because there is pervasive disagreement on these and because each has fundamental interests in advancing his or her own judgment. So we cannot justify this democratic equality instrumentally by reference to any further specific outcome principles.

From the public egalitarian standpoint, democracy is the best we can do to make sure that the society advances the interests of each equally. The standard by which we evaluate this situation from a public standpoint cannot go beyond the idea of an equal say, because any particular outcome standard is controversial. So the democratic process, by virtue of the fact that it gives each equal abilities to shape the common world in which they live and thereby equal abilities to advance their interests, is the only publicly clear and acceptable realization of equal advancement of interests in the light of the facts and interests in judgment. And since we do not justify it by reference to any other outcome principle, it is intrinsically justified.[11]

THE PRIORITY OF DEMOCRATIC EQUALITY

To be sure, within the context of democratic institutions, individuals advance their own more particular versions of equality in substantive law and policy and some of these are likely to be wrong while others may be right. Each

[11] See Harry Brighouse, "Egalitarianism and the Equal Availability of Political Influence," *Journal of Political Philosophy*, vol. 4, no. 2 (June 1996), pp. 1996, for another argument for democracy along egalitarian lines. See also Christopher G. Griffin, "Democracy as a Non-Instrumentally Just Procedure," *Journal of Political Philosophy*, vol. 11, no. 1 (March 2003), pp. 111–121.

thinks that his or her view is more defensible than the others but each also understands the facts and interests in judgment. So from the standpoints of individual citizens within the democratic process, particular pieces of legislation will be just or unjust or good or bad. And so, even when legislation is passed, those who think it unjust or wrong will attempt to change it at a later time. The distinctive points of view of each citizen on the justice or injustice of legislation do not evaporate in the democratic process. So democracy only gives partial satisfaction to the principle of publicity. In view of the disagreements that citizens have over what constitutes equality in the society, even when collective decisions are made in a way that take everyone's interests equally into consideration, the outcomes will be thought to be unjust and inegalitarian by many. This follows from the fact that there is disagreement.

So while democracy realizes public equality, the proposals that citizens make within the context of the democratic forum do not fully satisfy publicity. But it is clear that these proposals can be objectively right or wrong, so some citizens' proposals for substantive law and policy will be mistaken and perhaps some proposals will be good ones. There are procedure independent standards for evaluating the outcomes of the democratic process, even though they are not public standards. Moreover, many times the majority will choose the lesser proposal in the democratic process. And if the controversial conception of equality embodied in legislation or policy happens to be objectively mistaken, the democratic process does not thereby make it correct. It does not change unjust legislation into just legislation.

What I have argued is that even in these cases, resolving the matter democratically is intrinsically important. Why is it so important to resolve disputed questions democratically when the issues being resolved are so important? Why not just try to ensure that we get the right answers to the disputed questions? Why is it the case that we must content ourselves with resolving the disputed questions in the context of the democratic process? In these cases I argue that the value of the democratic process has a certain priority over the values involved in the substantive issues of law and policy.

The democratic origin of the legislation makes it such that those who disobey it treat others publicly as inferiors because democracy is the public realization of equality. The legislation is legitimate if it has been made democratically, so individuals owe it to each other to obey it. The competing conceptions of equality in the democratic forum remain controversial notions but if the process that selects them publicly treats all citizens as equals then they are legitimate outcomes of the democratic process. Why does democratic equality have this priority?

First, a qualification is in order. The grounds for democracy only ground a limited scope for democracy, as I will argue in more detail later. Since democracy is grounded in public equality, other rights that are grounded in public equality are limits to democracy. I will argue in Chapter 4 that liberal rights are grounded in public equality and later I will argue that an economic minimum is grounded in public equality. And I will argue that those rights that are grounded in public equality constitute limits to democratic authority. So, the legitimate reach of democracy is compatible with public equality and does not compete with other equally fundamental or more fundamental rights.

Second, democracy is a realization of public equality while the issues within its legitimate reach do not lend themselves to publicly clear solutions. There is conscientious and informed disagreement on these issues. Democracy is a realization of public equality because the interests that ground democracy are preeminent political interests that publicly stand out when the facts of judgment hold. So the grounds for the priority of democracy are that democracy realizes public equality and the issues over which democracy exercises legitimate power do not have answers that realize public equality. And we have seen in Chapter 2 why public equality has preeminence over other forms of equality.

For people to establish justice among themselves, they must do so according to their own best judgments. When we consider the facts of fallibility, disagreement, diversity, and cognitive bias and in general the imperfections of human beings as well as the interests people have in trying to come up with a conception of justice we must realize that the ultimate institutional question is, who has the authority to judge? We cannot simply ask, is it just that this person is treated in this way? We have to ask, who gets to make the decision? And this is a question of how power is distributed and whose judgment has authority.

I may well think that the majority has made a poor decision in some circumstance not ruled out by the limits to democratic authority. And it is my right to think this, express it, and try to change matters through the democratic process. But if I think that I may change it regardless of what others think then I must have an argument that says something about why my judgment ought to be given more weight than that of others. And it is here that the question of the interests behind each person having a say come into play. If I were to change things regardless of what others think, I am in effect saying that my judgment on these matters is better than theirs in a way that is contradicted by all that I know about the limitations of people's capacities for judgments. I am in effect treating myself like a god or the others like children. Since that is not the relationship between us and since they have the same interests in having their judgments respected as I do, I must respect their judgments.

Intuitively, if one dissents from an outcome that has been democratically chosen and one attempts to bring about another outcome by means of revolution or intrigue or manipulating the system, one is acting in such a way that cannot be thought of by others as treating them as equals. One is putting one's judgment ahead of others' and in the light of the facts about judgment and the interests in respect for judgment, one is in effect expressing the superiority of one's interests over others.[12]

Many might be tempted to object that the interests in health care, education, and other such interests are weightier interests than the interests in having a say in how one's society is arranged or in being able to express one's views about these matters. After all, what is the loss involved in a person not being able to say what he thinks or play a role in the formation of society? It seems to be a small one. But, in fact, we can see that the loss is incalculable once we recognize that we must solve these problems in accordance with our best judgment about what justice and the common good require and we appreciate

---

[12] Someone might worry that there is little or no loss to an individual if he or some other particular person is disenfranchised. After all, few, if any, decisions hang on a single vote. So no interests are likely to hang on a single vote. So the argument that I have provided, the objection might go, does not actually ground individual rights to participate in democracy.

This objection misconstrues the real threats to the voting rights of persons. The important threat involves the disenfranchisement or political disadvantage of groups of persons. If an individual is dropped by mistake or even maliciously from the voting rolls, this is a small setback to the individual but it is not a basic setback to the interests of that person nor does it advance the interests of any other group in the society. Some groups try to advance their interests by disenfranchising or diminishing the power of other groups. So the danger in democratic societies is that some groups try to disenfranchise or diminish the strength of other groups' voting rights.

The above objection also supposes falsely that individuals have voting rights in order to advance their own individual and idiosyncratic interests. But, in fact, individuals have rights in a democracy to participate in essentially collective endeavors of their own choosing in order to advance shared interests and the common good. What creates the effective power that advances the interests of individuals is the coalescing of groups of persons into united forces for influencing the collective decision-making process. Very crudely, women join together to improve the conditions of women, African-Americans join together to advance conceptions of the common good and justice that include them. No individual African-American is going to make the difference; only the larger group makes the difference. But the larger group must be formed out of the choices of the individual members. And the members of this group must determine its aims. Moreover, a group's power is in significant respects increased as more individuals join and cast their votes with it. And in an egalitarian method of decision-making, it is just that the number of people who support it and the importance they assign to its concerns determine the power of a group. So the central importance of the individual right is that it is the basis of the judgment of which interests and conceptions of the common good are pursued by groups and it contributes to the strength of the group to which it voluntarily aligns itself. The setback to the fundamental interests of persons occurs when groups of persons are not allowed to participate or when their participation is limited or when their influence is not commensurate with the number of people who are members and with the importance those people place on the concerns the group advances. So while it is the groups that wield the influence, it is individuals who determine the size and importance of the groups in an egalitarian society.

the facts about judgment and the relations of judgment to our interests. For a society to silence or impose political disadvantages on some dissenting group of persons or for it to deprive them of the right to organize and promote their views in order to influence the collective decision-making is for it to deprive itself of all that it can learn about itself and about those others. How much is lost and exactly what is lost is not known, but it is highly likely that a great deal is and that the interests of many people will not be advanced as a consequence.[13]

Under these circumstances, the adherence to democratic decision-making constitutes a kind of touchstone in the public realization of the equality of citizens in the light of disagreement. Democracy is necessary if we are to find a way of resolving disagreement that remains faithful to public equality. This is what makes democracy a uniquely just solution to political conflict and disagreement. It is what ensures that democracy legitimates outcomes even when they are unjust in the eyes of some. What democracy does (together with liberal rights and a minimum) is ensure public equality to the extent that it can be established in human societies. And it is against the background of this public equality that further attempts to realize justice, which are not fully public, can be made legitimate.[14]

---

[13] One example of this kind of loss is laid out in great detail by Amartya Sen in his *Development as Freedom* (Cambridge, MA: Harvard University Press, 2001), p. 152. There he argues that democracy tends to advance the interests of the poor. As an illustration, he argues that famines do not occur in democracies, while they do occur elsewhere, precisely because the interests of the poor are not represented.

[14] There may be some cases in which the suspension of public equality and the consequent setback of the interests connected with it are less problematic than the setback to justice from observing public equality. It is important to see how limited they must be since the injustice of the outcome cannot violate public equality and so cannot violate democracy, liberal rights, or the economic minimum. We will see this in Chapter 7. The questions are, are there cases in which the setback to public equality is less weighty than the loss to the interests in less public concerns and what is one to do with these possible cases? The problem is that in the normal case of disagreement with the outcome, a person would have to make a special exception for himself from the legal framework involved in decision-making by saying that in this instance he is right and thus ought to be able to act contrary to the generally accepted procedures for decision-making. But this seems to violate the idea of equality. Such a person may be justly accused of placing his interests before those of others. So if I say that only I may do these things and no one else may, given the facts of diversity, disagreement, fallibility, and cognitive bias, this would have to be seen as an indefensible hubris and a treatment of others as inferiors.

Equality seems to demand that we have a general rule for this kind of case. Obviously, the rule that says that anyone who disagrees with the outcome may opt out would defeat the collective decision-making procedure altogether. Another rule would assert that when anyone thinks that justice requires X and acknowledges that X is not a publicly accepted principle but nevertheless thinks that the importance of this consideration outweighs others' interests in judgment, then that person gets to make the choice on her own. The implementation of this general rule would severely weaken collective decision-making. Many are likely to overestimate the importance of

TAKING STOCK

The argument to this point has been long and complex and involves a number of layers. Here I will provide a brief outline of what we have done so far. I argued in favor of a fundamental principle of equality of advancement of interests in Chapter 1. I argued that the principle of equal advancement of interests avoids the common objection to equality called the leveling down objection. The principle of equal advancement of interests is a common good principle. The principle of equal advancement of interests is the ground of public equality. The question is how are we to realize equality in our social world? The requirement of publicity, or in other words, the requirement that principles for evaluating social relations, rules and institutions not merely be realized but be seen to be realized, is grounded in equality and the fundamental interests of persons in political society. When people attempt to establish justice among themselves, the facts of disagreement, diversity, fallibility, and cognitive bias along with the interests in correcting for cognitive bias, being at home in the world and being recognized and affirmed as an equal in society all support the idea that only public principles of social justice are compatible with treating persons as equals. Hence the principles of social justice are the principles of public equality and social justice consists in the public realization of equality. So when attempting to realize equality among persons in a social world, we must secure informed and conscientious agreement among those persons that they are being treated as equals; we must secure agreement from the egalitarian standpoint.

If we evaluate the establishment of justice within society from the egalitarian standpoint, we see that there is agreement on the principle that each person ought to have an equal say in the process of establishing justice. We can see this once we acknowledge the background conditions of disagreement, diversity, fallibility, and cognitive bias and we acknowledge the interests people have in having a say in this context. Only democracy can ensure that people are being treated as equals in the making of collective decisions when these background conditions and interests are taken into account. Furthermore, we can see that from the egalitarian standpoint, the case for democracy is essentially noninstrumental; democracy is not a mere means to the realization of some other end state. The reason for this is that, aside from the maintenance of democracy, liberal rights, and an economic minimum, there are disagreements on how to treat people as equals in substantive law and policy. Since

the considerations they advance and underestimate the importance of the public equality lost and many are likely to think that others, who have used this rule, have underestimated public equality and overestimated the importance of the considerations they advance.

there are disagreements on so many matters aside from democracy, liberal rights, and an economic minimum, democracy is justified noninstrumentally from the egalitarian standpoint. Hence, democracy is one essential part of public equality and it is intrinsically valuable when looked at from the egalitarian standpoint.[15]

In what remains, I will address four worries that might arise concerning my egalitarian conception of democracy. Then I will address two fundamental objections to the argument I have made here. I will discuss the objection that equality may require the complete or near complete decentralization of power rather than the democratic control of collective decision-making. Then I will discuss the objection that democracy cannot be intrinsically justified because power ought to be distributed in accordance with the relevant knowledge.

FOUR WORRIES ABOUT DEMOCRATIC EQUALITY

The account of the grounds of democracy supports a robustly egalitarian conception of democracy. There are three main elements to this egalitarian conception of democracy. First, it ensures equality in the formal apparatus of democratic decision-making such as equality in voting rights and in the formal opportunities to run for office and to create political parties and interest groups with which to exert pressure on the legislative assembly. Second, it supports robustly egalitarian opportunities to influence the democratic process in public deliberation and negotiation among interest groups. I will discuss more in Chapter 5. Third, an egalitarian conception of democracy prescribes mechanisms for eliminating the effects of differences of wealth and social power on the democratic process. I have discussed how to realize this conception of democracy in great detail elsewhere, so I will not go into them here.[16]

---

[15] To be clear, though the argument does rely in part on the expressive power that giving democratic rights to individuals has, it is not primarily an argument from the expressive power of democracy or at least not solely from it. The idea behind the argument is that democracy has power to express equality because of its actual realization of equality against the background of the facts of diversity, disagreement, fallibility, and cognitive bias. Democracy does not merely express the equality of the members of society; it does it because it is a way of actually treating the members as equals. Its symbolic significance derives from the fact that democracy is an egalitarian way of treating people. And it is only because the symbolic importance is rooted in an actual equality that it has the significance that it does have. The symbolic significance of democracy that is so important to my account cannot be replaced by public assertions that people are equals.

[16] See my *The Rule of the Many* (Boulder, CO: Westview Press, 1996), parts 2 and 3 for discussions of the implications of a principle of equality for a conception of the nature of citizenship,

In this section, I want briefly to discuss four difficulties that might be attributed to an egalitarian conception of democracy. First, I will answer the worry that a majoritarian conception of democracy can be oppressive. Second, I will answer the objection that an egalitarian conception of democracy countenances leveling down and I will discuss this with reference to the choice between representative and direct democracy. Third, I will show that the principle of democracy that I have defended does not allow for age discrimination among adults. Fourth, I will answer the objection that the grounds I have offered for democracy are as compatible with rule by lotteries as with democracy. In the last part of this chapter, I will address two fundamental objections to my account of democracy.

The account I have given of democracy supports a roughly majoritarian method for making final decisions. The argument above asserts that people have certain fundamental interests in having a say in how their society is organized. But it does not imply that they always get what they want. For given the facts of disagreement and diversity and the unity of the society for which decisions are to be made, it is inevitable that one gets what one wants out of this process only some of the time. Only such an arrangement is compatible with treating everyone's interests equally. The principal alternatives to a majoritarian decision rule are unanimity or supermajority rules. But unanimity and supermajority rules as collective decision rules tend to be inegalitarian because they tend to favor the status quo and those whose interests are protected by the status quo. Only a majoritarian method for ultimate decision-making has the neutrality among options and the anonymity among persons to qualify as a fully egalitarian rule for collective decision-making.[17]

But some may worry that majority rule can be oppressive because majorities can act tyrannically. This worry can be defeated once we see the qualifications to the majoritarian conception of democracy that are derived from the principle of public equality. The qualifications are that majority rule is only defensible within a certain limited scope which is determined by the principle

legislative representation, political parties, interest groups, and deliberative institutions in the context of the modern state. See also my paper "Political Equality and the Independent Power of Private Property," in *Problems for Democracy* eds. John Kultgen and Mary Lenzi (Amsterdam: Rodopi, 2006) for a discussion of how the exercise of property rights can amount to an exercise of political power and how to reconcile this with democratic norms. See also my "Social Choice and Democracy," in *The Idea of Democracy* eds. David Copp, Jean Hampton, and John Roemer (Cambridge: Cambridge University Press, 1993) for a discussion of egalitarian voting rules.

[17] To be sure, the egalitarian standpoint from which this argument is made is itself a kind of unanimity standpoint, but this unanimity standpoint does not have a default rule that favors the status quo and so does not violate equality. When we look from that standpoint at how to establish justice, we can see that it is necessary to give each person an equal say in the process of establishing justice if we are to treat them as equals. And that equal say itself demands that decisions be made in a majoritarian fashion.

of public equality. So majority rule has no special status when applied to issues where the principle of public equality delivers clear verdicts such as the maintenance of democratic rights of all sane adults and the basic liberal rights as well as the guarantee of an economic minimum. Violations of these clear implications of public equality fall outside the sphere in which democracy has intrinsic value. Furthermore, majority rule loses its authoritative force when it produces persistent minorities or discrete and insular groups that never participate in winning coalitions in decision-making. I will lay out the argument for these limits by showing how they are grounded in public equality in more detail in Chapter 7 of this book.

PUBLIC EQUALITY, LEVELING DOWN, AND REPRESENTATIVE DEMOCRACY

The egalitarian conception of democracy may lead some to think that my account supports a kind of leveling down. If equality is at the basis of democracy then a more equal but far less effective system of collective decision-making would be superior to an unequal system that was more effective at advancing everyone's interests.[18]

I will discuss this worry with reference to the issue of whether direct democracy is superior to representative democracy. It appears that in representative democracy some people have decision-making power that others do not. The representatives in a legislative assembly have the powers to make laws and policy while most citizens do not have this power. Does this imply that representative democracy is inegalitarian while direct democracy is not?

Such an inference would be mistaken for two connected reasons. First, I argue that while some institutions of representative democracy are inegalitarian in some respects, there are institutional mechanisms that can make representative democracy compatible with equality in the most important respects. Briefly, I argue that modern states ought to have a democratic division of labor that can reconcile the need for a division of labor in the modern state with the demand for equality. In this division of labor, citizens are charged with the task of defining the aims the society is to pursue while legislators are charged with the tasks of implementing and devising the means to those aims through the making of legislation. As long as the legislative assembly proportionally

[18] See for example, David Estlund, "Political Quality," *Social Philosophy and Policy*, vol. 17 (2000), pp. 127–60, for this kind of worry.

represents the aims that citizens have chosen and the legislators are faithful to those aims while pursuing the appropriate compromises and means, the requirement of political equality can be met.[19]

In contrast, a system of direct democracy in a modern state would be so cumbersome and unwieldy for citizens it would undermine any sense that equality is being realized among citizens. Most citizens simply would not have the time to devote to the complicated issues involved in making legislation. The process would inevitably be hijacked by elites with axes to grind. That is why a division of labor is necessary. It would also substantially undermine the power of citizens to decide on the structure and organization of society. Without the division of labor that the representative system supplies, citizens would be capable of doing a lot less than they would with such a division of labor. Hence, citizens would have much less power and thus power would inevitably be transferred to other sectors of the society. Hence, not only is representative democracy compatible with democracy, it is superior to direct democracy on the score of equality.

These points are connected with another reason for favoring representative democracy over direct democracy. It must be acknowledged that there will always be some residual inequality under representative democracy. I would argue that representative democracy is still preferable on the principle of equality I have defended. The reason for this is that under representative democracy, because there is an efficient division of labor for decision-making, the citizenry is likely to have a lot more power over the society (even granting limitations on the legitimate scope of democracy) than under direct democracy. The consequence of this is that the interests advanced by this increased power will be better advanced. As a consequence, representative democracy will constitute a Pareto improvement over direct democracy. Since the principle I defended in Chapter 1 says that Pareto superior inequalities are more just than Pareto inferior equalities, the implication is that representative democracy would be more just than direct democracy even if the later were in some sense more equal. To be sure, the fact that there are inequalities in representative democracy implies that there is some injustice in it but it is not an injustice that can be improved by replacing it with direct democracy.

Of course, in a political society this fact must be publicly clear to citizens. And it seems that in the case of representative democracy, the advantages of the division of labor are so clear that this can qualify as a publicly clear

---

[19] See my *The Rule of the Many*, chapter 5 for a defense of this conception of citizenship and chapter 6 for a defense of a kind of proportional representation as an egalitarian way to make legislation.

improvement. Thus, I think we can explain two clear intuitions about representative democracy on this account. First, we can explain why the inequality is desirable and then we can explain why there is something to regret in it, relative to what we think ideally just.

POLITICAL EQUALITY AND AGE GROUPS

Another worry about the conception of democracy on offer here is, do the arguments above support a conception of political equality where people always have equal political rights or is it legitimate for political rights to be age differentiated? For example, Philippe Van Parijs has argued that it may be legitimate to suspend or diminish the political rights of the elderly on various grounds. The question is, does this violate the principle of political equality defended so far? The reason for this question is that there is an important respect in which these proposals may not deprive individuals of power relative to other individuals. Even if the elderly (or any other adult age group) are fully disenfranchised, individuals still face the same lifetime prospects of political power. All persons have equal votes until a certain age and then lose power after that age. In effect, they are given the same lifetime prospects for power. Hence, perhaps these proposals do not violate the ideal of political equality. Let us call this the *broad conception* of political equality.[20] Let us call the conception of political equality that requires that equality be preserved throughout a person's life the *narrow conception* of political equality.

The principles above support the narrow conception of political equality. There are two reasons for this. One reason for this is that the very same problems that usually arise between persons are also likely to arise (although in a slightly attenuated form) between age groups. People have distinct interests at different stages of their lives. People's lives form wholes wherein the different stages are distinct parts of these wholes. The interests associated with the stages are themselves parts of the good on the whole of a person's life. Individuals' lives are structured in part in terms of how they wish to live this sequence of stages of life.

At the same time, in a democratic society, laws and policies can change at any stage in life whether one plans for it or not. Changes such as these have important effects on whether one can carry out one's life in the way that one thinks best. This is not something for which one can insure oneself

---

[20] "The Disenfranchisement of the Elderly," *Philosophy and Public Affairs*, 27 (1998), pp. 292–333, p. 306.

entirely since even the rules governing insurance can also change over time. In a society governed by law that can be changed, it is not the case that individuals can make choices in earlier parts of their lives that guarantee outcomes at later stages of their lives. Hence, if individuals' interests in organizing their lives and being able to depend on (or adjust) that organization over time are to be recognized, they must have a right to have their interests considered whenever the conditions on which they depend are subject to change. And I have argued that under the conditions of cognitive limitations that we find ourselves in, this implies that they must have a voice in these decisions.

So the first argument for the narrow conception of political equality is an essentially protective one. Because political decisions are being made and reconsidered all the time, citizens cannot simply set things up for themselves for the future and depend on the arrangements. Each person must be able to advance the conditions necessary to their well-being at all times and so they must have a say at all times in the determination of the conditions that affect their lives. And the basic reason behind this is that the facts of judgment apply as much, or nearly as much, to different age groups as to different classes of persons. The judgments of younger individuals regarding what is good for older individuals are fallible and cognitively biased toward their own interests. To the extent that the younger can change things for the older in a way that could not have been prevented by the older when they were younger, the older must retain the right to have a say over these possible changes.

A second problem of inequality arises when we consider that different individuals assign very different relative weights to different parts of their lives and assign different roles to those parts of their lives in the overall structure. Those who assign a more significant role to a particular stage in life are likely to do worse in a regime that does not allow them a say in collective decision-making at that stage in life than those who assign a much less significant role. This is because they will not have a say in whether and how the laws, on which their plans depend, change. For those who assign little value to that stage of their lives this will not matter.

To give equal consideration to the interests associated with all these different forms of life in the light of disagreement over what laws are best, it is necessary that each person have a say in whether and how the laws are changed at the different stages of their lives. These considerations are such that individuals can see that if the elderly (e.g.) are disenfranchised, it will be a publicly clear expression of unequal concern for the interests of at least many persons for whom the later parts of their lives are very important. To give public equal consideration to those persons it is necessary to give power to persons at all stages of their lives.

Note that both of the above arguments suggest that a rejection of the narrow conception of political equality would imply a denial of the broader conception of political equality. It suggests that some people's overall interests, when considering their lives as a whole, will be less taken into account on the system that allows age discrimination in assignment of voting rights. Therefore, the arguments that support the broader notion of political equality also support the narrower conception.

ARE EQUAL LOTTERIES AS FAIR AS DEMOCRACY?

Some have wondered whether the kind of egalitarian argument put forward for democracy in this book could not just as well support some system in which decisions were made by lotteries wherein each person had an equal chance to affect the outcome.[21] The thought is that since the lottery treats people as equals, the fairness of democracy that results from its public realization of equality would hold of the lottery system as well. There are a lot of different possibilities here but I think that all of them suffer from the same defect. Let us look at some of the different possibilities first.

One system would give each person an equal chance to rule, say for a year or some other determined time. In a large society like the United States, each person would have a 1 in a 100 million chance to rule. If her number comes up, she would be a kind of queen for the year. Let us call this the Equal Chance to Rule doctrine. There could be a number of variations on this doctrine, for example a number of people might end up ruling as opposed to just one, but they are roughly the same. Another variation on this doctrine would give each person the right to trade the chances before the lottery was put into effect. We will discuss this more in what follows.

Another doctrine might require a system of point voting. In such a system each person gets an equal vote in the decision-making, but the vote only gives that person a 1 in a 100 million chance of making a difference. On this doctrine, the system of voting would be very much like an ordinary system of voting except the outcome of the voting would not determine which alternative wins. The outcome would be a kind of lottery in which the chances of an alternative for winning would be proportional to the number of votes it had received overall. So the alternative that received 51 percent of the vote

[21] See David Estlund, "Beyond Fairness and Deliberation: The Epistemic Dimension of Democratic Authority," in *Deliberative Democracy* eds. James Bohman and William Rehg (Cambridge, MA: MIT Press, 1998), for an argument to this effect. I thank Holly Smith for pressing me on this objection many years ago.

would now have a 51 percent chance of being selected. We can imagine this system with or without a system of representation. It could be used to choose representatives. Representatives could use this method of voting to choose legislation. And, of course, the population at large could use it in directly voting for legislation.

Is there anything wrong with these systems of voting from the point of view of equality and therefore fairness? They all seem to assign equal voting rights or something equal to everyone. In my view they all fail to realize equality adequately. Of course, the worst one is the equal chance to rule doctrine but the point voting systems also fail in important ways. What is the nature of this failure?

We can see the failure of all these forms of lottery systems as systems of political equality if we think of the analogous case of substituting equal distribution of chances at material resources for equal distribution of resources. In the normal case, when we think that a set of resources ought to be distributed equally among a group of persons, we think it is unfair to give each person a chance at those resources and then to distribute everything to that person who turns up the lucky card. For example, suppose that we could choose between paying three equally deserving workers the same wage or paying them with equal chances at all the wages. And suppose that we chose the latter alternative and the consequence was that one of the workers got all the income. Would this be fair? Or more relevantly, would this be as fair as paying each the same wage? I submit that this would not be as fair and that everyone will agree that this would not be as fair. Equal lotteries would realize some kind of equality but the equality realized would be thinner than the equality realized by equal wages.

In effect, the lottery system of wages is a very thin form of equality because it contracts the reach of equality to just the initial lottery. It eliminates equality at other stages. For example, the equal wages arrangement gives people equal opportunities to engage in exchange with each other and with other people. The equal lottery arrangement breaks off the equality at the moment of the lottery itself.

We could imagine, of course, a different lottery system in which people trade their chances for promises. So I give my lottery ticket to one person, thereby increasing her chances of winning, in return for her promising me that she will do something for me if she wins. This new system, which we could call Tradable Equal Chances at Wages, would get us closer to the equal wages scheme. In fact, under the tradable equal chances we could end up with equal wages at the end if some person had made promises to everyone else that he would redistribute his lottery gains equally to everyone. Presumably that would only happen if all had transferred their tradable chances to him. In the absence of complete and unanimous transfer of chances, even if everyone had transferred nearly all of their chances to him in exchange for promises of wages, there would still be a chance that everything would go to someone else who had not made any promises. That would end the egalitarian distribution at the moment of the lottery itself. The initial equality does not reach beyond the initial distribution in that case. In the equal wages system the equality does reach beyond the initial distribution to affect subsequent distributions because people have capacities to negotiate and exchange with others and the outcomes of those negotiations and exchanges are determined by the initial distribution as well as the actions of the equal persons.

In sum, if we simply distribute nontradable chances to wages, then the reach of equality is very limited. If we allow trading in chances of wages, the reach becomes greater and tradable chances are fairly close to equal wages; but there is always the chance that, through no decision on anyone's part, the equality will end as a result of the lottery's operation. In this latter case, it looks as though the lottery system does not allow equality to determine the outcome while in the equal wages case, equality is determining the outcome of trades. Hence, lottery equality is a very thin form of equality when compared to wage equality; it becomes closer to wage equality to the extent that we can trade in the chances but even here (except in the unusual case where all have traded away their chances to one person) chance still has the ability to determine outcomes in a way that seems to ignore equality.

In general, we have recourse to simple lotteries (lotteries without tradable chances) when we must dispose of a nondivisible good and where there cannot be any mutually advantageous negotiation over how that nondivisible good is used. Lifeboat cases are like this. If one person must be removed from a boat so that the rest may survive, and there is no negotiation possible that is mutually advantageous, then we have recourse to a lottery. The simple lottery precludes mutually advantageous negotiation but since it cannot be engaged in anyway, it does not matter.

Now the equal chance to rule doctrine precludes a huge amount of negotiation and deliberation where it would otherwise be possible under an ordinary system of voting. In an ordinary system of voting, selecting who is to rule or represent the group is subject to a great deal of deliberation, negotiation, and compromise. These activities are highly advantageous to all the participants and the distribution of voting power and other kinds of power make this an egalitarian process. What a system of ordinary voting does is extend the reach of equality into these areas of great importance, while the equal chance to rule contracts the reach of equality to a fairly small set of issues and it allows inequality or chance to rule the rest.

One could respond to this by saying that in equal chance to rule, there will be a significant rotation of persons through the system of rule. The likelihood is that different people will win the lottery each time. This gives these people some kind of equality beyond the mere equal chances. This observation is correct but it shows the weakness of the lottery system as a form of equality in a new way. For in this rotating system of rule, the nature of the rotation is determined by chance and thus the agenda for decision-making, which is determined in significant part by the rotation, is determined by chance. In an egalitarian system of decision-making one would want the agenda for decision-making to be determined in an egalitarian way as well since this is crucial to the outcome of decision-making. Once again, the thinness of the lottery equality is exposed.

In addition, once one person has won the lottery and not as a result of any kind of negotiation or compromise with others, the opportunities for negotiation and deliberation on the agenda for decision-making and on the exact character of the items to be decided on is nearly completely thrown away or put at the discretion of the ruler. In an ordinary system of voting, in contrast, all of these issues would be subject to the negotiation and deliberations of the members.

We could try to amend the equal chance to rule in the same way we amended the equal chance at wages arrangement. Give each person the opportunity to trade his chances for promises from the person to whom the chances are given. This arrangement would suffer from the same defects as the equal tradable chances at wages. It gets us closer to a genuine equality, but it still allows chance to come in and overturn all the negotiations and compromises made by the participants as long as there is at least one person who has not traded away his chances. Of course, point voting does this less than the equal chance to rule. But it does it to some extent. The key feature of point voting is that it takes away from everyone the chance to be decisive. No one and no group can ever hold in its hand the possibility of deciding the outcome given what everyone else has done. The consequence of this is that it lessens the value of engaging in negotiation and in engaging in deliberation. It leaves much more to chance while the system of ordinary voting extends the reach of equality into these areas.

And it is in this way that the kind of equality realized by lotteries is thinner than the equality realized by a system of ordinary voting. Extending the reach of equality in effect makes more of the activities involved subject to equality. In that respect, it makes the process fairer to the participants. And thus an egalitarian approach to collective decision-making must reject a lottery approach except in those cases where equality can reach no further anyway.

TWO FUNDAMENTAL OBJECTIONS
TO DEMOCRATIC EQUALITY

In this last part of this chapter, I want to discuss two fundamental objections to the argument for democracy that I have developed here. The first objection agrees with the thesis that some publicly equal way of making decisions is required when there is disagreement about what justice and the common good require. But it suggests that in this situation, decisions should be disaggregated and there should be no collective decision-making at all except perhaps as minimally necessary. Here some have argued from the existence of pervasive disagreement to a kind of libertarianism. The second objection states that the argument for democracy ignores a very powerful and central reason for not giving each person an equal say in the collective decision-making. This argument states that because some have superior wisdom to others and because the decisions involved affect every person's interests, those who have the most wisdom ought to have all the political power or at least more political power than the others.[22]

PUBLIC EQUALITY, PROPERTY, AND POLITICAL POWER

The first objection to my account of democracy accepts the need for people to make their own judgments about what ought to be done in society when the background facts of diversity, controversy, fallibility, and cognitive bias are in play. But instead of arguing that these circumstances call for each person to have an equal say in a collective decision process, this position argues that each person ought to be able to make decisions about his or her own life without the interference of others.[23]

---

[22] Each of these objections are instances of very general types of criticism that have been made of democracy deriving from Plato, Aristotle, and various kinds of anarchist critiques of democracy. They, along with the Hobbesian objections I have discussed in my earlier work, are the main objections that have been made to democracy throughout history. See my *The Rule of the Many* (Boulder, CO: Westview Press, 1996), chapters 4 and 5, for a critical discussion of the kinds of criticism inspired by Anthony Downs' work *An Economic Theory of Democracy* (New York: Harper and Row, 1960). See also my "Social Choice and Democracy," in *The Idea of Democracy* eds. David Copp, Jean Hampton, and John Roemer (Cambridge: Cambridge University Press, 1993), for a critical discussion of the claim that Kenneth Arrow's General Possibility Theorem in social choice theory shows that there is something incoherent about democracy, a claim defended by Russell Hardin in his "Public Choice and Democracy," also in *The Idea of Democracy*.

[23] This criticism is a reconstruction of a number of positions that I have thought about and discussed with people. One source of this idea comes from Robert Nozick's, *Anarchy, State*

The full libertarian position is similar in a crucial respect to the democratic view. They both attempt to resolve the problem of disagreement in the establishment of justice by giving individuals power to act on their own judgments. The democratic theorist does this by giving each person an equal say in a collective decision-making process while the full libertarian does it by giving each rights against the interference of others and rights to acquire, control, and benefit from full liberal property rights and then allowing each person to do as he or she pleases with those rights. Each of these views permits a fairly open-ended use of these rights so that people may live in a way that accords with their judgments.

The libertarian position allows for a certain kind of political freedom as well. For on this account, each person has a right to exit any political society he desires, though, of course, political societies have the right to deny him entrance. The right of exit is really the centerpiece of the whole account. And the thought is that a society is a free society when each person has the right to exit any association (including political societies) of which he is a member. So, in principle, this allows for there to be socialist societies, religious political societies, capitalist societies, and ethnically based societies. It allows that there be any kind of society that people want to have, as long as one is free to exit that society. So people do have some right to choose the terms of the society of which they want to be members or at least exit those societies they do not want to be members of. Of course, this choice must ultimately be made against the background of full libertarian property rights. Individuals may choose to join a society with their property and may voluntarily transfer it all to that society or to organizations within that society.

The reconciliation of the establishment of public equality with disagreement cannot be achieved simply by giving each person full rights to property and allowing persons to associate freely with each other and do as they like on their own pieces of property. The fully libertarian idea of letting each person go his or her own way is only an appearance of a solution to this problem. I want to advance three reasons why the fully libertarian view cannot provide a satisfactory way of reconciling the requirement of public equality with the facts of disagreement. First, a libertarian system of property rights imposes a unitary system of rules on everyone and limits the liberty of each member of the society. The limits on liberty that such a system imposes are not obviously any greater or less than the limits imposed by other schemes since the property of a particular person imposes limits on the liberty of all other

---

and Utopia (New York: Basic Books, 1974), part III. See also Chandran Kukathas, *The Liberal Archipelago* (Oxford: Oxford University Press, 2003), for a related view. I thank Mark LeBar for extensive and instructive discussion on this kind of objection.

persons in society. Property establishes duties in other people to refrain from using someone else's property except on terms that the other person dictates. The others who are bound to obey the duties do not consent to take on the duties.

Second, a fully libertarian system engages each person in the project of respecting the property rights of others as well as supporting a legal regime that protects those rights. The regime established by such a conception of justice is no less a source of disagreement than any other regime imposed by alternative conceptions of justice. And yet individuals must lend their support to that system regardless of what they think of it, on the libertarian account. They have some say within the scheme of rules but they have no say over the scheme of rules, which they must support. From this system there is no exit on the full libertarian view, there is only exit from particular associations of property holders. For the rest one is committed to supporting the arrangement.

The third reason for rejecting it is that a fully libertarian scheme threatens to treat many people as inferiors. This comes in two different forms. One, a fully libertarian scheme threatens to create a status of second-class citizenship for members of the society. The reason for this is that a regime in which individuals have full liberal rights over their property normally generates huge inequalities of property. The consequence of this situation is that individuals who end up without any external property at all may end up in a situation wherein in order to be a member of any society at all or to support their livelihood, they must consent to the condition of second-class citizenship. Such citizenship may include no say over how the society is organized while others do have a say. It may include a reduction of basic liberal rights of association, expression, and private pursuits for the sake of subsistence. Two, the full libertarian allows for some to be beneath the threshold of a minimum amount for a decent life. This is because the full libertarian allows for radical inequalities of wealth to occur. And it allows for those inequalities to be transferred to subsequent generations, so that one may easily fall beneath the minimum for reasons entirely beyond one's control. That these are conditions to which one can be subjected through no fault of one's own, due to the conditions in which one is born, seems to me to be a very serious charge against the full libertarian approach to politics.

One might respond to this criticism that the same could hold for democracy. It would appear that in a democracy the majority could take away the rights of the minority and thus reduce them to second-class citizenship. I will show in Chapters 4 and 7 of this book on liberal rights and the limits to the authority of democracy that these outcomes are not consistent with the principles that underwrite the authority of democracy. So the criticism cannot be turned back on a democrat who has a clear conception of the ideals that animate the concern for democracy.

Still the libertarian could do something similar by simply modifying the libertarianism to include guarantees of the basic rights of expression, association, and private pursuits and by guaranteeing a minimum for each person who enters the world. This is not a small concession and would alter dramatically the account of justice the qualified libertarian would offer. Still it is a consistent position.[24]

What remains a problem for this qualified position is that it cannot really be said to provide a way of resolving disagreement that treats individuals publicly as equals. For it is still the case on the qualified libertarian doctrine, that a person born into the world with a very low endowment of resources cannot honestly be said to have much power to determine what association he will be a member of and what the terms of that association will be. Someone who is born into an enormous share of property clearly has much greater power to shape the world he lives in to accord with his judgment than the poor person has. In addition, the poor person is required to respect that person's greater power and to support it by supporting the institutions that protect property. Such a person cannot plausibly be described as being treated publicly in a way that treats his judgment as important as that of the very wealthy person. And so, given the background facts of diversity, disagreement, fallibility, and cognitive bias and the interests in correcting for that cognitive bias as well as the interests in being at home in the world and being recognized and affirmed as an equal, it seems clear that such a person is being treated in a way that publicly embodies the lesser importance of his interests when compared to those of the wealthy person.

This conclusion is reinforced by the fact that the wealthy person does not have power only with regard to how to dispose of her property. That power is often easily converted into power over how the community is organized and the public environment in which people live. Such a person is able to influence many others by virtue of her wealth. In contrast, the poorer person not only has little influence over the world because he has little property, he has the duty to respect and support the decisions of the wealthy person. Wealth and poverty are not the only differences between persons that have the effect of marginalizing and disempowering some to the advantage of others. A scheme that allows these forms of disempowerment and marginalization as a normal

---

[24] This is something Kukathas would not allow since it violates the consciences of those who reject these provisions and it forces them to accommodate those who need them. Again, a version of the puzzle I have raised above is, why should this violation of conscience be thought of as worse than the violation of the consciences of those who reject the fully libertarian scheme?

part of its operation cannot be said to be publicly treating the interests of all its members as of equal importance.[25]

PUBLIC EQUALITY, KNOWLEDGE, AND POWER

Let us consider a second criticism of the democratic view on offer. The idea that democratic decision-making is an intrinsically just way of making decisions about the structure of society seems paradoxical in a crucial way. This idea along with some commonsense observations about society commits us to a set of propositions that appear to be incompatible with each other. On the one hand, a moral ideal of political equality implies that all adults have moral rights to participate as equals in political decision-making. This appears to commit us either to the idea that differences in competence relevant to making good political decisions are not important or to the idea that there are no fundamental differences in the relevant competence among adults. On the other hand, we clearly do think that the competence relevant to good political decision-making is an important qualification for holding a share in political decision-making power. This is shown by the fact that we do not and ought not to allow children or insane adults to have a share in political decision-making. We can also see that adults differ in important ways regarding their abilities

---

[25] Chandran Kukathas argues in favor of this kind of society (though without emphasizing private property) on the basis of a conception of the nature and role of the freedom of conscience. He says: "The worst fate that a person might have to endure is that he be unable to avoid acting against conscience." He also says: "Our basic interest is...in not being forced to embrace or become implicated in ends we find repugnant." See his *The Liberal Archipelago*, p. 64. Acting against conscience seems to mean embracing or becoming implicated in ends we find repugnant. And being unable to avoid acting against conscience seems to mean being forced to embrace or become implicated in ends we find repugnant. It is hard to see how this position can avoid falling into incoherence. Many people, probably most, will find repugnant the protection of a society in which highly oppressive groups exist and which requires only the right of exit from these groups. But people will necessarily be implicated in supporting that system inasmuch as they will have to respect the rights and support the legal apparatus that protects it. Furthermore, it is inevitable in such an arrangement that most will simply not be able to find regimes that they find entirely to their liking. How could it be otherwise? Of course, few people will reject the freedom of conscience as a powerful principle of political organization. But the vast majority of these have in mind a more limited conception of freedom of conscience than the one offered by Kukathas. Kukathas partly grounds his view on an extreme skepticism about powerful states. (Kukathas 2003: 194). I find Kukathas's statements of extreme skepticism about the possibility for nonoppressive liberal democratic states greatly overstated. His examples are generally of nondemocratic states or of states that are at best nominally democratic.

I have grounded a qualified respect for the judgment of each person and a qualified right of each person to have a say in the society of which he is a part on the basis of the interests people have in their judgments being accorded respect. This position avoids the paradoxes that Kukathas's position seems to court.

to make good political decisions. Hence, given the importance of political decisions to the lives of citizens, it seems foolish to say that all adults have moral rights to participate as equals in political decision-making.

Part of what we want to understand is why individuals who are minimally competent, but clearly possess different degrees of competence above the minimum, should all have equal political rights. Intuitively, since individual voters have a share of power over the lives of others and must make morally significant decisions regarding how social life is to be organized, they are in a position to do morally significant harm to others by, say, enacting unjust laws or unduly restricting liberty. As a rule the less competent are more likely than the more competent to do harm. This reasoning seems to make all gradations of moral competence relevant and suggests that requiring a minimum of competence for the possession of power and making power proportional to competence are in part based on the same idea. Why is one reasonable and the other not?

The problem is internal to the point of view of the democratic citizen. On the one hand, every citizen is expected to acknowledge the right of every other citizen to an equal vote in the democratic process as if they were equally competent or as if competence did not matter. On the other hand, in a complex system of representative democracy, when citizens exercise their democratic rights by choosing party leaders, opinion leaders, sources of information, and so forth, each is expected to choose as if some were more competent than others. These choices are often grounded on a sense that some editors of newspapers or magazines are more reliable sources of morally relevant and accurate information than are others or that a party leader will more reliably steer the party in the right direction and maintain its integrity. Such choices are fundamental to any kind of representative democracy. The point of view of the citizen thus seems irremediably schizoid when it comes to the ranking of competence of fellow citizens. Is democracy simply paradoxical? What is the place of considerations of competence in the justification of democracy?

The evident differences in moral competence among citizens have seemed to many to imply that democracy is an intrinsically unjust or undesirable scheme for collective decision-making or at best a merely useful way to arrange political decision-making.[26] I will not discuss the different possible

---

[26] See Richard Arneson, "Democratic Rights at National and Workplace Levels," in *The Idea of Democracy* eds. David Copp, Jean Hampton, and John Roemer (New York: Cambridge University Press, 1993), pp. 122 and 133–8. The *locus classicus* of parts of this argument is in Plato, *Republic* trans. Desmond Lee (Harmondsworth, UK: Penguin Books, 1991) and Aristotle, *Politics* trans. T. A. Sinclair, rev. J. T. Saunders (Harmondsworth, UK: Penguin Books, 1983), book III and in democratic theory it is J. S. Mill, *Considerations on Representative Government* (Buffalo, NY: Prometheus Press, 1991), chapter 8.

implications of the competence argument in what follows. I aim to defeat the underlying argument and defend equality.

In my view, the conception of democracy as grounded in public equality defended in this chapter and Chapter 2 can help us see how the objection from competence can be defeated. In what follows, I will lay out two conceptions of how one might test for superior competence. I show how both of these tests fail from the point of view of the egalitarian standpoint. I then raise an objection to the egalitarian standpoint namely that it presupposes either the equality of competence or the irrelevance of competence. In other words, the worry is that arguments from the egalitarian standpoint to equality beg the question against the antiegalitarian. I then argue that the egalitarian standpoint does not presuppose equality in competence or the irrelevance of competence. It rests, rather, directly on the principle of equal advancement of interests and the facts of judgment as well as the interests in judgment. Hence the egalitarian standpoint is vindicated and the democratic implications of the standpoint survive the challenge of differential competence.

THE TESTS OF COMPETENCE

The starting point for an investigation of the role competence ought to play in the construction of political institutions is the egalitarian standpoint. The question we must ask is whether there is a way of showing that some are more competent than others that can be seen to be so given the kinds of limits to cognitive ability that we have postulated and given a conscientious effort on the part of citizens. I will argue that the ways in which people have tried to demonstrate different levels of competence will not satisfy from the egalitarian standpoint, that there is no public way of demonstrating the superiority of competence in a way that satisfies citizens from the egalitarian standpoint. But as we will see, there is some question as to whether invoking the egalitarian standpoint in this argument is defensible or question begging. I will elaborate on this worry and show how it can be dealt with.

There are two tests by which one might attempt to show that some are superior in competence to others: substantive and procedural tests. In substantive tests of competence we determine persons' relative moral competence by giving each a list of questions or tasks and then deciding who has performed better in answering the questions or performing the tasks.[27] In this kind of test, whatever measure we design for determining the relative moral capacities

---

[27] In effect, this is the way IQ tests are constructed.

of citizens will presuppose a substantive conception of interests and morality. A measure relying on one substantive conception of value may give evidence of the superiority of some while a measure relying on another conception of value may suggest the greater capacity of others.

But the problem with this is easy to see. If there is controversy on the nature of interests and values, there is controversy on the various measures that rely on them. In a pluralistic society where individuals disagree sharply on conceptions of the good and many of the elements of justice, there are likely to be many incompatible standards for assessing moral competence.

The pervasiveness of controversy in these matters is increased by the fact that moral competence is a very complex disposition that is not well understood. The competence argument shows us that the morally competent person must take many kinds of considerations into account. Abilities to judge each of these kinds of considerations well and balance them appropriately are somewhat independent. People can often be right about certain matters and seriously in error about others. In addition, moral competence usually refers to how well one approximates the truth in moral matters. Furthermore, the speed with which one is able to judge well, the nuance with which one judges, and the capacity to see particular circumstances in the right way are all relevant to the assessment of competence. Again all of these dimensions are somewhat independent of each other. And people rank them differently. This adds to the immense complexity of attempting to assess and compare overall moral competence.

If we were to distribute power in proportion to the distribution of moral competence, political power would be distributed in accordance with standards that are not accepted by people to whom the political system ought to be responsive. If citizens were to take into account the facts of fallibility, diversity, disagreement, and cognitive bias and the interests in judgment, many would have reason to believe that their interests were being neglected or at least not being given equal consideration in the society. Therefore a distribution of power based on such standards cannot satisfy the weak publicity requirement defended above. It fails, to that extent, to be just when we look at the matter from the egalitarian standpoint.

THE PROCEDURAL TEST OF COMPETENCE

Mill proposes that we look to the relative levels of education of the members of society in order to determine who are the most morally competent to make decisions. He argues that those who have had a higher education should receive more votes than the less educated. This test is relatively simple and it is a public one in the sense that members of the society can recognize when someone is better on this particular measure. In order to clarify the purpose and nature of this test, we must distinguish two different kinds of knowledge in this context: technical knowledge and competence from moral knowledge and competence. Technical competence has to do with the mastery of a skill, such as carpentry, or a science like physics. What is crucial to both of these enterprises is that they tend to generate expertise the results of which are products or predictions that can be seen by most people to be useful or not or right or wrong. By contrast, moral knowledge tells us what is useful or not by telling us what the ends of our actions or institutions ought to be. It tells us what the useful knowledge is useful for.

With regard to technical knowledge, the procedural test makes sense. We tend to think that individuals who are well trained in a science ought to have more power in applying that science. We see the point of a council of economic advisors having economists on it. On the other hand, moral knowledge is more problematic in this regard and I have argued that this is what we ought to focus on when we are talking about democratic rights. Still, a person can become more acute in moral competence as a consequence of spending a lot of time thinking about moral questions, hence, perhaps, as Mill thought, education ought to make a difference here as well as in the case of technical knowledge.

Let us assume away the issue of injustice explaining differential education and ask what would be right if each had a robust equality of opportunity to receive an education that qualified him or her for the assumption of power. If equality of opportunity were in place, would those who have superior education be entitled to a greater amount of power than those who do not? Presumably this is the strongest case for the Millian principle.

In reply to the defense of the procedural test, first, we must observe that it is inevitable that the system of education employs controversial standards for the assessment of the candidates for entrance into that system as well as for successful performance in that system. If this is true, one should object that when educational criteria are used for the assessment of the moral competence of citizens, they inevitably presuppose substantive conceptions of what is morally desirable.

Second, the well educated, who have gone through the system of education in a democratic society, are likely to have somewhat different sets of interests from those who have not gone through the system of education. The processes of socialization and other formative features of a course of education are likely to have an impact on what enables such persons to flourish or on what is in their interests. In addition, the social milieu in which such people live their lives is likely to be distinct in various ways from those who are not as extensively educated.

These two facts are likely to have two effects on the perspectives of these individuals. First, their interests will likely be distinct from those outside the group. Second, their understanding of their interests is likely to be more developed than their understanding of the interests of those who live in different circumstances. When we join these two observations with the facts of judgment, we can see that a scheme that gives greater political power to the well educated must inevitably appear to many to give their interests greater weight than the others. This conclusion and the principles of equality and weak publicity together imply that such a distribution of power would be unjust. Hence we can conclude that the educated ought not be given extra power lest we undermine the public realization of equal advancement of interests. Again, from the egalitarian standpoint, this kind of test cannot pass muster.

THE CIRCULARITY OBJECTION

Now suppose that someone asks why we should take everyone's views equally seriously. In particular, why take the standards of value underlying the different standards of competence equally seriously? It appears that the argument above assumes that it is legitimate to take all persons' viewpoints equally seriously since it assigns to each person a veto over any proposal. But if we take into account what appear to be the only plausible rationales for this equal treatment, we appear to have stumbled on a kind of circularity. The only apparent plausible rationales for taking each person's view equally seriously is that each has equal moral competence or that competence rankings ought not to count. We have criticized differential distribution of power in proportion to competence rank either by presupposing equality of competence in the premises or by supposing that inequality of competence above the minimum ought not to make a difference to how seriously we take each person's judgment.[28] But those who suppose that political power ought to be apportioned to moral competence reject both these presuppositions. In any case, neither has been defended. It looks like the egalitarian standpoint itself presupposes the principle that is under discussion and which we have been trying to defend

---

[28] David Estlund's argument against authoritarianism in "Making Truth Safe for Democracy," also exhibits this circularity. He gives each reasonable person a veto over the regime in question. And this supposes that people are equally reasonable or that it does not matter how reasonable people are. The authoritarian rejects both assumptions. The argument I provide to overcome the objection could save the reasonableness account too on this score.

by invoking the egalitarian standpoint. This implies that using the egalitarian standpoint and the attendant principle of weak publicity to defeat apportioning power to competence seems to beg the question against the authoritarian and the elitist.

I will try to show in what follows that this circularity objection can be overcome. To do so, let us define a standpoint where each person's view of justice is taken seriously but where we have made no commitment to equality as the inclusive standpoint. Given this standpoint it is only necessary that people have some say as to whether they can see that they are being treated as equals but that say need not be equal. The inclusive standpoint is inclusive but it may not be an egalitarian standpoint. What I want to show in what follows is that apportioning power in the inclusive standpoint to competence ranking is incompatible with even a minimal responsiveness to the interests of some of the members in judgment. Apportioning power or the respect we accord a person's judgment to competence will require that we not take someone's judgment seriously at all at some crucial point in the disagreement. Hence, we will not be responsive to that person's interests in judgment and thus there is a fairly clear case to be made that that person's interests are not treated with equal consideration with the others.

By comparison, I will argue that a regime that does not take a stand on competence in the inclusive standpoint, but which assigns each person an equal right to judge for himself on the issue of competence within the political institutions, never fails to be responsive to anyone's judgment and so seems to be egalitarian in a way that the merely inclusive standpoint based on competence rankings cannot be. Such a regime takes each person's competence rankings seriously because it gives each person the right to judge for himself on the competence of others in the course of political life. Hence, such a regime strikes a better balance between the requirement of equality and the need to take competence rankings seriously. The egalitarian standpoint is then vindicated from the point of view of equal advancement of interests.

THE ARGUMENT FOR THE REFUSAL TO GROUND POLITICAL RIGHTS ON COMPETENCE RANKINGS

The first step in reply to the circularity objection is to show that the problem of circularity arises as much for defenders of inequality as it does for its critics.

The competence inegalitarian idea behind the rejection of the egalitarian standpoint is that everyone's views ought to be taken seriously but some of these ought to be taken more seriously than others are. Both the claim that competence does not matter and the claim that competence is equal are rejected. Recall that we are assuming that the competence inegalitarian is attempting to realize equal advancement of interests. This latter principle is not at issue in this debate. And since we have argued that there are interests connected with judgment, the competence inegalitarian does wish to set up a regime that is at least minimally responsive to the judgments of each sane adult. He wants to set up a public standpoint that is inclusive even if it is not egalitarian with regard to competence. How might the competence inegalitarian do this?

Instead of an egalitarian standpoint, we have an inclusive standpoint wherein a distribution of power must at least be responsive to the views of each citizen but it need not be equally responsive to the views of each citizen. Such a standpoint cannot operate by simple unanimity, it must operate by some kind of weighting rule that gives each person a say but weights the views differently. From this standpoint, a distribution of power will be evaluated as to whether it treats people as equals or not. What we need to adopt is a hypothetical procedure of compromise that gives different weights to the different parties depending on their competence rank. The compromise procedure directs each to give up some of what he claims until a compromise is achieved. What each must give up is apportioned to competence rank.[29] Let us suppose, for simplicity of exposition, that we can measure competence levels in cardinal numbers. A thinks that he ranks a 10 in competence to B's 2 given standard of value Sa while B thinks that he ranks a 10 to A's 2 given Sb. We take them each seriously but we take A more seriously than B because we think A is more competent. So we attach greater weight to A's judgment than to B's in the compromise procedure. This assessment relies on a standard of value (one that is presumably closer to A's). So instead of splitting the difference in favor of equality the procedure inclines toward A. We end up with the ranking A 8 to B's 4 and thus give A more power. Now both A and B object to the division but B feels more put out than A. But since we take A more seriously than B we are willing to live with the result. Here we have been responsive to both parties' viewpoints but we have not reached equality. The way we have done this is by introducing inequality in the inclusive standpoint itself. And with the unequal say that people have in the inclusive standpoint, we justify unequal power in the political institutions. What is wrong (if anything) with this way of proceeding?

The main problem is that the ranking that gives more weight to A's judgment than B's will be contested presumably by B. To be responsive (at all) to B's complaint about the weightings, we must go through the compromise

---

[29] A hypothetical weighted voting system or a plural voting scheme would do as well. The objections are the same.

procedure again either by adjusting the weights or by going to a higher order compromise procedure. Either way we will end up without any result since B will complain until he gets more and then A will complain and so on. Presumably equality will not satisfy either one. There is no equilibrium point here if we try to be responsive to each person's complaint. On the other hand, we might simply tell B that the process is over since our judgment of his inferior competence is final. We take him and his standard less seriously. This means that in the inclusive standpoint we have simply presupposed A's superior competence and, of course, that it is relevant. So, the reasoning in the inclusive standpoint must end up either in no solution at all or defending A's claim to superior competence partly on the grounds that A is more competent. Hence, we discover the same kind of circularity that plagues the argument for equality.

Establishing a competence ranking when rankings are based on controversial standards seems to have this odd kind of structure. Taking a challenge to inequality of power based on competence rankings seriously enough to reject inequality or generate equality must either presuppose equality of competence or the irrelevance of differences in competence. So there is an implicit circularity. On the other hand, rejecting the challenge to inequality on the ground that the challenger is not an equal must be based on a similarly suspect move of presupposing a particular distribution of competence. Thus we seem to be at an *impasse of conflicting judgments.*

The impasse of conflicting judgments implies that if we allow one or the other presupposition to hold, then we are unresponsive to the judgments of those who object to the presupposition. If we fail to respond to B's objection to the initial weightings, then given the facts of judgment, we seem to be taking A's interests more seriously than B's. And the same goes for B. The same problem holds for equality of competence. With equality of competence we can support equality of power but then we favor the judgments and interests of those who hold the standards that support the egalitarian test. We also support a ranking that virtually everyone regards as false, although for different reasons.

Moreover, we must remember that those who are making these judgments about who gets to be taken more seriously in the inclusive standpoint are also in the political system. If we are assessing A and B for competence, we too are players in the political scheme and our interests are now at stake. All the properties of fallibility, diversity, disagreement, and cognitive bias apply to us as well. And the observations about the standards on which we base our competence rankings hold for us as well. They reflect our interests in various ways. We must not think of ourselves or of anyone who is making these rankings as having a god's eye point of view. We are just human beings with interests and imperfections just like everyone else.

When we consider that we are subject to the same imperfections as the others, we must conclude that when we take the competence rankings that we assign to others as final and thereby disregard the competence rankings of some of the others, we are no longer being responsive to the interests that they have that are connected with judgment. We are only being responsive to our own judgment here. This is not merely an unequal responsiveness; it is a lack of responsiveness at least on this crucial issue. We are simply saying we do not care about your view here, not because your view is inconsistent with equality but because it is inconsistent with our standard of ranking. Hence, an argument that apportions power to competence is not even compatible with a fully inclusive standpoint.

Notice, moreover, that a scheme that uses competence rankings to define the public standpoint itself would seem to disallow each person from judging for himself who is more competent than who. This is because the public standpoint would already have built into its structure differences in competence. It is hard to see how a coherent view would then permit individuals to make their own judgments of competence. Hence the unresponsiveness to the judgments of those who disagreed with the competence rankings of those who determine the distribution of power within the inclusive standpoint would be more thoroughgoing that might at first appear. It would seem to require an unresponsiveness to the judgments of these persons whenever questions of competence had to be decided in ordinary political life. And if it were not thoroughgoing, we would have some reason to doubt the coherence of the method of justification of the institutions.

Any argument for a distribution of power that starts with a competence ranking must be unresponsive to many, assuming disagreement on the rankings. This seems to me to be a fairly clear-cut violation of equal advancement of interests because it involves not only controversial assertions of competence but responsiveness to some and lack of responsiveness to others. But this implies, once we take into account the facts of judgment and the interests in judgment, that every distribution of power grounded in competence rankings treats the interests of some as having inferior significance. So using competence rankings of individuals to weigh the strength of their competing claims to power cannot accord with equality.

What this implies is that if the public standpoint from which distributions of power are evaluated is to be inclusive then it must be an egalitarian standpoint. If the standpoint is not egalitarian then it is not inclusive, which means that it is responsive to some and not to others.

But if we take the facts of judgment seriously as well as the interests in judgment, it is hard to see how the lack of inclusiveness in the public standpoint can be compatible with equality at all. So it must fail to accord with the underlying principle of equal advancement of interests. Therefore the principle of equal advancement of interests requires that the public standpoint be an egalitarian standpoint.

Therefore, the compromise procedure, with rankings at the start, is not an attractive realization of the public standpoint.[30] Hence, the challenge to the inference from the public standpoint to the egalitarian standpoint has been fully met. In order for a society to be responsive to its members, it must embody equality in its institutions in a way that everyone can come to see. If it cannot be seen to embody equality at the level of civil and economic concerns because of pervasive disagreements about these, then it must do so at the level of the institutions designed to resolve these disagreements.

We have rejected the idea that competence rankings can justify unequal responses to citizens; still, competence rankings play an important role in the organization of society. They can play three different roles. In a complex society with a division of labor we need to have a way to choose who is to perform each task. The optimal division of labor is one in which each task is performed by the most competent at that task. In addition, we often need advisors who are reliable guides to truth. The most reliable guides to truth are the best advisors. Furthermore, we must sometimes choose partners in joint ventures and it is important that we choose competent partners because we have to live with the results. So competence rankings play a very important role in social organization. And this holds for moral competence as well.

---

[30] Once we abandon the idea of using competence to weigh the initial claims of the participants in the hypothetical compromise procedure, we might simply allow the participants to engage in something like a bargaining procedure and compromising with the others. They would thereby determine the relative weights of their inputs in the public standpoint by means of a kind of first-order compromise procedure wherein each would start with an equal capacity to advance their claims but each would also start with differing assessments of their relative competences. The idea would be that my sense that I am superior in competence to you and your sense that you are superior are now directly subject to a kind of compromise. This kind of procedure would be a very odd one. It has no appeal as a method of responding to individuals' views. First, though the procedure weighs each person's claim equally, many will claim a greater share of power on the ground that they are more competent at assessing what equality demands. But it is not clear how this can be a stable solution. If I claim to be more competent than you are then it is not clear how I can be willing to compromise as an equal with your claim to be more competent than I am. Once we permit people to claim a greater share of power on the grounds of greater competence the dispute will rise to the second order very quickly. If we reject using competence rankings at the second order, as I have just shown we must, then we should reject individuals' use of competence rankings at the first order. But this entails that individuals will be in agreement over what they demand and thus no compromise will be necessary.

Second, the results of the compromise procedure never satisfy any of the participants since the results must always be a compromise with others. If the hypothetical compromise procedure is used to compromise between different conceptions of substantive justice, the resulting conception of justice will be more mixed up and in many cases less attractive to the participants than their opponents' starting points. The scheme will seem no more responsive than one not based on the compromise procedure.

We have defended the principle of weak publicity and shown that no distribution of power can be based on competence rankings and satisfy publicity. We have also seen that assessments of competence are important for a society. Can any distribution of power satisfy equality and publicity and make room for differential assessments of competence?

THE ARGUMENT FOR POLITICAL EQUALITY

Given the rejection of competence-based distributions of power, I propose that all have equal rights to judge for themselves in matters regarding moral competence. We have equal rights of judgment when each person has the right to decide for himself or herself on the competence of others. It allows that people will disagree in their assessments. Each person has the right to judge that some other person is more competent than himself and/or others and to think of that person as a kind of advisor or leader with regard to moral questions.

To argue for this principle we must show that it need not be based on a particular competence ranking and that it is grounded directly on equality and weak publicity. The principle is not based on a competence ranking. It does not presuppose that individuals are equally competent, or that we ought to think of each other as if we were equally competent or even that our competencies are incommensurable. Under equality, we are willing to give others a chance to persuade us of their views but we are not surprised when, by our lights, some turn out to be more reliable in producing better ideas than others. The principle allows that there may be differences in competence while not taking a stand on what they are. In contrast to this, an inegalitarian distribution of rights to judge would be directly opposed to equal consideration of interests if it were not based on the idea that those who have more rights are more competent.

Equality in the right to judge for oneself is founded on equality of interests, weak publicity, and the facts of judgment as well as the great importance of moral competence rankings. Since there is no way to assign a competence ranking for the society overall that satisfies equality and publicity, the best we can do is to refuse to judge as a society. Yet judgments of competence must be made so we must allow each to judge for himself or herself. Anything but an equal right to judge for oneself would clearly violate the principle of equal advancement of interests in the light of the facts of judgment. An unequal right to judge would either be based on inequality of competence or it would be directly based on unequal consideration of interest. Either way, it violates equality of interests and publicity.

This argument supports in turn the democratic rights to an equal vote and equality in the process of deliberation. Each has a right to judge for himself. These moral competence judgments must be used in organizing society. Hence someone or some group must have the power to make their judgments effective. To assign equal rights to judge to each citizen but a greater say in collective decision-making to a few citizens makes sense on one of two conditions: either we presuppose a particular unequal distribution of competence or we assume that some people's interests are more important than others' are. Either way, it would be clear to those who possess a lesser power that their interests were not being given equal consideration. In contrast, a person need not think that the scheme of equal rights to judge and act is grounded on equal competence or on the irrelevance of competence since it is coherent for her to think and act on the basis of unequal assessments of competence. Such a scheme must therefore be seen as grounded in equality of interest and the facts of judgment. Hence, equal political rights to choose according to one's own judgment are required by justice.

WHY A MINIMUM?

Why are the principles of publicity limited to minimally morally competent persons? The basic reason is that the facts of judgment do not apply to those who are less than minimally competent. The basic standard of minimal moral competence is that an individual is capable of elaborating, reflecting on, and revising ideas about justice. Once a person is capable of doing these things, the problems of the facts of judgment arise and there is a basis for respect for the judgment of that person. If a person is not capable of this kind of reflection on justice, then the facts of judgment do not apply to their appeals and there is no basis for the kind of respect for judgment we accord to those who are able to reflect on these matters. For instance, children are not normally capable of elaborating or reflecting on moral principles, they adopt moral ideas from their parents not out of a sense of conviction or from adequate reasoning but out of a desire to please and a sense of trust in their parents. For the same reasons, children do not have a developed sense of their own interests.[31] As a consequence of these points, children are not likely to have elaborated or reflected on ideas of justice and whatever ideas they do express are not likely to reflect their interests. Furthermore, they are not likely to learn a lot by appealing to already developed conceptions of principles. And their sense

---

[31] See Lawrence Kohlberg, *The Philosophy of Moral Development*, pp. 17–18.

of at homeness is not likely to be tied to principles. Moreover, their status is not undermined by exclusion from collective decision-making about matters pertaining to justice. Children do not understand what is at issue in debates about justice and the decisions that must be based on them. So their status as worthy of just treatment is not undermined, because the facts of judgment do not apply.[32] The facts of judgment, I have argued, create a bridge connecting the individuals' judgments with their interests. If the facts of judgment do not hold for some group of people, then there is no basis within a welfarist theory for thinking that failure to respond to a person's judgments is an injustice to them.[33]

[32] We ought to be responsive to children's complaints. Their complaints are sometimes clear signs of mistreatment and responsiveness can serve an educative function.

[33] Here, I disagree with those who say that we can extend democratic principles to others even though we cannot understand what they say. See Robert Goodin, *Reflective Democracy* (Oxford: Oxford University Press, 2003), pp. 215–21 and John Dryzek, *Deliberative Democracy and Beyond* (Oxford: Oxford University Press, 2000), chapter 6 for defenses of these kinds of views. Here it is important to distinguish between the question of the citizenship status of persons and the moral status of persons. I have argued that children and insane adults ought not in general have voting rights. Hence, they do have inferior statuses as citizens. But this in no way reflects a lesser moral status. They have an equal moral status with adults. Their interests are worthy of consideration and advancement as much as anyone else's. It is just that they are not able, through participation, to advance those interests. Hence they do not have rights of participation.

Of course, the trouble here is, how to advance the interests of children and insane adults? I have argued that those who have no right to participate are likely to see their interests set back. Won't this happen to children and insane adults? It is no use to give them voting rights since they are not likely to be able to advance their interests in this way. The only way that we can make some effort at advancing their interests is through some form of trusteeship.

In the case of children, this is done in part through the parents. The ties of parenthood and the feelings of love and the sense of duty toward their children, parental memory and knowledge of childhood, and the sharing of the social and economic world in which the child is living enable parents to perform this role well. Still, though parents know the interests of children usually better than the children themselves know them, the relation is imperfect. There is no way around the fact that here, the democratic principle cannot be fully satisfied. The case of insane adults is even worse. They too have equal moral status but they do not have the rights to speak for themselves and have a say in the political process because their interests are not likely to be advanced by their participation in this process. And the trustees in their cases are more distant from their interests than in the case of children. Here too the democratic principle is likely to go quite unsatisfied.

One last group that is worth mentioning here is the case of some nonhuman higher primates. We have some reason to believe that some higher primates have the kinds of capacities that are distinctive of persons. But we do not at the moment have any way of figuring out whether they make judgments of justice, what they are or whether they track their interests. So there is no way to integrate them into the democratic system. We can try as hard as possible to treat them as equals. But there is no way that we can give them a voice in democratic processes. Here too, we see a disturbing limit to democracy. The best we can do is to try to treat equals as equals but we cannot treat them democratically, which implies that there will always be a serious defect in our treatment of them. Of course, democracy is not worse here than other political systems. It is probably better since at least it gives every actual and potential trustee a chance at participation.

This defeats the objection that democracy is unjust because it gives unequally competent people equal power.

In conclusion, I have argued that a democracy with limited scope is grounded on the principle of public equality. And I have argued against a number of important objections to this account. In what follows, I will argue that liberal rights also rest on the principle of public equality. Then I will inquire into whether the further requirement of reasonableness, as understood by Rawls and Cohen and a number of deliberative democrats, ought to play a role in an egalitarian society. In the last chapters I will show how democracy has legitimate authority and what the limits to that legitimate authority are.

4

An Egalitarian Conception of Liberal Rights

Liberal rights such as the rights of freedom of conscience, freedom of association and freedom of speech are grounded in the interests of persons and the requirement that individuals be treated publicly as equals. The underlying rationale for liberal rights is essentially the same as that for democratic rights. They are grounded in the principle of public equality. In this chapter, I hope to show how liberal rights are grounded in the principle of public equality and I hope to display the advantages of this conception of the underlying rationale for liberal rights. The parallelism of justification is important, as I hope to show in Chapter 7, because it enables liberal rights to serve as limits to the authority of democracy.

There are a number of desiderata that a conception of liberal rights must satisfy. First, a conception of liberal rights must explain the peculiar complexity, nuance, and structure of liberal rights. It must explain the flexibility with which they are implemented in the face of competing considerations. Second, a conception of liberal rights must explain why liberal rights are so important. It must explain why the liberal rights should be protected despite the obvious costs to people that arise from that protection. An account of liberal rights that says nothing about these costs is defective. Third, a conception of liberal rights must explain why the liberal rights of a person cannot be overridden by the aggregated interests of many people.

My idea is to show that liberal rights are founded in the principle of public equality. Since the principle of public equality requires that the interests of the members of society be advanced equally in a publicly clear way, the argument for liberal rights will be in three main stages. First, I will show that liberal rights advance the fundamental interests of members of society when their interests are adequately understood and when the means to satisfying them are taken into account. Second, I will show that the interests that ground the liberal rights have a kind of undefeated preeminence that the interests that oppose liberal rights do not have. The costs of the exercise of liberal rights do not defeat the fundamental interests in liberal rights. For example, many of the various costs that exercises of liberal rights impose on others are ones that can be best remedied by the exercise of liberal rights. Third, I will argue that the liberal rights of each individual have a strong priority over considerations of the aggregated interests of many people, which is grounded in the egalitarian dimension of the principle of public equality.

The three stage argument on offer here attempts to reconcile two opposing and distinct theoretical intuitions about liberal rights that are usually thought to be at loggerheads. The interest-based stages of the argument provide a flexible and empirical approach to the grounds of liberal rights and to their importance. It explains the complexity and nuance we see in liberal rights. The egalitarian stage of the argument provides us with a conception of liberal rights as trumps. It explains what appear to be the deontological aspects of liberal rights: the precise way in which the liberal rights can function as side constraints. Though these two aspects are not logically incompatible, many theories of liberal rights tend to be one sided precisely because they emphasize one aspect to the neglect of the other. I want to show how they come together in one satisfying whole. It is the principle of public equality, which advances interests in an egalitarian way, that ensures that these two elements can come together in a satisfying way.[1]

In what follows, first, I will discuss the structure of liberal rights and distinguish my account of that structure from others' accounts. This initial stage will lay out some reasons for thinking that liberal rights must be grounded in large part in interests. Second, I will lay out the interests that are advanced by the liberal rights. Third, I will then argue that these interests are preeminent and undefeated because of the importance of the interests and because the liberal rights that protect them provide the remedies to the costs that exercises of these rights inevitably impose. I will conclude this section with a discussion of the cores of the different rights and the limits of those rights. Fourth, I will show how the principle of public equality, which grounds democratic rights as well, grounds the notion that liberal rights are trumps against considerations of the greater good. Finally, I will end this chapter with a discussion of some objections that are likely to arise to my account. In Chapter 7 of this book, I will argue that liberal rights are one basis of limits to democratic authority.

---

[1] It is useful here to make a statement about the methods behind my argument. I make frequent use of empirical claims throughout the argument in this chapter as in Chapters 2 and 3. In my view, these claims are unavoidable in a full conception of liberal rights. I do not defend these empirical claims except by trying to make them appealing to common sense and ordinary experience, by giving empirical evidence that I have seen and by trying to show that the major global alternatives to liberal rights such as Fascism, Communism, Theocracy, and other forms of Authoritarianism are far inferior to a society with liberal rights. Ultimately, they must be tested by the methods of social science. Political philosophy can only go so far in this venture. It must respect the results of science and it can point the way to further areas of social scientific study. Furthermore it can defend a certain approach to thinking about how institutions ought to be structured.

This argument is based on the idea that the interests and the principle of equality that ground democratic rights also ground the liberal rights.

One quick disclaimer is relevant before we start. I aim only at giving an account of the basic grounds of liberal rights here. I do not have the space to work out the implications of this view for all issues relating to liberal rights. I attempt for illustrative purposes to elaborate some implications of the theory here for example with respect to blasphemy, but there are a number of important issues that I do not discuss such as pornography, hate speech, and other important issues. I believe the theory here has implications for these issues and that the illustrations I give of other issues may provide some guidance in thinking through these problems.

WHAT ARE LIBERAL RIGHTS?

In this section I wish to lay out some reasons for thinking that liberal rights are grounded in significant part in interests. If we look at the long established practices of liberal rights we observe the following important properties of liberal rights. Liberal rights mark out a sphere of activity within which a person may act as he pleases without government intervention. Persons acting within that sphere are also to be protected from the interventions of others. In this sphere, each person is to be free from coercion and violence. Furthermore, the activities in this sphere may not be the basis of legal discrimination against persons with regard to holding political office or civil service positions or the legally mandated benefits of the state. In addition, each person has some protection from being fired from their jobs or being discriminated against in the conduct of economic activities. Finally, persons' exercises of their liberal rights are not to be unduly burdened by state regulations even when those regulations are not designed to curtail the liberal rights.[2]

This sphere of activity cannot be described as a sphere in which no non-consenting person is affected by one's activities or where the activities are purely self-regarding. The *self-regarding action approach* to liberal rights is

---

[2] In my view, what makes a thinker a liberal is that that person subscribes to all or nearly all these rights. Liberals are also likely to prefer democracy to other forms of government and they are likely to think that much economic exchange and production are best engaged in freely. There are no fundamental liberal philosophical ideas such that if one fails to hold them, one fails to be a liberal. What makes one a liberal is the belief that institutions characterized by the rights above are basic to a just and decent society. So it is quite possible for utilitarians to be liberals as much as Kantians and Hobbesians. And it is possible for communitarians to be liberals at least in a particular society. My focus in this chapter will not be on what liberalism really is but rather on the nature and limits of the justification of liberal rights.

incompatible with the fact that liberal rights permit activities in which one can do damage to others, exercise power over others, or simply cause inconvenience to others. For example, people have rights to break off financial and personal relationships with some of those who are dependent on them even if that means that the dependents suffer some damage. People have rights to damage politicians' reputations even if they end the careers of those politicians. People have rights to say things that are offensive to others. And people have rights to speak and associate with others even when these produce inconveniences to others, as in parades and leafleting campaigns. And in the case of personal property rights, people have limited rights to exclude others from the use, benefit, or mere occupation of some parts of the material or intellectual world and they have limited rights to define the terms on which people may contract to use, benefit, or occupy those things.

All of these rights permit either exercises of power over others or ways of doing damage to others without their consent but they are nevertheless permitted within the sphere of liberal rights. The idea is that it is important that people have these powers even if they sometimes do damage with them. Liberal rights give people the power to organize their relations with other people and thereby give them some power over other people. Indeed, liberal rights confer power on people to shape their individual lives in very much the same way as democratic rights confer power on individuals to shape the collective life of the community.

To say that liberal rights protect a sphere of activities is to say that they do more then merely prohibit people from interfering with others for the wrong reasons.[3] The *restricted reasons approach* to liberal rights asserts that liberal rights prohibit interference with another person on certain grounds. But religious liberty, for example, implies more than this. One may not *unduly burden* a person's exercise of religion even if it is for a good reason. For example, in many cases one may not require the Catholic Church in the United States to comply with laws banning discrimination on the basis of sex even though discrimination on the basis of sex is thought to be wrong and is banned in the case of many economic activities. Protections of free expression provide many other examples. To be sure, one may not abridge free political

---

[3] See Thomas Scanlon's early paper, "A Theory of Freedom of Expression," in *The Difficulty of Tolerance* (Cambridge: Cambridge University Press, 2003), for a view of this sort. Scanlon has since given up this type of analysis of the right of freedom of expression in his "Freedom of Expression and Categories of Expression," in *The Difficulty of Tolerance*. See also Peter de Marneffe, "Rights, Reasons and Freedom of Association," in *Freedom of Association* ed. Amy Gutmann (Princeton, NJ: Princeton University Press, 1998), pp. 145–172, esp. p. 146, for the view that moral rights are defined in terms of the moral wrongness of interfering for certain reasons. And see Ronald Dworkin, "Why Must the Press Be Free?" in *Freedom's Law* (Cambridge, MA: Harvard University Press, 1996), for a view that seems to come close to this kind.

or artistic expression on the grounds that the ideas expressed are false. In addition, however, a number of laws regulating the Internet for the legitimate purpose of stopping children from having access to pornography have been struck down by the US Supreme Court on the grounds that these laws also, even if unintentionally, interfere with the free speech interests of adults. And again, the rights of freedom of expression and freedom of association must be protected even when the exercise of these rights may produce inconvenience or upset or offense in others. The avoidance of inconvenience, upset, and offense are all legitimate reasons for government action, so the restricted reasons approach cannot explain why they are not usually sound reasons for the restriction of speech. The idea is that only the weightiness of the interests in keeping the sphere off limits to intervention can explain the right against nonintervention even when there are otherwise good reasons to interfere.[4]

Of course, all liberal rights have their limits but those limits are not merely defined in terms of classes of reasons for action. The limits of liberal rights are partly grounded in the balancing of the interests served by the liberal rights against those that might be damaged by liberal rights. The freedom of religion does not permit that one sacrifices the life of another person. Nor does it permit that one may go about disrupting public order willy-nilly. To be sure, though the free exercise of religion may not be unduly burdened by actions that are intended to protect public order, considerations of public order may, when sufficiently weighty, justify interference with religious activities.

In addition to the fact that neither the self-regarding approach nor the restricted reasons approach provides necessary conditions for liberal rights, neither one provides sufficient conditions either. Contrary to the self-regarding approach, the practice of liberal rights permits that people do not have the rights to kill themselves or to enslave themselves to others even when such action affects no nonconsenting individuals.[5] Though in general freedom of expression does prohibit the state's ban on speech on the ground that the speech is false, contrary to the restricted reasons approach, liberal rights to freedom of expression do permit some restrictions on the speech of a particular person on the grounds that the beliefs expressed are false and harm the persons in audience. For example, restrictions on false advertising are created for the purpose of restricting fraudulent speech and to some degree protecting people from having certain false beliefs that may be harmful to them. Restrictions on libel may also have this character. Though they are

---

[4] See T. M. Scanlon, "Freedom of Expression and Categories of Expression," in *The Difficulty of Tolerance* (Cambridge: Cambridge University Press, 2003), pp. 84–112, esp. p. 98.

[5] These restrictions have been defended by Locke, Kant, and Mill and they are embodied in the practices of all contemporary liberal societies.

primarily intended to protect the persons who are libeled, they also protect those who are made to have false beliefs about others.

I shall call the alternative view of the structure of liberal rights I am defending the *sphere of activity approach* to liberal rights. This approach seems to me to capture the structure of these rights. Like the self-regarding action approach, it says that a certain class of actions is to be protected from various kinds of interference. But it expands the class of actions much further than just self-regarding actions. And it identifies that class of actions by appeal to the underlying interests. Liberal rights would be severely constrained if the state had the authority to interfere with people's actions every time the state thought that some undesirable effects on others would occur. And the interests that underpin liberal rights would not be well served.

This account does not deny that liberal rights are sometimes the basis of restrictions on reasons for interfering with others. A liberal right to live one's life in one's own way in part implies that others may not interfere for the purpose of advancing one's own good. Many paternalistic reasons, though clearly not all, are barred as a basis for interference with a person's activity in a large number of cases. So while liberal rights are not to be defined in terms of restricted reasons, some of them do imply restrictions on the reasons for interference and discrimination.

The best explanation for why liberal rights have the complex structure they have, namely shaping spheres of activities in which individuals may act without threat of interference or discrimination or imposition of undue burdens, is that these rights are grounded in certain kinds of interests. The principal purpose of liberal rights is to advance persons' interests in living their own lives in their own way and in discussing with others what the best way of living is. It is the interests that ground the liberal rights that determine the shapes of the spheres of activity in which each person has rights to act. The interests also define the classes of actions that the liberal rights protect. Furthermore, the nature of the interests that underpin the liberal rights also enables us to define what kinds of action fall within the core protections of these liberal rights and which actions are on the periphery, as I will show in the section on the shapes and cores of liberal rights.

RIGHTS AND INVIOLABILITY

These observations can help us see the limitations of the approach to liberal rights Thomas Nagel and others develop. Nagel's approach attempts to ground liberal rights directly in the idea of the inviolable status of human beings. He says:

That the expression of what one thinks and feels should be overwhelmingly one's own business, ..., is a condition of being an independent thinking being. It is a form of moral recognition that you have a mind of your own.... The sovereignty of each person's reason over his own beliefs and values requires that he be permitted to express them, expose them to the reactions of others and defend them against objections. It also requires that he not be protected against exposure to views of arguments that might influence him in ways others deem pernicious, but that he have the responsibility to make up his own mind about whether to accept or reject them. Mental autonomy is restricted by shutting down both inputs and outputs.[6]

On this view the liberal rights have an inflexibility and absoluteness that is not even close to consistent with our practices regarding liberal rights. In the area of expression the view seems to support a blanket prohibition on all regulation of content. It is hard to see on this account, for instance, how there could be any justification for treating advertising differently from political or artistic expression.[7] And yet it has been a long-standing practice within liberal societies to require truth in advertising while permitting all kinds of falsehood in political and artistic expression. Furthermore, it is hard to see how the complex rules for libel could be made sense of on this account. Why should people be protected from libel? And why is there so little protection from libel afforded to public figures? In addition, there are long-standing practices in modern liberal societies that prohibit paternalism in some areas and there are others that permit paternalistic action on the part of the state. The state in all modern liberal societies regulates the trade of pharmaceuticals and food and many other goods and services on explicitly paternalistic grounds. And the basic practice of paternalistic regulation in areas where technical expertise is important is not itself in question though many particular instances of it may be. The reason for the troubling lack of texture in the inviolability theory is that the theory attempts to ground the rights on a fundamental status of inviolability, which status outranks in importance any of the kinds of costs or interests that we normally think ought to play a role in defining the shapes and limits of liberal rights.

---

[6] See Thomas Nagel's paper "Personal Rights and Public Space," in *Concealment and Exposure & Other Essays* (Oxford: Oxford University Press, 2002), pp. 31–52, esp. p. 43.

[7] See T. M. Scanlon, "Freedom of Expression and Categories of Expression," in *The Difficulty of Tolerance: Essays in Political Philosophy* (Cambridge: Cambridge University Press, 2003), pp. 84–112, esp. p. 96. For a more in-depth treatment see, Leif Wenar, "The Value of Rights," in *Law and Social Justice* eds. Joseph Keim Campbell, Michael O'Rourke, and David Shier (Cambridge, MA: MIT Press, 2006).

In contrast, the view I will defend attempts to ground the liberal rights in certain central interests. And it is able to explain the fine texture of these rights by recourse to a showing of the centrality to the right of some protections and the peripheral character of other protections. It is also able to explain this texture by reference to the abilities of persons to protect themselves from certain exercises of these rights.

But the view I defend also attempts to give an explanation of features of liberal rights that interest-based views have had trouble with. It attempts to show when and why liberal rights can serve as side constraints against the advancement of the greater good of society. It is the egalitarian dimension of the principle of public equality that serves to explain this part of the texture of liberal rights.

In what follows, I will lay out the foundations of liberal rights as I understand them. First, I will lay out the basic interests that liberal rights protect. I will do this for four basic liberal rights: freedom of conscience, freedom of private pursuits, freedom of association, and freedom of expression. Second, I will argue that the interests in these liberal rights are preeminent interests. The interests that ground liberal rights are weightier than those interests that normally compete with liberal rights. The argument for the preeminence of these interests also requires that a clear conception of the costs of the exercise of these rights be laid out. I will argue that the package of liberal rights is superior to other regimes at providing remedies for the costs of exercises of liberal rights. Hence, liberal rights have great weight because they protect fundamental interests and because they are capable of remedying the costs they themselves produce. Finally, I will show that the liberal rights of one person are trumps against considerations of the greater aggregated good of many individuals by invoking the egalitarian dimension of the principle of public equality.

THE FUNDAMENTAL INTERESTS GROUNDING
THE LIBERAL RIGHTS

Freedom of Conscience

I will discuss freedom of conscience, freedom of private pursuits, freedom of association, and freedom of expression in what follows. These are not the only fundamental liberal rights. Each person has a right to some basic personal property, to privacy, to a fair trial, and to be treated in accordance with due process of law. But I will discuss the four rights above as basic illustrations of how the others are to be treated.

Let us take each of these liberties in turn. Freedom of conscience is the right to believe and think what one thinks is true and defensible as well as to change one's mind about these matters. It is a right against being coerced or forced into believing some set of officially sanctioned beliefs. Let us call this the *noninterference condition* of freedom of conscience. It is also a protection against being discriminated against on the basis of ones beliefs by government regarding the benefits and protections government provides and with regard to the opportunities to run for political office and the opportunity to hold a position in the civil service. It also involves a limited right not to be discriminated against in economic transactions on the basis of one's beliefs. Let us call these the *nondiscrimination conditions* of freedom of conscience. Finally, the right of freedom of conscience includes the right not to be unduly burdened regarding the activities that are connected with those beliefs. For example, if a zoning regulation rules out public places of worship, without being explicitly designed to rule them out, such a regulation seems to be a violation of freedom of religion as well. Let us call this the condition of *nonburdened access*.

What are the basic grounds for freedom of conscience? I will offer grounds based on the interests individuals and society have in having freedom of conscience and then after discussing the interests behind the other liberal rights I will show how these interests are preeminent and undefeated by other countervailing interests. Finally, after a discussion of the interests in all the other rights is completed, I will show that the rights of each person to freedom of conscience and the other liberal rights are side constraints against the advancement of the greater good of society. This last part will invoke the egalitarian dimension of the principle of public equality.

The first ground of the freedom of conscience is the *interest* each member of society has *in acquiring true and justified beliefs*. How does one discover the best way to live or the right way to think about some topic? The idea is that in general one discovers this by means of trial and error, by testing ideas, and by subjecting them to critical scrutiny. Without going through this process of trial and error and critical scrutiny one is unable to have one's interest in getting at the truth of the matter advanced. Hence, trial and error is the best way of securing the interest in having true and defensible beliefs.

But in order to start the process of learning by trial and error one must be able to formulate without fear those beliefs that are most congenial to one. It is important that a person be able to reflect on her own beliefs and have her beliefs responded to by others without fear of interference or discrimination.

If a person's beliefs are never given consideration as a result of being banned, then that person's opportunity to learn from trial and error is closed off.

It is also important for the person to have access to a wide variety of other beliefs against which he can challenge his own views and from which he can learn. Again trial and error in the development of one's beliefs requires that one have access to many different beliefs and many different challenges to one's own beliefs. The banning of beliefs can therefore be harmful to a person's ability to learn from trial and error even if the person does not agree with them.

Furthermore, reflection on beliefs and on the alternatives to those beliefs develops one's capacity to reflect and evaluate beliefs and the development of that capacity helps one learn and acquire better and more defensible beliefs. Each person develops her capacity by learning from her mistakes and this cannot happen if the state tries to take over the process of learning for her own good. Furthermore the development of the capacities of thinking for herself and taking an active role in defining her life can only occur as a consequence of that person having to take responsibility for her own actions and beliefs. So banning beliefs or imposing beliefs threatens to stunt the development of this capacity and thus threatens to stunt each person's ability to learn and think for herself.

Moreover, each person must go through a somewhat different learning process, starting from different initial beliefs and learning from different types of mistakes. This is because each person is different in important ways. In a complex and pluralistic society, people are likely to have very different doxastic starting points and are likely to have very different epistemic problems blocking their efforts to achieve better understanding. So each person must follow a different trial and error path to achieve better understanding.

Now the interest in learning by trial and error, to the extent that it is satisfied in very different ways in different people, requires that no particular set of beliefs be excluded so that a maximum number of paths to truth remain open. To forbid some particular set of beliefs risks foreclosing a particular path to truth for some group of people and thus risks setting back their interests in truth. Hence, in order to secure each person's interests in acquiring the best beliefs, each person must have freedom of conscience. All persons' interests in getting a handle on the truth, and the diversity of persons who have those interests, ground freedom of conscience.[8]

Notice that this argument does not imply that the state has to think that a person's views are true or even possibly true. The epistemological argument for freedom of conscience is merely that a person's interests in true and

---

[8] The argument from the importance of trial and error comes from Mill, *On Liberty* ed. Stefan Collini (Cambridge: Cambridge University Press, 1989), p. 23.

justified belief are not going to be advanced by the state's banning the beliefs it regards as false. The claim is a comparative claim to the effect that the state is far more likely to advance a person's interest in learning the truth by allowing him and others the freedom of thought than by attempting to impose beliefs it regards as true.

Notice that this argument has an individual and a collective dimension. It is good for each person that he or she has freedom of conscience since he or she learns best in this way. And the banning of certain beliefs is highly likely to set back a certain group of persons' interests in truth more than others' interests. And so, the banning of beliefs entails a kind of inequality of concern for the interests of the members of society. It is also good for people generally that each person have this freedom because each person can also learn from other people's efforts to get at the truth and can learn from others freely responding to their views. Freedom of thought plays an important role in winnowing out deeply implausible or indefensible beliefs and thus protects the society from basing its actions and ideas on falsehood.

The second interest in freedom of conscience stems from the fundamental *interest in being at home in the world* that one lives in.[9] Being at home in the world implies that one recognizes the things in the world around one, and it implies that those things in some sense reflect oneself and in some sense are congenial to oneself or at least they make sense to oneself. There are a couple of different ways in which this can happen. One way to be at home in the world is through shaping the world one lives in and making it conform to one's needs, interests, and concerns. The other way to be at home is through developing a conception of the world that one lives in, making it intelligible to oneself, and understanding how it relates to ones needs, interests, and concerns. The latter way of being at home in the world is threatened if one is not permitted to have any belief aside from the official beliefs.

The idea is that each person makes the world her own in part by developing a conception of that world and of the values in the world. This is what makes the world intelligible to a person and it is what enables a person to achieve an orientation among the things in it. But it is also a way of making the things in the world her own. They become infused with her thought. Her thought penetrates the things and makes them familiar. She is capable of figuring out how the world is, or can be made to be, responsive to her needs and interests. By contrast, to live in a world about which one has no beliefs or very few genuine beliefs is to be in part alienated from that world. It is to have the world one lives in be opaque and inaccessible and perhaps even hostile.

---

[9] See G. W. F. Hegel, *Elements of the Philosophy of Right* trans. R. Nisbet (Cambridge: Cambridge University Press, 1991), for a discussion of this idea esp. section 7.

Where freedom of thought is not permitted, the official beliefs may fail to sit well with many, or they may be poorly related to the evidence as many see it, or they may fail to cohere with other beliefs many have. In these kinds of situations, many will be in a situation of not really having genuine beliefs about the world they live in regarding the subjects of the banned beliefs. They will experience the world they live in as something inaccessible to them because the beliefs they are required to have are unsatisfying and they are not permitted to have other beliefs.

Again, given the diversity of persons in a pluralistic and complex society the kinds of beliefs that contribute to a sense of at-homeness are likely to be quite diverse. And given that people change in a variety of ways, forbidding some beliefs is likely to undermine many people's interests in being at home in the world. So to the extent that we wish to advance everyone's good, we must permit freedom of conscience. Since people's beliefs about the world enable them to be at home in the world they live in, when one group imposes its beliefs on the other, the group on whom the beliefs are imposed is likely to experience a sense of alienation from the world they live in. Therefore their interests in being at home are sacrificed to the interests of others.

These last two arguments dovetail each other. While it is better, from the standpoint of being at home in the world, to have some false beliefs than no genuine beliefs at all, it is still better to have true and defensible genuine beliefs rather than false ones. So the interest in being at home in the world is better secured when each has more defensible and true beliefs and thus when each person's interest in the truth is promoted by freedom of conscience.

In addition to the above interests, are the interests individuals have in *correcting for the cognitive biases of others*. The beliefs that people hold about moral, spiritual, and political matters tend to have a cognitive bias toward the interests of those who hold them as I argued in the discussions of publicity and democracy in Chapters 2 and 3. So when one group imposes its beliefs on another group, there is a significant likelihood that the imposed upon group's interests are being subordinated to the first group's interests. Since the imposed upon group is required to make its beliefs conform to the imposing group and the beliefs tend to carry a cognitive bias toward the interests, experience, and backgrounds of the group that initially has the beliefs then it is likely that the imposed upon group will be living in a way that reflects the interests of a different group.

Furthermore, given the interests I described above, in a pluralistic society where the beliefs of some are imposed on all only some will have their interests advanced while the others will have reason to think that their interests are set back. This implies that those on whom the beliefs are imposed have good reason to think that they are being given inferior moral standing compared to the imposers. Since each person has an *interest in being recognized as having equal moral standing* with his fellows, his interests will be set back in a pluralistic society where the beliefs of some are imposed on him or some beliefs are banned. In general, those upon whom beliefs are imposed will, given the facts noted above, have reason to think that their interests do not count for as much as those of the dominant group in society. They will have reason to think that they are not considered worthy of being treated in accordance with justice.

It will be noted that these considerations are contingent empirical considerations. They do not establish an a priori argument for freedom of conscience nor do they show that freedom of conscience is absolutely necessary; this will become important in what follows. These observations imply that lack of freedom of conscience may not have the same impact on everyone; for instance, it may not have as bad an impact on someone who finds the official beliefs congenial or on someone who easily accepts what he is told. Another thing to note is that the argument so far will not establish that freedom of conscience has the same importance under all circumstances. For instance, in a society that is pluralistic, suppression of certain beliefs or the establishment of certain official beliefs is likely to have the effects noted above on most people. But in a society where almost everyone already believes the same thing, making those beliefs official beliefs is not likely to have all the unfortunate effects that are had in a society which is initially pluralistic.

Still, as a general rule, contingent facts strongly support liberal rights, if I understand them properly. For the vast majority of societies we know of, pluralism and diversity are simply fundamental facts. And to the extent that the trial and error method is more likely to give us good beliefs than not, the establishment of official beliefs is likely to set back the interests in having defensible and true beliefs for all the members of the society even in an apparently homogeneous society.[10]

The contingent argument I have given so far does not establish a right to freedom of conscience of sufficient strength. There are two things that need to be done to show that freedom of conscience is a powerful right, not to be

[10] In defense of this element of contingency in liberal rights, I offer the fact that most of the great accounts of liberal rights of the last two centuries have large elements of contingency in them. Obviously, John Stuart Mill's account in *On Liberty* displays this contingency. But in addition, Rawls's account of liberal rights must also be based on contingent facts. An argument from the original position will always depend on the general laws of psychology and society and on the effects of liberal rights on the self-respect of persons and more generally. And Rawls's arguments for stability of the right kind in *A Theory of Justice* as well as in *Political Liberalism* introduce an inevitable dimension of contingency into the basis for liberal rights. Even Kant's conception of liberal rights in the Doctrine of Justice introduces a large element of contingency by the fact that rights must ultimately be grounded in the general will. Finally, those conceptions of liberal rights such as Nagel's, which do not allow for this contingency, are simply incapable of giving an account of the complexity and nuance of liberal rights.

overridden by other interests or concerns. First, it must be shown that the interests that are protected by freedom of conscience are preeminent interests. This is for two reasons. First, in many cases the interests that ground liberal rights are more important interests than most of those that are likely to compete with them. Second, even when the competing interests are on a par with the interests that ground liberal rights, the liberal rights provide means to satisfy the competing interests so that the costs of the exercise of liberal rights are less than the benefits. These arguments attempt to show that when there is competition between some person's interests in freedom of conscience and another's interest in them not having freedom of conscience, the interests in freedom of conscience win out.

The second part of the showing that the right of freedom of conscience is a weighty one is to show that it cannot be overridden easily by the interests of large numbers of persons or by the similar interests of others. If the freedom of conscience were a right based only on certain interests it might be a right that could be overridden fairly easily. If the majority were sufficiently dismayed by the presence of what they take to be false beliefs, there would be reasons on the grounds of the interests of the members of society to sacrifice the interests of the minority to those of the more numerous majority.[11] This would be so even if the individual interests of the minority were weightier than the interests of the majority taken individually. At some point the aggregated lesser interests of the majority could outweigh the more weighty interests of the smaller minority.

It is only once we introduce the requirement that the equal advancement of interests must be publicly realized that we can show that a fundamental and very strong right to freedom of conscience can trump the interests of many other people. Only when the principle of public equality is in place can the dismay of the majority at the false beliefs of the minority be shown not to override the interests of the minority in freedom of conscience. I will complete these segments of the argument once I have discussed the interests underlying the other main liberal rights.

Freedom of Pursuits

The idea of freedom of private pursuits includes the freedom of worship, the freedom of occupation, freedom of aesthetic pursuits, all the freedoms connected with the freedom of association, and the freedom to own and dispose of as one wishes personal private property. The idea behind the freedom of

[11] See C. L. Ten's, *Mill on Liberty* (Oxford: Oxford University Press, 1980), chapter 2, for an extensive discussion of this worry.

pursuits is that each person is to be free to choose the aims that they wish to pursue in life and to determine the basic plans for achieving those aims.[12] It is not enough that a person has the freedom of thought and conscience to determine what she believes and what she thinks important; it is essential that a person be free to devise aims and basic plans for achieving those aims and that a person have at least some minimal capacity to shape the world she lives in to suit her needs and interests.

The freedom of private pursuits involves the right not to be forced or coerced into living in ways that others demand. It also includes a right not to be discriminated against by government for the benefits of government activity or for government offices on the basis of one's way of life as long as that way of life does not interfere with the proper fulfillment of the duties of one's job. And, it involves a right not to be discriminated against in essential economic activities. Finally, it involves a right not to have one's access to the means to living one's life unduly burdened.

Here it is important to see that the freedom of private pursuits is a right against certain forms of paternalistic and moralistic interference but it also gives one a claim to have unburdened access to the means of one's way of life. Here the example of a zoning ordinance not intended for paternalistic or moralistic reasons but that still makes the building say of reasonable church facilities impossible within one's town is also a violation of the freedom of private pursuits.

As Mill notes, the principle of freedom of pursuits does not imply that economic activity, such as production and exchange, may not be regulated. What it implies is that economic activity may not be regulated or prohibited on the grounds that the basic choice of aims and plans to achieve those aims are thought to be bad for the person who is choosing or harmless wrongdoing. Nor may such economic regulation unduly burden such choices. Choice of aims and basic plans to achieve desired ends may not be interfered with by others on the grounds that these aims or basic plans are bad for the agent or on the grounds that others disapprove of or are repelled by the thought of them. In essence, this freedom rules out certain kinds of paternalism on the part of government and others and it rules out the dismay or distress of others at the mere thought of these actions as legitimate reasons for interference.

The limit on paternalistic action, however, does not extend to all matters that relate only to the agent's good. This is a very complex issue that we will not have the space to deal with here. Suffice it to say, paternalistic action may

---

[12] The idea of freedom of pursuits is John Stuart Mill's term, see *On Liberty* ed. Stefan Collini (Cambridge: Cambridge University Press, 1989), p. 15.

be justified under certain circumstances involving the necessity for making decisions informed by expert knowledge. Although certainly not uncontroversial, regulations on food and drugs, on the design and manufacture of complex machines for personal and public use, on the use of complex financial institutions all constitute limits on what individuals may do. They are, in many cases, justified by appeal to the good of the individuals involved. The activities in question all involve the use of objects and institutions the evaluation of which require expert knowledge that we cannot expect people to have in general. Indeed we may not want most people to spend much of their time in acquiring some of the expert knowledge necessary to evaluate complex instruments and medicines on division of labor grounds.[13]

Still, it is clear that mere capacity to determine the ends that one may pursue is not a sufficient form of freedom of private pursuits. One must in addition be able to determine at least the basic plans by which one pursues those ends. It is not enough that one must be able to pursue one's own ends, one must be able to do it in one's own way, at least to some extent. In part this is because the way in which one goes about achieving outcomes is often as important and sometimes more important than the outcomes themselves. One does not judge the worth of ones life merely by the outcomes one has achieved nor do others judge one's life in that way. It is also because it is only the person who is pursuing different ends who can decide how those ends are to be balanced against each other and this plays a larger role in determining the plans one lives by. Finally, expert knowledge about the best plan to live by is not to be had even if one's ends are completely set; each must learn from his or her own experience and the experiences of others by trial and error in order to devise reasonable plans of life. In this chapter, I will have to be content with expressing this with the vague statement that citizens must have the freedom to choose and pursue aims and basic plans.[14]

Of course, this must all take place against a background of just institutions. So other people's liberal rights must be respected, others' democratic rights must be respected. And the basic decisions of a democratic assembly regarding

---

[13] For a debate between those who espouse limited paternalism where expert knowledge is at stake, see Joel Feinberg, who favors it in "Legal Paternalism," in *Paternalism* ed. Rolf Sartorius (Minneapolis: University of Minnesota Press, 1989) and Richard Arneson, who opposes it in "Mill versus Paternalism," *Ethics* (July 1980). For a discussion of other kinds of defensible paternalistic action, see Robert Goodin, *Utilitarianism as a Public Philosophy* (Cambridge: Cambridge University Press, 1995), esp. the chapter on "Liberalism and the Best-Judge Principle."

[14] The argument and conclusion of this section parallel the argument and conclusion of Chapter 5 of *The Rule of the Many* in which I maintain that citizens ought to choose the overall aims of society while legislators and administrators ought to be concerned with figuring out how to pursue those aims. I argue that this is the only way to reconcile the ideals of democracy with the need for a division of labor in a modern democratic state.

questions of efficiency and distributive justice and public decency must be respected.

I will not discuss the arguments for the freedom of pursuits separately except to agree with Mill that the argument for freedom of pursuits is an extension of the argument for freedom of conscience. It is important for people to be able to live as they see fit so that they may learn from their own successes and mistakes and so that others may learn from them. And it is important for people to form the world in which they live in terms of their own aims and plans so that they can be at home in the world they live in. Furthermore, it is important that a person be able to shape her own ends and plans because each person's conception of these matters is biased toward their own interests. If someone's basic ends and plans are chosen by others, the likelihood is that they will be a poor fit with the real needs and interests of the person. And to the extent that these interests are important interests, a society that sets them back displays a lesser concern for the interests of those activities which are curtailed for paternalistic or moralistic reasons. In this chapter, I will pursue these issues more deeply and relate them to the principle of equality in my discussion of the freedoms of association and expression.

Freedom of Association

A central and often the most central element in each person's plans of life is the associations she forms and joins. Hence the freedom of association is perhaps the most important component of the freedom of private pursuits. Each person has the right to join with others to pursue joint activities on terms to which each voluntarily agrees. The same conditions of noninterference, nondiscrimination, and unburdened access hold for this right as for freedom of conscience. This right of association fully extends to all joint activities except economic activities. Economic association may be regulated but not on the grounds that certain types of people may not associate with other people. Economic association is characterized by the general presence of incentives to defraud and exploit others in these relationships and so they do not come under the freedom of association.

What are the basic interests that underlie the right of freedom of association? One, each person has an interest in being at home in the world he lives in and this is done partly by making the world conform to what he thinks is important. One important way in which a person shapes the world he lives in is by organizing his relationships with others so as to form associations of various sorts or by choosing to join already formed associations that he finds congenial. A person might choose to join an association that advances or expresses his political, or moral or even religious convictions. He will want to join associations with other like-minded people, but he will also want to join associations that are organized in ways he finds congenial and that attract other people he finds congenial. Another essential aspect of being at home in the world is being with the persons who one finds congenial in various ways.

Not to be able to form associations with like-minded people or with people one finds congenial is to become deeply alienated in the world that one lives in. It is to live with people who do not understand one's point of view or who are incapable of empathizing with one's situation.

A further profound interest in association derives from the interest each person has in being recognized and affirmed by his or her fellows. In the association of the family each person is recognized and affirmed, ideally at least, as the unique individual in all the intimate ways that one tries to keep away from the public eye.[15] Friendship is also essential in this regard. The other associations of which one is a part also serve as vehicles for the recognition and affirmation of one's talents and aspirations. Here too, we must recognize that individuals are not fulfilled by being recognized and affirmed by just anyone. That is why the particularity of the associations we are members of is so important. I do not care very much about what a doctor thinks about the quality of my philosophical work but I care very much about what fellow philosophers think. I do not want to be seen in my more physically vulnerable moments by virtually anyone but I do want to be recognized and affirmed as the vulnerable and particular person that I am by my partner in life and to a lesser extent by my brothers and sisters and parents and close friends. I also want to be recognized and affirmed by people who share my aspirations and can appreciate my talents and I receive this fundamental good from those who are members of the very particular groups of which I am a member.

If one is not able to form associations with like-minded or congenial persons, one lacks a crucial support for the development of one's self-esteem and for the sense of the worth of one's projects and one's capacity for carrying them out.

Associational life is essential for instrumental reasons as well. Associating with others and cooperating with them is essential to the realization of many of one's projects. Sometimes the cooperation is intrinsically important as in the case of a musical ensemble and sometimes cooperation is instrumentally important as in the case of membership in associations that advance various causes. In the case of instrumental groups one purpose is to change things in the world either politically or socially. Here the interest in membership in

---

[15] See Hegel on the family in *Elements of the Philosophy of Right* on the importance of the family in each person's life.

these kinds of associations is connected with the interests in making the world conform to one's judgment. This kind of association is essentially connected with political equality.

Furthermore, associations can serve another important interest. Participating with others is an important part of the process of trial and error learning that people engage in. Talking with others, competing with others, and seeing how others perform activities that one is considering performing are all important sources of learning for each person. Participating in groups is essential to these forms of learning and thus plays a large role in each person's efforts to learn what is a good and satisfying life.

Finally, people's judgments about how the world works and how it ought to work are in various ways cognitively biased toward their own interests. Hence it is important that one be able to form associations according to one's own judgment. This is particularly the case because if one cannot do so, it is inevitable that one will be a member of associations that one has not chosen. If it is the case that a person lives in a world entirely dominated by other people's associations, it is likely that that person's life is being guided by ideas and judgments that are cognitively biased away from his interests and needs. Hence, in a world where one must be a member of associations not of one's own choice, one's interests are being set back for the benefit of others, at least in the normal case.

Why is *freedom* of association so important? First, the freedom of association is important because people are different from each other and find very different kinds of association satisfying and good. Moreover, the differences between people ensure that they find different people congenial. Second, freedom of association is necessary to the process of learning what kinds of association are good for one and congenial. It is necessary that a person be able to try out different kinds of associative life in order to determine what is the best form for him. Third, people change and come to find different kinds of association desirable as they undergo changes. All of the interests I noted above can only be satisfied in very particular ways for distinct individuals.

Here again, it is worthwhile noting that freedom of association brings both collective benefits and individual benefits and these two are deeply intertwined. Civil society is the realm in which voluntary associations flourish and multiply and in which each person can express and develop his or her own distinct abilities and aspirations as well as his or her own distinct character traits. But it is also an environment in which people can learn from others and benefit from the associations that others have formed. Hence freedom of association is essential to the advancement of the common good.

Given the importance of the interests described above and the great diversity of persons, when certain kinds of association are banned it is reasonably evident that some persons' interests are being subordinated to others' interests. In particular those who ban the associations seem to be subordinating the interests of those whose associations are banned. This threatens those persons' interests in being recognized as equals in society. Indeed, it suggests to each member of the banned group that their interests are less worthy of consideration and advancement than those of others and that they are being treated as if justice were not their due. Their interest in having equal standing with others is undermined. Hence, each member of the banned group has reason to think that they are being publicly treated as inferiors and this is an injustice to each of them to the extent that the public realization of equality is the fundamental principle of justice.

Notice, again, that the argument for freedom of association is at this stage still a partial argument. Only after we introduce the argument that the interests in it are preeminent and we introduce the principle of public equality will the full strength of the principle of freedom of association be established. For if we simply defended freedom of association by appeal to the interests that individuals have, we would not be able to defend freedom of association in all cases where a majority was deeply dismayed at the associational behavior of a few. The interests of the majority might in some cases outweigh those of the few. But once we introduce the thought that the few would be treated publicly as inferiors in denying them this freedom, we will see that the right of freedom of association rests on very firm grounds in the principle of public equality.

Freedom of Expression

The value of freedom of expression is founded primarily on the contribution that discussion among free people can make to each person's thought about his own life and about the common good. A person need not participate in the process of free discussion in order to receive the benefits of this discussion. In my view, no one has articulated the collective benefits of free expression better than John Stuart Mill in *On Liberty*.[16] It would be foolish to try to improve on his masterful arguments for the collective good of freedom of expression. The gist of his case can be summarized in the following claims. Only in a regime of freedom of expression and thought can a community go through the process of trial and error in evaluating moral, political, and religious beliefs that is necessary to determining which beliefs are true, which are false, and what kernels of truth can be found in the viewpoints of different people. And only in such a community can people come to a rational appreciation of the

---

[16] See John Stuart Mill, *On Liberty* (Buffalo, NY: Prometheus Books, 1986), esp. chapter 2.

justifications of different beliefs. Finally, for such a process of trial and error to have its optimal impact, no belief may be banned since any belief may prove to be the vehicle by which truth and falsehood as well as justification is recognized. In the long run, freedom of expression secures the collective benefit of improving the beliefs and values of people in society.

The collective benefits of free expression extend the collective benefits of freedom of conscience as Mill noted. These benefits enhance both the democratic process and the quality of the lives of individuals. They also provide some measure of protection to each individual and the society of the reasonableness of the opinions on matters of great importance to each and all.

As in the arguments above, I start with an exposition of the interests of each person in participation (either as speaker or as audience) and then I show how setting back those interests is a public violation of equality. Like freedom of conscience and association, freedom of expression is in the interests of individuals as well. This is what makes the freedom of expression a matter of justice. The individual benefit of freedom of expression is an extension of the individual benefit of freedom of conscience.

The interest in true and justified beliefs is advanced for an individual to the extent that each individual has the opportunity to express, or hear expressed, the opinions they hold. Trial and error and the challenges that arise in confronting one's own beliefs with those of others are the principal means by which each person can improve the quality of his beliefs. And each person is different and starts from different starting points and must follow different trial and error paths in order to improve those beliefs. So, it is essential that no expression of belief be banned. The banning of some beliefs ensures that some persons will not be able to go through the process of learning that each has an interest in going through. Obviously these processes also enhance a person's ability to think and reflect on conceptions of the good, politics, and religion. The argument for freedom of conscience proceeded by only taking into account what a person could learn through free thought. But the very same argument can now be extended to free expression. Being able to make one's thoughts available to others is a way of extending the process of trial and error that each person learns from in his own thinking. One benefits just from the process of having to clarify one's thought to others. And one benefits by hearing the responses of others and having to think of replies to them.

This benefit does not require that each person personally participate in the process of discussion. It merely requires that there be no obstacle to persons of different beliefs to participate in discussion on the basis of their beliefs. A person can learn just as much by having his ideas expressed by others and responded to as he can by expressing his ideas himself.

The interest in being at home in the world is also advanced in part by the freedom of expression. Freedom of expression advances the interest in being at home in the world in the two different ways that this can be done. On the one hand, freedom of expression allows individuals to participate in the discussion that helps shape the democratic process and the common legal arrangements through them as well as the more informal processes by which the culture of the society and individuals' lives are shaped and modified. It also helps shape the lives of persons within the more particular associations of which they are members. Thus expression plays a key role in the shaping of the world around one on the personal level as well as the collective level.

On the other hand, like freedom of conscience, freedom of expression enables one to express one's own view and have it treated with some respect. Thus it enables one to come to have a view about the world that one lives in. Or, since it enables other like-minded persons to express their views, it enables persons at least to hear the ideas they hold expressed and hear how they can be elaborated, justified and modified in accordance with evidence. So it enables each person to come to terms with the world he or she lives in by making it intelligible to him or her. It also enables a person to express or hear about how she can make the world intelligible in such a way that she can see how it responds to her needs and interests.

Freedom of expression advances the interest in being at home in the world in part by reinforcing the freedom of association. This is because freedom of expression enables people to communicate with like-minded people and connect up with them. It is also because like-minded people are able to express mutually supportive ideas and give support to each other that the freedom of association provides a powerful basis for advancing the interest in being at home in the world.

Freedom of expression also advances the interest in correcting for cognitive bias. To the extent that one is able to hear or express ideas that are congenial to one and one is not forced merely to listen to the ideas of other persons, one has that crucial protection against being imposed upon by the cognitive biases of others. In part it does this by reinforcing the freedom of association of like-minded persons. Again, since each person's viewpoint is biased toward her interests, a person being forbidden from speaking has a tendency to undermine the advancement of her interests in the social world she lives in. It tends to make it the case that the interests of others prevail in the formation of associations and thus of the social world in which a person lives.

This aspect of the support for free expression is parallel to the claim that exclusion from political power and political discussion undermines the advancement of a person's interests in the pursuit of the common good. This suggests that if a person is prohibited from speaking or if a certain set of ideas are prohibited from being expressed, that person's interests are being subordinated to others' interests. The interests of the silenced person and the person whose ideas cannot be expressed are being treated as inferior.

Finally to the extent that each person can see that the banning of beliefs can set back the interests of some sectors of society, it is clear that the protection of the right to freedom of expression also advances the interest of each person in being recognized and affirmed as an equal in society. To the extent that a person is excluded from speaking his mind, his fellows are treating him as having an inferior status. Indeed, given the above interests it appears that the silenced person is being treated in a way that suggests that his or her interests are less important than those of others and this implies a disastrous loss of status among one's fellows. These and the above are interests a person has in the right of freedom of expression, so it is evident that the excluded person is being treated publicly as if her interests were not worthy of equal consideration and therefore that that person is not worthy of being treated justly. Just as in the case of democratic rights, this involves a disastrous loss of standing among one's fellows. And the suspension of a person's rights to speak publicly embodies inequality among persons. And therefore it is unjust to that person.

As in the cases of the above freedoms of association and conscience, arguments can establish the general importance of these freedoms for the people in society as a whole. But only the arguments for the preeminence of the interests and the introduction of the egalitarian dimension of the principle of public equality can show that each person's right to freedom of expression is a powerful trump against the aggregated interests of other members of society. Given that the arguments above are based on the interests of the members of society, it is conceivable that there will be circumstances in which the misgivings of the majority will outweigh the interests of the society in permitting a few people to express unpopular views or views that seem blasphemous to others. The arguments from the collective benefits and the interests of individuals seem to leave such a possibility open. And though the right to free expression is not absolutely inviolable, no right is, it is intuitively clear that no individual's right to freedom of expression ought to be at the mercy of the sentiments of the majority regarding him or what he says. The egalitarian dimension of the principle of public equality provides the foundation for the strength of this right, as we will see.

One final point concerning the liberal rights is that they are mutually reinforcing; the interests they serve are best served when the liberal rights are taken as a package. So, as I have pointed out above, the freedom of expression extends the freedom of conscience and furthers the aims of acquiring true and justified beliefs. The freedom of expression is an essential support for the freedom of association to the extent that expression is necessary to the creation and maintenance of associations. Furthermore, free association furthers the interests in freedom of conscience and freedom of expression to the extent that associations of like-minded people further people's capacities to elaborate and deepen their ideas and express them to the larger society. As we will see in what follows the liberal rights also function as a package by providing remedies to the costs imposed on others by the exercises of liberal rights. This is an essential step in the argument that these interests are preeminent.

WHY ARE THESE INTERESTS SO IMPORTANT?

The interests in truth, being at home in the world, correcting for cognitive bias and being recognized and affirmed as an equal are preeminent and fundamental interests for us insofar as we think of ourselves as rational and moral agents in a pluralistic world. The liberal rights are of great importance because they protect and advance these interests in a pluralistic society. I will provide a quick recap of the facts of pluralism here. First, there is deep diversity of persons in societies as a result of the facts that those societies have complex divisions of labor and that persons are just naturally quite different from each other with respect to natural talents, handicaps, and capacities for understanding and enjoyment. This kind of deep diversity ensures that the conditions of people's development and well-being are quite different one from another. As a consequence the interests of each person are quite distinct from those of others.

Second, each person has cognitive biases that make her ideas about the good life and even justice tend to reflect her own background, distinctive experiences, and talents. As a consequence they have cognitive biases that ensure that their beliefs about morals, religion, and politics tend to reflect their own interests.

Third, there is pervasive disagreement and fallibility about how to live a good life. This is simply a fact that we observe all the time. But it is a fact that is easily explained by the wide diversity of circumstances in which persons are born and develop and the facts of cognitive bias.

Once we recognize these facts, we can see the great importance of the interests that are advanced by liberal rights. The interests in believing the truth, in being at home in the world, and in being recognized and affirmed as an equal are intrinsically important for us and are instrumentally important to us. The interest in truth is fundamental because it is the interest that gives purpose to having beliefs for rational beings. Everyone who has beliefs, has them because they think they are true. So, social institutions that are connected with belief formation and expression must have as one of their fundamental aims to promote belief of true propositions. And true beliefs are essential to elaborating and carrying out reasonable projects in life. So they are essential to the realization of all of our other interests.

The interest in being at home in the world in both of its dimensions is fundamental for a number of reasons. First, because we are rational beings it is intrinsically important to us that the world we live in makes sense to us. Second, only when one lives in a world that makes sense to one can one pursue one's well-being in that world. This interest stands out in pluralistic societies precisely because in such societies there is a danger that a majority or a most powerful group will force everyone else to live in a society that makes sense to themselves but not to the others. A setback to this interest is disastrous to all the other interests one has.

Here it is important to recall that the metaphor of being at home in the world can mislead the reader in an important set of cases to which it applies. I have argued that when one is at home in the world one is able to make sense of the world one lives in and have a sense of how one fits in with it and is connected with it. But the metaphor suggests that one is happy with the world one lives in. And though many persons who are at home in the world they live in will be comfortable within that world, this is not a necessary condition of being at home in the world. Those who believe that the world is inalterably fallen and sinful and those who believe, as Buddhists do, that all of life is impermanent and full of suffering are not likely to think that the world is a place in which one will feel comfortable or even that one ought to feel comfortable in that world. Because of their distinctive ways of understanding the world and distinctive ways of ordering the world in which they live that are connected to their worldviews, these people must think it is important to be at home in the world in the sense in which I have defined it. They would experience a sense of being at a loss in a world that is dominated by a very different worldview. And this sense may undermine their efforts to achieve a good life in accordance with the views they hold.

It is important to note that the interest in being at home in the world is a distinctively political interest. It is an interest that emerges as such only against the background of disagreement, diversity, and cognitive bias. For one does not think of one's ideas and one's actions as creating a home for oneself primarily. One thinks of them as the right ideas and the right actions and institutions. But the idea of being at home in the world emerges when one sees oneself as one among many persons who are quite diverse, who have disagreements, and in whom there is cognitive bias. It is at that point that one comes to insist on being able to live one's life according to one's own understanding. It is only at that point that one can see that one's interests depend on this. And, of course, one comes to see that other's interests depend on this as well.

The interest in correcting for cognitive bias is a fundamental one in a world where people have different beliefs and different interests. In such a world to be ruled by another's beliefs is to have one's interests suppressed in favor of the other. Here too, a setback to this interest is most likely disastrous to the other interests one has.

These two last interests are distinctively political interests, in the sense that they become highly salient in political environments where disagreement, diversity, and cognitive bias are pervasive. Recall that the interest in being at home in the world does not emerge as a salient interest until one finds oneself in a world where people have very different ways of making the world make sense. And the interest in correcting for cognitive bias straightforwardly emerges when one lives in a world with many other people with distinct backgrounds and interests.

The interest in being recognized as an equal is fundamental for two reasons. Equality is central to justice as I have argued and we are rational beings with the capacity to appreciate justice. As rational beings it is essential to us to live in a world where we recognize each other as equals in accordance with justice.

It is important to note that liberal rights do not imply a denial that there is a right answer to the questions of what will make a person's life go best. Indeed, the thought is that there is a fair degree of objectivity in the answers to these questions. The grounds for liberal rights imply that given the background facts I have outlined above, each person is best off, in the usual case, if she has the power to figure these things out for herself and if she has the power then to shape the contours of her social and material world to accord with those interests and the moral aims that she thinks ought to be pursued. Just as in the case with democratic rights, the idea behind liberal rights is that disagreement about matters of one's well-being, about which there are objective truths, is best met with an egalitarian distribution of power to individuals.

COSTS OF LIBERAL RIGHTS

In a pluralistic society the grounds for equal liberal rights includes more than the interests and their preeminence described above.[17] We need to establish that the interests that ground the liberal rights are undefeated in order to show that they ground a strong right. This will depend a bit on a proper conception

---

[17] I thank Joseph Chan for showing me how the argument needed to be clarified here.

of the costs of the liberal rights and an argument to the effect that either those costs are less important than the benefits of liberal rights or they can be mitigated by the exercises of liberal rights.

Let us consider a number of types of interests at risk as a result of the exercise of liberal rights and that might be thought to justify repression of freedom of conscience, association, and expression. One, there are a variety of *interests in intellectual and cultural homogeneity*. First, there are interests in not being offended or upset by other people's views. Second, there may be an interest in being with like-minded people. Two, there are *moral interests* that stem from trying to act in accordance with conscience. First, there are interests in being able to convert people to one's own views and way of life. Second, there are interests in suppressing activities that express disrespect for values and things that one thinks worthy of respect. These moral interests are interests in the exercise of conscience. Not all persons' moral interests conflict with the interests of others. Some see it as incumbent upon them to suppress or punish blasphemy or heresy while others do not believe they have an obligation to interfere with others' blasphemous actions. But nearly all persons do have the sense of some obligation to act in accord with conscience. Third, there are considerations relating to the threat to justice that the freedoms of conscience, association, and expression on political matters might imply as a result of the fact that people are permitted to think and express mistaken ideas about justice. Three, there are a variety of *material interests* at stake. First, there are interests in the possession of wealth which could be set back by the social divisiveness that differences in belief and practice may trigger. Second, there are interests in security, which could be set back by permitting dangerous views to be thought and expounded.[18] Four, each person has *personal interests* in not being harassed by others or insulted or defamed. Finally, there is the cost that some people will end up with false beliefs and defective conceptions of the good and hence that their *epistemic interests* will be set back.

Some of these costs are exacted in each case of the exercise of conscience, as in the case of offense, harassment, defamation, and perhaps even the costs to the interests in some element of homogeneity. Others costs are cumulative in the sense that they tend only to be seriously threatening when many people exercise their rights. So the threat to justice of wayward ideas about justice and the threat to culturally desirable homogeneity are primarily the cumulative results of many actions as are the threats to the material interests.[19]

---

[18] See Thomas Hobbes, *Leviathan* ed. Edwin Curley (Indianapolis, IN: Hackett Publishing, 1980), chapter 18.

[19] See Joshua Cohen, "Freedom of Expression," *Philosophy and Public Affairs* (Summer 1993) and Thomas Scanlon, "Freedom of Expression and Categories of Expression," in *The Difficulty of Tolerance* (Cambridge: Cambridge University Press, 2003), for discussions of the costs of

So we can see that epistemic, cultural, moral, personal, and material interests can provide considerations against permitting the full panoply of liberal rights. The presence of these interests shows that there are genuine costs to the protection of the freedoms of conscience, association, and expression. And we need to take into account the costs of the liberal rights in order to determine whether the liberal rights are defensible. Why suppose that the interests that ground the freedoms of conscience, association, and expression are normally undefeated even when considering these opposed interests?

THE UNDEFEATED PREEMINENCE OF THE INTERESTS IN LIBERAL RIGHTS

There is not a simple way of showing that these interests do not defeat the interests people have in the liberal rights. I will attempt to answer the challenges posed by each of these opposing interests in stages. First, I will argue that the liberal rights provide remedies to many of the cultural and personal costs imposed by exercises of liberal rights. This is the *private protective function* of liberal rights. Second, those costs that cannot be eliminated by the liberal rights can be shown to be benefits in some respects. Third, I will argue that the liberal rights also have a *public protective function* that provides some remedy to the threats to the justice and security of the society that arise from the exercises of liberal rights. Fourth, I argue that the costs of prohibiting things like blasphemy or desecration of sacred places are greater than the costs to individuals imposed by the exercise of liberal rights. So, one would have to treat the interests of the alleged blasphemer less seriously than those of opponents of blasphemy in order to justify prohibition of blasphemy. Fifth, some alleged personal costs of liberal rights are ones that in fact people do not have liberal rights to impose, such as private libel or defamation. These limits are explained by the account of liberal rights I offer. The explanation is sketched out in the section on the shapes and cores of liberal rights. Sixth, I argue that, though the freedoms of speech and association of opponents of equality (whether illiberal or undemocratic) must be protected, a political society does have a right to attempt to promote a just ethos in the society by means of civic education, by public educational campaigns, and even by providing support to groups that defend equality. I will advance this point in the section on the rights of the intolerant. Finally, seventh, I argue that there

---

freedom of expression. Both of these discussions distinguish very helpfully between direct and "environmental" costs.

are certain principled limits to democratic authority and to the exercise of liberal rights that can be shown to follow from the theory on offer. These last two points will be advanced in Chapter 7.

The Private Protective Functions of the Package of Liberal Rights

One main argument for the undefeated preeminence of the interests protected by liberal rights is connected to the fact that the whole package of liberal freedoms provides significant protection for the interests that appear to be threatened by the liberal rights. For example, the freedom of association and freedom of private pursuits provide significant protection of the interests in cultural homogeneity as well as the interests in not being harassed or insulted by others. They do this, partly, by creating associations of relevantly like-minded people who can thereby shield themselves in part from the activities of the larger society. Someone who wishes to avoid the company of differently minded people can simply remain within the confines of the group of like-minded people. Someone who wishes to avoid the insult and offense that may arise as a consequence of contact with individuals in the larger society can avoid that contact in significant measure.

Furthermore, associational freedom and privacy enable persons to receive emotional and moral support from like-minded or sympathetic persons when persons in other parts of the society criticize or insult or offend them. Obviously families and friendships are central to a person's well-being in these circumstances. But associations of professionals or clubs or associations of like-minded people also serve to buffer the potential injuries that arise from exposure to the larger society.

All the positive arguments for freedom of association support this private protective function of the freedom of association once we accept that the liberal rights are taken as a package. So injuries that arise from the exercise of conscience or the freedom of speech can be partly avoided or diminished by the exercise of rights to freedom of association and privacy. It should be noted that the remedy can work the other way around as well. Oppressive conditions that arise in various associations can be remedied in part by the freedom of association, in particular by the right to exit a group. But they can also be partly remedied by recourse to the exercise of free speech in calling attention to wrongs or harms that occur in the groups and mobilizing the resources of the larger society against the oppressive conditions.

The private protective function of liberal rights does not eliminate all unwanted intrusions of other people's activities. First of all, most people cannot avoid participating in activities in the larger world. So they inevitably face the possibility of seeing or hearing unwanted exercises of conscience or expression on occasion. Second, it is especially difficult to avoid all contact with those exercises of conscience that produce cumulative effects in the society as a whole. Third, the activities of people who are not within one's association may threaten the association itself to the extent that other members may be persuaded by third parties to leave the association or to try to change it.

Still the private protective function of liberal rights significantly reduces the extent to which some of those costs must be borne by others. So when we consider the interests in freedom of conscience and the costs, we are looking at costs that can be significantly reduced by the voluntary action of those who wish to avoid them.

Moreover those encounters that liberal rights cannot eliminate do have a positive side to them for each person as well as a negative side. I have argued above that encounters with views that one rejects or that one finds offensive can play an important role in one's own thinking. One can learn from having to think about other positions and this learning is a benefit on the whole. One can learn about one's own views by considering challenges to them. One can learn about other people by hearing what they have to say.

Furthermore, with liberal rights one has a right to choose whether to protect oneself from outside intrusion or to expose oneself to the potentially threatening or offensive behaviors of others. Unlike in a regime where certain kinds of activities are forbidden by the state because they are offensive or morally impermissible or threatening to the maintenance of orthodoxy, in a liberal regime a person can decide whether and when to expose herself to these potentially threatening influences. The consequence of this is that each person can determine, in accordance with her own conception of her needs, interests, and capacities, when exposure to other ideas and practices would be problematic and when they would be potentially beneficial or at least not threatening.

So, liberal rights provide protection for those interests that are threatened by the exercise of liberal rights. The interests that are protected here are primarily the interests in cultural and intellectual homogeneity and the personal interests in not being offended or insulted. And the liberal rights provide the option to individuals whether to opt for this protection, which individuals can decide to use in a way that suits their interests and needs.

The liberal rights do not however provide complete protection for each person's interests in cultural or intellectual homogeneity or the personal interests in not being offended or insulted. To do this, the society would have to impose conformity on itself. And though this might advance some people's interests, there remain two strong moral reasons for thinking that these interests ought not to prevail. The first is that such homogeneity would be costly to everyone by cutting off all the benefits that arise from diversity. The second reason is that in order to establish cultural uniformity the society would have to disregard the interests in correcting for cognitive bias, being at home in the world and truth of those who do not accept the cultural imposition. The consequence of this is that the imposition of cultural uniformity is a blow to the interests of all and an especially serious blow to the interests of some. It is also a blow to equality as it appears to advance the interests of some at the expense of the interests of others.

The sum of these considerations is that while there is a cost to liberal rights, the cost of prohibition of expression of views or association on the basis of potentially offensive views is greater than the cost of the liberal rights. The costs of the liberal rights are not as great as the costs of the prohibitions and the costs of the liberal rights can be significantly mitigated. So, the imposition of conformity on a minority would amount to sacrificing the interests of the minority for the sake of the lesser interests of those who would prohibit the expression or association of the minority. Thus, such an imposition would treat the interests of the minority as having less worth.

As I will argue in the section on liberal rights as trumps, the right of the minority will override the aggregated interests of even a majority that desires prohibition. The principle of public equality establishes these rights as trumps.

The Public Protective Function of Liberal Rights

The private protective function of liberal rights does not eliminate the risks to justice or to the moral interests in stopping valuable or sacred objects from being dishonored or damaged or to the material interests that arise from the freedoms of conscience, association, and expression. If a growing number of people become convinced of views that are antithetical to justice, this may pose a threat to justice that one cannot avoid by avoiding the public realm. To the extent that this change of view alters the informal norms of the society or it threatens to alter the laws by way of democratic decision-making, one cannot avoid it by exercising the private protective functions of liberal rights. In addition, to the extent that differing views produce social strife and thus threaten the security and material prosperity of the society, one cannot entirely avoid these consequences either by recourse to the private protective function of liberal rights.

These effects will often be forestalled by the effects of public exercises of liberal and democratic rights. We may call this the public protective function of liberal rights. This is a generalization of Louis Brandeis's famous maxim: "if there be time to expose through discussion the falsehood and fallacies, to avert the evil by the process of education, the remedy to be applied is more speech, not enforced silence."[20] For instance, one can argue that freedom of expression and freedom of conscience are more likely to lead to an endorsement of justice or at least to a rejection of serious injustice by the society. A full treatment of this issue will have to await the section on the rights of the intolerant.

One can also argue that lack of freedom of conscience is more likely to lead to civil strife than freedom of conscience, as Locke argued. Civil strife is more likely to arise as a result of some people trying to use the state to advance their particular religious or moral agendas, thereby enlisting others in religious and moral activities they disagree with or forcing others to conform to such ideas.[21] Where there is freedom of conscience and religion, the impulse to do this is lessened since the stakes are lessened. These are instances of the public protective function of liberal rights.

Blasphemy

Finally, there are costs to the public airing of blasphemy or the desecration or insult to sacred objects or places. These costs must be taken seriously. Many individuals with serious religious views are likely to experience a sense of serious injury when someone blasphemes against the objects of their religious worship. Here we must distinguish three different kinds of concern. First, people may experience feelings of offense at the blasphemous action. Second, a person may have an interest in being able to stand up and protect the object of the blasphemy. And third, there may a wrong that has been done to the object of worship. In the first case, the thought is that a wrong has been done to the individual offended and in the second case the person may believe that she has an obligation to stop the blasphemy. And in the third case, a wrong has been done to the object of worship. The first case is straightforwardly a conflict of interests while the second case implies a conflict between different conceptions of people's religious obligations.

The first case is one that we have already dealt with. The thought here is that though the offense to the religious person is a genuine harm, the religious person does have the resources to avoid this harm by avoiding the company of those who would inflict it. The religious person also has the resources to mitigate the harm by engaging the sympathy and support of like-minded people. Finally, though some instances of blasphemy are merely flippant exercises of insensitivity, many such exercises are the result of serious thought and

---

[20] See Whitney v. California, 274 U.S. 357, 375–76, 377 (1927) (concurring).
[21] See John Locke, *A Letter Concerning Toleration* ed. James Tully (Indianapolis, IN: Hackett Publishers, 1983).

reflection. To deny a person the right to say these things because they might offend others is to set back an important interest of that person for the sake of a somewhat less important interest in the other, which interest can be protected at least in part in other ways. It would amount to a sacrifice of the interests of some for the sake of the lesser interests of others.[22]

To take the second case, a person may think that he is under an obligation to try to stop blasphemy from occurring while the alleged blasphemer may think of herself as under an obligation to say what she thinks and stand up for her views. In cases like these, many have thought that the state ought to stop the blaspheming. I think that there are very strong grounds for rejecting this view. I do not deny that the person who wishes to stop the blaspheming has a right to try to stop it. But that person must be limited to persuasion and argument to do this. The freedom of speech and the freedom of association can be exercised to try to persuade people not to engage in blasphemy. These are the tools that liberal rights afford such persons and they are not inconsiderable tools.

What are the resources of the account I have provided so far for supporting this answer? The basic move in the argument for liberal rights as for democratic rights in the context of conflicts of opinion has been to understand the conflicts of opinion partly as conflicts of interest. Each person has a right to have her opinions respected because each person has interests in having that right. I have outlined the interests above. It seems clear to me that the prohibition of blasphemy sacrifices one person's profound interests for the sake of another's while the liberal right respects the interests of each in an egalitarian manner. The costs of prohibition greatly outweigh the costs of the right, if we are thinking in terms of the interests of the participants. To ban blasphemy would amount to setting back the interests of the alleged blasphemer so that another's interests in having his desire that everyone conform their behavior and speech to his opinions be respected. To allow blasphemy amounts to according an equal respect to each person's opinion on the matter. It allows the alleged blasphemer to speak her mind and it allows the opponent of blasphemy to speak his mind as well and it allows the opponent of blasphemy to try to persuade the alleged blasphemer to stop her behavior. The cost to the alleged blasphemer of not being able to speak her mind and not being able to associate with other like-minded persons is greater than the cost to the opponent of blasphemy, which is that people are not required

---

[22] The major concerns with blasphemy of modern societies have been with the threat to stability of the permission to blasphemy (on the grounds that religion is an essential support for political society) and with the offense blasphemy gives to religious adherents. See Leonard Levy, *Blasphemy: Verbal Offense Against the Sacred from Moses to Salman Rushdie* (New York: Alfred Knopf, 1993), for a historical account. See also David A. J. Richards, *Free Speech and the Politics of Identity* (New York: Oxford University Press, 1999).

to make their behaviors conform to his view of the matter. These costs to the opponent of blasphemy can in part be mitigated by efforts to persuade others. The opponent of blasphemy can discharge his obligation to try to stop blasphemy by means of efforts at persuasion. And he may even be able to stop some instances of it. And to the extent that this fails he may simply avoid the company of blasphemers by associating with other like-minded persons. So it seems clear that the costs to the alleged blasphemer of prohibition are greater than the costs of the right to the opponent of blasphemy.[23]

As we will see, this right holds up even if a majority thinks that the speech of the alleged blasphemer ought to be stopped. The principle of public equality protects individuals' interests even when the similar or lesser interests of a greater number oppose them.

But, what are we to think of the alleged wrong of blasphemy itself? We have so far dealt with the interests of each person in expressing his or her view and in protecting themselves from offense as well as in discharging their obligations toward the object of blasphemy. But I have said nothing about the wrong itself. How should this figure into our political theory of democracy and liberal rights? What kind of reason can it supply?

Aside from what I have said above, there is one further important remark to make about how blasphemy should be thought of in the context of the principle of public equality. This thought cannot be fully explained until we arrive at Chapter 7 on the limits of democratic authority. But the basic idea is that the authority of the democratic assembly is grounded in public equality. And the limits of democratic authority are also grounded in public equality. So some action of the democratic assembly that violates public equality undercuts the authority of that assembly in that instance. Now to the extent that the arguments in favor of the idea that liberal rights are a way of publicly treating the interests of persons publicly as equals are correct, it follows that liberal rights are public realizations of equality. But this means that the setting back of liberal rights is beyond the authority of democracy. A democratic assembly does not have the right to violate these rights. This implies that whatever claim the alleged wrong of blasphemy has upon us independent of our interests, the democratic assembly does not have a right to ban blasphemy. Such an action is beyond its authority since it violates public equality. So when we bracket the interests of the persons in society that are connected with blasphemy and we

---

[23] My account of the protection of blasphemy is close in many respects, though not as subtle, to Joel Feinberg's treatment of profound offense in *Offense to Others: Volume II of The Moral Limits of the Criminal Law* (New York: Oxford University Press, 1985), pp. 50–96. The main ways in which I differ is in thinking that offense does constitute a setback to interests (in contrast, see Feinberg, p. 74) and in the claim that the principle of equality is necessary to a full account of the grounds of liberal rights. This is defended in what follows.

attend to the question of the remedy for the alleged evil of blasphemy itself, we find that the democratic assembly cannot provide the remedy for this evil and retain its inherent authority.[24]

Shapes and the Cores of the Liberal Rights

Now that we have sketched the interests arrayed in favor of liberal rights and how they override or at least are undefeated by the interests against them we can see that the liberal rights are themselves quite complex so that the relation to other concerns does not rule out all restrictions on the possible exercises of interests. There are certain well-known limits to freedom of expression that need to be discussed in this context. For example, it is generally thought that the right to freedom of expression does not protect false advertising or libel of private individuals or the making of false alarms or incitement to violence. Furthermore, freedom of expression does not protect all expression, even of the appropriate kinds of content. It is thought legitimate to restrict expression in matters of time, manner, and place though here there are certain not well-defined limitations on these kinds of qualifications.

   Can we account for these limitations within the view elaborated so far? To what extent do false advertising, libel, false alarms, incitement to violence advance the interests associated with freedom of expression and to what extent do they fail to advance those interests? How do the harms that are produced by these kinds of speech outweigh whatever benefits they may bring?

   It has been traditionally thought permissible to regulate the time, manner, and place of expression up to a point for the sake of other goods. The reason for this is that the interests that underlie freedom of expression are not at stake in every instance of expression. The interest in expressing one's views are not at least centrally at stake in the regulation that specifies that one may not shout one's views at the top of one's lungs in the middle of the night in a residential neighborhood. And one may not follow someone around, hectoring them about the falsity or perniciousness of their views. As long as

---

[24] To be sure, it is still possible for someone to say that the evil of blasphemy outweighs the goods of democracy and liberal rights and public equality in general and that therefore one should be able to use political institutions to stop it regardless of these other values. There are really only two possible strategies in countering this possibility. One may hope that the religious views acquire an allegiance to the political principles as Rawls does in *Political Liberalism*. Or one may try to tame religious belief so that religious differences are more like ordinary differences of view and are not a matter of who attains salvation and who does not as Locke does in his *Letter Concerning Toleration*. I explore a version of this last strategy in my paper "Does Religious Toleration Make Any Sense?" in *Contemporary Debates in Social Philosophy* ed. Laurence Thomas (Oxford: Blackwell Publishers, 2007). Both of these seem to have happened in the twentieth and twenty-first centuries to many though not all religious believers.

those interests can be advanced in the light of day as well as in writing under circumstances where the relevant person has the capacity to express the views, the regulations protecting people from public nuisances do not set back the interests in freedom of expression.

We need to define a kind of central core of liberal rights that may not be compromised and beyond which reasonable people and democratic assemblies may disagree. It seems to me that the core of liberal rights should be defined in terms of the central interests that the rights are meant to protect and in terms of the capacity for protection afforded people from unfortunate exercises of the rights. For example, we might argue that the right to free expression does not extend to libel of private individuals on the grounds that the interests in truth, being at home in the world, and correcting for cognitive bias do not seem to be centrally at stake in the activity of defaming or libeling ordinary private individuals. Furthermore, the capacity to protect oneself from defamation or libel seems greatly diminished in the case of private libel. One cannot simply exercise the protective function of association or privacy to do this since the way one's interests are set back result from the influence on the opinions of third parties. It is hard to undo the damage to reputation that results from malicious defamatory or libelous statements.

In contrast, libel of public figures, while certainly deserving of censure when it is maliciously and recklessly done, engages the interests mentioned above more centrally. One has an interest in attacking public figures whose outlooks seem threatening to the society or whose ideas seem dangerously far from the truth or who hold positions of public responsibility. These public figures have a great influence on the public and represent certain ways of living or approaches to the organization of society or even styles of thinking. Thus they ought to that extent be more open to attacks and the standard of libel that protects them ought to be more stringent, so that open and free discussion about the issues they raise can be advanced. Furthermore, they do have the capacity to defend themselves because of their public standing as opinion leaders, political leaders, celebrities, or even public figures representing a particular way of life. Hence, a more stringent protection of free expression from libel suits advanced by public figures can be shown to be grounded in the basic interests underlying liberal rights and the protective capacities afforded by those rights.[25]

Limitations on public advertising seem also to be defensible on these grounds. The interests that are advanced by public advertising are primarily monetary interests. They are not the interests that are fundamental to the freedom of expression. Of course, once the interests in freedom of expression

---

[25] See New York Times v. Sullivan (1968), for this reasoning.

come into play in discussions of commodities, such as when there are arguments about their safety or their usefulness, the protections afforded freedom of expression must be extended to these. But there is no such need in the activity of advertising itself. Furthermore, the financial interests arrayed in favor of the advertised commodities make it hard for there to be significant occasions for rebutting the claims of advertisers so the protective function of free expression is likely not to be as well served. Hence, it is reasonable to demand truth in advertising.

The above observations provide just a few examples of how reference to the central interests protected by the liberal rights can help determine when certain types of actions should be protected by the rights and when they should not. They also show that some actions ought to receive a lesser degree of protection of others.

Public Equality and the Liberal Rights as Trumps

So far I have argued that the interests protected by the liberal rights are undefeated preeminent interests. They are themselves very important interests and they provide the means to protect individuals against the kinds of costs that the exercise of liberal rights can impose on others. But this argument does not establish that the interests protected by the liberal rights can outweigh in importance the aggregated interests of many people who might be offended by the exercise of these rights by some particular person or who might wish to have a more homogeneous cultural environment to live in. I have argued that the interests protected by liberal rights are preeminent and undefeated in the sense that each interest is very important and fundamental and can defeat the interests opposed to liberal rights. But I have not argued for the claim that when we add up the less important interests of many people and compare the aggregate to the interests protected by the liberal right of a person who holds an unpopular view, the liberal right trumps the aggregated good of the others. For all I have argued so far, if the exercise of freedom of conscience by a particular person offends a large proportion of the population or it disrupts the otherwise homogeneous culture with which a large proportion of the population is comfortable, the person's interests must give way to the interests of the great majority.

It is here that the egalitarian dimension of the principle of public equality plays a key role. I argue that even if the denial of freedom of conscience could alleviate the dismay of the majority, denial of that right to the minority ensures that the minority would have good reason to think that they are being treated as inferiors in a public way. Since each and every person has a right to be treated in accordance with public equality, a society that denies freedom of conscience to its members is unjust in a publicly clear way. This shows that each person has a fundamental and equal right to freedom of conscience. And the same can be shown of the other liberal rights.

The publicly clear setback to interests that accompanies the denial of freedom of conscience implies that some people are being treated publicly as inferiors in a society where freedom of conscience or other liberal rights are denied to them. I will argue that the principle of public equality requires that liberal rights are trumps.

The trumping property of liberal rights is grounded in the egalitarian dimension of the principle of public equality directly. The basic idea proceeds from the premises that each person has fundamental interests in having their liberal rights protected and that the principle of public equality serves as a constraint on the advancement of the interests of the members of society. From these two claims, the argument states that to sacrifice one person's fundamental interests in the liberal rights so that many others may have less fundamental interests served is a way of treating that person publicly as an inferior. Public equality requires in effect that the interests of persons be compared in a pairwise fashion so that one may not sacrifice one person's interests for the less important though more numerous interests of others.[26]

Let us look at this argument more closely. Remember that the principle of public equality is a principle of egalitarian distribution. It says that persons must have their interests equally advanced in a society by some publicly clear measure, that is, in terms of the basic interests I have described in favor of and against liberal rights. To make the argument clear, we can think initially of a regime of liberal rights as a roughly equal distribution of the benefits and costs. The interests advanced by the liberal rights are roughly equal and the interests set back by the liberal rights are of roughly equal importance across persons (again, always thinking in terms of a crude but publicly clear measure). Now the desire to impose constraints on the liberal rights of some group (say A) arises because some other group (say group B) thinks that its interests are being sacrificed as a result of the exercises of the liberal rights of the members of A. B's thought might even be that they are being sacrificed for the sake of A. They think that the costs of liberal rights are not being equally distributed and they want to rectify this by limiting the rights of A.

---

[26] It seems to me that Joshua Cohen's otherwise excellent "Freedom of Expression," in *Philosophy and Public Affairs*, vol. 22, no. 3 (Summer 1993), pp. 207–63 is an interest-based account that fails to grasp the need for showing how the liberal rights trump other concerns. His account is open to the objection that many people's lesser interests might outweigh the interests an individual has in the liberal right.

How should we think about this demand? Surely we should concede that there can be inequalities in the distribution of the costs of liberal rights and these inequalities might even be measurable by a publicly clear standard. So now we have a departure from equality due to a supposed inequality of costs imposed by liberal rights. The liberal rights are respected in this state but the costs of the liberal rights fall unevenly on the members of the society (more on B than on A). Let us call this inegalitarian state I1.

Now let us describe the consequence of the proposed restriction on A's liberal rights for the sake of diminishing the costs imposed on B. I have argued that the interests behind the liberal rights are weightier than the interests that are set back by the exercises of liberal rights. This implies that the interests set back by denying A's liberal rights are weightier than the interests of B that are set back by A's exercise of their liberal rights. As a result the denial of A's liberal rights will bring about a greater departure from equality than the inequality that results from the differential costs of everyone's exercise of their liberal rights. Hence the state I2, in which A's liberal rights are denied, is more inegalitarian than I1. And I claim that the difference in inequalities is assessed by a reasonably clear public measure. Therefore, the denial of liberal rights to A would amount to an unacceptably unequal distribution of the advancement of interests by the publicly clear standard of measure. And this implies that the members of A are being treated publicly as inferiors, since their interests are not being as well advanced as those of B.

Now this argument extends to cases of setting back the interests in liberal rights of one for the sake of the lesser interests of many people. Such an action would bring about an unacceptable publicly clear inegalitarian distribution of interest advancement between the one person and all the others. One person's interest would have been sacrificed for the sake of the others' lesser interests. The denial of liberal rights to some for the sake of diminishing the costs of the liberal rights for others will involve a greater departure from equality (as measured by a publicly clear standard) than the unequal distribution of the costs of liberal rights.

To appreciate this, notice that the requirement of publicly equal distribution of interest advancement implies that one only allow pairwise comparisons between the winners and the losers. The limitation to pairwise comparisons is entailed by the egalitarian principle of distribution. For any conception of egalitarian distribution, equality and inequality are measured in terms of whether each person is as well off as any other person. And departures from equality are measured in pairwise terms as well. Now because the interests in liberal rights are weightier than the set back interests, the pairwise differences between the winners and losers will be greater in the case of denial of rights than in the case of the differential costs of liberal rights. And if we suppose that the measure of inequality is in terms of the sum of the differences from those pairwise comparisons, then the inequality that results from denial of liberal rights will be significantly greater than the inequality that results from the unequal distribution of costs even if many more people are experiencing the costs.

Here is an idealized example. Suppose that the numbers below represent cardinally the public measure of well-being of each person. A person who has the benefit of liberal rights and who does not have costs imposed has 5 points. A person who is offended by others' exercise of liberal rights but who also has the benefit of the liberal rights has 4 points. And a person who has a particular liberal right denied in order to avoid offense to others, whose liberal rights are not denied, has 2 points. The states I1 and I2 described above are represented by the following numbers under the supposition that there are ten people.

$$I1 \quad 5 \quad 4 \quad 4 \quad 4 \quad 4 \quad 4 \quad 4 \quad 4 \quad 4 \quad 4$$
$$I2 \quad 2 \quad 5 \quad 5 \quad 5 \quad 5 \quad 5 \quad 5 \quad 5 \quad 5 \quad 5$$

According to one standard measure (according to which we sum the differences between each person) the amount of inequality in I1 is 9. The amount of inequality in I2 is 27. And if we increase the number of people whose exercises of rights are offensive and thereby whose rights are to be restricted in I2, the inequality increases.

So, if we are to implement the principle of public equality, then we must protect the liberal rights of persons even when there is some inequality in the imposition of the costs of the liberal rights.[27]

It is important to remember here that we are talking about equality and inequality as measured by some publicly clear measure. This is what public equality requires. We do not know exactly the comparisons of well-being among the different persons in society and these must necessarily be controversial. So we attempt to realize equality in some way that is publicly clear. This means that the interests involved in the comparisons must be important and fundamental ones and they must be ones that have some fairly clear public measure and for which we have pretty good public means for determining which are more important than which. Equal liberal rights are, I have argued above, ways of achieving equality in a way that is publicly clear. So are democratic rights. Other measures will necessarily be more

[27] I thank Charles Beitz and Jeff McMahan for impressing on me the need to clarify this argument.

obscure and incapable of bringing about the public recognition that they are egalitarian.

I have given an extensive argument for the principle of equality as a principle of distributive justice in Chapter 1. Also, the egalitarian account of liberal rights sheds light on the peculiar property of liberal rights as trumps without undermining the complexity and nuance that an interest-based conception of rights has to offer. These are two independent arguments for this conception of liberal rights.

I think that there is another argument for the egalitarian conception of rights that I have offered. This argument is based on an implication of the egalitarian view. Recall that the egalitarian principle in Chapter 1 says that all inequalities are unjust. It avoids leveling down by saying that not all equalities are more just than all inequalities. But it does insist that whenever there is inequality, even if the inequality is Pareto superior to all feasible equalities, there is some injustice. In the context of the liberal rights case above, this would suggest that the uneven distribution of costs of everyone's exercise of his or her liberal rights may involve a kind of residual injustice even if we cannot make the situation more equal.

So the fact that some are offended or disturbed by what others say while others do not experience the same difficulties in society may involve some injustice. In any case, this is what the egalitarian view suggests. Does this make sense? I believe it does. Of course, we have to be very careful here to get a clear grasp of what is at issue. Sometimes people are offended by what others say on the basis of their own false ideas and we think they should know better. Sometimes we think that saying things that offend others will help them get a clearer grasp of the truth. These kinds of cases can make us wonder whether there is any wrong or harm done because we hold out the hope that the offensive words will actually benefit the person. In these cases, we may think that the harms are only apparent or merely short term.

To get a clear case, imagine the situation of a person who is set in his religious ways and beliefs and imagine that we think that this person's religious views are false though not dangerous. But we also know that this person will be offended by the expression of certain ideas that are blasphemous or heretical in the context of his faith. I think our sense in this context is that there is a certain injustice to this person when they experience offense and upset when these ideas are expressed. They experience a setback to their interests. Again, this injustice may not be institutionally rectifiable without creating even more injustice, as I argued above. But it is something. And indeed most people will make some significant effort not to offend this person and will think it a wrong when others do not do the same. And I think it is quite intuitive to say that if some person seems to be experiencing these effects disproportionately, there is some injustice.[28] Minority religions are often in this situation in societies and it is plausible to say that there is injustice in the fact that the costs of liberal rights fall more heavily on them than on others. We usually make some effort to avoid this kind of offense. And we may even be justified in imposing some time, manner, and place restrictions. This is one of the insights of multiculturalism. So I think that the egalitarian view sheds light on the peculiar aspect of liberal rights that we think there is some residual injustice in the uneven distribution of the costs of exercise and that we think that individuals ought to modify their behavior so as to avoid needless imposition of costs in these contexts even though we do not think that institutions should be altered to diminish the liberal rights.

In conclusion, we can see that the public egalitarian conception of liberal rights sheds light on a number of important properties of liberal rights. The interest-based component sheds light on the complexity and nuance of liberal rights. It explains their apparent messiness. The egalitarian component explains how liberal rights, conceived along interest-based lines, can be trumps against the aggregated greater good of society.[29] But it also explains a residual sense of injustice when the costs of liberal rights clearly fall disproportionately on some group.

Public Equality and the Rule of Law

The argument so far has suggested that the grounds of liberal rights are in the principle of public equality. The principle of public equality says that

---

[28] It is important to recall here that the principle of equality does not require that if one person is offended, then others should be offended as well so as to even up the score. I have argued in Chapter 1 against the idea that the principle of equality, properly understood, implies leveling down.

[29] One might worry that the account generates a kind of utilitarianism of rights. The reason for this is that the principle of equality seems to have a kind of states of affairs cast. So if the question is, when is a right sacrificed for the sake of similar rights of other people, since there is no apparent index connected with doing and allowing or intention and foreknowledge, it would appear that the view would allow that the rights of a few should be sacrificed for the sake of the rights of more. But this may not hold after all. The reason for this is that in the main case, the issue would be whether the rights of a few were violated by the basic structure or the rights of more were violated by the structure. Both of these would be problematic. It is hard to see how an institutional system would be forced into such a choice without treating people publicly as unequals. The reason why the problem may not be real here is because all of the alternatives are thought of as results of the institutional arrangement and it is unclear how it could be legitimate to put the rights of a number of people at risk such that it became necessary to threaten the rights of fewer people in order to protect the greater number. In a sense, the idea is that all of the rights violation are doings of the institutional structure. This does not provide a completely general solution to the question of utilitarianism of rights but it does provide a solution for the case of institutions.

institutions should advance the interests of the members of society equally in a publicly clear way. So the conception of the grounds of liberal rights involves first an elaboration of the interests at stake in liberal rights and a showing that the interests that favor the liberal rights are not defeated by the interests that may be set back by those rights. Second, the egalitarian dimension of the principle comes in to show how liberal rights cannot be defeated in the normal case by the aggregated lesser interests of others.

But the argument so far leaves some cracks in the grounds for liberal rights. It is not difficult to imagine cases of exercises of liberal rights where the interests protected by the liberal rights seem weaker than the interests that are set back by the exercise of such rights. For example, imagine the frivolous but brilliant blasphemer who causes no end of grief to the devout religious person. It is not hard to imagine that in some such cases, the interests of the frivolous blasphemer are less weighty than those of the religious devotee. And these kinds of cases can be easily replicated. Imagine frivolous or merely malicious but brilliant attackers of public persons' reputations. The theory I have described so far cannot rule out such cases. And the theory seems to suggest that the right can be curtailed in these cases. What are we to think of this kind of case? Does the right of free expression run out with the frivolous blasphemer? Or does the frivolous blasphemer have a right to torment the religious devotee?

I think our judgment must be complex here. There is a sense in which the frivolous blasphemer is acting in a way that ought not to be protected by fundamental considerations of justice. This person is wronging the religious devotee and it appears that there is some kind of injustice here because the interests of the blasphemer are slight and the interests of the religious devotee are serious.

But this is not the end of the discussion because there are reasons connected with institutional structure that we would rather not in general prohibit frivolous blasphemers from acting as they please. There may be injustices in these cases but we may not think that the state or the legal system is the proper instrument for rectifying these injustices. We may think that the state is too crude an instrument in this context and that it will likely end up suppressing expression that ought to be protected by public equality.

The final component of the conception of the grounds of liberal rights is based in the idea of the rule of law. The idea of the rule of law implies that the interests that ground the liberal rights are not to be balanced, at least in the normal case, on a case by case basis. Individuals are to be treated in accordance with publicly promulgated settled laws. These laws are justified by the interests that ground the liberal rights and by the correct balance of these interests with the costs of the liberal rights as well as the principle of public equality. The consequence of this principle of the rule of law is that we cannot simply select an instance of problematic behavior and say that it ought to be prohibited without giving a general rule for all such cases.

One argument in favor of the rule of law is that it establishes a stability of expectations among persons. Individuals know what to expect and know how to avoid coming into conflict with the state. Were state action toward individuals generally determined on a case by case basis reflecting in each case a judgment of the balance of the interests for and against the action, individuals would have a hard time predicting what the actions of the state were. This would undermine their abilities to live lives in accordance with their own design as well as to make the plans that are necessary to the achievement of many of their purposes. This would imply a setback to the legitimate pursuit of interests.

The stability of expectations argument is a venerable one. But there is another argument in the tradition as well.[30] And this argument can best be expressed with the help of the principle of public equality. What the rule of law does is undermine one very clear and public way in which individuals can treat others as public inferiors. When state policy is made by means of case by case reasoning reflecting the balance of interests in each case, two significant dangers arise. First, those who are responsible for making the case by case judgments have a significant incentive to impose costs on others that they do not impose on themselves. Since they must formulate policies in each instance and some of these instances will involve policies in which their own interests are at stake, there will be a tendency for a bias toward one's own interests to reveal itself. The consequence of this will often be more favorable treatment of oneself or others closely connected with oneself than of others. There may in some cases be a danger of outright domination of others in favor of one's own interests.

Second, a danger arises not only in cases of outright cynicism but also in cases where individuals act in a conscientious manner. If we invoke the facts of fallibility and cognitive bias we can see that there is a significant likelihood that those who are charged with the task of balancing interests on a case by case basis are likely to advance their own interests when they must deal with a case involving themselves.

These two dangers imply that persons who are subjected to this constant case by case reasoning will have reason to think that their interests are not being given as much consideration as the interests of others. Consequently they will have reason to think that their status as equals in the society is called

---

[30] See John Locke, "Second Treatise on Civil Government," in *Two Treatises on Civil Government* ed. Peter Laslett (Cambridge: Cambridge University Press, 2000), section 137.

into question. As a rule then, they will have reason to think that they are being publicly treated as inferiors.

The rule of law is one important means by which this kind of public inequality is averted. It ensures at least that whatever decisions a person makes must also apply in many other cases including ones in which he himself or people close to him are involved. Thus it diminishes some of the opportunity to favor oneself and it certainly diminishes the appearance of doing so. It is therefore a necessary condition on the public realization of equality in a society.

So in order to deal with the frivolous blasphemer we must have settled and known laws. But what would the law be? We can imagine a criminal law or a system of tort law that criminalizes frivolous blasphemy or makes it a possible basis for civil suit. But now the question is, how are we to judge when the blasphemy is frivolous or not or malicious or not? Furthermore, how do we determine that the interests of the frivolous blasphemer really are significantly of less importance than those who are the alleged victims? If we have not very stringent standards for judging when blasphemy is frivolous, we may end up either criminalizing a lot of nonfrivolous blasphemy or subjecting such nonfrivolous blasphemy to the threat of lawsuits. And even if the application of the law would often successfully exonerate the nonfrivolous blasphemy or avoid imposing civil damages, it would still have a significant chilling effect on discussion of important theological issues because of people's understandable fears of getting tied up in the legal system.

But there is a more serious problem here. To determine whether the interests of the blasphemer are less weighty than the interests of the offended party, the judge or jury would have to balance the interests in this instance. But the balancing of interests in this kind of case is a hazardous enterprise. And given that the judges or the juries that decide these cases may have feelings of sympathy with the views of the alleged victims, the determination of the balance of interests may not be always very impartial. Hence, there would be a serious danger to public equality in allowing a rule against blasphemy.

My sense in these kinds of cases is that considerations of institutional structure suggest that frivolous or malicious blasphemers ought not to be handled by the law at all. There are too many risks of government heavy handedness and bias in the application of such a law and these threaten the fundamental interests protected by the liberal rights. And this holds even though we do not think that the frivolous blasphemer has fundamental interests at stake.[31]

---

[31] Another solution is the New York Times v. Sullivan solution. Make it possible to sue for damages for offenses due to frivolous or malicious blasphemy but make the standards of proof of frivolity or malice so high that people rarely, if ever, sue. The advantage of this is that it does express some disapproval of these actions while not threatening the fundamental interests.

So on the view defended here, there is no fundamental right to frivolous or malicious blasphemy but there are considerations of public equality that militate against using the law to protect persons from frivolous blasphemy.

The Liberal Rights of the Intolerant

The argument for liberal rights I have given here implies that individuals who advance antiliberal, antidemocratic, and antiegalitarian views have the same rights as all the others. At first this may seem strange since those who advocate for the antiegalitarian views seem to be contesting the very principle that grounds their rights. There seems to be a kind of pragmatic inconsistency in their claim to an equal right to express and organize for these antiegalitarian views in the normal case. Furthermore, we might think that when they espouse the antiegalitarian views, they themselves are violating the principle of public equality. They seem to be treating those who they think are worthy of inferior treatment as inferiors by insisting that they ought to be treated as inferiors. Finally, they seem to be trying to bring about some deeply inegalitarian state of affairs and are making some contribution to bringing that inegalitarian state of affairs about. Why do not these three considerations tell against giving the full panoply of liberal rights to these people?

The basis of my response to these three arguments is the argument I have just given for the liberal rights grounded in the interests of persons and the principle of public equality. The interests of antiegalitarian persons in speech and therefore the clearly public violation of equality that would attend banning antiegalitarian expression and association are for the most part the same for these people as they are for the rest of the society. The interest in true and justified beliefs holds for these persons as well as anyone else. Remember that the interest in truth, according to the argument presented above, is not advanced by imposing beliefs on people, it is advanced when people have the opportunities to test their beliefs and consider alternatives. And the interest in correcting for cognitive bias seems to have the same implications for the antiegalitarian as for others. So too are the interests in free association protected by the liberal rights.

There are also collective benefits from airing of antiegalitarian views. They are the benefits of knowing what these views are, what the basis of the views are and also being able to hear the refutations of these views. They also involve the hearing of positive reasons offered for equality. In general the public protective

---

On the other hand, one can imagine the high standards of proof being chiseled away over time thus threatening the fundamental interests.

function of speech itself makes a useful contribution to the generation and maintenance of egalitarian ideas.

The interest in being at home in the world may not speak as strongly in favor of treating the intolerant as equals. For recall, I argued in Chapter 2 that interest is for being at home in an egalitarian world while the antiegalitarians attempt to bring about a nonegalitarian world and are not satisfied with an egalitarian world. Or at least they are not fully satisfied with it if their affective response to equality is consistent with their views. So being treated as an equal does not fully advance their interest in being at home in the world.

Furthermore the interest in being recognized and affirmed as an equal is not as well satisfied for these people as well as for others. The interest is a partially objective interest that everyone has whether they believe in equality or not. So even if they do not adhere to the principle of equality, they can have their interests in being recognized and affirmed as equals fulfilled or set back by the way others treat them. But they cannot have that interest fully satisfied since they may not appreciate equality. So the two interests that require satisfaction with equality are not fully satisfied for the antiegalitarian.

To say that the interest in being at home in the world is not satisfied for antiegalitarians in an egalitarian world does not imply that their interests in being at home in the world would be satisfied in a world where subordination of some was the norm. I have argued in Chapter 2 that there is no interest in being at home in an antiegalitarian world, at least with respect to the inequality. And this is because interests must be connected with what is intrinsically valuable. But at the same time interests must also be connected with one's appreciation. So if one does not appreciate some aspect of a world, even if it is intrinsically valuable, that aspect does not advance one's interest in being at home, at least in the respect of the quality one fails to appreciate.

Nevertheless, the antiegalitarians do not have these interests better satisfied by being prohibited from expressing their views or associating on the basis of those views. For prohibition will not make them satisfied and it will set back their interests in truth and correcting for cognitive bias as well as their interests in being members of associations of like-minded persons. Furthermore, even if they are not likely to be satisfied with equality, their interests in being at home in the world and in being recognized as an equal will be partly set back by an inequality that disadvantages them. Though they may not care for equality for all, they are likely to be deeply dissatisfied by being treated as an inferior. And so, at least in part, the interests in equality still count as considerations in favor of equality of rights for them.

All in all, the interests are not quite as strongly arrayed in favor of the protection of the liberal rights of the antiegalitarians as they are for egalitarian members of society. But they nevertheless do speak in favor of their having liberal rights and do not speak against their possession of liberal rights. Given these clear setbacks to the interests of the antiegalitarians from the denial of liberal rights, it seems clear that antiegalitarians are being treated publicly as inferiors when their liberal rights are denied. Therefore the principle of public equality demands that the antiegalitarians be afforded the liberal rights.

With this argument in mind let us consider the three arguments for banning antiegalitarian views. The first argument from inconsistency is a nonstarter. One, the mere fact of pragmatic inconsistency does not disqualify a view from being expressed. Indeed, the fact of inconsistency could well be a basis for learning of all the persons involved. Two, the principle of public equality is an objective principle and does not require for its operation that those protected by it agree to it. Though the advocacy of inequality displays a lack of regard for equality it does not follow that public equality does not protect such advocacy. As I noted in Chapter 2, the publicity component of public equality only requires that people can see that they are being treated as equals. It does not require that they agree with the principle of equality. So there is no difficulty in treating people who are opposed to equality in accordance with the principle of public equality. And there is no difficulty in seeing that the banning of the expression of beliefs opposed to equality is a public violation of equality.

The second argument, which states that advocating for inequality amounts to treating some as inferiors, does strike me as a more serious argument than the first. This argument has been given by some feminists as a reason for banning pornography. They argue that pornography amounts to treating women as inferiors. Indeed they argue that pornography silences women as a result of leading men and even some women not to take them seriously.

We should separate two claims here, though we will treat them in one single argument. The first is that advocating for inequality amounts to treating some as inferiors. The second is that advocating for inequality may have the causal effect that some are treated as inferiors. The first claim must be assessed against the background that the democratic and liberal rights are assured and that each has a basic minimum of material goods. If these latter conditions are satisfied, then it appears that the society is treating its members publicly as equals.

But what if many members of the society advocate for unequal treatment for a single group? Even if they do not get their way in the formal institutions of society, a culture of inequality may arise in such a way that the members of the disadvantaged group may think of themselves as publicly treated as inferiors, if not by the institutions then by the public culture of the society. The generation and maintenance of stereotypes of the disadvantaged group and the subtle ways in which the disadvantaged group can be insulted and never given the benefit of the doubt are ways in which this can happen without violating any laws or even running up against the limits to the authority of democracy.

What can we expect from a democratic society by way of response to the threat of antiegalitarian sentiments? First, we can expect that the public protective function of the liberal rights will likely have the effect of marginalizing the antiegalitarian ideas. Second, as we will see in Chapter 7, the limits of democratic authority are such that any legislation passed on the basis of these antiegalitarian ideas will be beyond the legitimate authority of a democratic assembly. Beyond these two safeguards, it seems to me that a democratic society has a right to counteract these kinds of influences either by officially expressing adherence to egalitarian principles or by giving some support to groups that promote this kind of position. A democratic society has the right and in some cases even the duty to take steps to improve the egalitarian ethos of the public culture but it may not do this by banning views. It must do this by promoting the egalitarian ethos through persuasion or support for egalitarian groups or even through requirements on the system of education.

A democratic society may not ban the kinds of groups that advocate for these kinds of ideas nor may it ban the expression of the ideas. To do any one of these two things would amount publicly to be treating the advocates as inferiors.

There is one set of circumstances in which the suspension of liberal rights may be permitted. John Rawls argues that the basic liberties ought only to be suspended when there is what he calls a constitutional crisis of the most severe kind.[32] This is a crisis where the very institutions of government that are charged with the task of protecting liberty and ensuring democracy are threatened with imminent destruction.

It strikes me that the Rawlsian standard is certainly a sufficient condition for justifying restriction of liberal rights but it is not a necessary condition. John Stuart Mill defends a less stringent standard which permits prohibition of the content of speech only when the exercises of conscience and speech are intended to incite and are likely to bring about imminent violence or other severe violations of the basic interests protected by liberal rights.[33] This action need not threaten the very existence of government, it only need threaten imminent violence or other serious harm to the individuals who are verbally attacked. In these instances, it will be defensible to restrict the

---

[32] See John Rawls, *Political Liberalism* revised edition (New York: Columbia University Press, 1996), p. 354.
[33] See John Stuart Mill, *On Liberty*, p. 56.

liberal rights of those who are engaged in such incitement. In this case, we are restricting something at the margin of the liberal rights of some in order to protect the regime of liberal and democratic rights from imminent attack or to protect the liberal and democratic rights of a particular person or group of persons.

Let us summarize the things that a democratic society may do to counteract antiegalitarian mobilization. First, and most important, the public protective function of the rights of freedom of expression and association can be exercised by ordinary citizens. In the normal case in a reasonably just and democratic society that protects the democratic and liberal rights of all citizens and that secures an adequate material minimum for all citizens, the likelihood is that the best remedy for bad speech is more speech. The second thing a democratic society may do is attempt to promote equality through education, public announcements, and support for egalitarian groups and an egalitarian ethos. Third, as we will argue in Chapter 7, since the authority of a democratic assembly runs out when it tries to infringe the democratic or liberal rights of members of the society, a democratic society may protect itself against the possibility of antiegalitarian legislation by imposing limits on legally permissible legislation. In all of these cases, a democratic society must avoid attempting to ban views or ideas or particular kinds of association. Fourth, only in the cases where none of these remedies succeeds and antiegalitarian groups incite violence or violation of the basic rights of the members through their speech or association may a democratic society step in to restrict the freedom of speech and association in those contexts.

SOME OBJECTIONS TO THE EGALITARIAN ACCOUNT OF LIBERAL RIGHTS

In this section, I want to consider two objections to the view I have defended and offer some responses to those objections. The first objection I consider is meant to be a counterexample to my account of liberal rights. It asserts that my account does not rule out the possibility of scientists attempting to brainwash the intolerant into believing the principle of equality and its implications for liberal and democratic rights. It argues that this is compatible with my view and yet that it is indefensible and contrary to freedom of conscience. The second set of objections questions the adequacy of the egalitarian account of liberal rights on the grounds that the principle of equality can offer no objection to the equal diminishing of everyone's liberal rights.

The Problem of Perfect or Near Perfect Brainwashing

The account offered here of the foundations of liberal rights is grounded in the facts of disagreement, fallibility, cognitive bias, and diversity among persons and the fundamental interests that emerge in those circumstances. But this suggests a potential objection to the view. To consider this objection we need to suppose a situation in which one person forcibly brainwashes another with the predictable effect that the brainwashed person comes to have a completely true, coherent, and desirable set of beliefs and one that fits well with the experience of the brainwashed person. Is this a violation of freedom of conscience, and if so, is it wrong?

My view would seem not to be able to exclude this kind of brainwashing, since it seems clearly in the interests of the brainwashed person to have the sorts of beliefs under consideration. All of the interests at the ground of the various rights of conscience are interests that either would not be set back or would be positively advanced in this brainwashing case. It is clear that the interest in learning the truth would be advanced by this instance of brainwashing. By hypothesis, the beliefs one is brainwashed to have are all true and they are well supported. It is also clear that the interest in being at home in the world would not be set back. By hypothesis, one would now have a completely coherent set of beliefs that were true and that cohere with one's experience. There would be no occasion for alienation from the world one lives in. The interest in correcting for cognitive bias would also not be set back. Indeed, by hypothesis we are imagining that the person now acquires all true beliefs and that those administering the brainwashing are not biased.

It is a little less clear how the interest in having one's equal status recognized and affirmed would be affected. In one respect, since one is guaranteed that one's beliefs will turn out to be true, coherent, and well supported, it is clear that one's interests are being advanced and therefore it appears that one's interests are not being given short shrift. But clearly one's capacity for judgment is not being given the same respect as that of the brainwasher. The brainwasher is accorded the right to change one's beliefs. So this by itself seems to set back the interests in status.

But the setback is not as great as in the ordinary case of assumption of power of some over others. The reason for this is that, given the facts that we have described above, it is clear that the interests of the brainwashed are not being set back. Since we are not thinking of the brainwasher as cognitively biased and the interests in being at home in the world and learning are not set back, the loss of status does not include a sense that one's interests are less worthy of consideration. So there is no implied loss of fundamental moral status or even of the status associated with justice.

Still, the forcible brainwashing case described above is a case of infringe-ment of freedom of conscience.[34] To put this example in a more realistic per-spective, let us look at how brainwashing would clearly be wrong and unjust in the ordinary circumstances we know. In normal circumstances, where the conditions among persons would be marked by the facts of disagreement, fal-libility, cognitive bias, and diversity, the person doing the brainwashing would be a fallible agent who is cognitively biased toward his own interests. The brainwasher would, in brainwashing the victim, be putting his own interests before those of the other. In addition, given the limited capacity for brainwash-ing, the brainwasher would likely put beliefs in, which would not be entirely compatible with the other beliefs or experience in the victim's belief set. Those beliefs may not correspond to the kinds of evidence the brainwashed person normally has. Thus the victim is likely not to have a coherent set of beliefs with which to face and interpret the world around him. The interest in learning would not be advanced since the new beliefs would not be connected with the particular learning path, experience, and background of the person. Finally, since all of these facts obtain, it will be clear that the interests of the victim will have been publicly subordinated to those of the perpetrator and so it will be the case that the status of the victim will be that of a second-class citizen in the arrangement.

The Analogy with Parental Authority and Divine Grace

When we suspend the ordinary conditions and think of the brainwasher as stimulating all true and relevant beliefs in the victim and making the beliefs cohere with all the other beliefs and experiences of the victim, the situation looks quite different from the ordinary case. What I want to say about this kind of case is that while it is clearly an infringement of freedom of conscience, it is not clearly unjust. In order to see this we need to compare this situation with two other cases. The first case would be that of divine grace and the second case would be that of the relation between parent and child.

The perfect brainwashing case seems a bit like a case of divine grace. In divine grace, as in the case of God knocking Saul off of his horse on the road to Damascus, we have something like coercive brainwashing taking place. God does not appeal to Saul's rational capacities; that has not stopped Saul from persecuting the Christians before. It is hard to see how it will help in this case. God exercises overwhelming force to overpower Saul's ability for reflection to get Saul to change his mind and become Paul. There is a sense in which

---

[34] I thank Andrew Williams for pressing this objection.

this is an infringement of freedom of conscience because God is not trying to persuade Saul; God is simply changing Saul's mind. Yet I think that most people would not regard this action as wrong. Why not? The reason, I think, lies in the thought that God is not subject to the facts of judgment in the way that ordinary humans are. God is not fallible or cognitively biased toward his own interests. Furthermore, God is capable of changing people's minds in ways that make the new cognitive states true and fully coherent as well as relevant to the interests of the person changed. In this kind of case, we can accept the thought that God is concerned with advancing our interests even though he is not consulting us.

The other case I have in mind is the case of parents and children. Parents have such an advantage over children in terms of cognitive and emotional maturation, we give them power to direct the lives of their children and give them power to direct the cognitive development of those children. Especially when children are infants, the parents tend to advance the cognitive development of children by partially nonrational means and sometimes by coercive means. But in these cases, we do not think of the parents as acting wrongly even though they are in some sense infringing on the freedom of conscience of their charges. It is because of the obvious superiority of the parents over the children that we permit this. This superiority is one of cognitive capacity and emotional maturation.

The superiority of parents over children is not one of moral status. The interests of children are of equal worth to those of the parents. It is simply clear that the parents have the capacity to do a good job of directing the lives of their children. Again it seems that though parents are fallible, they are far less so than children. And given the usual love of parents for children, parents tend not to have as strong a cognitive bias with respect to their children. In addition, the cognitive bias is not as important a factor between parents and children because they will end up sharing a great variety of interests because of the similarity of background. Furthermore, the child's interest in learning is better advanced by the mixed methods of parents than it would be by a method that was completely nonpaternalistic.

With these two examples of defensible interference with freedom of conscience in mind, I now want to address the case of the objection. The objection, it seems to me, presupposes that the brainwasher is superior to ordinary human beings in something like the way that parents are superior to their children and the way in which God is superior to human beings. Indeed the degree of superiority is somewhere between the former and the latter kind. The brainwasher has to have a degree of superiority over human beings that far outstrips the superiority of parents to children. This is necessary because we are assuming that the brainwasher is not fallible, at least about the things that the brainwashing concerns. And we are assuming that the brainwasher is not cognitively biased.

But most important for the case of brainwashing of the intolerant, we also assume that the brainwasher knows much more about the cognitive states of his subject than the subject himself knows. He is capable of introducing coherence and capable of giving the victim a sufficiently coherent and experienced compatible set of beliefs so that the victim does better as a consequence of it than the victim would do on his own. He is also capable of ensuring that he does this in a way that does not diminish the subject's capacity for reflection. In other words, the brainwasher must be in possession of a vast amount of knowledge about the subject, which the subject does not have. This is a case of transcendent superiority.

In my view, given this transcendent superiority and the interests people have in acquiring the truth as well as enhanced capacities for acquiring the truth, the likelihood is that this kind of brainwashing would be defensible. It is hard to say this for certain because we do not have any experience with this kind of superiority. We have, on the other hand, a lot of experience with fraudulent claims to superiority such as the claims of vanguard parties to direct the people to their own interests. But these have all been fraudulent precisely because the supposed vanguard persons were subject to the same facts of judgment that everyone else is.

So we are not likely to have clear intuitions about this kind of case. But to the extent that we have intuitions about the cases of the relations between parents and children and God and human beings, we might be able to use these to form some kind of preliminary judgment about the brainwashing case. My sense is that to the extent that the brainwashing case is somewhere between the parent child case and the divine grace case, we have reason to think that it may be a defensible instance of infringement of freedom of conscience.

What this response to the objection suggests is that the argument for freedom of conscience requires not only that those who have the freedom have a certain minimum capacity for judgment, it suggests that there is a maximum capacity as well. So that if we have a being that has vastly superior capacities to those of human beings and is capable of helping human beings to achieve an understanding of the truth while assuring coherence and enhancing the capacities for reflection, then that being will not fall under the circumstances of judgment that delimit the freedom of conscience. So there is a kind of factual equality that is presupposed by freedom of conscience and, I suspect, other rights. That factual equality is determined by a minimum threshold of capacity as well as a maximum threshold of capacity. All those who fall between these two thresholds are such that if they infringe on each other's freedom of conscience they publicly treat each other as subordinates. But once we think in terms of relations between people within that range and those outside the range, we must invoke other principles though, of course, the principle of equal worth of interests will still hold.

It seems to me that this idea holds not only for the case of liberal rights but also for democratic rights. Thus Aristotle's observation seems partly right: if we could actually find a person preeminent in all the virtues to rule over us, we would not insist on the universal participation of citizens.[35] But such a person or group of persons would have to be divine or semidivine.

One difference between the democratic rights and the rights against brain-washing ought to be noted. The infringement of the democratic rights does not involve the invasion of a person's mental states. This makes a difference, for as Mill observed, there are some important interests that are set back even if we are ruled by a divine being. The interests that are advanced by one's having to take an active role in the formation of one's life are set back. These are interests in the development of our mental capacities that are set back if we have no occasion to use the faculties. Mill eloquently argued that these interests were quite profound and so we have reasons to think that even divine rule misses something important by setting back the interests that are connected with participation. By contrast, under the assumption that the brainwasher could actually give us these character traits, the objection would not apply to this kind of infringement of freedom of conscience. It might, of course, apply to the more usual infringements, that is by means of coercion.

As I have said, it is not even clear that we would suspend equal liberal or democratic rights in the cases I have described. The reason for this is that we do not really have clear intuitions about this kind of case. But the evidence from the analogous cases of parental power and divine grace suggest that equal liberal and democratic rights might be suspended with justification under these circumstances. But these are not the circumstances we face as human beings and so they are not relevant to how we think about political order.[36]

---

[35] Aristotle, *The Politics* ed. Stephen Everson (Cambridge: Cambridge University Press, 1996), p. 90.

[36] What if the brainwasher is vastly superior but not publicly recognized as such? In the examples above, it appears that there is a kind of public recognition that the brainwasher is superior. The analogies with parental authority and divine grace are also, at least at first blush, cases of publicly recognized superiority. In the case of parents, children usually have a certain degree of trust in their parents and recognize that their parents are acting for their own good. In the case of divine grace, it is usually recognized by those who have been blessed with divine grace that they have been blessed with it. And so in these cases, there is a kind of public acknowledgment of the superiority of the agent of intervention. Thus this kind of intervention is compatible with persons seeing themselves as having their interests equally advanced even though they do not have an equal say in how to advance them.

But we can imagine at least a case where a being has vastly superior moral and intellectual powers and makes a claim to rule on the basis of these powers but where those over whom

Equality and Liberal Rights

The thesis of the main argument is that disenfranchisement of individuals or classes of individuals and deprivation of the liberal rights of some people is a publicly clear violation of equality. The work of the argument seems to be entirely focused on equality and the work that it does. So the thought is that taking away someone's voting rights or liberal rights is a way of treating that person as an inferior. But one might wonder about a number of possible cases that seem to be serious deprivations of democratic and liberal rights that may not be ruled out by this egalitarian reasoning.

First, we might wonder whether taking away the liberal rights from everyone is defensible even if it is egalitarian. Second, we might wonder whether taking at least some broad set of rights away from everyone because of serious security concerns is defensible even it accords with equality.[37] Let us call these cases of apparently *antiliberal equality*.

Why Illiberal Equalities are Violations of Public Equality

I have two arguments in favor of the claim that general curtailments of liberal rights are violations of public equality. The first one is based on an analogy to democratic rights. One thing that characterizes democratic rights is that one cannot curtail the democratic rights without enhancing the power of some. The simplest case is that of dictatorship. By taking away the democratic rights of citizenship, one does not eliminate political power; one puts it in the hands of some group or person. One cannot do otherwise. Since democratic rights are rights to exercise power over the state and the elimination of democratic

power is to be wielded do not recognize that superiority in power. Thus, the vastly superior being has the capacity and the will to correctly impose a regime that advances the interests of all the members equally but the members refuse to accept it. What are we to say of this kind of case?

We should notice that the analogies to parental and divine intervention hold in this kind of case as well as the above cases. It is quite possible for parents to have children who are not appreciative of the contribution the parents make to their well-being. And so it is quite possible for parents to have to impose their wills on their children in a way that they receive no thanks for their efforts. And though in many of these kinds of cases, we have justifiable suspicions that the parents are not treating the children properly, it is also quite possible to have some such cases wherein the parents are acting completely for the interests of the children. And, of course, it is a commonplace of religious belief that God's benefits to human beings go unrecognized by those human beings.

Still the analogies are weaker than in the cases outlined above where the superiority is publicly recognized. We do have suspicion of parents whose children are constantly complaining even if we do not take this as definitive evidence of injustice. And religious belief has often been thought of as fraudulent or ideological when it merely embraces the status quo and the miseries of the worst off.

[37] These objections were stated by Michaella Mueller.

rights does not eliminate the state, there are still some who exercise power over others. In this respect, the suspension of democratic rights is a genuine public violation of equality.

Might the same be said about the suspension of liberal rights? Though it may well be that one can suppress the free speech rights of everyone, the fact is that this is not how these suppressions work. The way the suppressions work is that they end up suppressing certain kinds of activities and certain kinds of speech and certain kinds of associations and not others. One cannot suppress all forms of speech or even all forms of political speech. And though one can suppress certain kinds of association, one cannot suppress all associations. Though one can suppress certain kinds of activities, one cannot suppress all activities or speech. As a consequence, the authorities will always be selective in enforcing the general suppression. This implies that the general suspension of liberal rights is always going to involve a much greater setback to some people's interests than to others. Hence there is an inevitable public inequality that arises in the case of the attempted general suppression of liberal rights.

One might think that it is possible and defensible on an egalitarian view to engage in general surveillance of everyone. But this would be a mistaken conception of the egalitarian view of liberal rights. That this is not right can be seen from the fact that restrictions on surveillance are in part instrumentally justified. Restrictions on the state's capacity to engage in surveillance on others and to circumvent the process of fair trials are justified instrumentally as well as intrinsically. That is, these restrictions are essential to protecting other rights and interests of citizens. The state can stop people from speaking freely, or associating freely with others if it can harass them without much effort. It can harass them by publishing information about them that is embarrassing or easy to misunderstand. It can harass them by seizing things or persons and jailing them without giving them recourse to a fair trial. To the extent that the rights to association are essential to the advancement of interests, it is clear that the retrenchment of the rights that protect these freedoms is going to be a setback to the interests of most people. And to the extent that this retrenchment will inevitably be applied selectively to groups by the authorities, it is clear that this will have very different impacts on different groups of people. Hence, it can be seen that this is a public violation of equality.

A second argument vindicates the claim that antiliberal equalities are in fact public violations of equality. I argued in Chapter 1 that the leveling down objection failed against the conception of equality when properly understood. We can now use that conception of equality to show how a general retrenchment of liberal rights is a public violation of equality. If we look at the case of the general curtailment of liberal rights and we make use of the argument for liberal rights we have proposed, it is clear that the general curtailment makes everyone worse off than they could have been without the curtailment. In this respect, the curtailment violates the principle of equality.

To be sure one can imagine circumstances where general curtailment of liberal rights might be defensible. If the curtailment is done in order to stop some grave and immediate threat to public order then the curtailment may not be a public violation of equality. This would be because the curtailment might be thought to enhance the security that is necessary to public order and thus the curtailment may be necessary to the long-run survival of the liberal regime. It may well be that there is reason to be skeptical in this type of situation but the basic idea is that it is legitimate for people to debate and decide the matter and thus it is within the legitimate sphere of democratic authority.

But this kind of curtailment can be justified only under extreme circumstances which are very rare. Furthermore, the curtailment must be carefully bounded in time and character. In other circumstances, the general curtailment of any or all liberal rights would be a violation of the principle of public equality defended in this book.[38]

---

[38] One case that seems to challenge the egalitarian view I have defended is punishment. The punishment objection takes the form of a dilemma. Either the punishment is a violation of equality, in which case it is a rejection of equality under the supposition that punishment is at least sometimes just. Or the punishment is not a violation of equality in which case it undermines the case for the idea that all removals of liberal rights are cases of public violations of equality.

I will answer the second horn of the dilemma first. The second horn says that if punishment is compatible with equality then it is a counterexample to the claim that all disenfranchisement is a violation of public equality.

The answer to this objection is a methodological one. It states that questions of distributive justice must be answered before questions of retributive justice are answered. The idea is that a conception of retributive justice can only be in place when a full conception of distributive justice is in place. As a consequence, it is appropriate to characterize distributive justice before we attempt to answer the question of retributive justice. So it is legitimate to try to give an account of distributive justice without consideration of punishment. The theory described in this book is such a conception of distributive justice. It does not give us a complete conception of justice until an account of punishment and other responses to injustice are given. But it is legitimate to give such an account independent of the question of punishment.

The reason for this methodological principle is that retributive justice is a response to injustice. One can have an account of retributive justice only after we have an account of the nature of justice that is protected by retributive justice. This general approach holds for all responses to injustice such as compensation, restitution, punishment, reparations, and others.

The consequence of this general approach is that we have justification for thinking of distributive justice first on the supposition that we have perfect compliance among all those who have duties of justice. And so the principle that states that suspension of democratic or liberal rights is a public violation of equality is a principle that holds prior to the introduction of the issue of punishment. I thank John Pollock and Richard Lippke for pressing me on this point.

CONCLUSION

This concludes the elaboration and defense of the account of public equality in this book. I have argued that justice is equality and that social justice is public equality. And I have argued that democracy and liberal rights are realizations of public equality and are therefore fundamentally justified. In this I have tried to show that the grounds of democracy and liberal rights are parallel. I have also attempted to demonstrate how this conception of democracy and liberal rights provides us with a more nuanced account of these rights that are on offer elsewhere.

In what follows I will add one more piece to the account of democracy: the role played by public deliberation. In Chapter 5, I will outline what I take to be the role played by deliberation and I will critique one prominent alternative account of democracy that assigns a very different role to deliberation. In Chapters 6 and 7, I will use the accounts of democracy and liberal rights I have offered in Chapters 1–5 to define the nature of democratic authority and the limits of that authority.

5

Equality and Public Deliberation

Public deliberation about proposed legislation and policy is one of the key elements of a well-ordered democracy. In a well-ordered democracy, citizens discuss and debate different conceptions of justice and the common good as grounds for choosing political parties and candidates for election and ultimately as grounds for legislation and policy. But there is some debate about the nature of the value of deliberation and what exact form public deliberation ought to take in a democratic society. According to the *wide conception* of public deliberation, citizens debate and discuss proposals for legislation and policy on the basis of arguments grounded in differing conceptions of justice and the common good and in different empirically grounded ideas about how society works. Each citizen proposes arguments to others with the aim of rationally persuading those others to accept their views about how society ought to be organized. But each citizen is also willing to listen to the opposed arguments of other citizens and ready to modify her position when the better argument recommends it. And she is willing to go through a long-term process of debate with the aim of determining which views are best supported by good argument. All of this is in order to determine what the best policies and legislation for the society are with an eye to making the best political choice.

Such a process of deliberation embodies a number of fundamental values. First, it embodies the ideal of equal respect that lies at the foundation of democracy. Citizens embody this value in their attitudes and in the behaviors that express these attitudes. They do so by being ready to listen to and learn from others and by being willing to accept the force of the better argument wherever it may come from. Second, it embodies the commitment of each citizen to advance justice and the common good in her society. To the extent that citizens genuinely try to learn from one another and attempt to discern the most defensible ideas, citizens show that they desire to advance morally desirable aims. Third, the process of public deliberation is a public realization of equality to the extent that the process is reasonably egalitarian. Citizens' abilities to receive hearings for their views are not undermined by a skewed distribution of wealth or power. The process of public deliberation ensures that all the major interests and points of view in society are given a fair hearing. And no citizen is ignored on the basis of invidious distinctions of race, religion, ethnic identity, gender, or class.

These values and constraints are characteristic of what I call the wide conception of public deliberation. In what follows I will display the underlying grounds of this conception in the principle of public equality. Some have argued recently for what I call the *narrow conception* of public deliberation in addition to the above values and constraints on deliberation. According to the narrow view, citizens must advance proposals and the arguments for them only on the basis of a shared fund of political ideas. They must not appeal, on this account, to controversial views in arguing for law and policy. Such a view asserts that in addition to the above values and constraints imposed by the wide view of deliberation, a principle of reasonableness or reciprocity must constrain the process of public deliberation. And they argue that the narrow conception of public deliberation is required by the values of justification or respect for persons or equality.

My purpose in this chapter is to articulate and defend the wide view of public deliberation and to show that this conception is fully adequate to all the values that underpin deliberation. I will explain the value and function of public deliberation in a society that realizes public equality. Public deliberation has instrumental value in a democratic society since it leads to the development of an informed, rational, and morally sensitive citizenry. But once there is a process of public deliberation in place, justice requires that this process be an egalitarian process. By an egalitarian process I mean a process of deliberation and discussion which expresses equal respect for every citizen, which ensures that each citizen has equal opportunities to contribute to the formation of the agenda for collective decision-making and which ensures equality in the cognitive conditions for citizen decision-making. These basic ideas are grounded in the principle of public equality that has been defended in this book. The second issue I want to address in this chapter is whether in addition to the values of equal respect and equality, public deliberation ought to be constrained by the idea that citizens ought only to advance proposals on the basis of shared political ideas. I argue against the most important philosophical proponent of this view and attempt to show that the considerations that are thought to support the narrow view of public deliberation actually support the adequacy of the wide view.

In what follows, I lay out the conception of deliberation I am concerned with. I then discuss the instrumental values of public deliberation. I proceed by characterizing equality in the process of public deliberation. Then I give the grounds for the value of the egalitarian process of deliberation. Once the wide view of public deliberation and its grounds have been examined I move on to characterize the principle of reasonableness that distinguishes the narrow view. I look at three arguments for the narrow view and show that they fail and I show that the underlying considerations behind these arguments actually tell against the narrow view.

DELIBERATION

The process of public deliberation is a process in which individuals and groups advance proposals for the organization of society and arguments for those proposals and in which they listen to the proposals and arguments of other individuals and groups. They engage in this process with the aim of learning from the process of debate. Ideally, citizens desire to shape and modify their proposals in ways that reflect the most rationally defensible accounts of the values of justice and the common good as well as the best available empirical knowledge in the society. To be sure, disagreement is likely to remain after even the most fruitful periods of public discussion and debate. This disagreement is founded on the facts of cognitive bias, fallibility, and diversity. Those facts ensure that people will go into the debate with different views and they will come out of the debates with different views. Despite the persistence of disagreement, the process of public deliberation can be a highly useful activity for the society.

When I speak of public deliberation, I am thinking of a society wide process that takes place over a number of years. People rarely change their minds over a period of days or weeks or even months. But minds are changed by the persistent accumulation of evidence and argument over long periods of time. Over time, ideas are modified and some are entirely rejected. Hence, though the process of electoral campaigning is a crucial node in the process of public deliberation, it is by no means the whole of it or even a substantial proportion of it. To be sure, the debates that take place in electoral campaigns play a central role in determining the policies and legislative agenda for the subsequent period. But the quality of these debates will be greatly enhanced or set back depending on the quality of the society wide discussion and debate that has taken place over the previous years. Let us examine the grounds of the value of public deliberation.

THE INSTRUMENTAL VALUE OF PUBLIC DELIBERATION

What grounds the value of public deliberation? First, public deliberation may be valuable because of its results. Three kinds of results are often hoped for from public deliberation: improvements in the quality of legislation and policy, legitimacy, and virtue. One result is that public deliberation generally improves the quality of legislation by enhancing citizens' understanding of their society and of the moral principles that ought to regulate it. Societies that experience a great deal of good-faith discussion and rational debate among all citizens on the merits of alternative proposals tend to be more just or to protect liberty better. Here, the justice of laws and social institutions may be increased by the process of discussion. A second result is that the laws of these societies may tend to be rationally justified more often in the eyes of their citizens than those of societies that do not undergo intensive processes of deliberation on legislation. Deliberation, it is often said, leads to reasoned agreement among citizens on the merits of legislation. In this case, the legitimacy of the society is increased by the process of deliberation. A third result is that certain desirable qualities in citizens are enhanced when they must participate in the process of deliberation. People who participate frequently in deliberation as free and equal citizens are more likely, many think, to develop traits of autonomy, rationality, and morality. In this instance, the *virtues* of citizens are increased by the process.[1]

It is important to emphasize the independence of the values of justice, legitimacy, and virtue from the deliberative process that is thought to be causally responsible for their realization. Rousseau seems to have thought that these values were less likely to arise in a society where public deliberation plays a role in the passage of legislation.[2] Others argue public discussion only diminishes agreement on matters of principle and policy and thus undermines the legitimacy of the social institutions. I do not mean to endorse these claims, but to emphasize the point that the values discussed above are at most contingent results of public deliberation. They only support an *instrumental* value of public deliberation.

The justice and virtue effects of public deliberation on democratic outcomes would appear to be reasonably likely outcomes of democracy at least if the public deliberation takes place in a political context free of fear and intimidation or ridicule and a wide variety of points of view can be expressed and heard in the public forum. Discussion and deliberation promote greater

---

[1] See John Stuart Mill, *Considerations on Representative Government* (Buffalo: Prometheus Books, 1985), chapters 2 and 3, and *On Liberty* (Buffalo: Prometheus Books, 1990), chapter 2, for this kind of view. See also Cass Sunstein, *Democracy and the Problem of Free Speech* (New York: Free Press, 1993), chapter 8, for this kind of view. And see my *The Rule of the Many* (Boulder, CO: Westview Press, 1996), for a development of these instrumentalist claims.

[2] Jean-Jacques Rousseau, *The Social Contract and Discourses* ed. G. H. D. Cole (London: J. M. Dent, 1973), p. 185, and Bernard Manin, "On Legitimacy and Political Deliberation," *Political Theory* (August 1987), pp. 338–368, esp. p. 345.

understanding of the interests of the members of society as well as how the common features of the society relate to those interests. They allow us to submit our understandings to the test of critical scrutiny. John Stuart Mill states the reason forcefully:

The whole strength and value then of human judgment, depending on the one property, that it can be set right when it is wrong, reliance can be placed on it only, when the means of setting it right are kept constantly at hand. In the case of a person whose judgment is really deserving of confidence, how has it become so? Because he has kept his mind open to criticism on his opinions and conduct. Because it has been his practice to listen to all that could be said against him; to profit by as much of it as was just, and expound to himself, and upon occasion to others, the fallacy of what was fallacious. Because he has felt that the only way in which a human being can make some approach to knowing the whole of a subject, is by hearing what can be said about it by persons of every variety of opinion, and studying all modes in which it can be looked at by every character of mind.[3]

Under the assumption that minds informed in this way will often make better decisions and that a society wherein all the members of the society participate in this process of discussion and debate will at least be able to root out policies based on unsubstantiated prejudices, we have reason to think that a society that promotes public deliberation will make better decisions. It is likely to be more sensitive to, and understanding of, the interests of a broader portion of the population than one where citizens do not have the opportunity to express and discuss their interests. Its decisions will be informed by a better knowledge of the facts important to the realization of the aims of the society when a wide variety of people and groups have the opportunity to examine the facts and test each others' views on these matters. Citizens' ideas of justice and the common good that provide the ultimate justification for many policies will usually avoid egregious forms of arbitrary treatment that arise when a decision-making group is not aware of other groups in the society. The more fallacious and superstitious forms of reasoning about all these matters will generally be undermined. In short, the process of public deliberation will serve as a kind of filtering device taking out the egregious forms of ignorance regarding interests and justice.

These are modest claims that appeal to our common sense but we ought to remember that empirical evidence for such large-scale effects of public discussion is fairly thin and not all of it is positive. Most of the supporting research has been done only on small groups and so its generalization to the context

---

[3] John Stuart Mill, *On Liberty*, p. 108. See Philip Kitcher, "The Division of Cognitive Labor," *Journal of Philosophy* (January 1990), pp. 5–22, for an epistemic defense of diversity in scientific theorizing.

of democratic societies must be treated with caution.[4] So we can only give a tentative endorsement to these claims. They call for more empirical research.

In addition, the virtue effect of deliberation is endorsed by common sense. In a society where public deliberation is the norm, having the traits by which one can contribute to public deliberation is highly functional for individuals or at least for groups. Where one is unable to make a contribution to the public discussion that informs policymaking and one has distinctive interests and points of view, those interests and points of view are not likely to be accommodated in the policies that are chosen. At the same time, in a society where public discussion is ignored or suppressed, individuals are not likely to have reason to discuss their views with others and they will have less reason to think carefully about many of their views.

To be sure, not all citizens engage in public deliberation and many do not even consider participating. But even these are likely to be affected by the model of those who do participate. A society in which a substantial proportion of people participate intelligently provides ample examples of rational, autonomous, and morally engaged persons. The ethos of rational discussion cannot but have desirable impacts on those who do not participate.

To the extent that participation in discussion on a regular basis enlists the abilities necessary to that participation, it is likely to enhance the character traits of citizens. And to the extent that public deliberation calls upon a set of morally important qualities, such as rationality, autonomy, and respect for others, there is some reason to think that these traits, which are important in politics, will be promoted more in a society that encourages deliberation among all of its citizens.

Here too, the empirical evidence for this kind of commonsensical claim is scanty. More empirical research is called for here. We can see some ways in which public deliberation might promote poor character traits in some circumstances as well. For instance, a capacity for pandering and manipulation may prove to be superior to the more desirable ones in some contexts. Crude appeals to group identity and national superiority as well as to religious fears may also sometimes be highly advantageous to demagogues. Or perhaps in some societies which greatly value public deliberation indecisiveness will result.

---

[4] See Cass Sunstein, *Why Societies Need Dissent* (Cambridge, MA: Harvard University Press, 2003), for some evidence for these kinds of claim. See also "Discussion of Shared and Unshared Information in Decision Making Groups," *Journal of Personality and Social Psychology*, vol. 67, no. 3 (1994), pp. 446–461, esp. p. 459 on the sharing of unshared information and how this contributes to the qualities of outcomes. See also Herbert Blumberg, "Group Decision Making and Choice Shift," in *Small Group Research: A Handbook* eds. A. Paul Hare, Herbert Blumberg, Martin Davies, and Valerie Kent (Norwood, NJ: Abex Publishing Corporation, 1994), pp. 195–210, esp. p. 200.

Does public deliberation increase the tendency among citizens to agree on political matters and thereby increase the legitimacy of the actions of the state? This outcome is unlikely in a large pluralistic society. Discussion and debate increase the diversity of opinions on many matters. While discussion may eliminate some disagreements such as those that are the result of mere prejudice and superstition, it is likely to generate disagreements also. If discussion is set in an egalitarian context, then many more points of view will have to be debated to the extent that previously neglected sectors of society come to the fore. One need not be a skeptic about knowledge of matters in politics to see that debates about these matters are extremely hard to resolve. Differing points of view cannot be eliminated when there are participants with differing social and economic backgrounds and experiences in life and the evidence always falls short of proof. His highly speculative developmental moral psychology notwithstanding, what Rawls has called the burdens of reason weigh against achieving agreement on matters that are of great importance in politics including issues relating to the common good and social justice.[5]

Would it be desirable for deliberation to increase the tendency toward agreement? While agreement may contribute to the stability of society, disagreement and diversity of view are among the most fertile conditions for the realization of the justice and the virtue effects. The problem is that in a world in which the facts of diversity, fallibility, and cognitive bias are ubiquitous, prolonged periods of agreement suggest the presence of intellectual stagnation and oppressive domination of one group over others. Furthermore, given the likelihood that egalitarian institutions will in fact produce a lot of disagreement, the idea that we will in fact achieve agreement on the right principles of justice if and only if we structure our democratic institutions in the right way is clearly false.[6] The best we can do toward achieving an understanding of justice and the common good is by means of a trial and error process wherein a diversity of points of view is always present to test any particular view. Hence, we ought not to be aiming at consensus on moral and political matters. As long as public discussion acts as a process of trial and error for excluding forms of

---

[5] See *A Theory of Justice* (Cambridge, MA: Harvard University Press, 1971), p. 473, for a discussion of the moral psychological impact of institutions regulated by the two principles of justice and *Political Liberalism* (New York: Columbia University Press, 1993), for a discussion of the burdens of judgment. Rawls thinks that the burdens of judgment only afflict comprehensive conceptions of the good and not conceptions of justice.

[6] It is important to distinguish those views (such as those of Habermas and Rawls) that claim that justice is defined in terms of what reasonable people agree to in idealized conditions from claims that consensus in the process of democratic deliberation is possible and desirable. The former views can be entered into the process of public deliberation as alternatives to be considered though they are unlikely to receive unanimous consent even among reasonable people in any actual democratic society.

ignorance, it serves a useful purpose for individuals as well as for society while increasing the amount of disagreement in the community.

EGALITARIAN PUBLIC DELIBERATION

These instrumental considerations favor the use of a process of public deliberation as a kind of collective benefit. But a properly functioning process of public deliberation ought to be constrained by egalitarian principles as well. There are three dimensions of distribution that are important to our assessment of a process of public deliberation: the distribution of cognitive conditions for the effective exercise of citizenship, the distribution of opportunities for influencing the agenda for collective decision-making, and equality of respect that citizens hold for each other. The principle of public equality will require that these distributive aspects of deliberation be egalitarian in a publicly clear way.

First, we can evaluate a process of public deliberation in terms of its distribution of the cognitive conditions of citizens for participating in an informed way in the democratic process. Favorable cognitive conditions for the effective exercise of citizenship are of great importance in a democracy. Those who do not know what policies will advance their interests or their conception of what is best are not likely to have much real power compared to those who do know. Compare a person at the wheel of an automobile that is ready to drive, who does not know how to drive it, with someone who has a car who does know how to drive it. The first person is powerless because of his ignorance of how to use the resources at his command; the second, who has the same resources, does have control. This parallels the comparison between those who vote on the basis of some real understanding of politics and those who have little. There is a considerable differential in power because while the ignorant might sometimes be able to block the knowledgeable from getting what they prefer, the ignorant will never get what they prefer at all except by accident.

Furthermore, confused or distorted conceptions of his interests or moral aims can undermine a person's ability to advance ends. Compare the person who has a car, and knows how to use it but has only confused and contradictory ideas of where he wants to go, to the person who knows where she wants to go. The first person is at a considerable disadvantage in power compared to the second. He will drive around aimlessly without achieving any end while the second person will be able to achieve some end that she desires. This is a real difference in power.

Finally, a person whose conception of her interests is more or less arbitrarily arrived at is at a disadvantage in relation to a person who has thought about her aims and has some basis for pursuing the ends she does. The person who has a poorly reasoned or unreflective conception of her aims is a person who is unlikely to achieve much of worth to herself. She will be easily subject to confusion, arbitrary changes in opinion as well as manipulation by others. Since it is important to advance the interests of a person, as well as morally worthy aims, it is important for her to have some reasoned grasp of her interests. So the provision of cognitive conditions for the effective exercise of citizenship is essential to the evaluation of democratic institutions. And the distribution of these cognitive conditions is of fundamental concern in a democratic society.

Public deliberation is one of the main cognitive conditions for effective citizenship. It is the main process by which citizens learn about the issues and alternatives facing society. In it citizens come to appreciate alternate conceptions of justice and the common good. Citizens also learn about the interests of other citizens and about competing conceptions of the available empirical knowledge within the society. Finally, they learn a great deal about their own interests and their ideas about the common good to the extent that people respond to their accounts of their interests and the common good.

The process of public deliberation can be evaluated in terms of the way it distributes these cognitive conditions of citizenship. Does it enable all citizens to learn from the process? A process that is dominated by particular groups in the society that do not represent the interests of all the members of society is likely to favor the interests of those groups. It is not merely important that there be a robust process of discussion and debate in society, it must also be the case that there are equal opportunities for all the different interests in society to be heard. Otherwise the process will favor the development of the cognitive conditions for some over that of others and the consequence will be a real inequality in the distribution of political power.

Second, we can evaluate the process of public deliberation in terms of its distribution of the capacities to influence the agenda of collective decision-making. The process of public deliberation plays a key role in defining the agenda for collective decision-making. It determines the key issues and it determines what the main alternatives are in those issues. Individuals and groups contribute to the formation of the agenda for decision-making by presenting new issues for discussion as well as new alternatives for discussion and by contributing to the discussion of the issues and modifying the positions of others on the alternatives. In this respect, the process of public deliberation plays an essential role in democratic decision-making. A successful process will ensure that a wide variety of relevant considerations are taken into account and that issues and alternatives are important and properly formulated. But in addition the process of public deliberation can affect the opportunities of different groups to bring important and relevant considerations to the fore. It can be evaluated in terms of whether some groups are excluded from the process or whether some groups' opportunities are enhanced at the expense of others. To the extent that this plays a fundamental role in determining the agenda for decision-making, the process of public deliberation can play a fundamental role in determining the distribution of power in democratic decision-making.

These last two considerations argue in favor of egalitarian public support of interest group associations and political parties and support public financing of electoral campaigns. To the extent that the interest group associations of disadvantaged citizens are likely to have far less resources than those concerned with the interests of more advantaged citizens, the views of the disadvantaged are likely to receive much less of a hearing in the democratic forum. As a consequence, there will be little opportunity to learn from the responses to these views. And this will tend to undermine the cognitive conditions for effective citizenship for these groups. It will also tend to undermine their chances for influencing the agenda for collective decision-making. As a consequence, their influence on democratic decision-making will be correspondingly diminished and their interests are likely not to be advanced.[7]

Third, we can evaluate a process of public decision-making in terms of whether every person and group has been accorded equal respect from all the others in the process. When one is considering the making of legislation or policy one expresses respect for others by listening to what they have to say and by trying to take it into account or by rationally arguing against what they have to say. This attitude has two basic merits. One is that it treats the other as a rational being with a perspective on value that is to be taken into account and that one can learn from. Two, it expresses the idea that it is important to take someone else's opinions into account when one is considering law and policy that affects their interests. To the extent that the other person's views are likely to reflect their interests and are likely to include some account of those interests and to the extent that we expect people normally to have better conceptions of their interests than others do, we take their interests seriously when we try to take their points of view into account. This is just an instance of the considerations that ground democracy on my account. So not only is it important to have democratic institutions that give each person an equal say and that provide the cognitive conditions for informed participation, it is also

---

[7] I have discussed egalitarian institutions for interest groups and political parties in much more detail in *The Rule of the Many*, chapters 7 and 8.

important that each citizen be willing to listen to the views of other citizens for the same kinds of reasons. To be sure, this does not require that one listen every time a person says something. It is important to have at some point considered seriously the views of others. Thus the mutual respect embodied by democratic deliberation is grounded in the need to treat others as rational beings and as beings with interests to be taken into account.

THE GROUNDS OF EQUALITY IN PUBLIC DELIBERATION

The importance of public deliberation and the egalitarian constraints are grounded in the interests that underpin the democratic and liberal rights and in the principle that these interests must be advanced in a publicly equal way. Individuals have four basic interests in being able to participate in the process of democratic deliberation: the interest in correcting for cognitive bias, the interest in being at home in the world, the interest in learning the truth, and the interest in being recognized and affirmed as an equal. And the principle of public equality demands that these interests be advanced in a publicly egalitarian way.

Since I have discussed how these interests are advanced by both the democratic and the liberal rights, the presentation here can be brief. Once there is a process of public deliberation in place, we can see, given the facts of diversity, fallibility, cognitive bias, and disagreement why it is important to have an egalitarian process of deliberation in place. The facts of diversity and cognitive bias ensure that the views and arguments of persons will reflect different interests and will be sensitive to different concerns. As a consequence, each person's understanding is fallible and there is a great deal of disagreement. This is one of the reasons why people engage in public deliberation and these facts give us reasons for structuring public deliberation in certain ways.

Given the facts of diversity and cognitive bias, each person has an interest in correcting for the cognitive bias of others. To the extent that deliberation plays a role in shaping the bases of legislation and policy, each person wants to make sure that the legislation is not biased in favor of other groups and takes her interests into account. So each has an interest in participating in deliberation so as to have opportunities to influence the agenda for collective decision-making. And since each person can correct for cognitive bias in the collective decision-making only if she is properly informed about the issues and alternatives, each citizen has an interest in having the cognitive conditions for the effective exercise of citizenship. Finally, one further bulwark against cognitive bias obtains when each citizen attempts seriously to take the points of view of other citizens into account. Thus each person wants to be able to contribute on an equal footing with others to public deliberation in order to correct for the cognitive biases of others.

Furthermore, participation in the process of deliberation advances the interests of each citizen in being at home in the world. Since having the cognitive conditions for the effective exercise of citizenship and having opportunities for affecting the agenda of collective decision-making are essential to playing a role in shaping one's society, it is clear that these are necessary to advance the interest in being at home in the world that is at the basis of the democratic right. And to the extent that others are taking one's views seriously and come to have some understanding of one's interests, they are more likely to help create a world that accommodates one's interests and concerns. Finally, the interest in being at home in the world can be advanced by an egalitarian process of public deliberation in the sense that one acquires a clearer understanding of the people around one and understands how one's interests mesh and do not mesh with those others.

Since each person can learn from the process of public deliberation to the extent that others are willing to respond to his views, each person has an interest in truth in being able to participate. The interest in truth is most clearly advanced by the feature of public deliberation that enhances the cognitive conditions for citizenship. But it is also advanced by the opportunities to influence the agenda that public deliberation affords and by the equal respect afforded on in the process. Both of these ensure that people will take one's views seriously and attempt to respond to them and so advance one's interest in truth.

Finally, since the process of deliberation is one in which individuals express mutual respect by being willing to listen to and entertain each other's arguments, the interest in being recognized and affirmed as an equal by others is advanced by being able to participate in the process. And since being able to participate as an equal in the process of deliberation advances the interests of each individual, it expresses the equal importance of each individual.

In the light of these fact and interests, the principle of public equality requires that the process of public deliberation be structured in an egalitarian way. Individuals must have the resources so that they can make themselves heard in a democratic society and so that they can contribute to ongoing debates in the public forum. Individuals have no less reason for insisting on resources for participation in the process of public deliberation than they do for insisting on being able to vote. The process of public deliberation is so important for creation of the cognitive conditions of effective citizenship and the shaping of the collective decision-making agenda that any person or group that was not able to participate would have good reason to think that their interests were not likely to be advanced by the collective decision-making of the society. As a consequence, if some group is excluded from the process of public deliberation due to its unfavorable position in the distribution of wealth and power, it would have reason to think that its interests were not being advanced in the democratic society and it would have reason to think that it was not being recognized and affirmed as an equal in that society. Or if some group consistently has significantly less resources for the purpose of participating in debate, then the individuals in that group have reason to think that they are being treated as unequal.

To be sure the exact institutional requirements for ensuring equality in the process of public deliberation are likely to be a lot more contentious than the requirements of one person one vote or the equal liberal rights. Nevertheless, a political society must make it one of its main purposes to ensure some kind of robust equality in the process.

MUST DEMOCRACY BE REASONABLE?

So far I have characterized what I have called the wide conception of public deliberation and given an account of the grounds of its value. In addition to assigning importance to moral discussion and debate in a democracy, a number of theorists add the constraint that this discussion and debate ought to be framed by considerations that all reasonable citizens can sign on to. Debate in a well-functioning democracy ought to be limited to a shared basis of public reasons. The requirement that debate be limited to considerations on which there is reasonable consensus imposes severe constraints on a legitimate process of moral discussion and debate in democracy. Indeed, I would venture to say that most people in most contemporary democracies do not satisfy these constraints. I call the conception of deliberative democracy that includes this constraint the *narrow* conception of deliberative democracy.[8]

In my view, the reasons offered do not support the thesis that the narrow conception of deliberative democracy is superior to the wide conception and I think that there are some disadvantages to accepting the narrow conception. The basic principle that distinguishes the narrow account of deliberative

---

[8] The principle of reasonableness is employed and defended by other democratic thinkers as well, most prominently by Amy Gutmann and Dennis Thompson, in *Democracy and Disagreement* (Princeton: Princeton University Press, 1996) and *Why Deliberative Democracy?* (Princeton: Princeton University Press, 2005) as well as Samuel Freeman in "Deliberative Democracy: A Sympathetic Account," *Philosophy and Public Affairs*, vol. 29, no. 4, pp. 371–418. In this chapter I focus on Joshua Cohen's arguments.

democracy is the principle of reasonableness. Joshua Cohen gives three basic arguments for this principle: an epistemological argument, a moral argument, and an argument from democratic values. In what follows, I articulate the principle of reasonableness. Then I explain and critique the three arguments Cohen offers for holding the principle of reasonableness. Along the way, I argue that the chief considerations employed to defend the principle of reasonableness actually argue against the principle. Not only is the principle not defended, it ought to be rejected.

THE PRINCIPLE OF REASONABLENESS

The *principle of reasonableness* or the *criterion of reciprocity* asserts

People are reasonable, politically speaking, only if they are concerned to live with others on terms that those others, understood as free and equal, can also reasonably accept.[9]

A key component of the principle of reasonableness is the need to acknowledge the *fact of reasonable pluralism*. This fact is

Conscientious, good-faith efforts in the exercise of practical reason, by politically reasonable people, do not converge on a particular philosophy of life.[10]

The principle of reasonableness is the distinguishing feature of the narrow conception of deliberative democracy. "Reasonableness" is a basic normative notion in Cohen's account of a well-ordered society. And so a criterion of reasonableness is meant to provide a principle for the evaluation of all basic political and economic institutions of the society in which one lives and it is thereby meant to guide the deliberations of democratic citizens as they attempt to design those basic institutions.

We need to clarify three notions to understand the principle of reasonableness that I have quoted above. First, we need to clarify the idea that one *can reasonably accept* terms of association or cooperation. Cohen says: "a consideration is an acceptable political reason just in case it has the support of the different comprehensive views endorsed by reasonable citizens."[11] I take this to imply that a sufficient condition for saying that a particular person can reasonably accept terms of association is to say that the terms, and the considerations the society accepts as underpinning the terms, are at least compatible

---

[9] See "Reflections on Habermas on Democracy," *Ratio Juris*, Vol. 12, no. 4, December 1999, pp. 385–416, p. 396.
[10] See "Reflections on Habermas on Democracy," p. 396.
[11] See "Reflections on Habermas on Democracy," p. 398.

with that person's reasonable doctrine. And a sufficient condition for saying that a particular person cannot reasonably accept terms of association is to say that the terms, or the considerations the society accepts as underpinning the terms, are incompatible with that person's reasonable doctrine. For instance, terms of association that affirm some religious belief, say by establishing the religion, cannot be reasonably accepted by someone who is an atheist. And a religious person cannot reasonably accept terms of association that establish atheism, as in the case of the Soviet Union.[12] But also if the terms of the society are seen by the society to be grounded in some controversial set of religious or moral considerations, those who reject these considerations cannot reasonably accept the terms.

Second, a *reasonable comprehensive doctrine* is an epistemically reasonable doctrine held by a reasonable person. It is a doctrine designed with a view to justifying terms of association on terms that others can reasonably accept. The atheist whose doctrine affirms that the state must eradicate religion in a political society marked by the fact of reasonable pluralism does not hold a reasonable comprehensive doctrine. While such an atheist desires to eradicate religion, it is not true that this desire shows that he cannot reasonably accept a political society that allows the survival of religion.

I stated a sufficient condition for rightly saying that a person can reasonably accept terms of association. It should be possible to say when an unreasonable person can or cannot reasonably accept terms of association. This idea is not thoroughly discussed in Cohen or Rawls. Presumably to say that an unreasonable person can reasonably accept terms of association is to say that such a person could reasonably accept those terms were that person reasonable. We do not have the space here to consider the conditions that make this counterfactual true.

Third, a doctrine is *epistemically reasonable* to the extent that it is coherent, intelligible, and survives conscientious critical reflection.[13] This condition imposes a kind of minimal condition of epistemic legitimacy on comprehensive doctrines. The different formulations that Cohen gives of this minimal

---

[12] As Cohen and Rawls use these terms, to say that A can reasonably accept terms of association T is to say that A cannot reasonably reject those terms. And to say that A cannot reasonably accept the terms T is to say that A can reasonably reject those terms. So, given a particular reasonable comprehensive doctrine, reasonable rejectability, and reasonable acceptability are exclusive. Of course, it is possible for terms T to be both reasonably rejectable by one person and reasonably acceptable to another when those persons have different reasonable comprehensive doctrines. And, of course, one person might change from reasonably rejecting terms to reasonably accepting those terms because of a change in reasonable comprehensive view.

[13] See Cohen, "Moral Pluralism and Political Consensus," in *The Idea of Democracy* eds. David Copp, John Roemer, and Jean Hampton (Cambridge: Cambridge University Press, 1993), pp. 270–291, esp. pp. 281–282.

condition are all meant to be quite undemanding so as to avoid the charge that a particular epistemological doctrine is being presupposed.

From the above definitions, we can see how the principle of reasonableness is a criterion of reciprocity. It states that reasonable people propose terms of association that other reasonable people can reasonably accept. I want to focus, in this chapter, on a key component of this requirement of reasonableness. It is a necessary condition on being a reasonable person that one seeks to justify terms of association to others on the basis of considerations that they can accept, as long as they are reasonable. Reasonable persons try to find a shared basis of justification among reasonable citizens of a political society. The reasonable person seeks consensus as a basis for the justification of terms of association of a political society.

It is important to be clear on what this consensus is. First, it is a consensus among reasonable persons. Hence, the fact that some unreasonable persons do not agree with some basic considerations is not sufficient to show that those considerations are not the shared basis the reasonable person is looking for. Second, the consensus arrived at is not a complete consensus. The fact of reasonable pluralism rules out complete consensus on all the items in the comprehensive doctrines of the citizens including all the political ideas of the citizens. Reasonable persons do not seek to advance those aspects of their ideas about justice and political morality that they know others cannot reasonably accept. Third, the consensus that reasonable citizens search for is a consensus on the list of considerations that are relevant to the justification of terms of association. They may not agree entirely on the relative weights of these considerations and they may not agree entirely on the exact interpretation of these considerations. Cohen thinks that as long as justification proceeds from a shared list of considerations, disagreement on the exact principles and policies people propose as terms of association is compatible with each person being able reasonably to accept the terms of association. Cohen argues that once the limited consensus on the list of considerations has been arrived at, disagreements based on the different weights people place on considerations and their different interpretations can legitimately be resolved by majority rule.[14] Majority rule cannot however legitimate decisions that are not based on the considerations in the agreed upon list of considerations.[15]

---

[14] See Cohen, "Procedure and Substance in Deliberative Democracy," in *Deliberative Democracy* ed. James Bohman and William Rehg (Cambridge, MA: MIT Press, 1998), pp. 407–37, esp. p. 414.

[15] Even with all these qualifications and caveats on the kind of consensus sought after, the consensus does not have to be entirely actual even among reasonable persons. For some may wrongly believe that the terms proposed are incompatible with their reasonable doctrines. Some such false beliefs ought not to count against saying that they can reasonably accept the terms. But others presumably do count against saying that they can reasonably accept

Finally, the consensus concerns considerations that are relevant to evaluating the basic political institutions of society: in particular, the constitutional essentials and the principles of basic justice. Though much of Cohen's discussion proceeds without this last restriction, I will limit my discussion to these issues for the sake of ease of presentation.

The principle of reasonableness requires that one seek a kind of consensus among citizens as a basis for the justification of political institutions. A basic implication of the idea of the reasonable is that persons, when proposing terms of association for the society, must refrain from justifying those terms on the basis of what they regard as the whole truth concerning matters of justice and political morality. They must exclude from their justifications those parts of what they regard as the whole truth that are incompatible with the political ideas of other reasonable persons.

My question is, why must we refrain from proposing terms of association on the basis of reasons that we believe to be true or appropriate considerations but that we know to be incompatible with the reasonable comprehensive doctrines others accept? This question is particularly important in the light of the great amount of disagreement over ideas about justice and political morality we see in political life. The principle demands a great deal of restraint on the part of those who participate in politics. What are the arguments for this principle?

In what follows I discuss three types of arguments and I argue that they all fail. First, I discuss two versions of what I call the epistemological argument and show that both versions fail. Indeed, both versions of the argument are essentially self-defeating. Second, I discuss what I call the moral argument for the principle of reasonableness. I show that it fails and that in fact the considerations given by the argument point away from the principle that we ought to seek a shared basis of justification. Finally, I discuss the democratic argument and show why I think it too fails as a defense of the principle of reasonableness.

EPISTEMOLOGICAL ARGUMENTS FOR THE
PRINCIPLE OF REASONABLENESS

Cohen gives an epistemological argument for the principle of reasonableness that Rawls seems to endorse.[16] The key premises in the argument are (a) if it is

the terms. Presumably, reasonable acceptance is not closed under implication. But what the exact boundaries are is uncertain. I do not think that these difficult issues need to be settled for the purposes of this chapter. See Gerald Gaus, *Justificatory Liberalism* (Oxford: Oxford University Press, 1996), for a nuanced treatment of this issue in the context of this kind of theory.

[16] See John Rawls, *Political Liberalism* (New York: Columbia University Press, 1993), p. 61.

reasonable for us to adopt a belief and even a comprehensive doctrine as true and it is reasonable for others to deny the truth of that belief or comprehensive doctrine (the fact of reasonable pluralism), then *as far as others are concerned* "what lies between our taking our views to be reasonable and our taking them to be true is not a further reason but simply our belief in those views."[17] (*b*) If what lies between our taking our views to be reasonable and our taking them to be true is not a further reason but simply our belief in those views, then "an appeal to the whole truth will seem indistinguishable [to others who disagree] from an appeal to what we believe."[18] (*c*) The "mere appeal to what we believe carries no force in justification."[19] Therefore, given the fact of reasonable pluralism, if the terms of cooperation are to be justified to others, they must be justified to them on a basis of justification (or reasons) they can accept.

Note carefully that the first premise's claim that what I take to be justified may not be justified *as far as others are concerned* is not a psychological claim, it is a normative claim. To say that "as far as others are concerned what lies between our taking our beliefs to be reasonable and our taking them to be true is simply our beliefs in those views," is to say that from that other person's point of view, we are merely asserting our belief. It is to say that the beliefs are not justified at all from that other person's standpoint. To be sure, when I appeal to my beliefs, *I* do not appeal to them qua beliefs but qua truths. Truths, of course, do have force in justification and so I am able to justify the exercise of power for myself and for those who agree with me. In contrast, for those who disagree with my comprehensive view there is nothing more than my appeal to my belief in the comprehensive view when I use it in justification. I am merely stating a psychological fact about myself. And this has no force in justification for others.

But what support is there for the thesis that, given reasonable disagreement, *as far as others are concerned* "what lies between our taking our views to be reasonable and our taking them to be true is not a further reason but simply our belief in those views?" Cohen asserts that "reason does not mandate a single moral view."[20] He claims that in the context of reasonable pluralism it

---

[17] Joshua Cohen, "Moral Pluralism and Political Consensus," in *The Idea of Democracy* eds. David Copp, John Roemer, and Jean Hampton (Cambridge: Cambridge University Press, 1993), pp. 270–291, esp. p. 284.

[18] Joshua Cohen, "Moral Pluralism and Political Consensus," p. 284.

[19] See Cohen, "Moral Pluralism and Political Consensus," p. 283.

[20] "Moral Pluralism and Political Consensus," p. 284. Rawls suggests this same idea when he speaks of a plurality of conflicting and *incommensurable* reasonable views. As I understand Rawls, he is suggesting that the merits of different comprehensive views cannot be compared to one another. But I am not sure of this interpretation. See Rawls, *Political Liberalism*, p. 135.

is rationally permissible (though not mandatory) "to take the sectarian route of affirming one's own view, that is, believing it as a matter of faith."[21]

One way to understand these remarks in a way that supports the first premise is that subjective justification is the only kind of justification of beliefs there is. By *subjective justification* I mean justification on the basis of a body of premises and modes of reasoning the relevant subject actually accepts whether they are based in true or false premises, good or problematic methods of reasoning. As long as the body of beliefs is intelligible, coherent, and has survived critical reflection, the beliefs that are parts of the view are justified. And they are justified solely for those who hold the coherent and intelligible set of beliefs and whose critical reflection it has survived.[22] Justification is always indexed to a body of particular beliefs and methods of reasoning and belief evaluation. There is no other kind of justification. As a consequence, no single moral point of view or set of ideas is justified *simpliciter*. As examples, we might think here of Thomistic rational theology and Darwinian evolutionary biology. The propositions of Thomistic biology cannot be justified in evolutionary biology but are not defeated by them either since they are not parts of the same body of thought and inference. And the same goes the other way around. Hence, Cohen says that if I disagree with another person's reasonable view and accept my own reasonable view, then the controversial parts of that other person's view are not justified as far as I am concerned.

We can see how this might provide a defense of the idea that reasonable persons will not impose their views on others who cannot reasonably accept the views. Reasonable persons want to justify their proposals to others. But, justification to another, on this view, must proceed from within the body of beliefs and inferences the other person accepts (as long as that person is reasonable and her views are epistemically reasonable). If the exercise of power is to be justified to another it must be on a shared basis of justification.

Cohen's argument, on the subjectivist interpretation, is implausible. The argument, as I have interpreted it so far, hinges on a narrowly subjectivist conception of justification. But why should we agree that this narrowly subjectivist account of justification is the relevant notion for political justification? There are at least two main worries here.

First, the subjective conception of justification seems to impose *too little constraint on the process of justification*. Some people and peoples conscientiously exercise reason but spend much less time on it or are in possession

---

[21] See Cohen, p. 282.

[22] A view can be coherent and yet still employ problematic modes of reasoning, e.g. most people would regard predicting the future on the basis of the reading of tea leaves to be a highly problematic mode of reasoning about the future. But most people would not say that the mode of reasoning is incoherent.

of fewer resources with which to develop. These problems may arise because these people are burdened with other problems. Some exercises of reason are blocked for reasons internal to the comprehensive scheme. Some are in various ways very confused. Some may be based on very limited experience. They may be conscientiously held and have survived the critical reflection of members of the group but still fall short in important ways. In the light of these facts, to say that any comprehensive system of beliefs that is coherent, intelligible, and survives critical reflection is reasonable and therefore that there are no relevant considerations outside this scheme of belief that are relevant to supporting it or undermining it is absurd. It is to imply that those systems that have developed after a great deal of effort and progress cannot be compared to those that have developed under the most inauspicious circumstances and have not had the benefit of a highly developed intellectual tradition.[23]

To be sure, when we disagree with another's views, that the other has subjective justification for those views is a fact about the person that may make that person *blameless* in holding the false beliefs or acting on such a belief. But if we think that the person is mistaken in what she deems to be justified, we clearly want to say that the justification is highly defective or even defeated. We make a distinction between subjective justification and undefeated justification in this context.

To see this let us observe how the conception of subjective justification is not the same as coherentist justification, to which it seems to bear some resemblance. I take my observations about justification to be platitudes about justification that coherentists and opponents of coherentism all try to accommodate within their views. And I do not wish to take a stand on these epistemological theories in this chapter. A plausible coherentism will try to show that the claims of superior justification that people make are claims to a superior degree of coherence with accepted modes of reasoning and available sources of evidence once they are followed *without flaw*. The coherentist, to be sure, does appeal to the beliefs, modes of reasoning, and procedures for collecting evidence in a person's evaluative set to determine whether they are justified in believing something. And coherentists can say that the subjectively justified person is at least justified in some respect, the respect in which we take them to be blameless. But coherentism has room for another more demanding notion of justification. It requires that the beliefs be coherent with all of the

---

[23] Perhaps Cohen could say that only well-developed exercises of reason can be reasonable. This might help with limiting the absurdity of the requirement of justification but it does so at the cost of limiting the set of doctrines that can be described as reasonable. Presumably Cohen's criterion of coherent, intelligible, and surviving critical reflection is meant to cast a very wide net. Furthermore, there are still degrees of development of views that seem to vitiate the requirement to respect all these views.

beliefs, modes of reasoning, and procedures for collecting evidence the person subscribes to as well as the evidence that is available given those beliefs, modes of reasoning, and procedures for collecting evidence. And for undefeated justification it requires that the procedures and modes of reasoning be followed without flaw and until all evidence and considerations have been properly taken into account.

The idea here is that while a set of ideas may be justified subjectively for a particular person, it may be the case that were that person to have followed their methods and modes of reasoning without flaw, they would have acquired very different beliefs. They might have discovered evidence that they had not previously known about. They might have seen that some of the inferences they made were problematic. They might even have seen that some of the modes of reasoning they use are problematic, once evaluated by means of the set of standards for evaluating beliefs when followed without flaw. For these reasons, the subjective justification can be defeated by the very same standards that the person upholds as relevant to the assessment of beliefs.

By contrast, to say that someone is subjectively justified does not imply that their views are coherent with all of the elements of their evaluative set when carried out without flaw. For example, I would assume that creationism is a coherent and intelligible view that has survived the critical reflection of the members of a group. But since the members subscribe to the epistemic value of empirical evidence for deciding matters relating to how the world works (in their everyday lives) and the empirical evidence defeats creationism, the justification of creationism is defeated from a plausible coherentist standpoint. That would hold even if the group had never realized the relevance of empirical evidence to the view or simply did not have the tools to collect the kind of evidence necessary to evaluate it. On the subjectivist conception of justification, however, creationism could still be fully justified and thus a reasonable view. Coherentists would agree that there is a serious defect in the justification of the view.[24]

Can Cohen appeal to the more demanding coherentist notion of justification in support of the first premise? It seems clear that Cohen would have to abandon the first premise on the grounds that someone could easily think that what separates his view from those of another is not his mere belief but

---

[24] See Keith Lehrer, *Theory of Knowledge* (Boulder, CO: Westview Press, 2000), p. 171, for these ideas of subjective or personal justification and defeated justification. See also Gerald Gaus, *Justificatory Liberalism* (Oxford: Oxford University Press, 1996), p. 31, for the idea of "open justification," or the idea that a person can have reason to believe a set of ideas once they subject their beliefs fully and without error to the standards they actually are committed to. Subjective justification, as I am using the term, is what Gaus calls "closed justification."

a superior justification that implies the defeat of the other's justification. And this thought will be defensible in the case of many major religious, moral, and philosophical differences. Hence the epistemological argument for the principle of reasonableness does not go through.[25]

A second worry is that the limitation to subjective justification is clearly *not true to the positions that are taken by reasonable persons* in a controversy. Each person, to the extent that she thinks that the other points of view are coherent, intelligible, and conscientiously sustained through reflection, measures her view against those other views and deems her view superior on the basis of reasons not adequately taken into account by the other positions.

In order to maintain that one has justified one's own views one must think that one has reason to believe that one's own views are superior to their competitors. And to the extent that one thinks that one's own reasons are superior to those offered by the other, one must think that the other's justification is defeated by considerations that one has adduced for one's own position. But this implies that one must think that the other has reason to believe what one believes as well. And those reasons are the same as the ones one has. This is a requirement of justification. Justification is, for each person, essentially unitary and comparative in this way.

To be sure, as a matter of psychological fact, others view one's own scheme of beliefs as false and perhaps only barely reasonable (and sometimes not even that). But this does not touch the implicit normative claim one makes when one believes that one has good reason, considering the alternative views and their arguments, for believing what one believes and that those reasons obtain for all.

If one thinks that one's own comprehensive view is better supported by reason than another person's, what reason could one have for thinking that, *as far as that other person is concerned*, one's views are no better supported by reason? The only possible basis for claiming that my views are no better supported by reason than others' are, as far as those others are concerned, would be the narrowly subjectivist conception of justification discussed above. But this is clearly incompatible with the thought of reflective persons that their beliefs are better supported by reason. To say that one's beliefs are better supported by reason is to be committed to the idea that one's justification is superior to the others in a way that defeats the other justifications. Therefore, if the consequent of the first premise is to be sustained by the idea that justification

---

[25] It must be conceded that the coherentism that I have outlined can allow for divergences among the evaluative sets of persons and thus can allow for divergences in open or undefeated justifications among these persons. But these divergences are likely to be few and far between and will not explain the great majority of disagreements we see in politics.

is only subjective justification, it must be by denying the claim of every holder of a comprehensive view to hold a superior view to those of all the others.

If these last claims are right, the epistemic condition described by the consequent of the first premise seems to call for suspension of judgment on everyone's part at least with regard to the relative merits of the different comprehensive views. If I really thought that there was no more reason for me to believe what I believe than there is for what others believe, then I would not have reason to believe what I believe. I would be compelled to suspend judgment. Indeed, if the consequent of the first premise is true and I recognize that truth, then it is not clear how I can believe the antecedent of the first premise. The first premise collapses into incoherence.

Nothing I have said implies that it is not hard to apprehend certain facts that are important to assessing different views. For instance, some reasons may depend on experiences that are rarely had and, as a matter of psychological fact, may not be taken into account by others. One may excuse others for not taking these into account. But if one thinks the experiences support one's views, one must think that the experiences are reasons for others. One must think that there is some room in the other's view for thinking about these experiences. In any case, the idea that faith and revelation are the sources of controversial comprehensive views has been greatly overemphasized by writers such as John Rawls, Thomas Nagel, and Cohen. The great majority of controversial comprehensive views do not think of themselves as grounded in these kinds of experiences.

Note that the insistence that one's views are justified does not require that one think that one's views are conclusively justified or certain or even that one has conclusively defeated other views, but it does require that one has reason to think that one's views are the most justified. This conception of justification is perfectly compatible with a reasonable fallibilism about one's own beliefs.

Of course, all the proponents of opposing comprehensive views believe that reason favors their views over the others' views. We must acknowledge this kind of irresoluble rivalry. But we are not required to infer from this that what lies between thinking one's view is reasonable and thinking it true is just that one believes it. One can acknowledge as a matter of psychological fact that others conscientiously think one is wrong, while still thinking that one has better reasons for believing one's views than other people's views and that they would have more defensible beliefs if they believed the same. Once one has concluded from a careful examination of other people's views that there are good reasons to reject them in favor of one's own views, the fact that they also think our views are defective does not establish epistemic symmetry between our views. Acknowledging such symmetry is incompatible with the idea that one's views are defensible. There may well be a reason why we ought to treat others and their views with respect but it will have to be based on a different principle from the one suggested by this interpretation of the argument.[26]

To sum up, the notion of justification necessary to shore up the first premise is a narrowly subjective conception of justification. We do have recourse to such a notion when we try to make sense of how another might plausibly have arrived at certain beliefs given the other things they believe. And we normally hold people epistemically blameless if they have subjectively justified beliefs. But it is not the main notion of justification of beliefs that we normally use in assessing beliefs. We often think that a person has subjective justification for a certain belief and that that justification is defeated by other considerations they have not properly taken into account. We have recourse to a stronger notion of justification when we are evaluating and attempting to improve our beliefs as well as those of others. Given this stronger sense of justification, it makes no sense to say that, as far as the other who disagrees with us is concerned, the difference between saying our belief is reasonable and saying it is true is merely that we believe it.

AN OBJECTIVE ACCOUNT OF THE FIRST PREMISE

There is an alternative way to support the first premise. It is to say that reason does not favor any view objectively speaking and so we must simply accept that the different comprehensive views are radically incommensurable, epistemically speaking. On this view, reasonable pluralism entails that there is no more *reason* to believe what we believe than what others believe. Choice between reasonable comprehensive doctrines is merely a matter of faith.

If we accept that there is no more justification for accepting our view than others and we acknowledge the great variety of comprehensive views, we must see that as far as our reasons go, our beliefs may be with equal chances true, false, or neither. In effect we have a kind of skepticism with regard to the justification of comprehensive doctrines. As a consequence, one comprehensive view is no better, with respect to justification, than any other. This is another interpretation of Cohen's claim that "reason does not mandate a single moral view." And perhaps he thinks that his view follows from that simple unobjectionable phrase.

---

[26] Some of this argument is similar in some respects to Joseph Raz's critique of Nagel in his "Facing Diversity," in *Ethics in the Public Domain* (Oxford: Oxford University Press, 1993), pp. 60–96, esp. pp. 88–94.

Cohen's argument interpreted as an argument from objective skepticism to the principle of reasonableness fails for a variety of reasons. First, the defense of objective skepticism is faulty. The fact of reasonable disagreement among persons who reasonably accept different and incompatible comprehensive doctrines does not imply skepticism in the sense that there is no good reason for preferring any doctrine over any of the others. The facts of reasonable disagreement are perfectly compatible with some doctrines being more supported by reasons than others are even if none are conclusively defeated or conclusively justified.[27]

A second trouble with the argument interpreted as proceeding from claims about objective justification is that it is straightforwardly internally inconsistent. For now the consequent of the second premise can be generalized to say that any appeal to the truth is indistinguishable from appeal to what one believes. In addition to implying that others rightly think that my appeal to truth is merely an appeal to my belief, I now rightly think that my appeal to truth is nothing but an appeal to my belief. But if this is so, then the third premise will undercut any arguments I make. So there will not be any justification. I should be suspending judgment.

Third, there is a serious internal difficulty for this particular grounding of the principle of reasonableness, in that it implies a highly controversial variety of skepticism about our beliefs in comprehensive doctrines and it states that a condition of reasonableness is that each person must accept this skepticism. This is a claim that Cohen and Rawls want desperately to avoid.[28] It is, first of all, highly controversial among all of those doctrines that he claims to want to reconcile. Most adherents of these doctrines are committed to the idea that the basic elements of their belief systems are defensible on grounds common to all and that they are more warranted than other views. Indeed, some views imply that their doctrines are more or less incontrovertible in the light of commonly available facts. Now many do not go that far but they still assert the epistemic superiority of their views over all others.

If acceptance of deliberative democracy relies on these highly controversial epistemological claims, then it is not clear that it can be accepted as a basis of community among very different comprehensive views. Adherents of these views will be justified in thinking that they are being made to live in accordance with principles that they cannot accept. If so, deliberative democracy

---

[27] Here I disagree with Wenar's claim that the ideas of the burdens of judgment and their implications imply skepticism. Although I do share his worry that Cohen and Rawls are dangerously close to that view. Persons can conscientiously, intelligibly, and coherently believe different things when examining the same evidence even though some of the beliefs are more reasonable than others. See Leif Wenar, "Political Liberalism: An Internal Critique," pp. 32–62.

[28] See Rawls, *Political Liberalism* (New York: Columbia University Press, 1993), pp. 62–63.

and indeed political liberalism have not made much progress over the so-called comprehensive liberalisms.

In any case, there does not seem to be any warrant for the kind of strong skepticism that seems to be endorsed here. If so, then we should reject this claim as a basis of the conception of the reasonable person that Cohen offers.

The plausible sounding phrase "reason does not mandate a single moral view" could be given a weaker and much more plausible interpretation. It could be thought simply that reason does not supply *conclusive* justification for any view or even conclusive defeaters for many opposing views. Such a claim is compatible with saying that some views are more in accordance with all the evidence than all the others, but it would not require belief in those views. By analogy, all the available evidence may better support one scientific theory than any other theory, but because the evidence is inductive and the conclusion universal, belief in the theory may not be required by reason. Whatever the merits of this latter position, it is not sufficient to defend the claim of the first premise that only belief lies between the reasonableness of one's view and one's holding it to be true. For this position allows that some positions may be more reasonable than others, objectively speaking. And this would undercut the claim that only belief lies between our taking our view to be reasonable and our holding it to be true.

If we deny that choice between different reasonable doctrines can only be made on faith, what argument is there for the premise that whenever we exercise power, those over whom power is exercised must be given a sufficient justification on a basis of justification they accept? Is it plausible to assert this if we think that our views are better supported than other people's views? It will be the burdens of the moral argument and the democratic argument to attempt to ground the principle of reasonableness in a way that avoids controversial or implausible epistemological doctrines. To these I turn.

THE MORAL ARGUMENT: RESPECT FOR REASON

Another way of supporting the contention that the reasonable person justifies himself to others on a basis of justification each can accept might proceed from the premise that the reasonable person has respect for the products of reason. The argument I am envisioning proceeds in three simple steps. First, everyone must respect each person's free exercise of her own reason. Second, in order to respect the free exercise of each person's reason, one must respect the products of her reason, in particular her reasonable comprehensive doctrines. Third, in order to respect the products of each person's reason, one must not require her to live in ways that are incompatible with their reasonable comprehensive doctrines. This argument seems to be implied when Cohen says, "Adjustment [to the fact of reasonable diversity] is reasonable because some forms of diversity are the natural consequence of the free exercise of reason."[29]

Respect for the free exercise of reason, on this account, implies that one may not require persons to live in accordance with doctrines that are incompatible with the products of their own reason even if, objectively, reason tells one that those products are mistaken. Despite the fact that some doctrines are less epistemically reasonable than others, respect for the reason of other persons requires us to make sure that our impositions on others are justifiable to them on bases they accept.[30]

Notice that this implies also that we may not live under those terms of association that we regard as most reasonable if they are incompatible with the reasonable doctrines of our fellow citizens even if we think those other reasonable doctrines are flawed. The principle of restraint stops each person from living in accordance with what she takes to be the most defensible conception of justice.

I have two main objections to the argument from respect for reason. They both are fatal dilemmas for the argument. The first says that the argument from respect for reason either implies a controversial comprehensive doctrine or does not support the principle of reasonableness. The second says that the argument either implies a need for complete consensus or fails to establish the principle of reasonableness.

My first objection is that the argument from respect for reason implies a controversial doctrine or it fails to support the principle of reasonableness. First, we must determine whether this notion of respect implies a controversial comprehensive doctrine. Second, we must determine whether the respect for the free exercise of reason requires each to put aside his or her sense that some doctrine is more reasonable than another when justifying political proposals.

The two issues are related. They set up a fatal dilemma. On the one hand, if respect for the free exercise of reason does require us to put aside our sense that a particular doctrine is more epistemically reasonable than another is when justifying political proposals, then it does presuppose a controversial

---

[29] Joshua Cohen, "Moral Pluralism and Political Consensus," in *The Idea of Democracy* eds. David Copp, John Roemer, and Jean Hampton (Cambridge: Cambridge University Press, 1993), pp. 270–291, esp. p. 285.

[30] The idea of respect for reason seems to be what Charles Larmore has in mind in his "The Moral Basis of Political Liberalism," *Journal of Philosophy* (December 1999), p. 602 by the notion of respect for persons. The difference in expression suggests that Larmore adheres to a rationalist conception of the person.

comprehensive doctrine of a Kantian sort. On the other hand, if it does not require us to set aside the epistemic superiority of a particular reasonable doctrine in setting up political institutions, then it cannot provide the argument Cohen thinks it does for the principle of reasonableness.

If respect for the free exercise of reason requires us to ignore the greater epistemic reasonableness of a doctrine, then it presupposes that the value of respect for the free exercise of reason is lexically superior to any other reasonable value or combination of values or at least nearly so, that is, it must always be satisfied before any other reasonable value. Here is the argument.

Suppose the value of the free exercise of reason is not lexically superior to all other values. Then some values and combinations of values override the value of the free exercise of reason and its products in some cases of conflict. If the most epistemically reasonable conception of value implies the existence of a value greater than the free exercise of reason, then it recommends that the free exercise of reason be overridden in some cases of conflict with this value. Therefore, if there is a most epistemically reasonable conception of value and it is incompatible with some other reasonable conception of value, then, at least in some circumstances, one ought to take into account that epistemic superiority in deciding how to organize terms of association among those who hold these two conceptions.

Therefore, if the value of the free exercise of reason is not lexically superior to all other values then, at least in some circumstances, one ought to take into account the greater epistemic reasonableness of some doctrines in deciding how to organize terms of association. As a consequence, if one ought not take into account the greater reasonableness of some doctrines in establishing terms of association, then the free exercise of reason is lexically superior to all other values.

The idea that the value of the free exercise of reason is lexically superior to all other values is a highly controversial claim. Welfarist, contractarian, and most rationalist views as well as many religious views reject the view. Indeed most moral views reject the idea. So it must necessarily express commitment to a controversial claim about all reasonable comprehensive doctrines. Both Cohen and Rawls intend their views about the basis of cooperation to be themselves acceptable to all.[31] This is why they both eschew skepticism as a basis for the principle of reasonableness.[32] And so an argument from the

---

[31] See, again, Rawls, *Political Liberalism*, pp. 62–63, for the idea that the account of the reasonable cannot presuppose controversial doctrines.

[32] I reject Larmore's claim that the respect for persons, as it functions in the argument for political liberalism does not imply significant part of a comprehensive doctrine. See Larmore, p. 623.

lexical priority of respect for reason to the principle of reasonableness would be self-defeating.[33]

From these remarks we can see that the argument from the respect for reason generates a fatal dilemma. On the one hand, a commitment to this extreme Kantian conception of value undermines Cohen's claim to provide a shared basis of justification among different reasonable comprehensive conceptions. On the other hand, if the reasonable person takes account of differences in the epistemic reasonableness of comprehensive doctrines in establishing terms of association, then, the reasonable person ought to advance the most reasonable conception of value that he or she has. This last claim implies that the reasonable person may impose terms of association that others cannot reasonably accept. The argument in favor of the principle of reasonableness loses its force.

WHY RESPECT FOR REASON DOES NOT SUPPORT THE PRINCIPLE OF REASONABLENESS

The second objection is that either the argument from respect for reason requires complete consensus within the society on basic principles of justice or it is incompatible with the principle of reasonableness.

The idea is that there is something disrespectful to someone's reason in requiring him or her to live in accordance with principles he or she does not accept. But consider the situation in which someone is proposing terms of association for her group on the basis of reasons that she reasonably accepts but that some reasonably reject. Cohen thinks that it is disrespectful of the dissenters' reason to impose those terms on them, which they reasonably reject.[34] What Cohen does not appear to see is that, by the same token, we must say that it is disrespectful of this proponent's reason to require her to *forgo* living in accordance with principles she reasonably accepts (i.e. to forgo living in accordance with the whole truth as she sees it).

This can be seen from the following typical example. Suppose that I believe that, as a matter of basic justice, the distribution of jobs ought to be determined by the distribution of qualifications: the most qualified person ought to

---

[33] It is important to note that nothing I have said so far implies that the Kantian comprehensive liberalism is incoherent in itself. All that is being said is that this particular grounding of liberalism is incompatible with the Rawlsian aim of finding a mutually acceptable basis for social cooperation.

[34] Recall here that we are talking about the need for agreement on the list of considerations. Cohen thinks, as we noted above, that all that is needed to respect others is that one bases decisions on a list of considerations everyone can reasonably accept. For resolving disagreements on the relative weights of these considerations, Cohen thinks majority rule is legitimate.

be given the job.[35] I believe this to be a requirement on treating people justly. As it happens many reject the use of desert-based considerations altogether for assigning jobs. And let us suppose that I have good reasons for thinking that desert-based considerations are important and that others have reasons for thinking they are not important. They think that jobs ought to be distributed in accordance with the principle of what will produce the most efficient outcome or perhaps in accordance with Rawls's three principles.[36] Now, of course, I think that efficiency is an important value in the organization of work so I agree with the others that this value ought to have weight in determining the organization of work. But I also adhere to desert-based considerations while the others reasonably reject them. I think, in other words, that the organization of work and society is unjust if it is not regulated by a principle of desert, while others think that desert considerations only undermine efficiency. If my desert-based proposal wins then the others must live with terms of association that they reasonably reject. Desert was not on the list of considerations they reasonably accept. If my desert-based proposals fail because a majority of others reasonably reject them, then I must live with terms of association that I reasonably regard as unjust.[37]

I do not see that Cohen or Rawls has given any arguments that this is less of a sacrifice of one's reason than living in a society that conforms to principles I do not accept. Indeed, it is not clear that there is any fundamental difference between the two kinds of accommodation. Rawls's idea that someone's appeal to the whole truth in designing institutions is unreasonable would seem to apply symmetrically to someone's appeal to their rejection of a view in designing those institutions.

Let us call this situation the *deliberative impasse*. Either one must impose on one person terms that she does not accept or one must require another to live under terms that he regards as fundamentally inadequate. From this

[35] It should be noted here that different theorists disagree as to the content of the principles that are the focus of reasonable agreement. Samuel Freeman seems to be inclined to think that Rawls's justice as fairness is the object of reasonable agreement. See his "Deliberative Democracy: A Sympathetic Account," *Philosophy and Public Affairs*, vol. 29, no. 4, pp. 371–418, esp. p. 411. Rawls has recently broadened his account of what reasonable people could agree to. See his "The Idea of Public Reason Revisited," in *The Law of Peoples* (Cambridge, MA: Harvard University Press, 1999), p. 143. He includes a family of liberal political conceptions of justice in the domain of conceptions reasonable people can agree to. This family is much smaller, of course, than the set of principles that are actively debated in modern democracies.

[36] See John Rawls, "The Idea of Public Reason Revisited," p. 141.

[37] See David Miller, *The Principles of Social Justice* (Cambridge, MA: Harvard University Press, 1999), for a defense of the fundamental importance of desert claims. Obviously examples of disagreement on principles of basic justice abound. People disagree on the importance of considerations of utility, self-ownership, community, and many others to issues of the basic justice of society.

observation, it is hard to see why respect for reason would require one and not the other. But then respect for reason does not provide any guidance when there is disagreement and it certainly does not support the principle of reasonableness.

If these claims are right, then the principle of reasonableness requires complete consensus on the considerations that people take to be important to questions of basic justice. They show that even if there is an overlapping consensus on certain doctrines there is a problem in excluding the beliefs that are not in the overlap.[38] The problem is that exclusion of the beliefs that are not in the overlap is as much an expression of lack of respect for the reason of citizens as inclusion of views that are not in the overlap. So the principle of respect for reason pushes us to say that reasonable persons propose terms of association only when they are the object of complete consensus among persons concerning considerations relating to basic justice. But we know that consensus on all the considerations relevant to basic justice is impossible. Indeed, Rawls and Cohen agree on this point, which is why they attempt to show that an overlapping consensus is possible. The argument from respect for reason on this account does support the principle of reasonableness but it seems to require complete consensus on considerations relevant to basic justice. And this is a serious flaw for principles for pluralistic societies.

One might object to the above argument by saying that the solution to the deliberative impasse is to find a neutral baseline such that in order for one to introduce any terms of association backed by political power one must justify those terms or remain at the baseline which itself does not need justification. When there is a deliberative impasse, one reverts to the baseline. When I am not able to justify my proposals to others, the dissenters do not impose the baseline upon me nor do they treat me as an unequal if the baseline condition is what is chosen. When there is a baseline of this sort, there is an asymmetry in the requirements of justification. Every departure from the baseline must satisfy a burden of proof while remaining at the baseline need not. In order to have my way, either it must be at the baseline or I must provide justification to others.[39]

In cases like the above that involve competing conceptions of social and political order, I do not see how there can be a baseline solution as an alternative to deliberative impasse. First of all, the choice of baseline is likely to be as controversial as any other choice of political principles.

---

[38] An overlapping consensus is a consensus among reasonable persons once the controversial elements of their doctrines have been excluded. It is the consensus reasonable persons are supposed to have on Cohen's view and on the basis of which terms of association are justified.

[39] This kind of baseline is used in Gerald Gaus's, *Justificatory Liberalism* (Oxford: Oxford University Press, 1996).

For example, the idea of the minimal state has been proposed as such a baseline solution to conflicts of view over more ambitious conceptions of the role of the state. The reason given for this is that the minimal state involves a smaller state than more ambitious schemes. It seems to limit liberty less than other schemes. The minimal state is a baseline, some might claim, because there is more liberty in it. But this is clearly not generally true. It is a matter of the particular circumstances. Some might assert that the minimal state is a baseline because there is more coercion in more ambitious states than in minimal states. But why believe this?[40] Another possible support for this is that the minimal state is the most cautious use of political power. But this depends on where one starts from. In the early twenty-first century, attempting to bring about a minimal state would be a hazardous and highly uncertain enterprise. Finally, some may assert that the minimal state is a neutral baseline because it interferes only minimally with the rights of property and liberty understood in a classical liberal sense. But now we need a highly controversial view of justice just to get off the ground.

Furthermore, we can ask why we should accept some controversial conception of liberty as a baseline. Why not accept some notion of equality as the baseline or some notion of the common good or a harm principle? The fact of controversy here seems to belie the idea that there is a neutral baseline at all.

The basic problem is that there is no morally basic baseline that can serve as the starting point for justification of the exercise of political power. Any such claim to a baseline will be highly controversial and as a consequence, it does not bear a lesser burden of proof. No scheme of rights, powers, and liberties that determines the distribution of resources and liberties bears a greater burden of proof than any other; they are simply different.[41] The addition of the alternative of the minimal state or laissez-faire seems only to add to the deliberative impasse; it does not resolve it. The citizen who reasonably rejects a proposal that another citizen reasonably accepts is no more burdened by a state that implements the proposal than the citizen who reasonably accepts the proposal is burdened by the lack of implementation of the proposal. Therefore, it is clear that a neutral baseline cannot save us from the problems generated by the deliberative impasse.

---

[40] See G. A. Cohen, "Capitalism, Freedom and the Proletariat," in *The Idea of Freedom* ed. Alan Ryan (Oxford: Oxford University Press, 1969), for an effective dismantling of this argument.

[41] Gaus has proposed to me in discussion that there may be a baseline in politics that is analogous to the case of belief. Some think that in the case of belief, if we do not have good reasons for belief then we should suspend judgment. Suspending judgment is a kind of neutral baseline for belief. But I think that this is precisely what is disanalogous to politics. Political commitments cannot be suspended in the way belief can be; the society one lives in will satisfy some political commitment or another.

Let us take the other horn of the dilemma. Let us suppose that complete consensus is impossible and there is no neutral baseline. There is a deliberative impasse. The only way to ensure that one person does not have to live on terms he does not accept is to require another to live on terms she does not accept. What does the idea of respect for reason have to say in this circumstance? It seems plausible to think that the respect for reason always tilts in favor of the most epistemically reasonable doctrine when the above impasse occurs. And this will imply that each person, who believes that her doctrine is best supported, should attempt to advance her own view when others disagree. Otherwise, the proponent is disrespectful of her own reason if she willingly forgoes living in accordance with principles that she thinks are most epistemically reasonable in order to accommodate views that she takes to be less reasonable (though perhaps minimally reasonable). By hypothesis, she has to give up living in a way that her reason tells her is best.

On this horn of the dilemma, respect for reason is not capable of providing support for the principle of reasonableness because it is not capable of providing support for the idea of reciprocity that is part of the principle. That idea, recall, is that it is reasonable for me to accept terms of association only if those terms can also be reasonably accepted by others. What I have argued is that in the inevitable case of disagreement, respect for reason cannot generate this kind of reciprocity. The failure of respect for reason displayed by abandoning proposals that one thinks are the most defensible because others disagree with them seems to me to be greater than the failure of respect for reason incurred when one makes others live on the basis principles that are the most defensible but that they reject. The only way to defend the kind of reciprocity that is part of the principle of reasonableness is to take an impartial stance toward the different views at issue and not compare their relative merits. But this, I contend, is incompatible with the respect for reason unless one accepts some variant of the epistemological argument I have refuted above.[42]

We have then a second fatal dilemma for the argument from respect for reason to the principle of reasonableness. On the one hand, the principle of respect for reason does support the principle of reasonableness but pushes us to require complete consensus on considerations relevant to basic justice, which consensus is not even remotely possible in pluralistic societies. On the

---

[42] Of course, none of this problem need arise in a social world in which everyone agrees on all the basic principles of justice. As I understand Rawls, an overlapping consensus does not require full agreement on all the principles. It merely requires that there be agreement on some principles and disagreement on others. Then each person must restrain himself in trying to implement those principles on which there is disagreement. If so, then the problem I have outlined is a serious one. But if Rawls refers to the first kind of consensus as the overlapping consensus, then I contend that this is quite impossible in the world we live in.

other hand, in the absence of consensus, the principle of respect for reason leads us to reject the principle of reasonableness in favor of saying that we should advance the most epistemically reasonable considerations relevant to questions of basic justice.

Those who wish to live under the most reasonable type of regime need not abandon respect for rights to life and liberties. Nor need they be committed to violent means for establishing the most reasonable regime or the suppression of others' liberties of conscience and association. Those who aim to live under the most reasonable type of regime may think it is morally appropriate to engage in peaceful (even democratic) means to achieve their controversial aims. And, most important, those who wish to live under the most reasonable regime may think that among other things, such a regime is democratic and liberal. The above argument in no way commits one to authoritarianism.

THE DEMOCRATIC ARGUMENT FOR THE PRINCIPLE OF REASONABLENESS

Cohen offers a third argument for the principle of reasonableness. He argues very briefly that the principle is required by the fact of reasonable pluralism coupled with the demand that citizens be seen as free and equal.[43] Cohen says:

[Because of] the background of democracy—the idea of citizens as free and equal— and the fact of reasonable pluralism … the relevant justification must be addressed to citizens, by which I mean that its terms must be acknowledged as suitable by those subject to political power. Given that citizens have equal standing and are understood as free, and given the fact of reasonable pluralism, we have an especially strong showing of legitimacy when the exercise of state power is supported by considerations acknowledged as reasons by the different views endorsed by reasonable citizens, who are considered as equals. No other account of reasons is suited for this case.

On my reading of this passage the key idea is that in order for political authority to treat individuals who reasonably disagree as free and equal it must exercise power only on the basis of reasons they all reasonably accept. If an authority exercises power on the basis of a reason that some do not accept then it is (assuming it acknowledges the reasonable disagreement) treating those persons not as free and equal. As I understand this, the authority is treating these persons as inferiors or subordinates.

For example, a majority in a democratic society believes the reasons the dissenters have for rejecting the policy concerning matters of basic justice

---

[43] See "Reflections on Habermas on Democracy," p. 405.

at issue are not very good ones and so the majority chooses the policy the dissenting citizens reasonably reject. Ought we to say that the majority treats the reasonably dissenting citizens as inferiors? As far as I can tell, I do not think so. The citizens' *views* concerning the issue at hand are being treated as less reasonable than the ideas the majority is acting on. But this is not the same as saying that the citizens are being treated as inferiors. We must distinguish between treating a person as an inferior and treating a person's ideas or policy proposals as inferior.

There are a number of ways in which one can think of persons as inferiors. One way to think of persons as inferiors is to think of them as having *lesser capacities* for insight, good judgment and reasoning, or as having generally wasted their capacities for no good reason.[44] Another way to think of people as inferiors is to think that *their interests are less important* than those of others. A third way is to think of them as morally *depraved or evil* and thus not deserving of the same rights and advantages as others are.

Commitment to these kinds of inferiority is expressed by depriving a person of a right to a say in how the common world they live in is organized and to those things that are necessary to a right to an equal say. It is also expressed by depriving a person of basic liberal rights of expression, association, and conscience as well as by the denial of equality before the law. Furthermore, simply ignoring a person's views or not taking her arguments seriously in the process of making collective decisions also expresses a sense that she is an inferior. These are the basic ways in which one can treat others as inferiors.

On the wide view of deliberative democracy, there are three components to treating the other as an equal in a political society. First, one treats others as equals by respecting the democratic process and basic liberal rights: by giving each equal opportunities to affect the outcome of decision-making and present their arguments. Democratic and liberal institutions make no commitment about the relative capacities of individuals and instead allow citizens to choose for themselves who they wish to ally themselves with or who they wish to associate with and trust as we saw in Chapter 3. And democratic institutions implicitly express the equal importance of each person as a being with interests. Second, to the extent that one has taken the other persons' interests and capacities into account in the best way one knows how, that is, one's proposals take them into account, one has treated them as equals. Third, to the extent that one has listened to others' arguments in the democratic forum, attempted to give arguments that defeat their arguments, and submits to the "force of the better argument," one has treated them as equals in the

---

[44] Cohen understands treating others as equals this way in "Democracy and Liberty," in *Deliberative Democracy* ed. Jon Elster (Cambridge: Cambridge University Press, 1998), p. 192.

process of discussion by taking them seriously and not ignoring their views. Must one also be reasonable, in Cohen's sense, in order to treat others as equals?

It is clear that one does not treat another person as an inferior merely by thinking that some or even many of their ideas are less defensible than one's own. Indeed, one can think of another as superior in the senses listed above while rejecting their particular views.

The question is, does one treat another as an inferior when, having the best justified views on a particular subject (by one's own lights), one proposes terms of association to the democratic assembly on that basis? The answer to this must be no for anyone who recognizes that people disagree with each other and that policy proposals are always controversial.

Of course, if we accept Cohen's epistemological argument, the above egalitarian argument for the principle of reasonableness may work. For, given the epistemological argument, if another reasonably disagrees with me on the basis of a different comprehensive view from my own, then I appeal only to my belief in justifying forcing him to live in accordance with my views.[45] Then I treat the other as an inferior to the extent that I make laws on the basis of my beliefs but I do not permit the other to base laws on his own belief.[46] I have given myself a right that I do not similarly offer to others and, consequently, I have treated the other as an unequal.

I doubt that even this implies a genuine inequality. The above argument fails to take into account that the proposals are made to a democratic assembly. For suppose we live together with the dissenters in a democratic society wherein each has the right to advance his views in the public forum and wherein only some can get their way. It would seem that the democratic way of making decisions treats everyone as equals in this context.

But, once we reject the epistemological arguments, disagreement on comprehensive views in no way suggests that one treats the other as an inferior when one proposes terms of cooperation on the bases of considerations they cannot reasonably accept. Here is the basic argument.

First, clearly, one need not think that someone is an inferior if one disagrees with her on some very deep questions. One does not have to think that her capacities are inferior or that she is depraved or that her interests are of less importance.

Second, disagreements among rational persons are normally ones in which each of the parties thinks that she has superior reasons on her side. And every

---

[45] See p. 207 above.
[46] In "Democracy and Liberty," p. 206, Cohen connects what I call the epistemic argument to the democratic argument in this way.

person can recognize this. Under these circumstances, the effort to advance one's proposals in the democratic assembly is an attempt to bring about the most supported terms of association for all. Therefore, a person's advancing a proposal is not a mere form of self-assertion over others.

Third, once we acknowledge the deliberative impasse, we are in a situation where it is either one person's views or another's that are implemented. There is no neutral baseline on which we can fall back when we disagree about terms of political organization. Some proposal must be adopted. Therefore, the mere adoption of a controversial proposal cannot by itself imply that those who disagree are treated as inferiors. The only way in which the process of decision can be thought to treat some as inferiors is if the decision expresses the idea that they are inferiors or if the decision is made in a way that excludes or diminishes the participation of some of the members.

But we have established that the mere fact that one person disagrees with another does not imply that he thinks of the other as an inferior. And since each is advancing a view on the basis of reasons that each takes to defeat the others' views, no one is treating the others with contempt by simply ignoring them or not taking them seriously. Hence, to the extent that a decision must be made, the fact that it is made on controversial grounds cannot express the idea that the dissenters are inferiors. And since the decision is made democratically, so that each has an equal say in the process, the making of the controversial decision does not amount to treating the dissenters as unequals. Therefore, I see no reason for thinking that the principle of reasonableness is a further necessary condition on treating others as equals.[47]

Now that we have the fundamental argument in mind, let us consider another way in which democratic institutions can fail to treat individuals as equals in a way that may appear to support the principle of reasonableness. Democratic institutions do not foreclose the possibility that a society may have permanent minorities, that is, groups that always or nearly always lose on all the issues that arise in the ultimate voting decisions. If there exists within a society an insular minority that has very different views from the majority which itself has a great deal of agreement on views, there is a danger that

---

[47] One commentator has objected that "the devout Catholic who is told that his Catholic views are inferior may find it psychologically very hard to distinguish this from a claim that he is inferior." I am afraid that I do not see this. Though there may be some who might have this reaction, I do not see how, in a society where many deeply different views flourish, this would be a general reaction. Of course, when someone's deeply held views are rejected by the democratic assembly as a basis for association, that person is apt to feel somewhat alienated from his political world. But this is likely to happen more or less to anyone in a democratic society where there is substantial disagreement about how it ought to be organized. One way of seeing the point of democratic institutions is as a way of distributing this inevitable feeling of alienation in an egalitarian way.

the minority will always find itself governed on the basis of reasons it rejects. Suppose the majority's views never coincide with those of the minority and the majority never makes any attempt to accommodate the minority members' views. This is a rare case in democratic societies but it has occurred and continues to occur in some parts of the world.[48]

To be sure, the majority may be acting in a principled way in that it does take the minority's interests into account as they are understood in the majority comprehensive view.[49] But, in this kind of case, one can imagine that the members of the minority are deeply alienated from the political institutions and policies that regulate their lives. They do not agree with the majority conception of their interests and they find the majority norms of morality and religion quite foreign. In brief, they are not at home in the world as organized by the majority. In these kinds of situations, a case can be made for saying that the members of the minority are being treated as inferiors if nothing is done to alleviate this alienation.

How does this kind of situation relate to the principle of reasonableness? The main condition that produces the kind of cleavage described above occurs when the minority and the majority are adherents of deeply conflicting comprehensive views and social practices. Under these circumstances, the majority simply always gets its way and never listens to the views of the minority because they are so different and because the solidity of the majority ensures that minority votes are never needed to ensure a collective decision. In this kind of situation, it really appears that the majority is exercising authority directly from their comprehensive doctrine without a concern for the views of the minority. Here we can see the basis of the anxiety that Rawls expresses in the following passage: "There is no reason why any citizen, or association of citizens, should have the right to use state power to decide constitutional essentials as that person's, or that association's, comprehensive doctrine directs. When equally represented, no citizen could grant to another person or association that political authority."[50] In the case of permanent minorities, it is as if political authority in a democracy has been simply conferred on the majority. When the majority acts on its comprehensive doctrine, the minority is bound to be deeply alienated from the decisions made by the majority. I do

---

[48] The plight of indigenous peoples in the Western Hemisphere comes to mind here.
[49] This kind of case must be distinguished from the case of majority tyranny where the majority simply mistreats the minority on the basis of crazy views about justice or hatred. In the case of permanent minorities, the majority may well be treating the minority as equals in accordance with its own distinctive conception of the minority's interests and its own norms of equality.
[50] See *Political Liberalism*, pp. 62 and 226 (the same passage recurs).

not want to go further here into the basis of this alienation or the importance it has for political life, I will discuss this in more detail in Chapter 7.

I want to make a number of comments on this possible support for the principle of reasonableness. First, it ought to be noted that this is not how democracies usually work. In general, even after vigorous debate on the issues, decisions are made by alliances of different groups who vote in favor of policies on the basis of different reasons.[51] No person is granted authority to make decisions on the basis of his or her comprehensive view. Only the democratic assembly as a whole has authority, and majorities in the democratic assembly rarely agree on the reasons behind their decisions. Furthermore, majorities are usually shifting coalitions of groups. The case that Rawls's description seems to point to is a very special case in a democracy. Strictly speaking, even in the case of permanent minorities, the majority does not exercise authority because of its comprehensive doctrine; it does so because democratic decision-making is supposed to be a fair and authoritative process that treats everyone as equals.

The case of permanent minorities is a case, I would argue, in which the members of the minority are being treated as inferiors and I believe that it provides some insight into the motives for appealing to the principle of reasonableness. But our judgment here does not support the principle of reasonableness. First, the principle of reasonableness really is not capable of sorting things out in this kind of case since there is no shared basis of reasoning. Indeed, the case seems to be another counterexample to the principle of reasonableness as a necessary condition for treating others as equals because there are egalitarian ways of accommodating such insular minorities. One may grant them limited political autonomy or one may attempt a formal or informal type of consociational arrangement or the majority can simply attempt to accommodate the minority views in its decision-making.[52]

Second, the principle of reasonableness has a far greater reach than this kind of case. It is meant to exclude considerations that are not based in shared conceptions whenever they occur in the public political arena. And though the case of permanent minorities is a case of treating the members of the minority as inferiors, the normal case in which citizens base policy proposals on controversial comprehensive views is not sensibly thought of as a case of treating the dissenters as inferiors. Participants in normal democratic

---

[51] To use Robert Dahl's felicitous phrase, democracy is in fact polyarchy or "rule by minorities." For these expressions and the idea of democracy that lies behind them, see Robert Dahl, *A Preface to Democratic Theory* (Chicago: University of Chicago Press, 1956).

[52] For examples of some of these kinds of arrangements, see Arend Lijphart, *Democracy in Plural Societies* (New Haven, CN: Yale University Press, 1977), and Donald L. Horowitz, *A Democratic South Africa? Constitutional Engineering in a Divided Society* (Oxford: Oxford University Press, 1991).

processes defend policy proposals in terms not everyone can accept but they see that the democratic decision itself gets its authority only when enough support has been garnered for the chosen proposal.

To the extent that citizens have equal votes, equal resources with which to negotiate with others and equal resources with which to participate in the process of discussion and debate over principles, and to the extent that citizens are willing to listen to their fellow citizens with an open mind and willing to take everyone's interests equally into account when making democratic decisions, they are treating each other as equals (with the proviso that there are no permanent minorities) as much as can be done in a society where people disagree. I do not see what argument can be given for the claim that action in accordance with the principle of reasonableness is necessary to treat persons as equals.

Someone might argue that the interest in being at home in the world provides some support for the principle of reasonableness.[53] If one has an interest in being at home in the world, then one has an interest in the world conforming to what one thinks is right. But if this is right, then there seems always to be a reason for being reasonable. In being reasonable one is protecting others' interests in being at home in their world, which they share with us. I do not deny that this consideration has some force but I think it fails to establish the principle of reasonableness for the reasons I gave against the principle in discussing the argument from respect for reason. The trouble is that if I must compromise my sense of the whole truth to accommodate someone else's comprehensive view, then I have sacrificed my interest in being at home for the sake of another's interest. I do not say that one ought never do that. But I do not think that it is required and in any case, the principle of reasonableness is not satisfied by this since some aspect of my comprehensive view has been sacrificed. In effect, what I have called the deliberative impasse undermines the inference from the interests of all persons to being at home in the world they live in to the principle of reasonableness. The implication of this is that in a pluralistic society or indeed any moderately complex society, no one is fully at home in their world. This is what gives a point to the principle of equality: since there are conflicts of interests including the interests in being at home in the world, we want to structure the world so that each person's interest in being at home in the world is advanced equally. And democracy gives us a publicly clear way to do just that.[54]

---

[53] I thank Matthew Clayton for pressing me on this.

[54] I want to raise a final worry about the connection between the principle of reasonableness and democracy. In my view, we have reason to think that the principle of reasonableness is inegalitarian, Cohen's position notwithstanding. There are two worries here. First, the view that Cohen espouses excludes religious reasons and religiously based policies as well as other

In conclusion, the arguments used to support the principle of reasonableness and the associated narrow conception of deliberative democracy fail to
hit their targets. The epistemological arguments, the moral argument, and the
democratic argument do not support the principle of reasonableness. Indeed,
we have seen that the main considerations behind each of these arguments
and the combination of them suggest that the wide conception of deliberative
democracy is superior to the narrow conception.

comprehensive moral views such as Kantianism, Utilitarianism, Communitarianism, and a
whole host of other positions that are commonplace in the politics of democratic societies.
Second, Cohen's account of democracy does not seem to assign any fundamental value to the
inclusion of unreasonable people. Recall that the ideal deliberative procedure includes only
the reasonable in its characterization of the democratic process. What reason is there then
for the inclusion of the unreasonable? To be sure, the view does not directly entail the legal
exclusion of these comprehensive views and the exclusion of views is only from the formal
political forum of discussion that occurs in electoral campaigns and legislative debates, to name
the most important. Still the inclusion of unreasonable views seems to be a concession to reality
in the sense that it may be difficult to exclude unreasonable views without also excluding some
reasonable views. The worry is confirmed by the very limited role Rawls assigns to citizens in a
liberal democracy. He says: "Citizens fulfill their duty of civility and support the idea of public
reason by doing what they can to hold government officials to it." See "The Idea of Public Reason
Revisited," p. 136. This gives citizens something dangerously close to a merely instrumental role
in the democratic process and if it does not literally do so, it is not clear why Rawls would be
opposed to such a limited role.

6

The Authority of Democracy

Now that the grounding of democracy in public equality has been laid out, we must address the question of the authority of democracy. This question arises because in the conception of democracy I have elaborated, while democracy has a kind of intrinsic value, citizens also attempt to realize their differing conceptions of justice within the context of a democratic society. They argue for competing conceptions of the common good and justice, and they attempt to organize winning coalitions around these controversial conceptions so as to realize them in law and policy. This means that citizens can evaluate the democratic decisions from two distinct points of view. On the one hand, they can evaluate the democratic decision on the basis of its resulting from an intrinsically just process. On the other hand, they can evaluate the outcome of the process in terms of the justice of the substantive law and policy. Inevitably, given the pervasiveness of disagreement, the democratic process will produce decisions that many citizens will think unjust. And in some cases they will be right. Even though democracy is intrinsically valuable there are still procedure-independent standards for evaluating the democratic process. But this raises the problem of the authority of democracy. When the outcome of democratic decision-making conflicts with a citizen's best judgment about what justice requires in substantive law and policy, what is the citizen required to do?

The answer to this question must necessarily be complex, I argue. To say that democracy has authority implies that the citizen is required to go along with the democratic decision even in those cases where he or she thinks the decision unjust. But the authority is not unlimited; there are some cases in which the injustice of the result outweighs or defeats the justice of democracy. An account of the authority of democracy must explain how and when democracy can be authoritative even when it makes unjust decisions and how and when certain kinds of injustice can defeat the authority of democracy.

I argue in what follows that the idea that democracy is grounded in the principle of public equality can give a unified and satisfying explanation for the authority of democracy and for the limits to democratic authority.

In this chapter, I show how the principle of public equality grounds the authority of democracy. And in the next chapter, I show how the principle of public equality grounds the limits of the authority of democracy and I give an account of those limits. These two chapters lay the foundations of a democratic constitutionalism.

In what follows, I will start with a section characterizing some main desiderata that a successful conception of political authority must satisfy. In the next section, I will lay out what I take to be three concepts of political authority that have been prominent in recent discussions and argue for the importance of one of them. In the section after, I will define what I mean by saying that democracy has authority. And in the following section I will show how the principle of public equality grounds the authority of democracy and I will address some objections to my account. Finally, I will discuss the complexity of democratic authority. In the next chapter, I will explain how the limits of democratic authority are grounded in the principle of public equality and what those limits are.

SOME REQUIREMENTS ON A CONCEPTION
OF POLITICAL AUTHORITY

There are a number of desiderata of a conception of legitimate political authority that I want to lay out here. First, only a reasonably just state can have legitimate authority. Second, only a state that accords respect to the differing opinions of each citizen can have legitimate authority. Third, a proper conception of legitimate authority must respect the fact that a settled and just legal system is necessary to the establishment of justice among persons. Fourth, the legitimacy of authority is not predicated on a utopian degree of agreement among citizens on the substantive conception of justice that must guide the state's creation of law and policy.

The importance of the first two desiderata can be appreciated from a discussion of two central difficulties with the account of legitimate authority provided by Joseph Raz. The normal justification thesis is the most prominent approach among philosophers; it is usually associated with a kind of instrumentalist approach to political authority. As Joseph Raz puts it:

The normal way to establish that a person has authority over another person involves showing that the alleged subject is likely better to comply with reasons which already independently apply to him if he accepts the directives of the alleged authority as authoritatively binding and tries to follow them, rather than by trying to follow the reasons which apply to him directly.[1]

Authority is legitimate, never because there is anything inherent in the authority that confers this status, but merely to the extent that obeying it brings about better compliance with reasons that are independent of the authority. This is generally thought of as an instrumentalist approach to authority.[2] The reasons that are independent of the authority are thought of in terms of the outcomes of the exercises of authority, which outcomes are valuable however they are brought about. So those who hold to the NJT think that the legitimacy of authority is to be evaluated on the basis of the outcomes of the exercise of authority.[3]

The normal justification thesis is not defensible as a general account of legitimate authority or the authority of states more particularly. There are two main difficulties with this approach that I want to highlight here. The first problem with the normal justification thesis, particularly on its instrumentalist version, is that it divorces the issue of the legitimacy of the authority from the justice of the authority. To see this problem, it is important to see that the authority the thesis justifies is piecemeal. Whether the authority is legitimate varies, depending on the subject and the issues over which it is wielded.[4] The worry is that the instrumentalist and piecemeal nature of authority on this account allows it to attribute legitimate authority to ferociously unjust regimes. It does this because the circumstances that ferociously unjust regimes create often are such that it is better morally speaking to comply regularly with a number of their demands than not. For instance, think of the example of George in Bernard Williams' story of the scientist who is an opponent of Nazism and who is asked to run its laboratory for the making of chemical weapons. George does not think that the Nazis ought to have chemical weapons but he also realizes that many other scientists are willing to advance the Nazi aim of developing them. He believes that if he operates the laboratory, he can slow down its efficiency, say because he is less competent than the others or because he is not enthusiastic.[5] Indeed, let us suppose that George would

---

[1] See Joseph Raz, *The Morality of Freedom*.

[2] It need not imply a commitment to consequentialism however. A legitimate authority, on this account, may enable me to improve my compliance with reasons that derive from deontological considerations.

[3] Leslie Green, *The Authority of the State*, pp. 56–59, gives a qualified endorsement of this approach and Raz, in *The Morality of Freedom*, seems entirely instrumentalist regarding political authority. Let me say now that I do not think that this instrumentalist interpretation of the NJT is necessary. But I do not have time to go into this here.

[4] See Raz, *The Morality of Freedom*, p. 80.

[5] See J. J. C. Smart and Bernard Williams, *Utilitarianism For and Against* (Cambridge: Cambridge University Press).

succeed best at concealing his intentions were he to take the commands as authoritative, and obey the commands regardless of their content and in a way that excludes independent deliberation. So he has reasons for becoming the director of the laboratory and accepting as authoritative the commands of the state so as to remain in charge. In this kind of context, there are cases in which people like George would act rightly if they were to adopt the unsavory role but it is clear to me that the persons who issue the orders that they must take as authoritative are not legitimate authorities. The reason for this is that they are deeply unjust. And yet, the relation between the state and George is a relation of legitimate authority on the normal justification thesis. George does fare better in terms of what he has reason to do by submitting to the directives the authority gives him and not considering their rightness directly.[6]

This is not an unusual case, unjust states often impose odd compromises like this on their subjects. They implicitly threaten morally terrible consequences if their subjects do not comply with commands that require them to participate in evil activities. Sometimes the subjects should resist, but many times the subjects do better by going along. But even if complying without question is the right thing to do, the authority that issues the directives is clearly not legitimate.

This first argument shows that the normal justification thesis does not supply us with normally sufficient conditions for legitimate authority. The problem is that political institutions must have some reasonable degree of justice in order for them to have legitimate authority. Another trouble with the thesis suggests that it is not a necessary condition either.

The legitimate authority of the state, on the NJT, must be based on the prospect that individuals' compliance with morally important reasons would be improved as a result of their acceptance of authority. The trouble with this instrumentalist approach is that it ignores the moral significance of disagreement among equal citizens about the proper organization of their political communities.

Defenders of the normal justification thesis might say that the phenomenon of disagreement just shows that some are wrong about politics. They might insist that people's false political views have no direct relation to what they or we have in fact reason to do.[7] Thus, an entity has authority over me as long as it is right, even if I disagree strongly with what it is telling me to do. Suppose I believe that the state is deeply mistaken about what I ought to do in some sphere of activity and that acceptance of authority in this sphere will lessen

---

[6] For further discussion on this, see Steven Wall, "Democracy, Authority and Publicity," in *Journal of Political Philosophy*, vol. 14, no. 1, pp. 85–100 and my response "Democracy's Authority: Reply to Wall," *Journal of Political Philosophy*, vol. 14, no. 1, pp. 101–110.

[7] See Joseph Raz, "Disagreement in Politics," *American Journal of Jurisprudence*, (43) 25, 1998.

my conformity with reason. The above instrumentalist account suggests that it does not ultimately matter whether that authority has even taken my views into consideration in its decision-making. For instance, I may be the owner of a factory and believe that the state has no right to regulate the conditions of employment in my factory (beyond the provisions of the criminal law). I may believe that state regulation of this aspect of my activities is entirely unjustified; indeed, most people in the society may think this. But let us suppose that those who are in control of the state are correct in their contrary assessment that employment conditions ought to be regulated. It appears, on the instrumentalist account of authority, that the state need not in any way take into account my views of the matter when it authoritatively orders me to put controls on my factory. The state is improving my compliance with reason, by hypothesis, by forcing me to act in accordance with its dictates regardless of what I think.

This indifference to the presence of opposing views in the society is highly problematic. Part of the point of political organization is to make decisions when there are serious disagreements regarding the matters to be decided. And these disagreements take place against the background of the facts of diversity, fallibility, and cognitive bias as well as the interests persons have in judgment that attend these facts. This is what politics is all about. Hence, we need to come to common decisions in the absence of agreement on justice.

Now the theorists, whose standards are used to evaluate the political institutions, are also ordinary persons whose distinctiveness, fallibility, and cognitive bias ensure that their standards are biased toward their own interests. And the same holds for anyone who uses these standards. They are not outside the political system, and they do not occupy a divine standpoint free of the facts of judgment and interests. Their standpoint in the political society carries with it all the frailties and cognitive bias that anyone else's does.

The instrumentalist proposes standards for the evaluation of society, which she expects to be implemented regardless of people's opinions about those standards. She may of course take those opinions into account if they causally help or hinder the realization of her favored standard, but she does not think the differing opinions give any inherent reasons for modifying her favored standards. But someone who proposes standards for the evaluation of political institutions and expects them to be implemented without regard for the judgment of others is somehow placing himself and his judgment above that of others in a way that a parent places her judgment above that of an infant or a god places its judgment over that of a human being. They are in effect asserting a kind of higher level natural authority over others since they expect their standards to be realized regardless of what others in actual political societies think.

But this kind of relation of natural authority does not exist among ordinary sane adults in political societies. All sane adults are situated in the same kinds of limiting conditions with regard to judgment, and all have the same kinds of fundamental interests in having their judgments advanced. The consequence of these points is that to give one person natural authority over others is necessarily to accord their interests greater weight than those of the others, as I argued in Chapter 3.

Since there is no defensible natural authority of some sane adults over others, legitimate political authority must be grounded in part in the fact of disagreement among equals and must respect the judgments of each as an equal. Only in this way can the conception of authority be compatible with the roughly equally situated limitations of each person's cognitive capacities and with the principle that all persons' interests are of equal worth.

To put these points in terms of the conception of publicity defended in Chapter 2, the instrumentalist implicitly assumes that she occupies a kind of distinct and superior standpoint from which to judge political institutions. This is a standpoint that lies outside the normal constraints and problems of human cognitive activity. And from this standpoint, she imposes her favored proposals on others. In fact however, there is no such superior standpoint among sane adult persons. The only standpoint from which we can defensibly assess political authority in a way that treats everyone as an equal is the egalitarian standpoint. This is a standpoint that takes each person's judgment equally seriously and in which each evaluates institutions under the assumption that individuals are all subject more or less equally to the facts of judgment. From this standpoint, we determine what each can see to be treating each as equals and justify authority by this means.

To be sure, once authority is established in a way that treats the judgments of each equally, each may present his or her controversial proposals for consideration within the framework justified from the egalitarian standpoint. The normal justification thesis, assumes, in contrast, that the basic standards for the instrumental evaluation of political institutions are not to be treated as proposals that people offer to each other as equals but rather as special truths that superiors impose on inferiors for their benefit. This, I contend is incompatible with the equality of sane adult persons. And so this conception of authority must be rejected.

There are two lessons from this discussion that are relevant for what follows. One, for a state to be authoritative, it must be reasonably just either in the substance of its laws or in the process by which it makes those laws. Two, an authority that fails to take the points of view of citizens into account runs afoul of powerful considerations of justice even when it acts on the basis of a correct view of what ought to be done.[8]

This latter requirement on a conception of political authority is often taken to be a ground for the consent theory of political authority. According to this theory, the voluntary consent of a person to a putative authority is a necessary condition for that authority over that person to be legitimate. The consent theory is meant to provide a ground of political authority that respects each person as an equal since the authority over that person is legitimate only if that person gives his voluntary consent to it. And consent is a necessary condition of authority regardless of the goodness or justice of the state in question.[9]

The consent theory of political authority falls afoul of the third requirement of a conception of political authority. The third desideratum of a conception of political authority is that it respect the moral necessity of the state. The main purpose of the state, I have argued, is to *establish* justice among persons within a limited jurisdiction. And justice is something we owe to one another on a constant basis. This means that for the most part the legal system of a reasonably just society determines how one is to treat others justly if one is to treat them justly at all. What the state does, if it is reasonably just, is settle what justice consists in by promulgating public rules for the guidance of individual behavior. To say that the state is morally necessary is to say that one cannot act justly within its jurisdiction without complying with the rules it makes just because it has made these rules.

Let us recall the basic arguments for this view. Public rules for the guidance of behavior are important to justice because, first, justice underdetermines what system of rules we must adopt.[10] Many different systems of rules can realize the same principles of justice. To act justly it is essential for us to be on the same page with others, to coordinate with them on the same rules. Since the rules are likely to be quite complex, individuals must take the rule maker to be authoritative in order to act successfully on the basis of the same rules. To take some examples, rules defining property rights, such as when they are acquired, when a voluntary exchange occurs, when exchange is not exploitative, when one person's use of his property imposes too much of an externality on others, and when a person loses his property as a result of lack of use, are all very complex on their own and require that there be public rules.

---

[8] Even if all the above considerations are correct, there may still be a non-instrumental instance of the normal justification thesis that eludes these criticisms. Indeed, the view I defend may come under the thesis. See note 22 below.

[9] See John Simmons, *Justification and Legitimacy: Essays on Rights and Obligations* (Cambridge: Cambridge University Press, 2001) for this kind of view.

[10] As Raz puts it, morality underdetermines the law, in his "On the Authority and Interpretation of Constitutions," in *Constitutionalism: Philosophical Foundations* ed. Larry Alexander (Cambridge: Cambridge University Press, 1998).

If two people act in accordance with different rules specifying these general principles, one will end up treating the other unjustly. Also justice is at least in some significant part concerned with assuring the common good and certain kinds of distributions of power, opportunities, education, and income. The complexity of these rules and the variety of possible rules that could realize the same principles of justice simply make it impossible for people in any even moderately complicated society to be able to have coordinated expectations on them without accepting an authoritative rule maker.

Second people disagree about what justice requires in detail as well as in more basic ways. If they are to act in accordance with their own conceptions of justice, they are likely to treat each other quite badly and to think that the others are treating them badly. This is likely to lead to substantial conflict and is not going to serve the cause of justice. The existence of a public rule maker eliminates much of this source of conflict and thus enhances the ability of each to act justly, as long, to be sure, as the rule maker is reasonably just.

A third reason for having settled public rules that are made by an authoritative rule maker is grounded in the importance of publicity for social justice. To be treated in accordance with the rule of law is a public way of treating a person as an equal. Without public rules and a common authoritative rule maker, the public realization of equality is impossible. Once again, the complexity of rules required for justice and the variety of ways in which justice can be realized make the likelihood of individuals being able to see that they are being treated justly by others nearly zero in many cases of detail without a known and settled system of law. Once there are public rules made by an authoritative source, each person is at least guaranteed a treatment in accordance with commonly accepted rules.

Finally, in addition to the need for an authoritative rule maker, there is a need for a neutral judge to adjudicate cases in which there is conflict about the rules. The judicial institution is necessary for the public realization of equality to the extent that the judicial institution has a chance of dealing with matters in a reasonably impartial way. Without a judicial institution with the power to decide controversies and a police power to enforce these decisions, justice becomes merely the property of the highest bidder or those with the most power. Hence, under these circumstances, the only public way to treat people as equals is to have an authoritative judicial institution backed by police power. But in order for such a judicial power publicly to treat people as equals, there must be settled law in accordance with which it makes its decisions. Hence, we have another argument for having an authoritative rule maker who makes public laws for all.

To say, then, that the state establishes justice among citizens is more than to say that it is engaged in an admirable activity or that it is promoting justice in the same way that some morally admirable nongovernmental organization does.[11] The reasonably just state is engaged in a morally necessary activity in the sense that someone who fails to comply with the reasonably just state's publicly promulgated rules is normally violating a duty of justice to his fellow citizens. For instance, a person who does not believe that he is obligated to obey the state because he has not consented will view others' rights of property as suspect because they are defined by the legal system. Why should he abide by these rules? My claim is that the reason that he ought to abide by these rules in many cases is because this is how the society has resolved a whole variety of disagreements in order to get people to treat each other reasonably well. In contrast, consent theories of political authority suggest that one is permitted to ignore this scheme and disregard the legal rights of others as long as one has not consented to it. But this is surely to condone injustice toward ones fellow citizens. To be sure, the consent theorist can allow that a nonconsenting person ought to respect the property and rights of others to the extent that that person can see that they are morally defensible independent of the state. But this does not provide the kind of assurance that is necessary in a political society where the rights of persons are so deeply determined by the legal system. Though consent seems an appropriate basis for legitimate authority in morally permissible or even admirable associations, it is not the basis of political authority.[12]

The last desideratum of a conception of political authority is that it not rely on a utopian requirement for consensus on political norms.[13] A conception of political authority that relies on consensus on the substantive norms

[11] See John Simmons, *Justification and Legitimacy: Essays on Rights and Obligations* (Cambridge: Cambridge University Press, 2001), p. 153, for a statement of this sort.

[12] An interesting special case of this problem arises when we see what it would take to establish consent as a ground of political obligation. If a state were to try to implement a system of consenting as a condition of legal obligations, it would have to institutionalize that system. That is, it would have legally to define what constitutes valid consent and non-consent and what are the precise implications of these actions. It would have to determine what constitutes voluntary consent under fair conditions and what does not and it would probably have to establish dissenters' colonies to which the non-consenters may go. The system would be presumably quite complex and would have to take into account many complex possibilities; it would be the subject of many disagreements. And this system would have to be established by law. The trouble with this system is that, by the nature of consent theory, its legitimacy would also depend on consent. So even if one could find reasons for thinking that consent is a basis of obligation to the state, the theory would permit people to opt out of the scheme of consenting itself. And of course, this would hold for any method by which the state attempts to publicly regulate the system of consent. The whole system would be, I submit, self-defeating. See Harry Beran, *The Consent Theory of Political Obligation* (London: Croon Helm, 1987) and A. John Simmons, *Justification and Legitimacy: Essays on Rights and Obligations* (Cambridge: Cambridge University Press, 2001) for this suggestion.

[13] See John Rawls, *Political Liberalism* rev. ed. (New York: Columbia University Press, 1996) for a statement of the liberal principle of legitimacy that seems to be committed to a utopian

undergirding law and policy is one that simply cannot apply to societies of diverse human beings with limited and cognitively biased abilities of judgment. This should be obvious at this point. The whole idea behind political authority is to be able to make decisions in the context of serious political disagreements wherein there are deep conflicts of interests.

THREE CONCEPTS OF AUTHORITY

Before I discuss the grounds of the authority of democracy, it is important to make some basic distinctions between concepts of authority. There are three concepts of legitimate political authority: legitimate political authority as justified coercion, legitimate political authority as the capacity to impose duties, and legitimate political authority as the right to rule. The first notion of legitimate authority as justified coercion is a minimal account of authority. The basic idea is that an agent has legitimate authority over other agents with respect to a certain set of issues if the agent is morally justified in coercing the other agents to do what the coercing agent wishes concerning those issues. This concept of authority captures the idea that a state that has legitimate authority may coerce its subjects at least within some range of alternatives. And the concept has an appealing simplicity and straightforwardness to it. And it gets at one of the main worries that people have concerning the state, namely the fact that it coerces its citizens to do things that they may not even agree to.

The second notion of legitimate authority is the capacity to impose duties on the subjects of the authority. The idea is that an agent has legitimate authority over other agents if the agent can impose morally binding duties on those other agents. This gets at the idea that many people think they are obligated to obey the legitimate authority. The existence of the authority and the exercise of authority create duties in the subjects, again at least with respect to a range of issues. The capacity to impose duties does not imply a right on the part of the authority, for the duties may not be owed to the authority. I will call this type of authority *instrumental authority*.

The third notion of legitimate authority is the idea of a right to rule. A robust right to rule is first and foremost a valid claim of the authoritative body against others upon whom certain duties are imposed. The valid claim is correlated with a duty owed to the authority on the part of the subjects of

degree of consensus. I say more about this in Chapter 5 in my criticisms of the principle of reasonableness.

the authority and others not to interfere with the activities of the authority. The valid claim also generates duties in the subjects to comply with these rules and commands of the authority, which obedience they owe to the authority.[14] Authority as a right to rule includes a liberty on the part of the authority to make decisions as it sees fit and it includes a power to impose duties on citizens. This kind of authority will be the focus of much of the discussion that follows, let us call it *inherent authority*.

It is not, I think, a useful aim of philosophers or political thinkers to determine which one of these conceptual accounts of political authority is the right one. Each one of them grasps a kind of legitimacy of political authority that is worth taking into account and distinguishing from the others. The idea of legitimate authority as justified coercive power is a suitable way of getting at the authority of hostile but justified occupation powers. And the idea of legitimate authority as the right to rule over subjects who owe obedience to the authority and that has a right not to be interfered with by foreigners is surely an importantly distinct and ideal type of authority, which is rarely implemented. It is the kind of inherent authority that is realized, I will argue, by a democratic assembly that satisfies the principle of public equality defended in Chapters 2 and 3. The kind of legitimacy that is merely correlated with duties to obey or not to interfere is a useful intermediate category between those two. As we will see, courts and government agencies can hold this instrumental authority.

Two things are worth noting about the idea of the right to rule. One is that intuitively it seems to be the primary notion of legitimacy while the others are dim reflections of this primary notion. To inquire about the legitimacy of an authority is in the first instance to inquire into its right to make decisions for others. The demand for legitimacy arises when an agent has the power to make decisions for others and makes controversial decisions. It is to ask of a person: "who made you the boss?" And if the answer is, "my decisions are morally justified," we are likely to think that our question has not been fully answered. If the answer is, "I am the expert on these matters," we are likely to be more satisfied except in the case of political decisions. In the case of political decisions, which are necessarily controversial, the answer we are looking for is not the justification of the decision or a claim to expertise but rather a valid

---

[14] Strictly speaking, an authority can have a right to rule without the subjects having a duty to comply. The authority may have a "justification" right to rule. This means that the authority has a permission to issue commands and make rules and coerce others to comply and its possession of this right is justified on moral grounds. This "justification right" is not much more than the first notion we discussed above. See Robert Ladenson, "In Defense of a Hobbesian Conception of Law," *Philosophy and Public Affairs*, vol. 9 (1980) for a defense of this kind of account.

claim on us to respect the status of the decision maker even when we disagree with the substance of the decision.

Two, the idea of legitimate authority as a right to rule in the strong sense described above does describe a kind of ideal of political community. The idea of legitimate authority as a right to rule to which citizens owe obedience gives each citizen a moral duty to obey, which it owes to the authority. So this form of legitimacy is grounded in a moral relationship between the parties that goes beyond the fact that they are fellow human beings. The establishment of a robust right to rule depends on the fact that each citizen rightly takes as a reason for obedience that it has a moral duty owed to the authority. Since a legitimate political authority with a right to rule is predicated on the fact that citizens have moral reasons to obey it grounded in its right to rule, the right to rule engages citizens at a deep moral level. The exercise of political power is founded in a moral relationship between moral persons that recognizes and affirms the moral personality of each citizen.

By contrast, a society in which it is *merely* the case that coercion is justified is one in which the subjects are permissibly treated as means to morally defensible purposes. The subjects do not owe anything to the authority or have any duties to obey it. So, in the case of an authority that is merely justified coercion, the subjects' reasons for obedience may merely be their desires to avoid punishment. And that is the level at which the authority deals with them. Such a society does not engage the subjects as moral persons; it merely attempts to administer the activities of persons so as to bring about, in a morally justified way, a desirable outcome. At the extreme, a prisoner of war camp or even a hostile but justified military occupation gives the authorities justification for coercion. The people who are subjected to that treatment may have no duties to obey and they do not regard each other or the authorities as members of a unified political community. Indeed, they may have duties to resist the supposed authority.[15] They are merely fellow human beings. To the extent that a political society is best when it involves the mutual recognition and affirmation of the moral status of each person, the kind of society that involves merely justified coercion of some by others is a pale shadow.

And the intermediate instrumental form of political authority is incomplete in the respect in which the exercise of political power involves the mutual recognition and affirmation of the status of each person. It is the case that subjects have duties but those duties are not essentially connected to anything in the authority. The subjects instead act more in accordance with reasons that

---

[15] As may be the case when one army justly invades territory occupied by another army but where the soldiers of the other army still have duties to obey their commanders.

are independent of the instrumental authority when they obey the authority. The instrumental authority is helping subjects act in accordance with duties they already have but which they cannot be expected to discharge on their own. Hence, there is a vaguely paternalistic character to this kind of authority. As a consequence, the relation between the authority and the subjects need not be a relation among equals. So to the extent that a society ruled by an authority that has the right to rule is an ideal of a moral community, the other types of authority are lesser forms of a morally ideal political community.

As we will see in what follows, democratic authority is a kind of right to rule while the other kinds of authority in a democratic state such as bureaucratic, judicial, and executive authority are essentially kinds of instrumental authority that are grounded in the fact that they are implementing democratically chosen purposes.

WHAT IS THE AUTHORITY OF DEMOCRACY?

One term that surprisingly does not show up in many normative discussions of authority in the modern state is democracy. Indeed, it is striking how rarely discussions of authority turn to democracy as a possible source of authority for the state.[16] First, let us explain what it is and in the next section I will argue that the authority of democracy is grounded in the principle of public equality.

The authority of democracy consists in the right of the democratic assembly to rule by means of law and policy and the duties of citizens to obey the assembly's decisions, which duties are owed to the democratic assembly. It also includes duties on the part of foreigners and foreign powers not to interfere in the rule of the democratic assembly.

The first thing to note is that the authority of democracy consists in the possession of a right by the democratic assembly to make law and policy for the society over which it has jurisdiction. This right is most fundamentally a valid claim, grounded in public equality, to shape the common world of citizens by means of law and policy. It is a claim of the assembly against each citizen and against those who are outside the society. It implies duties on the

---

[16] The term does not show up at all in the index to Christopher Morris's *An Essay on the Modern State* and is used only as part of the general description of many modern states as "liberal democracies." Joseph Raz, in *The Morality of Freedom* (Oxford: Clarendon Press, 1986) Part I, does not entertain the possibility that there might be a special connection between democracy and authority; and Leslie Green does not consider democracy as a source of authority beyond a discussion of the ill-fated consent-based approaches to democracy and authority. For a notable exception to this, see Allen Buchanan, "Democracy and Political Legitimacy," *Ethics* (October 2002).

part of citizens not to interfere with the activity of the assembly and to obey law and policy. It also implies duties on the part of others not to interfere with the legal and policy decisions of the assembly.

This right includes a liberty on the part of the democratic assembly to make law and policy as it sees fit. Of course, this liberty, as we will see in greater detail in the next chapter, is a limited liberty. The liberty holds only within the range specified by the principle of public equality. We have seen that democratic rights are grounded in public equality as are basic liberal rights and we will see that public equality requires that each have an economic minimum with which to exercise their rights and that public equality requires that democratic decision-making not end up by creating permanent minorities within the population of citizens. Within these limits, the democratic assembly has the liberty to choose the legislation and policy.

This right entails a power to create and change the duties and powers of citizens, again within the limits set by public equality. The decisions of the democratic assembly create duties whose contents are specified in the laws and policies of the assembly. And the assembly can alter the duties of citizens by changing and repealing legislation.

If democracy has authority then it implies a duty of citizens to obey the democratic decisions because of their democratic provenance. So the duties of democratic citizens are content independent duties. Citizens have duties to obey democratic decisions not because of the content of the decision or the consequences of their obedience but because of the source of the decision in the democratic assembly. As we will see, this proposition will need to be refined to reflect the underlying grounds for democratic authority and its limits. The more precise statement says that it is because the decision is made by a process that embodies public equality that the decision must be obeyed by citizens.

This duty preempts or at least normally outweighs other duties that democratic citizens have to bring about substantive justice in law and policy. In other words, when the democratic assembly makes a decision about law on the basis of a controversial conception of justice, citizens have duties to go along with the decision even if they think the conception, and therefore the decision, is mistaken. They must put aside their own conception and obey the decision of the assembly. And they are justified in doing this, I say, even if their own conception is in fact superior to the one that is embodied in the content of the democratic decision. Thus the duty to obey is independent of the content of the decision and preempts or normally outweighs other moral duties and considerations.

The content independence and defeating power of duties to obey a democratic assembly has been a source of great puzzlement over the last thirty years as a result of Robert Paul Wolff's defense of philosophical anarchism.[17] The basic question is, how can I have content independent duties in effect to act in accordance with the judgments of other people? How can I ever have a duty to set aside my own conception of what I ought to do in order to act in accordance with what someone else tells me to do merely because that other person has told me to do it? Do I not have a duty to follow my own judgment whenever it conflicts with that of another? One advantage of grounding the authority of democracy on the principle of public equality is that we can answer this question in a clear and compelling way, or so I will argue in the next section.

To be sure, the right of the assembly to rule and the correlative duties obtain only when the democratic assembly makes decisions within a well-defined scope. If the democratic assembly makes decisions that violate the fundamental democratic and liberal rights of persons then, in that instance, the assembly does not have authority. If the assembly fails to ensure the right of each person to a decent economic minimum or becomes captured by a solid majority block, thereby producing permanent minorities, this significantly weakens the authority of the democratic assembly. In other words, if the democratic assembly violates the principle of public equality in its decisions or fails to uphold it, then its authority is significantly weakened and, in some cases, particular decisions have no authority at all. I will discuss these limitations in the next chapter.

I need to explain the idea of the democratic assembly in this formulation of the authority of democracy. First of all, I refer only to legislative authority here. Legislative authority is the most fundamental kind of authority in a democratic state and legislative authority is the authority that must be democratic. The fundamental importance of legislative authority is grounded in the fact that a just society must accord with the rule of law. Law is the most fundamental instrument by which a society that accords with public equality is shaped. The principle of the rule of law is itself grounded, as we saw in the previous chapters, in the principle of public equality.

There are, of course, other kinds of authority in the state such as judicial authority, executive authority, and administrative authority. All of these are essential in a large state and my argument here does not discuss them. We will discuss the instrumental authority of government agencies and courts when we discuss those institutions of the state that are subordinate to the democratic assembly later in the chapter.

Why focus on the democratic assembly and not the people? There are two reasons for this. First, we are concerned here with the people as a unified

---

[17] See Robert Paul Wolff, *In Defense of Anarchism* (New York: Harper and Row, 1970).

body politic. What has authority in a democratic society are not individuals considered separately but all the citizens assembled together in a body politic. Second, we are concerned with the body politic as a decision maker for the society. In order to bring about these two properties we need a kind of artificial union of all citizens since there is no natural union of citizens. And we need an artificial method for making collective decisions since there is no natural decision-making for a group of citizens. So we need a set of institutions that constitutes a unified body politic that can make collective decisions.

A properly constituted democratic assembly is the institutional embodiment of the unified body of the people as a collective decision maker in a political society. In a direct democracy, a properly constituted democratic assembly is the union of all the citizens who have chosen to participate and an egalitarian system of collective decision-making for that union. As part of that system of decision-making there must be an egalitarian process of discussion and deliberation and there must be a set of rules for decision-making. In the modern state, direct democracy is neither an efficient form of decision-making nor is it an egalitarian form of decision-making. I will focus instead on collective decision-making in a representative democracy.

In a representative democracy, to say that the democratic assembly is properly constituted implies that the representatives in the assembly have been elected in the proper way in a process of election that includes all sane permanent adult residents of the society. It also implies that the assembly represents citizens equally and properly. This means that the assembly represents the different aims the citizens have chosen for the society in a manner that is proportional to the amount of support those aims have in the society. To be sure, the distribution of support must result from a process in which people have had the opportunities to inform themselves about and think through the various alternatives that a fair process of discussion has offered.

Ideally, a properly constituted democratic assembly will require a system of party list proportional representation coupled with an egalitarian system of financing of political parties and an egalitarian process of discussion among the different interest groups and pressure groups in the society. The task of the democratic assembly is to take the different proportionally represented aims and find means for making compromises among those aims as well as determine ways in which to implement the aims in law and policy. The representatives are essentially delegates of citizens with regard to the aims the citizens choose and trustees with regard to the means of realizing those aims.[18]

---

[18] I have defended these ideas at length in my *The Rule of the Many* (Boulder, CO: Westview Press, 1996), chapters 6–8. For a subtle and in-depth treatment of the relation between legislature and bureaucracy that is mostly friendly to my approach, see Henry Richardson, *Democratic Autonomy* (Oxford: Oxford University Press, 2003).

A properly constituted democratic assembly provides the embodiment of the diverse array of views the citizens have regarding how best to organize the society and it transforms this diverse array into decisions on law and policy.

The right of the democratic assembly is not grounded in an organic conception of society or of its interests; it is grounded in the individual rights of all the citizens. The democratic assembly pools the equal political rights of all the citizens into one decision-making body. This must be so for two reasons. One, it is only when a properly constituted democratic assembly makes decisions that the citizens' equal political rights in collective decision-making are exercised in a publicly clear way. Two, the democratic assembly embodies the whole of the people in the sense that it represents views in proportion to the support citizens have chosen to give those views in a proper system of election and deliberation. In this way, it ensures the equality of citizens' input in the making of law and policy. Hence only through the decision-making of the democratic assembly can citizens' political rights be finally exercised and only through such a system can these rights be equally exercised.

On the first point, the citizens' equal political rights are not exercised merely in the processes of elections and discussion. Voting for representatives and talking as equals are not the final ends of political equality. Only if those processes ensure an equal say over how the society is actually organized can the citizens be said to have an equal say. This implies that only if the voting and discussing are parts of a process that is structured to give citizens an equal say over the society as a whole can the citizens be said to have an equal say. So, only if the equal political rights are embodied in the democratic assembly do citizens actually have an equal say.

To appreciate this notice that the relation of citizens to the democratic assembly is in significant part like the relation between a driver and the properly functioning motor and steering mechanism of an automobile. Just as turning the wheel and pushing a pedal are not the final aims of the motorist, so voting and discussion are not the final ends of the citizen. Just as the properly functioning motor and parts of the automobile are necessary to translate the turning of the wheel and pushing of the pedal into the desired motion of the car, so the democratic assembly is necessary to translate the chosen aims of the citizens into actual law and policy. In one case, the point is to drive the car; in the other case the point is to exercise equal control over the shared world.

On the second point, the equal political rights of citizens can be exercised only when they are exercised together in a unified process that gives them equal weight. The democratic assembly is more than a mere tool for the citizens. Because it represents views in proportion to the amount citizens have chosen to support those views, the assembly, when it is properly constituted, actually embodies the full array of positions that the citizens have chosen to support. And thus it embodies the equality of political rights of citizens. The properly constituted assembly embodies the chosen aims of citizens so that it is possible to engage in a rational and orderly decision process about what finally to do. It enables legislators to come up with rational compromises among the different views that reflect the relative strengths of the views in society at large. And it does this in a way that publicly treats each citizen as an equal.

So, the activity of the democratic assembly, when properly constituted, is the necessary and final moment in the exercise of the political rights of citizens and it embodies the equality of the political rights of citizens. In this way, the equal political rights of citizens must be pooled together in a collective decision-making body that gives each person's vote equal weight. This is a conceptual requirement for equal political rights. Citizens logically cannot have equal political rights unless they are ultimately pooled into an assembly that makes decisions. This is why the ultimate implication of the equal political rights of citizens is the right of the democratic assembly to rule.

One final point, the democratic assembly pools all the political rights of all the citizens even though the assembly does not contain all the citizens. This is because the citizens determine what the assembly aims at by choosing the basic overall aims of the assembly. This is the contribution the citizens make to democracy in virtue of which they are the ultimate source of authority in a democratic society. To the extent that the chosen overall aims of the citizens are properly and proportionally represented in the assembly, the citizens determine the most important element of what the assembly decides.

So if the democratic assembly is properly constituted, it genuinely embodies the people as a decision-making body and it pools all the equal rights of citizens into the assembly. The democratic assembly then stands for the citizenry as a whole and represents it. As a consequence, the actions of the democratic assembly are the pooled exercises of the political rights of all the citizens. So because all citizens have rights to an equal say and because the democratic assembly is the institutional method by which these equal political rights are exercised, the democratic assembly has a right to rule.

In addition, the legitimate authority of democracy implies that democratic societies have a right not be interfered with by other societies or persons outside the society. The distinction between a duty not to interfere and a duty to comply comes in handy when we consider the difference between the duties owed to a legitimate political authority by the subjects of that authority and the duties owed to it by other states and persons who are not subject to that authority. A state with a right to rule in the strongest sense may be owed obedience by its subjects, but it is usually owed only a duty of noninterference by those who are not a part of the state such as other states and persons in other states. It is worthwhile drawing a distinction here between internal legitimacy and external legitimacy.[19] It has a right that its domestic affairs not be interfered with by means of military force, economic and political sanctions, and other coercive methods.[20]

This external right is limited as well. First, if a democratic society goes on an aggressive war against another society, it does not have a right against that society to noninterference with its military activity. And if a democratic society is a constant and serious threat to another society, it may lose some of its rights to control its domestic affairs. Finally if the democratic society engages in constant and widespread violations of the fundamental rights of many of its citizens, it loses much of its immunity to external sanction; in this case it loses much of its internal legitimacy as well.

WHAT ARE THE GROUNDS OF THE AUTHORITY OF DEMOCRACY?

The argument for the authority of democracy must proceed in two steps. The first step is to show why the democratic assembly has a right to rule that correlates with the duties of citizens to obey. The second step is to show that the duty to obey is preemptive or at least especially weighty.

The first step of the argument is essentially achieved by recalling the arguments of Chapters 1 and 2. Each human being has a fundamental and natural duty to treat other human beings as equals and this implies that each person must try to realize the equal advancement of the interests of other human beings. But this duty is only fully realized among persons when each person attempts to treat others publicly as equals. Hence, each has a duty to attempt to bring about, and to conform his actions to, those institutions that publicly realize the equal advancement of interests. I have argued that democracy and liberal rights are necessary to the public realization of equal advancement of interests. So each citizen has a duty to bring about democratic institutions and to comply with those democratic institutions when they are realized at least as long as those institutions do not themselves violate public equality.

---

[19] See Allen Buchanan, *Justice, Legitimacy and Self-Determination* (Oxford: Oxford University Press, 2003) for the most important philosophical work to date on issues of legitimacy of states within the international system of states.

[20] Here is another place where the idea of political legitimacy as justified coercion is clearly defective. It cannot account for the right of the democratic society not to be interfered with. Indeed, as I have pointed out above, it is possible for one group of person to interfere justifiably with the justified activities of another group and so justified coercion establishes no right at all of the kind we intuitively attribute to democratic societies at least with respect to their domestic affairs.

Notice that each has a duty to comply with their own democratic institutions since these institutions are necessary to treating their fellows publicly as equals. The duty to treat people as equals is not fully discharged by trying to support the construction of democracy in other parts of the world. If one only did this and failed to act in accordance with a reasonably well-constituted democratic order, then one would be treating one's fellows publicly as inferiors. And this would be a very weighty violation of equality.[21]

This duty is correlated with the right of each citizen to an equal say. So each person has a duty to each other citizen to afford them a right to an equal say and to respect that equal say. But the political rights of all citizens are pooled in the decision-making activities of the democratic assembly. So the duty to comply with democratic institutions is correlated with the right of the democratic assembly to rule. And since this duty is owed to each citizen and the democratic assembly embodies the equal political rights of all citizens, the duty is owed to the democratic assembly.

The citizens' duties to the democratic assembly are, within certain scope limitations defined by public equality, duties to do whatever the democratic assembly tells them to do. Thus the duties are independent of the content of the democratic assembly's directive. The duties derive entirely from the fact that the democratic assembly has a right to tell them what to do. Hence the democratic assembly has a right to do wrong, within certain limitations.

Democratic decision-making is a publicly just and fair way of making collective decisions in light of conflicts of interests and disagreements about shared aspects of social life. Citizens who skirt democratically made law act contrary to the equal right of all citizens to have a say in making laws when there is substantial and informed disagreement. Those who refuse to pay taxes or who refuse to respect property laws on the grounds that these are unjust are simply affirming a superior right to that of others in determining how the shared aspects of social life ought to be arranged. Thus, they act unjustly and violate the duty to treat others publicly as equals.

The second step of the argument attempts to show that the right of the democratic assembly to rule grounds an especially weighty duty on the part of the citizens to obey and perhaps even a preemptive duty to obey.

Democratic equality has precedence over the other forms of equality that are in dispute in a political society, within the limits defined by public equality. The reason for this is because of its public nature. Public equality trumps other egalitarian considerations. So when there is a disagreement on what equality requires in substantive legislation and the process for resolving the

---

[21] Hence the view on offer of the authority of democracy satisfies what A. John Simmons calls the "particularity requirement," in *Moral Principles and Political Obligations* (Princeton, NJ: Princeton University Press, 1980).

disagreement is a publicly egalitarian one, then even if the equality chosen for the substantive legislation is mistaken in some way, those who see that it is wrong still have a duty to go along with the decision. They have this duty because the first duty of equality is to treat persons publicly as equals.

Of course, in the democratic forum and so within the limits defined by public equality, individuals will argue for more particular conceptions of equality, which they can see others reasonably disagree on. It is legitimate for them to argue for these contentious conceptions of equality and the implications they have for policy. It is even legitimate for them to try to put together majorities to decide in favor of this legislation by democratic means. And legislation that is contentious but nevertheless chosen by democratic means is for that reason legitimate. So if the legislation is passed then every member of the society has a duty to comply with the legislation grounded in public equality. Each person owes this compliance to the assembly, which pools the rights to public equality of all members.

Recall that the reason why the publicity of this equality carries so much weight is because of the importance of the interests that are involved in publicity. The interests in being publicly treated as an equal member of a society are the *pre-eminent* interests a person has where there is disagreement, fallibility, diversity, and cognitive bias in the process of establishing justice in society. The interests in public equality are pre-eminent for three main reasons.

First, the interests have great importance for each person in a political environment. The interest in being able to correct for the cognitive biases of others in the process of establishing the rules of social life is a fundamental bulwark against being dominated by those others. The interest in being at home in one's society is fundamental to one's capacity to advance one's well-being in the society. It is the pre-condition for the general advancement of one's interests in society. And when the establishment of justice in society is at stake and the basic rules of social life are at stake, what is necessary to making that world a home is absolutely fundamental to one's well-being. The interest in knowing that others recognize and affirm one as a person whose interests matter and matter equally among persons is of great importance especially when disagreement, diversity, and cognitive bias play such a large role in social life.

Second, public equality satisfies these interests in a way that is compatible with equality. We have seen how the interests themselves are conditioned by equality. For instance, the interest in being at home in the world is only realized when one is at home in an egalitarian world. The interest in being recognized and affirmed as an equal is straightforwardly egalitarian.

Third, these interests harmonize with the other fundamental interests a person has. These interests do not normally conflict with other fundamental interests. This is because one cannot be at home in a society that treats one clearly as an inferior either in body or in mind. One cannot be treated as an equal member in a society where one's basic interests in liberty, security, and material well-being are fundamentally threatened. I shall argue this more in the chapter on the limits of democratic authority. The last two points guarantee that these interests and the public equality that rests on them are not overridden by other moral concerns. It is for these reasons that the most basic terms of political association are to be justified by reference to the egalitarian standpoint and all political contention is to be set within the framework regulated by public equality.

And democracy realizes public equality in collective decision-making because it advances the fundamental interests of persons in political environments in a publicly egalitarian way. Each person can see that they have fundamental interests in correcting for cognitive bias, in being at home in the world, in learning about their interests and the common good as well as in being recognized and affirmed as an equal. And each can see that these fundamental interests are advanced by democratic institutions in a reasonably egalitarian way in the circumstances characterized by the facts of judgment and where people make competing claims to shape the common world. And given the facts of judgment, other forms of equality are not public forms of equality. So democracy constitutes a unique public realization of equality in collective decision-making.[22]

If these claims are right then only by obeying the democratically made choices can citizens act justly. Democratic directives give content independent reasons since one must accept a democratic decision as binding even when one disagrees with it. And the directives give pre-emptive or at least especially weighty reasons since they derive from a source that is meant to replace or at least override the reasons that apply directly to the situation at hand. But what is striking is that the democratic assembly has a right to rule since one treats its members unjustly if one ignores or skirts its decisions. Each citizen has a right to one's obedience and therefore the assembly as a whole has a right to one's obedience.[23]

---

[22] It is worth noting here that Raz's normal justification thesis could conceivably accommodate this conception of democratic authority. For one might say that one acts better in accordance with the principle of equality by deferring to the decision of the democratic assembly than by trying to advance equality on one's own. This would be a non-instrumental use of the normal justification thesis. I thank Joseph Raz and Matthew Clayton for suggesting this to me.

[23] Note here that democracy is not an absolutely necessary condition on the authoritativeness of political decision making. It is possible for a monarchy to issue legitimate authoritative commands on the grounds that its decisions are just. Of course, the justice of this method of decision making will be highly attenuated because the justice of the outcomes is not public. But we do not have to think that the outcomes are not just at all. But this authoritativeness will be piecemeal, and it carries no implication of a right to rule. It merely implies that subjects have reason to go along with some of the classes of commands if they are generally just.

Someone who refuses to obey the democratic assembly on the grounds that it has passed controversial legislation with which he disagrees cannot deflect the charge of treating people publicly as inferiors by some alternative action. For example, he cannot deflect the charge by trying to treat people in accordance with his own favored conception of substantive justice. This is because that conception is controversial and within the bounds of reasonable disagreement and so the imposition of his view on others constitutes a form of inequality against the background facts of diversity, disagreement, fallibility, and cognitive bias and the interests associated with these.

The principle of public equality also grounds the right of a democratic society to be free from military, economic, or political interference in its domestic affairs. To the extent that the democratic assembly pools all the political rights of all of its members, when an external society attempts coercively to interfere (by means of military force, or economic or political sanctions) for the purpose of altering the domestic laws and policy of a society, the members of the external society treat the members of the imposed upon democratic society publicly as inferiors. Naturally, this rationale does not immunize all the foreign policy activities of a democratic society. Nor does it immunize a democratic society that has engaged in severe and widespread violations of the fundamental rights of its citizens.

Someone might object that it is possible for the person who disobeys or tries unilaterally to change the democratic choice to say to everyone that they may all disobey the democratically chosen rule or try to bring about changes nondemocratically when they think the results are unjust. This might seem like it is compatible with equality, since the dissenter is affording the same rights of disobedience or unilateral change to everyone.[24]

But in fact, universal rights of disobedience are not compatible with equality properly understood. This kind of open and general permission to disobey when one disagrees is incompatible with a collective decision procedure. Given the pervasiveness of disagreement about justice every minority would be allowed to disobey or find some nondemocratic means for changing the outcome. But this would be incompatible with there being collective decision-making at all. So how is this incompatible with equality? There are two reasons. First, I argued in Chapter 1 that the proper principle of equality does not allow leveling down for the sake of equality. Pareto superior inequalities are more just than Pareto inferior equalities. Now the assumption I have been operating under is that limited collective decision-making is Pareto superior to complete or near complete decentralization. It enables people to take genuine control of the common world they live in and thus shape that

---

[24] I thank David Estlund for pressing me on this objection.

world to advance their interests as well as justice and the common good. Complete decentralization would undermine the ability to pursue justice and the common good as well as their interests. So even if the rule of general disobedience were egalitarian in the sense that everyone could equally partake of it, it would still be problematic from the point of the principle of equality I have defended in this book because it would be Pareto inferior to collective decision-making.

Second, I have argued that the decentralized world that results from the universal disobedience rule would not be very egalitarian. It would be dominated by some social forces to the exclusion of others. It would bring about publicly clear inequalities. I presented an argument for this in more detail in Chapter 3 when I considered the objection that decentralization is a better way of achieving equality than democratic equality.

So this person cannot deflect the charge by permitting everyone else to do the same as he. For this cannot possibly guarantee the public realization of equality. Such a system would undoubtedly be subject to the unregulated vagaries of shifting social power and would also essentially take away the power of citizens to exercise control over their society in an orderly and rational way. It is precisely these problems that a democratic assembly is meant to avoid. It is meant to provide for a highly regulated and efficient method for collective decision-making that embodies the equal political rights of all citizens.

The present argument allows us to see why the threat of philosophical anarchism is defeated. The first part of the argument shows that a conscientious person can see that her duty is to treat others publicly as equals and that failing to obey the democratic decision is a violation of that duty. The basic idea then is that one owes it to others, by virtue of the principle of equality and the fundamental interests of each in having her judgment about justice accorded respect, to comply with the decision of the majority about how to establish justice.

The second step of the argument shows that the duty to treat others as equals by respecting and obeying the democratic decisions pre-empts or at least normally outweighs the other duties a citizen has. It does this because the duty is grounded in public equality while the others are merely grounded in equality and because the duties of equality precede all other duties. The pre-emption occurs because it is precisely in the context of disagreement on the substantive requirements of equality for law and policy that the principle of public equality requires democratic decision-making. The principle of public equality then directs us to subordinate one's conception of equality and its implications for law and policy to democratic equality. So once a democratic decision has been made that does not violate public equality one must act on the basis of the decision and put aside one's own particular conception of equality at least as a guide to action. Of course one retains the right to try to change law democratically in accordance with one's conception of equality.

To be sure, the present argument does not give general grounds for a duty to obey the law. The laws of nondemocratic societies or highly defective democratic societies do not acquire legitimacy from this account. It does not even give completely grounds for a general duty to obey democratically made law. It gives sufficient grounds for the duty to obey democratically made law as long as it does not violate public equality.

It is worthwhile here to note how the conception of democratic authority manages to satisfy the four requirements on a conception of political authority that we enumerated at the beginning of this chapter. First, since the right to an equal say is a requirement of public equality and is engaged when there is reasonable disagreement about justice, the conception of democratic authority is consistent with the idea that only a reasonably just society can have government with legitimate authority. Second, the democratic assembly embodies the equal respect owed to each citizen in the process of decision-making by giving each citizen an equal say in the decision-making. Third, the democratic conception of authority respects the idea that a settled and just legal system is necessary to the establishment of justice among persons. It sets out a clear way in which citizens can treat each other as equals in a publicly clear way. Fourth, the democratic conception of authority does not rely on a utopian extent of agreement among citizens on the substantive conception of justice that must guide the state's creation of law and policy. Indeed, the democratic idea of authority is premised precisely on the facts of disagreement, diversity, fallibility, and cognitive bias and constitutes an egalitarian response to these facts and the fundamental interests that are connected to these facts.

DEMOCRACY AND THE COMPLEXITY OF AUTHORITY

There are many different sources of authority and different kinds of authority in a modern democratic state. It is important to note these differences of kind and function in order to understand political authority. As Christopher Morris argues, the state has rarely even approximated the unity that Hobbes suggested it should have. Just to list some of the different kinds of authority that exist within a normal state, there is to start with, some kind of constituent authority of those who make and ratify the constitution of the political society. In many political societies, this function is carried out by a distinct body which has unique authority over these questions and no authority over any other questions. The legislature has authority to make laws and define aims for the rest of the society as well as raise taxes and appropriate monies. These types of authority are not shared among the possessors; the legislature has authority that the constituent assembly does not have. In addition, those who execute the laws and set policies in order to carry out the law also have a distinctive authority. Though the legislature makes the law, and can define the basic framework of the executive branch, once that branch has its power defined, its job is to determine how to execute the laws according to its own best judgment. To be sure, the legislature can undercut any particular executive action by remaking the law the executive is supposed to execute. The executive branches of complex states include administrative agencies which also have limited authority of their own although they are ultimately under the control of the executive and their mandate derives from the legislature. They have limited authority to make decisions within the mandate defined for them by the legislature and the constraints of the executive. Of course, the judiciary has independent authority in all modern states and it makes a variety of decisions that are authoritative. Finally, there may be independent agencies that derive their mandate from the legislative but that have independent powers such as the central banks in most modern states.

The point of all this is to show that the authority of the state is quite a complex matter since there is usually a very complex division of authority. Is there any hierarchical structure to this? There is no hierarchical structure in the Hobbesian sense of a top down structure where the commands at the top are merely carried out by underlings. But there is a sense in which once the constitution has been put in place, the authority of the legislature has a certain primacy over the others. And this combination of complexity and partial hierarchy is what makes for complexity in authority in the state. On the one hand, one has good reason grounded in considerations of democracy to comply with the choices of a democratic legislature. On the other hand, one can see that the choices of a democratic legislature are not always properly followed through by the other branches of the state. And for the most part, the directives that one must obey are not directly from the legislature but from an agency claiming to carry out the will of the legislature. They usually issue from an executive agency or from a court. Usually when one asks whether one ought to obey a directive of the state, a number of layers of authority are at issue.

To what extent do the democratic credentials of a directive give us reason to obey it even when we are not sure that the directive, issued from a subordinate authority, is faithful to the democratic choice? One might think at first that the answer is that it provides no reason whatsoever since the basis of the authority is the democratic choice. But this would be too quick. If we take into account the fact that a separation of the parts of the state is necessary to the well functioning of any of the parts, then it may be that despite the fact that a state may sometimes issue directives unfaithful to their initial democratic provenance, one remains most faithful to democratic principles by acting in accordance with the directive.

Here is the argument. Democratic decision-making must in any large state be characterized by a division of labor in the process of decision-making. This is for various reasons. First, in order for the democratic decision to be made reasonably impartial, it is best for it to be made by persons other than those who apply it. Thus there ought to be a division between those who make and those who apply the law. This idea applies both to courts and to executive functions.[25] Second, the complexity of decisions requires that different aspects of decisions be divided up and given to different deciders. Hence, it makes sense for a democratic legislature to determine broad aims and principles that are to be applied with the help of a fuller knowledge of facts by various agencies and courts that can specialize in fact finding as well as in the sciences appropriate to a field of decisions. To eliminate such a division of labor would amount to undermining the ability of the legislature to make democratic decisions by imposing impossible demands on it as well as by setting up problematic incentives. Setting up this division of labor is necessary for a democratic process to work.[26] Assuming that the state we are dealing with is reasonably just and efficient in this context implies that the various subordinate decision-making parts of the state are carrying out their duties in good faith and with reasonable competence. In other words, making complex decisions by this means represents the best that a democratic society can do by way of just political decision-making. Now think of the fact that it is often hard to see how one can better carry out the mandate of a democratic legislature by acting in ways that are independent of the authorities who are meant to carry out its decisions. In some cases, it may be true that one can do better. These are the kinds of individualistic cases mentioned above wherein what one person does does not undermine the ability of others to carry out the democratic choice.

In effect, this means that the authority of government agencies charged with the tasks of finding ways of specifying and achieving the aims of the democratic assembly is essentially an instrumental authority. The same can

---

[25] See John Locke, *Second Treatise on Government*, for this defense of the separation between legislative and executive branches of government.

[26] I defend this account of the division of labor in the democratic state in great detail in *my The Rule of the Many*, chapter 5. For a further insight into the division of labor, see Henry Richardson's *Democratic Autonomy* (Oxford: Oxford University Press, 2003). In addition to applying the aims and determining the means to the aims of the democratic assembly, Richardson argues that the agencies must specify the aims of the democratic assembly.

be said I think of courts in a democratic society. They are meant primarily to serve the aims of the democratic assembly and to protect the realization of public equality. To the extent that they depart from these aims or significantly change them through interpretation, these branches fail in their duties to serve the democratic assembly.

To say that the authority of agencies is essentially instrumental is to imply that it is not to them that one owes obedience. Their activities enable citizens to discharge their duties of obedience to the democratic assembly. Citizens, in general, do best with regard to these duties, by treating the directives of the agencies and courts as giving them content independent and preemptive duties to act. Of course, there are times even under the best of circumstances when these agencies will fail. But if agencies are reasonably well constrained by the democratic process and they are properly monitored by the various groups in civil society as well as the democratic assembly, agencies are more likely to provide citizens with the right guidance as to how to satisfy the aims of the democratic assembly than the citizens can come up with on their own. And citizens will do best in general by treating the directives of agencies as authoritative.

These remarks are tentative and surely too crude a response to the challenge posed by the complexity of authority in modern democratic states. My suspicion is that the challenge cannot be completely answered and that the authority of democratic states is necessarily gappy on account of their complexity. For these reasons, I am compelled to accept the legitimacy of some of the skepticism many authors have expressed about the authority of democratic states.[27]

There is one institution of many modern democratic states that cannot be justified in the way I described above for agencies and ordinary courts. Constitutional courts with the power to review and strike down legislation, whether on appeal or during the process of passing the legislation, have a problematic kind of authority. They actually strike down the legislation of the democratic assembly, thereby rejecting the authority of the democratic assembly. The authority is problematic because it seems to violate public equality. When it strikes down the legislation of a democratic assembly, it acts contrary to public equality since it rejects the outcome of the process that is grounded in public equality. In a sense, it denies the right of the people to determine, as equals, the terms of association for themselves. Yet I say that the authority is problematic

---

[27] For extreme forms of skepticism about the authority of modern democratic states, see F. H. Hayek, *The Constitution of Liberty* (Chicago: University of Chicago Press, 1960) and more recently Danilo Zolo, *Democracy and Complexity* (University Park: Penn State Press, 1993).

and not merely illegitimate because there are circumstances in which it may be justified, or so I will argue in the next chapter. It may be justified when the democratic assembly acts beyond the limits of its authority or acts in such a way as to weaken its own authority by violating or failing to support public equality. In these circumstances, if such a court upholds the public equality that the democratic assembly is grounded in the court may have a limited though problematic authority. These issues are the subject of the next chapter.

7

The Limits to Democratic Authority

So far I have argued that democratic and liberal rights are underwritten by the principle of public equality. I have also argued that democratic decisions are authoritative in matters of substantive law and policy. The question I wish to address now is when do considerations of justice or injustice in the outcome override or defeat or in some way undermine the authority of the democratic assembly? We have seen that in the normal case, the democratic assembly has authority with respect to civil and economic rights. But it seems clear that the authority of the democratic assembly is problematic at least in cases of gross injustice. For example, we cannot countenance a democratic choice to introduce slavery for those who are among the minority. Surely this violation must be serious enough to override or defeat the authority of democracy. My answer to this question is that there are reasonably clear limits to the authority of democracy and they can be derived from the same principle of public equality that underlies democratic authority.

In this chapter, I give an account of the limits to democratic authority. First, I show how the basic democratic and liberal rights provide limits to the authority of the democratic assembly. Second, I argue that the provision of an economic minimum is necessary to public equality and that therefore a democratic assembly that does not do what it can to provide this thereby weakens its own authority. Third, I discuss the thesis that the democratic assembly ought to be constrained by a constitutional court with powers of review of legislation. I show how the principle of public equality can provide guidance as to when this kind of judicial review can be justified and when it is not. Fourth, I show how the conception of democracy as grounded in public equality implies that a democratic assembly that generates permanent minorities has its authority weakened.

Let us start with some intuitive cases of limits to democratic authority. First, it seems clear that the democratic assembly does not have the right to take away the democratic rights of the any part of the democratic assembly. It does not have the right to disenfranchise any citizens in the democratic assembly (except perhaps in the case of punishment). Second, it seems intuitively clear that the democratic assembly does not have the right to take away at least the cores of the liberal rights of any members of the democratic assembly (except perhaps as part of a punishment for crimes). So the democratic assembly does not have the right to take away the rights to freedom of expression, association, private pursuits, or conscience from any person or group in the assembly. Furthermore, I think it is intuitive that the right of the democratic assembly to choose is significantly weakened when a permanent majority has taken over the assembly and some minorities are permanently unable to have their way in the democratic assembly.

These limits to the authority of the democratic assembly are intuitive I think. But they can also be shown to follow from the conception of democratic authority that I have defended, or so I shall argue in what follows. I will argue for an additional limitation on democratic authority as well, which may not be quite as intuitive for many as the above limits. I will argue that the authority of the democratic assembly is significantly weakened when it acts in such a way as to fail to ensure that individual members of the society have a decent economic minimum with which to live their lives and participate in politics. I will show how this account of the decent economic minimum follows from the conceptions of democratic and liberal rights I have outlined and with the idea that these rights ground limits to democratic authority.

THE NATURE OF THE LIMITS TO DEMOCRATIC AUTHORITY

Let us recall that the authority of the democratic assembly is a right of that democratic assembly to rule. This means that the democratic assembly has the right to tell its members what to do and they have duties, owed to it, to obey the decision. The fact that a decision has been made democratically provides a very weighty consideration in favor of each member obeying that decision. And the weight of the consideration is grounded in the preeminent importance of the fact that the democratic assembly embodies public equality in its actions. This is what gives the democratic assembly the right to be obeyed. Decisions made in the democratic assembly carry all the weight that the principle of public equality offers.

In this chapter, I give an account of the nature and basis of the limits of democratic authority. To be clear about this idea of the limits of democratic authority it will be important to make some distinctions. A limit to democratic authority is a principle violation of which defeats the authority of the democratic assembly. First, I want to distinguish some different kinds of limits. One, there are considerations that count against obedience to the democratic decision. These are considerations that can be put in the balance with the weighty considerations that ground the duty of obedience. In some instances, these considerations are outweighed by the considerations that favor obedience and in other instances they override the considerations that favor obedience. Let us call this a *countervailing consideration* against democratic authority.

A different kind of limiting consideration I will call an *undercutting consideration* against democratic authority.[1] This kind of limit does not merely provide a consideration that can be weighed in the balance against considerations that favor obedience. This limiting consideration actually undercuts the claim to authority that the democratic assembly makes. In the case of this kind of limiting consideration, what happens is not that some consideration against obedience is advanced but that the authority of the democratic assembly is shown either to be significantly weakened or not to exist in the case at hand. The undercutting limit is much deeper than the countervailing kind of limit I described before. I will show in what follows that there is a set of very important undercutting limits to democratic authority. And this set of undercutting limits is made possible by the fact that the considerations involved are the same kinds of considerations that underwrite democratic authority.

It is also worthwhile to classify limits to democratic authority in terms of the basis of the limits. Some theorists have argued that there are *external* limits to democratic authority. This means that there are considerations that are independent of the grounds of democratic authority and of the operation of democratic authority, which provide limits to the authority. Some have thought that natural rights provide external limits to democratic authority in a way that grounds the basic liberal rights.

I do think that there are external limits to democratic authority but they will tend to fall outside the scope of this book. The external limits to democratic authority arise in cases where the democratic authority makes decisions about how to treat persons who are not part of the society over which the assembly has a right to rule. They also tend to be countervailing considerations. So, there may be considerations having to do with the correct decision about when to go to war against another state or how to conduct that war that may sometimes provide weighty reasons not to obey the democratic assembly. The reasons to obey the democratic assembly have to do with treating one's fellow citizens as equals. And there may be legitimate disagreement among

---

[1] I am borrowing the concepts "countervailing" and "undercutting" from John Pollock's, *Contemporary Theories of Knowledge* (Savage, MD: Rowman and Littlefield, 1986). A rebutting defeater (which is parallel to what I call a countervailing consideration) in epistemology is a consideration against believing a conclusion. An undercutting defeater is a consideration that undermines the reasons for believing a conclusion. The parallel here is that a rebutting limit to democratic authority is a consideration against obedience while an undercutting limit is a consideration that defeats the authority to make the decision in the first place.

citizens about the proper conduct of foreign affairs. But since there are persons affected by these decisions who have no say in the decision or have no trustee making the decision for them, sometimes considerations as to how to treat these persons will simply be external to the considerations that underpin democratic authority. But this takes us into the arena of international relations and the justice of relations among citizens of different states. This is obviously an important topic and no discussion of democracy can be complete without a thorough treatment of these issues but it must be seen as beyond the scope of this book.

A very different but common way of trying to derive limits to democratic authority is to say that some limits to democratic authority are essential to the proper operation of the democratic process of decision-making. So, some have argued that the right to freedom of expression is essential to the proper operation of the democratic process and they have argued that this implies that the right to freedom of expression ought to be protected against demo-cratic decision-making. They have also argued that freedom of association is essential to the democratic process to the extent that political parties and interest groups are essential to the proper operation of the democratic process. This is a kind of *internal* limit to democratic decision-making. The ground of the limit is in the protection of democracy itself.[2]

Clearly these are important considerations for grounding limits to demo-cratic authority. But I have two central worries about this approach as an account of the basis of the limits to democratic authority. One worry that some have expressed about this particular method of limiting the authority of democracy is that it would seem to be limited to protecting only political speech and political associations. This might leave the protection of private association and expression, connected with nonpolitical issues, unprotected. Intuitively, such an approach would seem not to provide as much protection from a democratic assembly as seems warranted.[3]

A more fundamental worry is that this way of grounding limits to demo-cratic authority cannot succeed unless it can be shown that democratic assem-blies do not have the authority to suspend democracy. The proposed strategy says that freedom of expression constitutes a limit on democratic authority because it is essential to the proper operation of democracy. But the strategy must then presuppose that legislation that undermines the proper functioning of democracy is beyond the limits of democratic authority. But this is what

[2] See Alexander Meiklejohn, *Free Speech and Its Relation to Self-Government* (New York: Harper and Row, 1948), and John Hart Ely, *Democracy and Distrust* (Cambridge, MA: Harvard University Press, 1980), chapter 4, for versions of this strategy.

[3] See Joshua Cohen, "Democracy and Liberty," in *Deliberative Democracy* ed. Jon Elster (Cambridge: Cambridge University Press, 1998), pp. 185–231, esp. p. 202.

an account of the limits of democratic authority should account for. The proposed strategy does nothing to answer this question and yet for the strategy to work this question must be answered. So in effect the first internal strategy for limiting democratic authority begs the most central question at issue.

In this chapter, I wish to show that there is a deeper kind of internal limit to democratic authority. The limit is internal because it is grounded in the same considerations that ground the democratic authority in the first place. The limits are not merely necessary to ensure the proper functioning of the democratic process; they are derived from the same values as those that underwrite the democratic process. I will show that in the case of democratic authority grounded in public equality, those considerations that are also grounded in public equality, such as liberal rights and a decent economic minimum, can undercut the claim of a democratic assembly to authority when it attempts to violate the cores of those rights. This account can also answer the question that remained unanswered for the earlier internal account that I described above. It can say why it is beyond the limits of democratic authority to undermine the democratic rights of citizens.

THE BASIC ARGUMENT FOR THE LIMITS
TO DEMOCRATIC AUTHORITY

Here I shall lay out the basis of the limits to democratic authority. I will lay out the grounds with the special case of disenfranchisement in mind. I will show how disenfranchisement is prohibited by the principles that ground democracy and then I will extend the account to the other cases.

1. Democratic assemblies have legitimate authority only when they publicly realize justice in themselves or they are instrumentally just.

2. Disenfranchisement of part of the sane adult population is a *public violation of equality.*[4]

3. Democratic assemblies publicly realize justice in themselves only when their decisions do not publicly violate justice.

4. (from 2 and 3) Therefore, when a democratic assembly votes to disenfranchise some of the population, it does not publicly realize justice in itself (nor is it instrumentally just).

---

[4] Except perhaps in cases of punishment for crimes. The apparent exception for punishment of crimes is only apparent. The assumption behind the arguments here is one of full compliance with the norms defended so punishment is not an issue here.

5. (from 1 and 4) Therefore, when a democratic assembly votes to disenfranchise some of its members, it does not have legitimate authority.

6. Just as disenfranchisement of part of the adult population publicly violates equality, so do suspension of the core of basic liberal rights, some form of radical discrimination against a part of the sane adult population, failure to assure a decent economic minimum, or the creation of persistent minorities publicly violate equality.

7. (from 4–6) Therefore, when a democratic assembly votes to suspend the core of liberal rights, or radically discriminates against a part of the sane adult population or fails to secure the decent economic minimum or creates a persistent minority, it does not publicly realize justice and so does not have legitimate authority.

The key premises here are 1–3 and 6. Premise 1 was defended in Chapter 6. Disenfranchisement is a violation of public equality if the arguments of Chapters 2 and 3 of this book are correct. Premise 2 states that disenfranchisement is not merely a violation of public equality, it is in effect a public violation of equality. That is to say that given the facts of judgment and the interests in having one's judgment respected, disenfranchisement is a publicly clear violation of a person's status as an equal and of the equal advancement of that person's interests. Were the majority to strip some minority of its democratic rights, then this would be a publicly clear way in which it acted as if its interests were of superior worth to those of the minority. Everyone would be able to see that the members of the minority were being treated as inferiors. Premise 2 is based on the thought that if a certain set of institutions is necessary to treating persons publicly as equals, then the absence of those institutions is a publicly clear treatment of those persons as unequals.

The argument that the democratic assembly does not have a right to rule can be made in two different ways given what I have said so far. The second is stronger than the first. The first argument is that for the democratic assembly to have a right to rule, it must generate a duty to obey in the citizens. But citizens never have a duty to violate public equality. The duty to promote and act in accordance with public equality is their most fundamental duty. So if the democratic assembly produces legislation that violates public equality, the citizens do not have a duty to obey and so the democratic assembly cannot have a right to make legislation that violates public equality.

This argument is important but, one, it does not go to the heart of the matter. It does not show how deep the limits to democratic authority are. And, consequently, two, it is insufficient to show that one never has a duty to obey the democratic assembly when it violates public equality. First, the argument provides only a kind of countervailing limit to democratic authority.

As we will see, there are deeper foundations for the limits to democratic authority. Second, since it suggests only countervailing considerations against obeying the democratic decisions that violate public equality, one could still ask whether the duty to obey the democratic assembly might not be stronger than the duty not to violate public equality in the form of the rights that are being violated. After all, they are grounded in the same considerations. So there is no reason yet to think that the consideration against there being a duty to obey is stronger than the consideration in favor of there being a duty. The question is, in this case, which action does the balance of considerations favor? It is not obvious that it always goes against obedience. But I think that at least with respect to decisions that violate fundamental democratic or liberal rights, at most one can have only pragmatic reasons for obeying the errant assembly.

THE MAIN PREMISE IN THE ARGUMENT FOR LIMITS TO DEMOCRATIC AUTHORITY

Premise 3 is the linchpin of a second more powerful argument grounding the limits of democratic authority. It states that the claim of authority is undercut at its root as opposed to giving merely countervailing considerations. It shows how the limit to democratic authority is established by eliminating the basis of the authority altogether at least in the instance of the decision in question.

Here is the argument. The thesis is that a democratic assembly that treats parts of its population publicly as inferiors no longer publicly embodies equality. The reason is that the institutions that embody public equality are not mere sets of rules; they are the organized and rule-governed behaviors of individuals who thereby express the equality of citizens in their participation. So if the institutional rules are used to perpetrate a public violation of equality then the institution no longer expresses equality but rather its opposite. Let us look at this argument in more detail.

First, if a majority in the democratic assembly uses the rules of the assembly to take away the voting rights of the minority in clear violation of public equality, then the majority cannot legitimately maintain that the rights they are exercising are morally grounded in the principle of public equality. If they were to think that their voting rights were required by public equality and they exercised them under this understanding, then they would be committed to maintaining the equal rights of all. By disenfranchising some and thus violating those persons' rights to be treated publicly as equals, the majority indicates that they are not committed to the thought that their use of these rights implies a commitment to public equality. They are in effect rejecting public equality as a norm over their behavior. The institutions have become, for them, mere tools in the service of treating some as inferiors.

Second, when the majority abandons its commitment to public equality by passing legislation that violates public equality, then the democratic assembly abandons its commitment to public equality. For the democratic assembly's action is merely the decisions that are made using the rules of the assembly.

But, third, the democratic assembly cannot embody public equality if it has openly abandoned public equality and treats, in a publicly clear way, some persons as inferiors. In support of this contention, note that a necessary condition of the assembly embodying public equality is that its activities express the equality of all citizens.[5] But it is clear that the activity of the assembly no longer expresses the equality of citizens when it clearly rejects public equality as a norm for its behavior. It can no longer be said to stand for the equality of the citizens. At least for the issue at hand, the democratic assembly becomes a mere collection of abusive persons taking advantage of their special place in society to use the rules for their particular interests.

Here is another way to get at this thesis. To say that the assembly publicly embodies equality is to say that the members of the society can see that they are being treated as equals by the assembly. But because the democratic assembly is a decision-making body it has two inseparably connected dimensions: the decision process and the decisions that are made. Both of these dimensions are essential to the public character of the decision-making body. Because the assembly has these two dimensions it is clear that there are two ways to defeat the public perception that persons are treated as equals by the assembly. One is that the process by which the decision is made is not egalitarian and the other is that the process is used to defeat equality in some publicly clear way.

So the idea is that if the majority acts in a way that is contrary to the principle of public equality properly understood, then the democratic assembly does not publicly embody equality in that instance. As a consequence, the democratic assembly does not have authority in that instance. The limits to democratic authority undercut the very claim to authority that the assembly makes.

Let me make some remarks on the argument I have just given. One, it is important that only publicly clear violations of equality defeat the public perception that the assembly treats persons as equals. The democratic assembly is likely to make many decisions that are regarded by some citizens as not treating all citizens as equals. But these violations of equality are not sufficient

---

[5] I have said in Chapter 3 that the expressive character of the democratic assembly is not sufficient for it to embody public equality.

to defeat the public perception that citizens are being treated as equals by the assembly. This is because of the considerations that underwrite the democratic institutions. Citizens know that agreement on the realization of equality in all matters of law and policy cannot be achieved because of the diversity, fallibility, and cognitive bias among citizens. So they understand that when these conditions obtain, it makes sense to make decisions in an egalitarian way. They do not expect to agree with all the decisions that are made by the assembly and do not think that this is required for public equality. But they do legitimately expect that certain publicly clear realizations of equality, which everyone can see to be realizations of equality, are to be respected and maintained. Only when these publicly clear realizations of equality are undermined by the assembly can citizens see that they are not treated publicly as equals. So only when these publicly clear realizations of equality are undermined is the authority of the democratic assembly undermined.

Two, I do not want to say merely that the majority cannot consistently complain in the name of public equality if it is stopped from doing what it wants to do (because what it wants to do is violate public equality). It is, of course, true that the members of the majority cannot consistently complain that they are being treated in violation of public equality if they intend to violate public equality by their legislative action. But the fact that someone cannot consistently complain that some form of treatment is an injustice to them is not a reason for thinking that that form of treatment is not an injustice to them. It may be inconsistent for them to make the complaint but the complaint may nevertheless be correct. So even though it may be inconsistent for the majority to complain that it is not being treated in accordance with public equality when it is stopped from making decisions that violate public equality, it does not follow that they are not being treated in violation of public equality.

The problem is that the majority rejects equality in a publicly clear way and that by its action it commits the assembly to the rejection of public equality. When the assembly is so committed to the rejection of public equality, it can no longer embody public equality.

Three, notice that the commitment attributed to the majority to abandon public equality does not entail that the majority actually thinks that it is abandoning public equality. The majority may think that it is remaining faithful to public equality for some reason. For instance, the majority may think that its disenfranchisement of the minority is justified by appeal to the idea that the minority is inferior in some way. The majority may think that the members of the minority are not persons. Or it may think that the members of the minority have the mental abilities of children or insane people. Or it may think that the members of the majority are such a threat to the well-being of the community that they must be excluded in order to protect the society. They may claim that their exclusion of the minority is compatible with public equality because of its conception of the minority. Or it may even have a strange view of what public equality requires. It may think that public equality does not require that the minority have democratic rights.

None of these thoughts is sufficient to defeat the claim that the majority has done something that commits it to the rejection of public equality. The basic principle of equality and the principle of public equality and its implications for democratic and liberal rights are not up for grabs. Normally, according to my account of the grounds of democracy and liberal rights, disagreement grounds a claim in the dissenter to have a say in the collective decision-making process and legitimates the outcome of collective decision-making when it conforms to the dissenter's view. But when we come to persons who reject equality or public equality or its implications for democracy we have reached the point in the theory where disagreement no longer has the power to legitimate an outcome of collective decision-making. The fact that the majority thinks that some group of persons are not persons or are not equals is not sufficient to legitimate a majority decision that treats those persons not as equal persons. According to the theory I have defended, a majority that believes such things should know better and the society is not required to respect these antiegalitarian judgments in the sense that it must accept as legitimate decisions that are grounded in this antiegalitarian judgment.

Four, it is important to be clear at this point on what the argument does not show. One might think that there is a parallelism between the following two propositions. (P1) The right of the democratic assembly to rule is undermined when its decisions violate public equality because the right is based on the fact that the democratic assembly embodies public equality. Some might also wonder whether (P2) the right of persons to freedoms of expression, association, and conscience and the right to vote, which are also grounded in public equality, may be undermined for persons who advocate for the rejection of public equality.

I want to argue that this parallel does not hold. The society must respect the freedoms of expression, association, and conscience and the democratic rights of persons even when they use them to oppose public equality and its implications even though it is not required to accept democratic decisions that violate public equality.

Such antiegalitarian individuals have interests in having their views heard, being able to associate with like-minded people and thinking for themselves. They also have interests in being able to advance their ideas in the democratic forum. Furthermore, none of these activities imply that the liberal rights or democratic rights no longer publicly embody equality. As long as the antiegalitarian views are merely expressed in individual exercises of rights, they do not defeat the public embodiment of equality in the scheme of rights overall. The reason for this is that the public embodiment of equality in institutions can only be defeated by a kind of society wide rejection of public equality in the use of those institutions. And this can only be done when the democratic assembly makes decisions that violate public equality or when the basic institutions fail to embody public equality. Such society wide rejections of public equality do constitute genuine threats to equality. By contrast, individual efforts to argue against public equality or its implications or to organize on the basis of a rejection of public equality do not yet carry the implication that "we" are rejecting public equality. And so the expression of opposition to public equality or its implications does not undercut the right to engage in such expression.

Another way to think of individual efforts to undermine public equality via the individual exercises of individual rights is to think of them as advancing mere hypotheses that are to be entertained by the democratic assembly. Individuals have important interests in being able to entertain these hypotheses, as I argued in the chapter on liberal rights, and to be able to develop them with other like-minded persons. The implementation by a democratic assembly of these ideas, however, goes beyond the mere entertainment of hypotheses actually to treating people in certain ways that they cannot avoid. So while the implementation by a democratic assembly of legislation that violates public equality undercuts the claim to authority made by the democratic assembly, the advocacy by individuals of violations of public equality does not undercut the right of those individuals to engage in such advocacy.

A closer parallel to the case of a democratic assembly violating public equality and thereby no longer embodying public equality is the case of the use of expression and association for the purpose of inciting violence against a particular group of persons or for the purpose of directly violating the rights of other persons. A person does not have the right to engage in activities of immediate incitement to violence for this is directly a violation of public equality.

Since democratic equality is inherently just only if it publicly embodies equality, in cases of disenfranchisement, the decision-making process of the democratic assembly is no longer just. And since the authority of democracy is grounded in its justice, democracy no longer has authority when it disenfranchises some of its people. Here we have derived a fundamental limit to democratic authority, which limit undercuts the claim to authority and does not merely provide countervailing considerations.

In what follows, I will lay out the grounds for thinking that liberal rights, the economic minimum, and the need to avoid permanent minorities constitute limits to democratic authority.

THE EXTENSION OF THE FUNDAMENTAL ARGUMENT TO LIBERAL RIGHTS

Premise 6 asserts that there is a fundamental parallelism between democratic rights and basic liberal rights. This parallelism is founded on the fact that the foundations of liberal rights are the same as those of democratic rights. Let us briefly recall how liberal rights are grounded taking the freedoms of association and the freedom of private pursuits as examples. Recall that given the background facts of diversity, fallibility, disagreement, and cognitive bias, each person has fundamental interests in being able to conduct their lives by their own lights at least in certain defined areas of human activity. The interest in being at home in the world is advanced when one has the right to associate with others one chooses to associate with and on terms one chooses. The interest in being able to avoid the consequences of being imposed upon by another's paternalistic judgment that is cognitively biased toward that other's interests is also advanced by the basic liberal rights. The interests in being able to learn from others and to learn from one's mistakes are advanced by one's having the rights to freedom of association to freedom of expression and the freedom of private pursuits. Furthermore, freedom of association furthers the interest in being recognized and affirmed as the individual person I am by others who I respect.

These and other interests are so fundamental to the well-being of a person that no society that set them back for all or some substantial proportion of the population could be thought to advance the common good. And no society that set them back for a few could be thought to be advancing the interests of each equally. Given the interest in correcting for cognitive bias and the interests in at homeness and learning, those whose freedoms of association were limited would have reason to think that their interests were being subordinated to those of the others in society. And those whose liberal rights were set back in this way would have reason to think that their equal moral standing was not recognized and affirmed by others. Thus, any fundamental undermining of the cores of a person's basic liberal rights would be a publicly clear violation of equality of advancement of interests.

Now consider the case in which a majority decides to enslave the minority; this is a clear violation of the principle of the public realization of equal advancement of interests. Why is this? If another enslaves me, that person assumes the power to decide what I ought to do and reaps the benefits from this. He thereby implies that my interests are not of equal significance to his. Or if he thinks that my interests do matter equally, he implies that my capacity for judgment is not worthy of respect. But, for all the same reasons that I gave for the importance of respect for the judgment of persons in cases of political decision-making and individual decision-making, the principle of public equality and the interests and facts on which it is based require that my judgment regarding how I am to conduct my life must be given equal respect and therefore must not be subordinated to those of others. Hence, enslavement is a violation of the principle of public equality.

Any radical suppression of basic liberal rights of members of the population would fall afoul of the basic requirements of public equality. People may disagree about what liberal rights are basic and what their boundaries are as well as what equality in these liberal rights consists in, but some kind of equality in basic liberal rights is necessary to the public realization of equality given the facts of judgment. What is not negotiable is the core of each person's liberal rights. A violation of any of these would constitute a radical suppression of the liberal rights of the person.

The consequence of these arguments is that just as the disenfranchisement of a group of persons is a public violation of equality so is the suppression of the cores of liberal rights for parts of the population a public violation of equality. And just as this fact undercuts the authority of democratic decision-making in the case of disenfranchisement, so it undercuts the authority of democracy in the case of violation of the cores of liberal rights.

AN ECONOMIC MINIMUM

The argument I have made so far suggests that a democratic assembly does not have the authority to suspend the cores of liberal rights or democratic rights. I wish to argue here that the authority of a democratic assembly is significantly weakened on those issues pertaining to the economic organization of society when it fails to do what can be done to secure an economic minimum for the members of the society. The structure of the argument for this claim is the same as the arguments for liberal and democratic rights serving as limits to democratic authority. But the nature of the limit is a bit different than in the cases of these other two rights.

WHY AN ECONOMIC MINIMUM?

But first, we need to give the reasons for thinking that assurance of an economic minimum is essential to treating persons publicly as equals. The basic reason for this is that the economic minimum is necessary to advancing the interests that are secured by the liberal and democratic rights. The idea is that without a basic minimum a person normally cannot successfully exercise the liberal and democratic rights. Without a basic minimum a person does not have the means even to present arguments in the public forum, he does not have the means to associate with others, he does not have the means to practice those things that may be required by conscience, and, of course, he does not have the means to engage in private pursuits. To the extent that these rights are grounded in interests that must be equally advanced, and the interests cannot be advanced without some basic means, the interests that ground the rights also ground the requirement of a provision of a basic minimum to each person in the society.

So someone whose rights to freedoms of association, expression, conscience, and private pursuits are protected but who does not have the basic means to exercise these rights can legitimately complain that she is not being publicly treated as an equal in the society. The interests she has in being able to exercise her rights are being sacrificed for the lesser interests of others and thus she is being treated publicly as an inferior.

Why only an economic minimum and not a more generous grant of income to everyone? Recall that the economic minimum is meant to serve as a kind of limit to the authority of democracy. A more extensive requirement on the distribution of income is something that a democratic assembly can decide to implement. And this can be decided on the basis of a conception of distributive justice that is shared by a sufficiently large majority. But we must accept that citizens can reasonably disagree on what the requirements on the state are that are derived from the requirement to treat persons as equals. For this reason, the argument for democracy that I have given in Chapter 3 implies that within a certain range, democratic discretion concerning distributive justice and the transfer schemes needed to implement it must be accepted. What this implies is that to the extent that there can be reasonable disagreement on how to treat a person as an equal as far as economic rights are concerned, there is likely to be a lot of disagreement on what the exact principles for the distribution of income ought to be.

The purpose of setting the requirement of an economic minimum is to honor this range of disagreements. We know that there is substantial and reasonable disagreement about what justice requires in the distribution of income; but we also know that the fundamental interests that underwrite the liberal and democratic rights cannot be advanced without some resources. To the extent that we are committed to advancing those interests, we must be committed to ensuring an economic minimum; but to the extent that there is disagreement about how much more each ought to have, we do not impose a more robust principle of distribution as a condition on the authority of democracy. Less than an economic minimum would fail to take the interests that ground liberal rights seriously; but to require more than an economic minimum as a condition of democratic authority would be to fail to take the interests behind democracy seriously.

The exact nature of the economic minimum would also by right be decided by the democratic assembly. I do not want to enter here into debates about exactly how much this minimum should be nor do I want to discuss the exact mechanism of transfer that would be required. Basic human needs, such as health care, education, a decent childhood, and others, are needs such that a serious lack in one of these can clearly be compared with someone else's good fortune. Someone who is seriously ill with no access to health care or has had no access to education or has been severely abused as a child is pretty clearly worse off than many others. And such a person is likely to experience serious obstacles to the exercise of their liberal and democratic rights. When there is a serious deficiency with regard to one of these interests, justice requires that some attention be paid to them. And no democratic assembly that ignored such fundamental needs of citizens could be regarded as fully legitimate.[6]

One qualification to the above argument is that it is not absolutely universally true that individuals need an economic minimum to exercise their liberal and democratic rights. Some may have special abilities that make this economic minimum unnecessary. But I want to say that the necessity of an economic minimum is necessary for the vast majority of people for most of the time. And this, it seems to me, is sufficient to ground a general claim on the part of each and every person to a minimum. The reason why is because we do not want the state to engage in the kind of case by case reasoning that would be necessary to separate out the few who do not need the minimum from those who do. The considerations behind this are grounded in the idea of the rule of law that I have argued has a special connection to public equality in Chapter 4.

---

[6] See John Schwarz, *Freedom Reclaimed: Rediscovering the American Vision* (Baltimore: Johns Hopkins Press, 2005), for a careful discussion of what the economic minimum in the United States ought to be.

DIFFERENT KINDS OF FAILURES
OF THE DEMOCRATIC ASSEMBLY

In the most straightforward case, the democratic assembly runs up against the limits of its authority by passing legislation that violates public equality. Thus passage of legislation that disenfranchises some part of the population or that strips the liberal rights of some part of the population clearly goes beyond the authority of the democratic assembly. In these cases, citizens no longer have duties to obey the democratic assembly. But the main effect of this loss of authority on the duties of citizens is localized in the sense that the citizens do not have duties to obey the offending piece of legislation, or at least the duty is not owed to the assembly. The citizen will still have duties to obey other pieces of legislation that are legitimate.

Here the language of limits to authority is most at home. The democratic assembly does something it has no right to do. These limits are negative limits and transgressing these limits has straightforward implications for the duties of the citizens. Moreover, the expressive character of transgression is the clearest in the case of legislation that expressly violates public equality.

But democratic authority can fail in other ways as well. The democratic authority may fail to do what is necessary to maintain public equality. Some clear-cut cases of this are when the democratic assembly fails to do what is necessary to ensure that everyone has an equal say in the process of decision-making. It may negligently set up electoral polls in a way that makes it difficult for some part of the population to participate in the process of decision-making. It may fail to make adequate provision of the materials of the electoral process such as votes, voting machines, and other things to all the various voting districts. Another such case is when the democratic assembly fails to ensure that the liberal and democratic rights of some are enforced and protected, such as when it fails to provide adequate police protection to certain neighborhoods. In these cases, it is failing to ensure that the very process of decision-making fully embodies public equality.

But it seems to me that the failure to maintain public equality is, more generally, a threat to the authority of democracy. We see this clearly in the case of the requirement of an economic minimum but it can be present in the case of all the other rights required by public equality. These are usually cases of negligence on the part of the democratic assembly. For instance, if the assembly fails to provide for the enforcement of the liberal or democratic rights of some minority that are being violated by some part of the population, this is a kind of failure of the democratic assembly that threatens its authority. Or if the democratic assembly fails to do what it can to provide the economic minimum, it fails in a way that threatens its authority.

There are two basic ways in which the democratic authority can be under-mined and these correspond to two types of requirements on democratic authority. The first requirement is a negative one. It says that the authority may not make certain decisions or laws that violate public equality. The second is a positive requirement. The democratic assembly is charged with ensuring that the society satisfies the requirements of public equality. So here the assembly is charged with the task of ensuring that people's rights are not violated by other members of the society. It is also charged with the task of assuring the economic minimum.

Failure to satisfy these requirements is a threat to the authority of democracy. The reason why is that democracy has authority only to the extent that it realizes public equality. But the assembly cannot realize public equality if the conditions of public equality are not realized in a way that can be attributed to the negligence of the assembly. The reason for this is that if the democratic assembly fails to do something that it can do to realize public equality, then it shows that it does not take public equality seriously in its decision-making. But if it fails to take public equality seriously in its decision-making, then it cannot fully embody public equality for the same reasons as when it passes legislation that violates public equality.

Of course, the implications for citizens of these requirements on democratic authority are distinct from those of the negative requirements. The failure of a democratic assembly to assure the economic minimum to its citizens cannot normally be attributed to particular pieces of legislation as it can be in the case of the assembly simply stripping a group of some of its liberal rights or its voting rights. This means that no particular piece of legislation can be identified as beyond the authority of the democratic assembly. And this implies further that there is no particular piece of legislation or policy that people do not have duties to comply with. So what is the nature of this limit? The thought is that when a democratic assembly fails to do what it can to secure an economic minimum for its citizens or it fails to implement a scheme of democratic decision-making that is fully democratic or it fails to enforce the liberal rights of some citizens there is a more general weakening of the authority of the democratic assembly. The authority does not just disappear for a particular piece of legislation.

The idea in the case of the minimum is that individuals have duties to do what they can to secure the economic minimum for each person. And these duties are grounded in public equality. What does this imply for the authority of the democratic assembly that fails to secure the minimum? What it suggests is that those laws that are the most serious obstacles to particular persons securing their liberal or democratic rights or the economic minimum are ones where the authority has run out. It also implies that those laws that are most supportive of the oppressive actions of the dominating group are not fully authoritative, even if they would normally be unobjectionable. And it also implies that those who are not even assured of a minimum or of the protection of their liberal or democratic rights are not required to treat the democratic assembly as having as extensive a right to rule over them as the others.

In the most extreme case, where the assembly acts systematically and seriously to undermine public equality in many different areas, the assembly may lose authority altogether. Systematic violations of liberal and democratic rights and systematic failure to assure the conditions of public equality out of negligence undermine the claim of the assembly to any authority at all. In this case, as Locke would have put it, the assembly is no longer authoritative; it simply becomes a gang of thugs trying to advance the interests of some particular group. The population must then attempt to bring about the establishment of justice. From the point of view of the officers of the state and those they benefit, this will appear to be revolutionary activity but as Locke pointed out, the rebellion would have already been initiated by the assembly itself by its complete violation of public equality.[7]

What are the remedies to these violations of public equality? It should first be noted that even when the democratic assembly acts beyond its authority in some particular piece of legislation, it does not follow that citizens ought not to obey. All that follows is that on that legislation, the citizens have no duty grounded in the right of the assembly to obey. They may still have reasons to obey that are more instrumental in character. In the simplest case, if the assembly has violated public equality with a particular piece of legislation, citizens may have a duty to go along just because to do otherwise might undermine the generally legitimate authority of the democratic assembly. But even in cases where this is not so, there could be other kinds of instrumental reasons for obedience. Lack of authority does not entail absence of reasons for compliance.

The first remedy to public injustice is to use the liberal and democratic rights to bring about change for the better. One of the main attractive features of liberal democracy is its capacity for renewal and reform from within itself. And this capacity for reform and renewal is present even if the society does not fully satisfy the principles that underwrite liberal democracy. A second remedy would be disobedience and mobilization for change. A third would be an attempt to establish justice when the authority has completely broken down in the sense of systematically violating public equality. But I want to discuss another kind of remedy here.

---

[7] See John Locke, *Second Treatise on Civil Government* ed. Peter Laslett (Cambridge: Cambridge University Press, 2002), chapter XIX.

SOME REMARKS ON CONSTITUTIONAL CONSTRAINTS
AND JUDICIAL REVIEW

One main remedy for the possibility that democratic assemblies overstep the limits of their authority is an institutional one. Some have argued that a democratic society ought to have a written constitution spelling out the basic rights people have, which is adjudicated by an independent court with the power to strike down legislation that violates constitutional law. In this section I will explore the extent to which the theory I have provided so far supports institutions of constitutional constraints and judicial review for the purpose of policing the limits of democratic authority. In the next section I will examine a recent philosophical argument against judicial review and I will show that it falls short of its target.

A CONCEPTION OF JUDICIAL REVIEW

I have argued that a democracy cannot have the legitimate authority to act in a way that undermines basic democratic rights or basic liberal rights. Though it may wish to disenfranchise a minority, the majority always has overriding reason to permit the minority to have a say grounded on the basic principle behind democracy and it always has overriding reason to respect at least the rudiments of the basic liberal rights of the minority (except in the cases of imminent threats of violence or serious disruption of public order). And, on the same basis, the minority always has a reason to insist that a majority's decision to suspend minority rights is mistaken on both counts. These reasons cannot be preempted.

In my view, this is where we should say that institutions should be constructed so as to preserve democracy and the basic structure of liberal rights. If a bill of rights with judicial review is necessary to achieve this result, the proper account of the justification of democracy does not rule this out. Democracy no longer has authority when it disenfranchises minorities or deprives them of their basic rights and there is always reason to protect these rights. Hence an institution that does so most effectively is defensible.[8]

I will lay this out a bit more carefully here. To be sure, a system of judicial review allows nondemocratic courts to overturn the results of democratic decision-making. How can this be legitimate? The nondemocratic court does

---

[8] Here I agree with the general thrust of Ronald Dworkin's argument in *Freedom's Law* [(Cambridge, MA: Harvard University Press, 1996), pp. 23–26] to the effect that there is a democratic rationale for limitations on majority rule.

not publicly embody equality. In fact, it seems publicly to violate equality. It seems to put power over the society in the hands of a minority.

The way to think about this problem is to consider comparisons between societies. Let us take one particular comparison. In one society only the democratic assembly makes decisions but it frequently violates public equality in the decisions themselves. In the other society, the democratic assembly makes decisions but its legislation is reviewed by a constitutional court to determine whether the decisions accord with public equality and can be struck down by the court when they are found to be in violation of public equality. And let us suppose that in this society the consequence of this review is that a significant proportion of the violations perpetrated by the democratic assembly are struck down by the constitutional court but few other acts of the assembly are struck down. In these circumstances, I claim, the society would better satisfy public equality overall with the help of judicial review than if the democratic assembly were to operate unchecked.

Let us see how this comparison works. It is clear that the constitutional court does not itself realize public equality. On my account, it has no inherent authority. But notice, in our hypothetical example, it acts generally only when the democratic assembly has overstepped its limits. It acts when the democratic assembly's action does not realize public equality and so when the democratic assembly has lost its inherent authority. This is a necessary consequence of the fact that in order to realize public equality, the democratic assembly must be both egalitarian in the process of decision-making and it must produce decisions that do not treat people publicly as inferiors. The realization of public equality by the democratic assembly is conditional on its making decisions that do not violate public equality. So in the example in which the democratic assembly oversteps its limits, both the constitutional court and the democratic assembly fail to realize public equality and neither has inherent authority.

In a sense, then, from the standpoint of the procedure the fact that the constitutional court does not realize public equality is no more a strike against it than is the fact that the democratic assembly fails to realize public equality. If the court had not intervened then the decision would have been taken by an assembly that does not realize public equality. If the court does intervene, then the decision is taken by the court that does not realize public equality. It looks like we have not gained or lost anything by substituting the court for the assembly in this case.

In our hypothetical example, however, there is a gain overall in public equality when the constitutional court rules properly. Of course, the court does not have the right to rule but when it makes decisions correctly, then the citizens have duties to go along because the decisions support public equality (by hypothesis) and they have duties to act in accord with public equality. So from the point of view of the compliance of citizens with their duties, the comparison I have offered favors the constitutional court's power to review and strike down legislation. While neither the democratic assembly nor the court have inherent authority, the court at least brings about greater compliance with equality. The citizens have duties grounded in public equality to go along with its decisions. And a court that normally does a good job in striking down legislation that violates public equality will have a kind of instrumental authority since citizens have reason to go along generally. So it looks like in our hypothetical example, the considerations in favor of a constitutional court dominate the case.

But the question becomes harder when we consider the possibility that the constitutional court makes some bad decisions, overturning democratic decisions that in fact accord with public equality. In those cases, we have a double loss: a decision is made in an antiegalitarian way and is itself antiegalitarian (since it defeats a legitimate democratic decision) and if the court had not intervened there would have been no loss to equality. So once we introduce bad decisions made by the constitutional court into our comparison, the picture becomes more complex.

Other things being equal, the loss to public equality that results from bad court decisions is greater than the gain to public equality when the court makes a good decision. This is because the loss that arises from a court making a bad decision (say striking down democratic legislation that accords with public equality) is a double loss while the gain from the court striking down bad democratic legislation is not as great. But this implies that a constitutional court can be justified only if the good decisions significantly outnumber or outweigh in importance the bad decisions.

What this reasoning suggests is that it is in principle possible for a constitutional court with the power to strike down legislation to be grounded in the fundamental principle underlying democracy. The argument is an essentially instrumental one. Whether the argument works depends on whether a democratic assembly with a constitutional check on its authority does substantially better in protecting public equality than a democratic assembly by itself.

But this view comes with some very strong qualifications. First, which institutions actually are necessary to protect democratic and liberal rights is a contingent question and probably has different answers for different societies that experience different kinds of social conflict. In some societies, the society may do significantly better in terms of the principle of public equality by having a constitutional court with the power of review while in others the society may do worse in terms of public equality. And different kinds of constitutional review may be desirable in different societies. Second, the burden that must be carried by an argument in favor of a constitutional court is quite heavy.

It is not enough just that it does a bit better than the unchecked democratic assembly. This is because, other things being equal, the loss to public equality due to the court's mistaken rejection of democratic legislation is greater than the gain from the court's correctly rejecting democratic legislation. So there is reason to think that if a constitutional bill of rights with judicial review is only somewhat more effective than an unmodified democracy in protecting basic democratic and liberal rights, the unmodified democratic method ought to be preferred. Third, I share the skepticism of many recent theorists about the ability of the Supreme Court of the United States to do this effectively. Its history is very mixed.[9] Still, we can see that it should be possible for a court to act well under some circumstances and so there is not a general principled reason for rejecting a constitutional court with the power of review.

WALDRON'S SKEPTICISM ABOUT JUDICIAL REVIEW

Jeremy Waldron has recently made some powerful arguments against the desirability of judicial review of democratic legislation. I take his view to be a serious challenge to the view I am presently defending, particularly since it appeals to basic democratic values. I will discuss two of his main arguments here. First I will discuss what I call the *internal argument* against Bills of Rights then I will discuss the *democratic argument*.

AN INTERNAL ARGUMENT AGAINST BILLS OF RIGHTS

The first argument can best be laid out in the following form.

1. A constitutional bill of rights is an attempt to limit the actions of a democratic legislature.

2. Such limits are imposed on the legislature on the grounds that individual citizens are not to be trusted in discerning what rights people have.

3. The moral abilities demanded of ordinary citizens in a democratic setting are quite similar to the moral abilities citizens need in exercising their liberal rights.

[9] See Robert Dahl, *A Preface to Democratic Theory* (Chicago: University of Chicago Press, 1955), for an unqualifiedly negative assessment of the Supreme Court of the United States's record in the protection of liberal and democratic rights up to that time. See also Mark Tushnet, *Taking the Constitution Away from the Courts* (Princeton: Princeton University Press, 1999), chapters 6 and 7, for an argument to this effect concerning the US Supreme Court in more recent history.

4. Attribution of liberal rights to persons implies that we trust their moral abilities.

5. If we trust people's moral abilities, then we must accept them in the case of democracy as well.

6. Therefore, grounds for constitutional bills of rights are incompatible with the grounds for the liberal rights that are to be protected by them.[10]

That there is some parallelism between democratic and liberal rights seems to me to be an important insight. This is a parallelism that I have defended and exploited in elaborating the arguments of this book. Both democratic and liberal rights give people the opportunities to exercise power over their own lives as well as the lives of other people. This parallel supports the idea that if we have reason to believe that people will act in a responsible way with their liberal rights then we have reason to think that they will exercise their democratic rights responsibly.

THE INTERNAL ARGUMENT SUPPORTS BILLS OF RIGHTS

Two main difficulties undermine the force of the internal argument. One, the parallel may not be quite as tight for Waldron's purposes as he suggests. First, choices about how to vote and choices about whom to associate with or how to live have radically different opportunity costs. This difference may lead to important differences in the time and attention that people are willing to devote to reflecting on these different matters. Many have argued that people are simply less likely to devote as much time and attention to matters of politics as to matters that concern their own lives.[11] This would have an impact on the quality of the decisions they make. It may make citizens less trustworthy in the context of democratic decision-making than in the case of individual decision-making. Second, the subject matter of democratic politics is quite a bit more complex than the question of how to live one's own life. And third, the relevant sources of knowledge are, in general, significantly more remote in the case of democratic decision-making than in the case of liberal rights. Democratic decision-making encompasses the lives

---

[10] See Jeremy Waldron, *Law and Disagreement* (Oxford: Oxford University Press, 2000), pp. 222–223.

[11] See Anthony Downs, *An Economic Theory of Democracy* (New York: Harper and Row, 1964), and Joseph Schumpeter, *Capitalism, Socialism and Democracy* (New York: Harper and Row, 1950), for two seminal treatments of this question. The literature discussing these problems is gargantuan now.

and interests of individuals who are quite different from us and with whom we have had no contact. These factors are likely to disincline citizens from attempting to gain the knowledge necessary for good democratic decision-making and make the search for such knowledge much more demanding. They are likely to have some impact in diminishing the quality of decisions people make relative to the decisions they make regarding their own lives and those around them.[12] This is a descriptive point relevant to the level of trust we should put in other people's political decision-making. While these matters deserve more attention, I will leave them to the side for the moment.

In any case, the internal argument is problematic in another important way. Waldron is right to point to the similarity between democratic and liberal rights. In fact, however, we do accept legal restrictions on what people do because we do not fully trust people to act out of respect for other's liberal rights and on account of the great importance to us of these liberal rights. So the internal argument could go in the opposite direction from the one Waldron suggests. We legally restrict people's individual actions toward others because we are not sure that those people will always act within the limits set by the rights of others. In addition, since the rights are so important to us, we prefer to reduce substantially the risk of violation. And so we impose explicit legal restrictions, backed by force, on how people treat each other. The fact is that a system of legal rights is grounded in a kind of balance of trust and distrust of the individual bearers of the rights. We trust people enough to allow them space to make their own choices but we distrust them enough to believe that we need coercion to stop them from occasionally making very bad choices. Clearly some balance of trust and distrust is reasonable in the case of democratic rights as well. The great importance of the interests threatened by undesirable exercises of these rights gives us some justification for imposing limitations on democratic decision-making in order to protect democracy and to protect liberal rights. Hence, the internal argument does not support the thesis that there ought not to be constitutional bills of rights. It may in fact point in the opposite direction, as we have seen.

THE DEMOCRATIC ARGUMENT AGAINST JUDICIAL REVIEW

Waldron's central argument against judicial review is what I call the *democratic argument*:

---

[12] I deal with some of these questions in detail in parts II and III of my *The Rule of the Many*.

1. Democratic assemblies have authority in matters of substantive justice.
2. If democracy has authority with respect to substantive justice, then any individual's or small group's views about justice must give way to the decision of the democratic assembly.
3. A constitutional bill of rights requires that some group of individuals (e.g. a constitutional court) be able to strike down democratic legislation on the basis of their interpretation of the enumerated rights.
4. Interpreting a bill of rights inevitably requires that individuals apply their own controversial standards of justice.
5. Hence, a constitutional bill of rights requires that some small group of individuals' be able to override democratic decisions on the basis of their controversial views about justice.
6. Therefore there ought not to be a constitutional bill of rights.

THE DEMOCRATIC ARGUMENT CRITICIZED

Let us focus on the democratic argument against constitutional bills of rights. Waldron is right to point out that people disagree on the shape of liberal rights and that respect for the judgments of rights bearers requires us to give each a say in defining the exact contours of the legal rights. And he argues that a constitutional bill of rights will take the power to define liberal legal rights out of the hands of most rights bearers and put it in the hands of a few. Against this, he invokes the main argument for democracy as a basis for rejecting the idea of a bill of rights.

But the premises are problematic. First, a minor quibble. A bill of rights that is entrenched against quick democratic change is compatible with the democratic assembly being the ultimate interpreter of the rights. Waldron is right to say that some democratic control over the precise contours of the rights in question is desirable in the light of serious disagreement on these matters. But such control is compatible with having a bill of rights, and versions of this control exist in some societies.[13] To be sure, we still must proceed on the basis of a trust in the assembly (and in the last analysis, the electorate) not to interpret the rights out of existence. The written bill of rights on this account serves as a constraint only if the legislature can be trusted not to misinterpret

---

[13] Indeed, it appears that some effective forms of democratic control over interpretation of the US Constitution existed before 1803 in the United States. See Akhil Reed Amar, *The Bill of Rights* (New Haven, CN: Yale University Press, 1998), pp. 23 and 98–104.

those rights completely. Still, the fact of disagreement need not undermine the usefulness of a bill of rights nor need the presence of a bill of rights preclude discretion on the part of a democratic assembly to define the exact character of the rights.

Second, given the kind of parallelism between democratic and liberal rights, one would think that the principle of respect for judgment that underwrites the democratic rights also supports liberal rights. But this implies that any serious limitation of liberal rights by a democratic legislature may express a failure of respect for those whose rights are limited. Why suppose that the failure of respect displayed in limiting a democratic legislature's decision-making is greater or more serious than that involved in limiting the liberal rights of certain persons, or even everyone? If we cannot always assume this, then we begin to see some reason for explicitly protecting liberal rights.

Hence, by this argument, the parallelism of democratic and liberal rights suggests that if one is to be protected by the procedural rules of the political society then there is no principled reason for the liberal rights not to be given special protection. The protection of one seems to have a parallel justification to the protection of the other.

IS EVERYTHING UP FOR GRABS?

This does not yet imply that there ought to be protection of liberal rights. For one may think that neither liberal nor democratic rights ought to be given special protection against the actions of majorities. Indeed, this seems to be the view Waldron favors. What Waldron suggests is that everything in a democratic society can legitimately be up for grabs, even the very basis of democratic rule itself as well as the fundamental liberal rights of persons.[14] I have argued that not everything is rightly up for grabs; even if democracy has authority over many questions, that authority must be limited. I want to show now that Waldron's own position must inevitably lead to limitations on democratic rule or fall into incoherence.

Waldron's account of the basis of democracy threatens to lead to a regress or self-defeat or to depend on the very consensus he is at pains to avoid.[15] The problem is that if in all disagreements, individuals must have a say in the resolution, then we are in danger of a regress as a result of disagreements about equality, democracy, and even the value of the theses that Waldron himself

[14] See Waldron, p. 303.
[15] I have argued for these points in more detail in my "Waldron on Law and Disagreement," in *Law and Philosophy* (July 2000).

proposes. In the light of the facts of pervasive disagreement, the regress is likely to have no end. The theory then ends up defending nothing at all.

The trouble arises for any conception of the principle of equal respect for judgment where the principle of respect for judgment is reflexive or, in other words, it requires respect for judgments about itself. Waldron's view seems to demand a kind of unlimited reflexivity with regard to viewpoint.

When the principle of equal respect for judgment has unlimited reflexivity with regard to viewpoint then the difficulties of infinite regress and antidemocratic legislation arise together. In view of the problem of regress, we have an uncontroversial reason for abandoning unlimited reflexivity regarding viewpoints about the proper method of collective decision-making. In particular, we ought not respect the decision of the majority when it undermines the political rights of citizens. We need this restriction simply to avoid the logical absurdity of infinite regress.

So far I have argued that a limit on the reflexivity of the principle of equal respect for judgment is necessary if we are to avoid the problem of regress. But this does not tell us that we can justify such a limit. For all we know now, the principle is hopelessly paradoxical and ought to be rejected. The question is, is there a way to justify the principle of equal respect for judgment that avoids the logical problems noted above?

One thing we could do is simply limit the principle of equal respect for judgment so that it does not extend to judgments about the principle itself. We simply say that we must respect all judgments except those judgments that reject equal respect for judgments. The trouble with this solution is that it seems to impose an arbitrary and ad hoc limitation on the principle of equal respect for judgment. We are told that we ought to respect judgments except one and we are given no explanation for this exception. The modification seems ad hoc.

Another way is to ground equal respect for judgment in a more fundamental principle that explains the principle and the restriction. The deeper principle would ground equal respect while limiting the reflexivity of the principle. Such a principle should support the idea that disagreements on a number of issues ought to be resolved as a matter of fairness by democratic means but limits the extent of disagreements that must be handled democratically. The basic principle itself should be nonnegotiable. There are two main views that attempt to ground the principle of equal respect for judgment in a deeper principle and thus avoid the problems of regress and self-defeat. The first is the view defended by John Rawls and many deliberative democrats. The second is the view defended in this book, which grounds the principle of equal respect for judgment in the principle of equal advancement of interests.

John Rawls and a number of deliberative democrats ground a restricted principle of equal respect for judgment in the criterion of reciprocity. Here, the idea is that I respect your judgment if you respect mine and vice versa. This would at least have the effect of excluding judgments that fail to respect the judgments of others and it has an intuitive appeal to it. I have discussed and criticized this principle in great detail in Chapter 5 so I will not discuss it further here.[16]

The view defended in this book grounds respect for judgment in the public realization of the equal advancement of interests. And this grounding avoids the problems of regress and self-defeat. Concern for the well-being of persons need not be beset with all the problems attendant on the reflexivity of respect for judgment. It provides a standpoint outside the disagreements people have from which to assess their relations with each other; at the same time, it recommends that those individuals be given a chance to resolve many of their disagreements democratically. A principle of respect for judgment derives from the principle of concern for well-being, as we have seen, because there are fundamental interests in persons having their judgments about justice being taken seriously and accommodated by the society. Equal respect for judgment derives from the idea of equal advancement of the interests of persons. The principles of equal advancement of interests and the derivative idea of equal respect for judgment together imply that a just society is one that publicly embodies the equal advancement of interests. Its institutions are constructed so as to make it publicly clear to citizens that their interests are being given equal consideration in their operation. When there is serious disagreement about matters of substantive justice among citizens, a just society can only publicly embody the equality of its citizens by giving them an equal say in resolving these disputes.

Moreover, each person has fundamental interests in being able to conduct their lives by their own lights at least in certain defined areas of human activity. Take for instance the interest in association and in judging whom to associate with, and the interests in partaking in free and open discussion about politics and the good life as well as the interest in judging the merits of different views by one's own light. These and other interests are so fundamental to the well-being of a person that no society that set them back for all could be thought to advance the common good. And no society that set them back for a few could be thought to be giving the interests of each equal consideration.

---

[16] See John Rawls, *Political Liberalism* revised edition (New York: Columbia University Press, 1996), chapter 2. I have also criticized this view in *The Rule of the Many*, chapter 1 and in my "The Significance of Public Deliberation," in *Deliberative Democracy* eds. James Bohman and William Rehg (Cambridge, MA: MIT Press, 1998).

The principle of the public realization of equal advancement of interests that I have defended in this book provides a large space in which the respect for judgments ought to hold, but it also sets limits to that respect. It does not permit that people effectively exercise power to undermine the public realization of equal consideration of interests. The result of having this restriction, however, is that we justify some restrictions on antidemocratic legislation. Hence, not everything can be up for grabs. Finally, in the light of the parallelisms between the grounds and nature of democratic and liberal rights, there is reason to impose restrictions on antiliberal legislation.[17]

With regard to the abolition of democracy, such an action cannot be *defensible* in a way that is consistent with the fundamental principle behind allowing people to have a say when there is disagreement on matters of substantive justice. Since the basic principle behind democracy is nonreflexive, democratic exercises of power may not undermine its realization. The parallelism between liberal and democratic rights noted by Waldron is underscored in this book by the argument that the basic principle that underwrites democracy also grounds liberal rights. But then the principle that underpins democracy makes it indefensible to undermine at least the basic components of liberal rights. Such actions are normatively incoherent in the same way that actions designed to undermine democracy are.[18]

In sum, there is in principle a way to justify constitutional courts in a democratic society on the basis of the very principles that underpin democracy. Such a justification must sustain a high burden of proof, however, in the light of the nondemocratic character of constitutional courts. Nevertheless, we must reject the views of those who have argued that constitutional courts are incompatible with democracy or the principles that ground it.

THE PROBLEM OF PERSISTENT MINORITIES

The final kind of defect in the authority of a democracy is the problem of persistent minorities. The idea that the democratic process confers legitimacy on the outcomes of the decision-making process faces an important challenge

[17] Limitations on the reflexivity of the principle of respect for judgment state that some judgments about the principle are not to be accorded respect. This implies only that the effective exercise of power in accordance with them is not permitted; it does not imply rejection of the free expression of these judgments. Or so I have argued in the above.

[18] We must distinguish between the *conceptual coherence* of a democracy voting itself out of existence or disenfranchising a minority of its members and the question of *the normative coherence* of such an action. There is no inconsistency in the idea that a democracy destroys itself. But if a democracy decides on legislation that is inconsistent with the fundamental principle that makes democracy desirable, there is some normative incoherence in this.

from one of the common pathologies of the democratic process. This challenge arises from the fact that democratic processes can bring about the existence of persistent minorities in the collective decision-making process. Some of the clearer cases of persistent minorities in recent times are the cases of indigenous peoples in many states throughout the world.

Here is a kind of ideal typical description of some of the common features of these cases. They are societies where there are (a) a number of social groups which differ from each other in a highly salient way, from the points of view of the members. There may be a plurality of religious groups (as in the Netherlands in the early twentieth century) or ethnic groups (as in Northern Ireland and Lebanon) or perhaps different political groups (as in Austria) or even linguistic groups (as in Belgium or Switzerland). (b) These differences are global in that they have significance for a wide variety of issues. (c) The preferences conflict in a way that compromise is necessary if both groups are to get some of what they want. (d) One group or combination of groups is considerably larger than the others so that it may be able to dominate in majority rule without compromise with any of the others. The consequence, in some cases, has been that the majority has attempted to dominate over the minority groups.

Obviously the concept of a persistent minority is a kind of idealization. Many such conflicts exhibit features which do not fit entirely neatly into the basic concept. For instance, indigenous peoples often do not want to have much to do with the states of which they are members. They want to minimize their interactions. In part this is because they find that they cannot get much of what they prefer out of the system of collective decision-making because they are a minority. In part it is because they simply do not think the rest of the society has much to offer them and thus they disagree as to the interdependence of interests. They do not seek compromise all the time, sometimes they wish to simply be left to themselves. This desire for autonomy on its own brings separate problems which I do not treat here.

PERSISTENT MINORITY AND MAJORITY TYRANNY

It is important to note a distinction between some of these cases. Some of them, such as Northern Ireland, are cases where one group has sought to dispossess the minority of its civil and political rights as well as its fair share of economic resources in the society. The minority has been unable to procure any reasonable share of the material resources at the disposition of the state. Its members' civil rights have been trampled on. Its rights of participation in the political process have been violated. These are cases of majority tyranny in addition to persistent minority. Though these violations of civil, political, and economic rights are sometimes a consequence of the kinds of social cleavages I mentioned above, they ought to be kept analytically distinct from the problem of persistent minority status. The case of majority tyranny involves a disregard for the rights of the minority or even an explicit attempt to dispossess the minority of those rights. The majority knows that the minority is being mistreated but does not care or actively endorses this mistreatment. Or the majority simply treats the minority in accordance with different standards altogether, which are suitable to an inferior group of people. The majority in some sense rejects the claims the minority has to equal consideration of interests or to being able to make the determinations about where their interests lie. Thus the majority acts either out of contempt for the minority's interests or out of contempt for the minority's understanding of its own interests. I have dealt with the problem of majority tyranny in my discussion of the democratic and liberal limits to democratic authority so I will say little more about it here.

By contrast, in the case of the pure problem of persistent minorities the problem is that the minority rarely gets its way on any of the properties of the common world it shares with the majority. It suffers from a kind of global alienation from the political process. Its members live in a world they do not really understand or recognize and which is not suited to their conception of social life. Nevertheless, this may not result from any tyrannous action on the part of the majority. The majority need not deprive the minority of its right to participate or its liberal rights or even its right to an economic minimum, it treats the minority in accordance with its considered judgment about what is just and unjust. Since it is the majority, its conception of justice as well as its conception of how to organize social relations and the cultural goods holds sway. By its lights it does not treat the minority unjustly or any differently from the way it treats itself. The majority may act in good faith in this context.

Now in the highly idealized and simplified cases of conflict and disagreement where there are two alternatives and a collective decision between them is to be made by an odd number of persons, majority rule is required by equality in the process of collective decision-making. It is the only rule in these contexts which satisfies two essential ingredients of equality. The rule is anonymous and it is neutral. It is anonymous when the same collective decisions result before and after any two people who vote in opposite ways switch their votes. This just shows that no one's vote is different in effect from anyone else's. It is neutral when no interests or points of view are favored in the group. Majority rule is neutral while unanimity rule is nonneutral, the latter favors the interests of the status quo or whatever default position there is when there is no consensus. Anonymity and neutrality are essential ingredients of equality. Therefore majority rule is intrinsically just under certain highly simplified circumstances.[19] In fact this conclusion will have to be qualified once we have taken account of the problem of persistent minorities.

Unfortunately these highly simplified circumstances are compatible with cases of persistent minorities. If a group uses majority rule repeatedly to decide issues over which there is disagreement among its members, there is a chance that a minority subgroup may lose in all (or nearly all) iterations of the rule. And if we include uses of the rule to amend legislation and determine the agenda, we can see that a group that rarely or ever gets its way is going to be highly alienated from the society of which they are a part. This seems unjust to most people as well as to me. "Rarely getting its way" is to be understood as rarely winning in any of the contexts in which majority rule is used. In effect, its preferences over legislation and policy will be always rejected in favor of a majority group. Here preferences are reasonable proxies for interests inasmuch as individuals have significant interests in having their preferences respected. Or so I have argued in Chapters 2 and 3. And individuals are more likely to have a good understanding of their own interests than others are. Thus rarely getting one's preferences satisfied will often imply rarely having those particular interests satisfied.

The theoretical problem that this raises is that it suggests that if the distribution of winnings is skewed in some way, then the process ought to be changed so as to achieve a more reasonable distribution of winnings. But this might appear to imply that equality in the process does not matter in and of itself. The democratic process is defensible on this account, it appears, only to the extent that it can produce certain outcomes. Thus if dictatorial methods are more likely to bring about the appropriate distribution of preference satisfaction, then they are better. Hence, we have a challenge to the intrinsic justice of democratic principles.

To sum up here, the challenge of the injustice of persistent minority status is quite deep since the foundation of democratic equality is a principle of equal advancement of the interests individuals have in shaping their lives in common. Individuals have conflicting interests in how their common lives are to be organized. Democracy provides a publicly fair means by which to resolve these conflicts by giving each equal resources in determining the outcomes of collective decision-making about their common life. In simple cases of collective decision-making this will involve giving each a vote and deciding by majority rule. But this equality is compatible with some minority never

---

[19] See Thomas Christiano, "Political Equality," *NOMOS XXXII: Majorities and Minorities* eds. John Chapman and Alan Wertheimer (New York: New York University Press, 1990), for this argument. The conditions of anonymity and neutrality and the proof that only majority rule can satisfy them under the simplified conditions were given by Kenneth May, "A Set of Independent Necessary and Sufficient Conditions for Simple Majority Decision," *Econometrica*, vol. 20 (1952), pp. 680–684.

or rarely getting its way. In these circumstances the minority does not have its interests in the common features of their society realized at all. It appears then that the principle of equal advancement of interests and the principles of democratic equality supposedly founded on it are on a collision course.

THREE OUTCOME STANDARDS

But let us explore this issue a bit more closely. There are a number of possible outcome standards that might be violated by the existence of persistent minorities. Three different outcome principles might be violated by the existence of persistent minorities. The first is the *equal preference satisfaction view*. This states that each person's preference with regard to the outcome of collective decision-making ought to be satisfied to an equal extent. This is the most extreme principle. Suppose we have three groups, A, B, and C. A and B agree on everything so they are really a persistent coalition. C is in the minority. Suppose we have issues x_1-y_1, x_2-y_2, $x_3-y_3 \ldots x_n-y_n$ that arise for voting and A and B consistently support x_i, while C supports y_i. This is a case of a persistent minority. Let us suppose further that the issues are not complementary and the preferences of A, B, and C are of equal intensity to each other as well as on each issue. How does the equal satisfaction principle work here? It states that C ought to have what she wants $n/2$ times while A and B ought each to have $n/2$ times what they want. Thus, they would each get satisfaction equal to each other.

If there were three such highly distinct groups of different size, then under the same assumptions as above, the equal satisfaction view would require that each won $n/3$ times on the issues. Such an outcome could be achieved in the long run by means of a lottery wherein each alternative had an equal chance of winning. If we relax the assumptions of sameness of intensity across persons and across issues, then we would need a complex system of interpersonal comparisons of utility in order to ensure overall equality of satisfaction. We would have even more difficulty if we relaxed the assumptions of noncomplementarity among the alternatives.

It is quite clear how the principle could be used to criticize the existence of persistent minorities. In those cases some are getting very little satisfaction of their preferences in the collective decision-making. It is also clear how this principle might be thought to be intimately related to equal advancement of interests. If the preferences that are not being satisfied are thought to be good proxies for the interests of the members of the minority, then we might have good reason to believe that equal preference satisfaction would be implied by equal advancement of interests. But the consequence of having such a principle would certainly be a thoroughly instrumentalist account of democracy and possibly require a number of nondemocratic institutions. Hence, if this is our standard, then the intrinsic defense of democracy would in effect collapse.

A similar claim might hold for *the proportional preference satisfaction view.* This view states that a person's preferences should be satisfied in proportion to the average size of the coalitions in which he belongs. Hence, in the example above, the idea is that A and B ought to have their preferences satisfied about $2n/3$ times and C ought to have hers satisfied $n/3$ times. This principle is less egalitarian in terms of outcome and it can be given more than one interpretation. A strong interpretation would require that outcomes accord only with the proportional principle. A weaker interpretation would require that outcomes accord at least with the proportional principle but that they may also accord with the egalitarian principle and any standard between them. On the weak principle, C should get anywhere between $n/3$ and $n/2$ of total preference satisfaction.

The strong proportional principle, like the egalitarian one, is a pure outcome principle that leaves virtually no room for the democratic process. The weaker principle, inasmuch as it is partly indeterminate, leaves room that can be determined by democratic procedures. Hence, it is not entirely in conflict with the procedural values in democracy. We might say that it is important that the democratic process be used as long as the outcomes fall within a certain range.

The third possible outcome standard might be a minimum preference satisfaction standard. Such a standard identifies a minimum level of preference satisfaction beneath which it would be unjust to permit a person or group to fall. This minimum would be a threshold. This standard is the easiest to satisfy and is the one least in conflict with the procedural values of the democratic process. It simply imposes a constraint on the democratic process without providing a fully outcome oriented view of the evaluation. At the same time it is sufficient to criticize the cases above.

SOME DIFFERENT SOLUTIONS TO THE PROBLEM OF PERSISTENT MINORITIES

Now that these three outcome standards have been identified we can discuss some theoretical solutions to the problem of persistent minorities. I will discuss three general categories of solutions one might have. There are the proceduralist–instrumentalist view, the outcome view, and the moderate proceduralist view.

The purely proceduralist view simply states that it does not matter if some get none of the outcomes they prefer. What matters is that they have the resources distributed to them by a principle of fair distribution of resources. Those who fail to procure what they prefer are not treated unjustly, but they are unlucky. Hence, persistent minorities have nothing to complain about.

To be sure, a proceduralist might argue that it is likely that persistent minorities are being unjustly treated in some straightforward way. Not only are they deprived of seeing their interests in collective features of society realized, they are also vulnerable to violations of civil, political, or economic rights by the majority. Such a response would argue that though the absence of satisfaction of minority interests in the collective features of the society provides no basis of complaint, the injustices which are likely to accompany such a minority weakness merit attention. The account of the limits to democratic authority that I have provided above would be sufficient on this account to ensure public equality. In this respect some method for ensuring at least a minimum of effective input would be desirable. Thus despite the view that little or no preference satisfaction in collective decision-making is not an injustice in the absence of violations of democratic or liberal or economic rights, the proceduralist may argue that rectifying some aspects of minority status can be justified in terms of protecting civil, economic, and political rights. The proceduralist view is supplemented by an *instrumentalist* approach which may justify restrictions on the democratic process for the sake of the protection of other rights. Such a view argues that the only problem behind permanent minority status is the problem of the tyranny of the majority.

The position opposite to the pure proceduralist/instrumentalist view is the *outcome view*. It assigns intrinsic value to one of the outcome standards and assigns no intrinsic value to the democratic process. The outcomes are distributions of preference satisfaction per se and there are four of them. Strictly speaking, only the strong proportional and equal preference satisfaction views are pure outcome views which threaten the legitimacy of democratic equality. Only they impose such stringent requirements on outcomes as to effectively rule out any separate role for democratic process.

CRITICISM OF THE PURE OUTCOME VIEWS

The problem with the proportional and egalitarian outcome views is that they run afoul of the characteristic problems of political societies that are part of the ground of democracy. They appear to be reasonable interpretations of the principle of equal advancement of interests but upon closer inspection they are not. I have argued that we cannot assume equal or proportional preference satisfaction views because we cannot make publicly clear sense of the comparisons that must be made in order to sustain them. There is too little information about the alternatives and their comparisons and there is a great deal of disagreement as to how they should be compared.

Egalitarian institutions must not only bring about or be egalitarian by some standard, they must be seen to be egalitarian by each of the members. Each member of an egalitarian society has fundamental interests in the equal advancement of their interests being manifest to themselves and to everyone. Equality cannot be publicly embodied with the use of the inscrutable standard of equality in well-being or preference satisfaction for the various reasons spelled out in Chapters 2 and 3.

But there is some reasonable chance that public equality can arise as a consequence of the implementation of equality in the process of collective decision-making. That each person has a vote, has adequate means to acquire understanding of their interests, and has the means for discussing with others their ideals and interests and making coalitions with others as well as getting equal representation in a legislature is a publicly manifest phenomenon. Without such manifest equality citizens cannot be assured that they are being treated as equals in an egalitarian society. This is why I argued that democracy is required by the principle of the public realization of equal advancement of interests.

From these considerations it is clear that equal advancement of interests in collective decision-making cannot be understood in terms of one of the outcome standards we discussed above. The only reasonable implementation of such a principle must be in the equal distribution of resources for making collective decisions. Such a distribution permits each of its members the chance to enhance their understanding of their interests as well as justice and to advance those interests in a way that is consistent with public equality.

MODERATE PROCEDURALISM

Now that we have rejected the pure outcome solution let us return to the pure proceduralist solution outlined above, which implies that permanent minorities have nothing to complain about. It claims that as long as the resources for affecting the process of collective decision-making are equally distributed, justice has been served for all parties. Thus as long as individuals have equal shares in the resources for acquiring information, for participating in discussion, for making coalitions as well as equal voting power, they are being treated justly. If permanent minorities arise out of this process, then they must resign themselves to their fates.

I have argued that public equality grounds democratic decision-making and it grounds limits to democratic decision-making. I have argued that democratic and liberal rights and the guarantee of an economic minimum are the bases of limits to democratic authority that are grounded in public equality. Here I want to add the need for a remedy to permanent minorities to that list of limits.

In my view this pure proceduralist view does not take sufficiently seriously the very interests that individuals have in having a say in their society, which can be set back when a group of persons are a persistent minority. They can be set back even when the majority is not attempting to exploit or injure the minority. The interests in playing a role in shaping the common world are important and provide part of the basis for our concern for democratic equality.

In Chapter 3, I argued that against the background of disagreement, diversity, fallibility, and cognitive bias, individuals have interests in correcting for that cognitive bias in the structuring of society. They also have interests in being at home in the world they live in. And they have interests in learning the truth about justice and their interests. Finally, they have interests in being recognized and affirmed as equals in the society of which they are a part. Our conception of the justice of a collective decision-making process is grounded in these interests. So even though the proceduralist is right that we cannot publicly define a clear outcone standard of justice by reference to these interests, they ought to be taken into consideration at least in contexts where they can clearly be seen to be ignored.

The fact is that we can clearly see in the cases of persistent minorities that those interests that ground the democratic rights are receiving less attention. These circumstances are different from the usual circumstance where it is difficult to compare how well people are doing. Here one group is getting very little if anything of what it desires. This permits us to make crude comparisons between their well-being and that of others. Clearly, if a group never or almost never has its way in the process of collective decision-making then it will not be able to provide a corrective to the cognitive bias of the majority in making the laws. They will not be able to make the larger world it lives in a home for themselves. And since other citizens will experience no need to listen to their ideas about justice and well-being, they will not learn much from the democratic process. Finally, since they can see that these interests are being neglected by the democratic process, they will have reason to think that they are not being treated as equals by the society at large. So they will not have their equal status recognized and affirmed.

This gives an important explanation why we think that the existence of persistent minorities is a problem. In such cases, we know that certain interests of great significance are not being satisfied. It may be hard or impossible in a publicly clear way to say the extent to which they are not being satisfied or to compare levels of satisfaction but the extreme deprivation involved with persistent minorities is not unclear. We know enough to have good reason to believe that the principle of equal advancement of interests is not being satisfied even if resources for collective decision-making are equally distributed. Thus to ignore such a state of affairs in the way the pure proceduralist recommends is unreasonable. Such a state of affairs is incompatible with public equality.

Contrast this situation with a society in which there is significant rotation in and out of the majority because there are crosscutting cleavages within the population. In this latter case, we know that each of the groups in the society is getting some of what it wants. We may not have enough knowledge to know who is getting the better of the arrangement because we do not have the kinds of information necessary to make this kind of comparison. In this context, the fact that decisions are made by majority rule in a reasonably egalitarian collective decision-making process is sufficient to legitimate those decisions, as long as they do not violate liberal or democratic rights. There could be no stronger publicly available standard with which to evaluate the arrangement.

In the light of these remarks, some minimum outcome standard may provide some guidance since it does not require the same kind of precision as the other outcome standards. The *minimum* outcome standard specifies that a group of people is being treated unjustly when its interests are not being satisfied above some threshold. The case of permanent minorities seems to be a case where individuals' interests in collective properties are not being satisfied sufficiently to meet the threshold requirement.

The minimum outcome standard is a way of acknowledging and attempting to explain the problem of minority status without invoking standards which are simply beyond the reach of political institutions. As in the case of the argument for the economic minimum, the minimum outcome standard respects a large range of disagreements while at the same time it takes account of the fundamental interests that are set back by permanent minority status. It does not provide a complete way to evaluate the outcomes of democratic processes in that satisfaction of the minimum standard is compatible with many different kinds of outcomes. Thus the minimum outcome standard is compatible with the basic intrinsic value of the democratic process. It merely places another limit on the outcomes that can be produced by the democratic process. It says that outcomes which fail to satisfy the minimum are publicly unjust.

These outcomes are clear public failures to satisfy the basic interests that underpin democracy. Hence, they are violations of public equality. Beyond that standard, it says nothing. This leaves room for the democratic process itself to legitimate many outcomes on its own. Thus, equality of resources in the collective decision-making process limited by a minimum standard for interests satisfaction seems to be the most reasonable principle for evaluating the collective decision-making process. This view follows from what I call *moderate proceduralism.*

Thus moderate proceduralism implies that the democratic process has intrinsic value but it recognizes limits beyond which some restraints must be placed on the process in order to accommodate a minimum of the interests which are at the foundation of the ideals of democracy. In addition to recognizing the instrumental value of certain constraints on democratic decision-making the moderate proceduralist also argues that at times, there is intrinsic worth to limiting the democratic process so as to protect the basic interests in collective properties of society.

Just like with the other limits to democratic authority, the need to avoid the creation of permanent minorities is a further requirement of public equality. The minimum outcome standard is a way to satisfy the requirement of public equality in collective decision-making while avoiding a state of affairs that is clearly inconsistent with public equality.

Notice that the minimum outcome standard is not sufficient for the public realization of public equality. So if a dictatorship attempted to realize the minimum outcome standard without instituting democracy, this would be a clear violation of public equality. The reason for this would be that it would be clear that above the minimum threshold certain interests were given priority, namely those interests associated with the class, religious, or ethnic group that supports the dictatorship.

A variety of procedural constraints have been discussed as means for mitigating permanent minority status. The separation of powers, or the use of bicameral legislatures or some form of federalism, or even some form of consociational decision-making, wherein executive and legislative decision-making must be done in a supermajoritarian way, may be used in this context to make sure that the minority has a say on some important matters.[20] Other methods are also possible such as requiring that candidates for elective office receive quotas of votes from some of the different groups in conflict or that party slates be ethnically mixed. Such devices have been

---

[20] See Arend Lijphart, *Democracies* (New Haven: Yale University Press, 1984), for a discussion of some of these institutional mechanisms. But see also Brian Barry, "The Consociational Model and Its Dangers," in *Democracy and Power: Essays in Political Theory I* (New York: Oxford University Press, 1992), pp. 136–155 and 153, for a more skeptical view.

tried with mixed success in a number of different countries, but they curtail equality in the process to some extent.[21] The first set of requirements tend toward a kind of unanimity rule while the second kind limit the agenda setting powers of the people implied by democratic equality. They do so however, not because they show that equality in the political process is not an important political value but because equality in the political process must be limited by considerations that stem from the same principles as political equality. They serve a remedial role in political decision-making much like affirmative action programs are supposed to serve in the United States. In some cases, the devices have been abandoned as a result of their successful use. Hence, the proceduralist can retain an egalitarian and resourcist view of the political process while justifying modifications so as to ensure other desirable qualities we look for in a political society.

THE CONDITIONAL NATURE OF THE JUSTICE OF DEMOCRACY

One question we might ask about the account I have given of the limits of the authority of democracy is whether it does not undermine the idea that democratic rights are intrinsically justified. In a sense, some outcomes defeat the intrinsic justice of democracy. They do not merely override the justice of democracy, they undermine the intrinsic justice altogether. Does this undermine the idea that democracy is intrinsically fair? The answer is no. First of all, on this account democratic decision-making retains its justice even when many of the outcomes are unjust. It legitimates those outcomes by the fact that they originate in fair procedures. Hence, even if overall we could say that the democracy was producing overall unjust outcomes, they would still be legitimate. Second, what the argument for the limits of the authority of democracy shows is that the justice of democracy is *conditional* on the realization of public equality but it is certainly not merely instrumental to the realization of public equality. Democracy, when it does not violate public equality, embodies public equality. Its justice is conditional on certain basic facts accompanying democratic process but its justice is not a mere instrument to the realization of those facts.[22]

---

[21] See Donald Horowitz, *A Democratic South Africa? Constitutional Engineering in a Divided Society* (Cape Town: Oxford University Press, 1991), p. 184.

[22] See Christine Korsgaard, "Two Distinctions in Goodness," in her *Creating the Kingdom of Ends* (Cambridge: Cambridge University Press, 1996), for the distinction between instrumental goodness and conditional goodness.

   To conclude, this argument shows that the way democracy loses its authority is by losing its intrinsic justice altogether. The democratic assembly simply does not have a moral right to violate the requirements of public equality or even to neglect them when it can do something to satisfy them. To the extent that democratic rights generally embody public equality, and basic liberal rights embody public equality, no one has a moral right to undermine democratic rights or the basic liberal rights of any of the citizens. The authority is lost because the right is lost altogether. Furthermore, when the democratic assembly neglects to do what it can to assure that the liberal and democratic rights of persons are protected and each has an economic minimum, its authority is to that extent weakened. And finally, to the extent that a democratic assembly is ruled by a permanent majority, its authority is similarly weakened as a result of the violation of public equality. These ideas provide not only the foundation for a conception of democratic authority but they also provide for the elements of a conception of constitutional limits on democratic power.

Index

Adams, Robert 19
Amar, Akil 284
agenda setting 111, 198, 201
approximations to ideal justice 39–41
Aristotle 117, 185
Arneson, Richard 17, 117, 146
Arrow, Kenneth 112
authority, political, *see* legitimate authority

background facts of judgment 56–60, 70, 78,
    88, 101, 112, 115, 119, 125, 154, 182,
    200, 233, 265, 271
  cognitive bias 58–60
  disagreement 59–63, 76, 112–16, 119
  diversity 56–7, 59
  fallibility of judgment 57–8
Barry, Brian 298
Beran, Harry 239
blasphemy 162–5, 173–6
Brandeis, Louis 161
Blumberg, Herbert 195
Brighouse, Harry 96
Buchanan, Allen 243, 249

Carritt, E. F. 22
Casal, Paula 30
Chan, Joseph 156
choice-insensitive principles 86–7
Christman, John 25
circularity Objection 121–2
circumstances of egalitarian justice 29
Clayton, Matthew 252
cognitive conditions of effective
    citizenship 197–8
Cohen, G. A. 25, 31, 58, 221
Cohen, Joshua 157, 168, 203–30, 263
common world 78–83
competence for citizenship 116–30
  distinction between different kinds of
    competence 120
  equal rights of citizens to judge 126–8
  minimum threshold of 128–9, 185
  maximum threshold of 185
  tests of competence 118–21
constitutionalism 278, 281–8, 298–300
culture 57, 82

Dahl, Robert 228, 281
Darwall, Stephen 18
De Marneffe, Peter 134
democracy
  argument against intrinsic fairness
    of 117–18
  argument for the intrinsic fairness
    of 88–96
  the priority of democracy over other forms
    of equality 97–100, 251–2
  conception of 102, 246
  the conditional but intrinsic justice of 299
  direct and representative 104–6, 117, 246
  equal political rights 117
  and judicial review 278–86
  the legitimate authority of 243–55
  limits to legitimate authority of 260–300
  parallelism of grounds for liberal rights
    and 189, 271, 288
  and persistent minorities, *see* persistent
    minorities
  and public deliberation 190–230
deliberative democracy, *see* public
    deliberation and reasonableness
desert 42–4
difference principle 23, 40–1
dignity of persons 14–16
Downs, Anthony 112, 282
Dryzek, John 129
Dworkin, Ronald 83, 86, 134, 278

economic minimum, *see* limits to legitimate
    political authority
egalitarian standpoint
  arguments from the egalitarian
    standpoint 71–3
  circularity objection to using it to establish
    equality 121–2
  and differences in competence of
    citizens 118–130
  and inclusive standpoint 122–5
  intrinsic justification 72
  instrumental justification 72
  and original position 70–1
  presupposition of 118
  what it is 69–71

Ely, John Hart 263
epistemic justification
    coherentism 209–11
    skepticism 213
    subjective justification 208
    undefeated justification 209
equal advancement of interests 12, 25, 60–3,
        127, 144, 249
    argument for 14–30
    in argument for equal right to judge
        competence 127
    in argument for public equality 60–3
    average utility and 40
    as constraint on desert principles 44
    as default principle of justice 44
    disruptive interference objection to 13
    feasibility of 37–41
    at the foundation of strong protections of
        liberal rights 167–72
    as ground of democracy 95
    as ground of equal respect for
        judgment 286–8
    as initial condition for desert principles 43
    leveling down objection to 13, 32–42,
        104–6, 172, 187, 253
    role of 30–2
equal moral status of persons 17–18
equal respect 199, 201
equal respect for judgment 285–8
    grounded in equal advancement of
        interests 287
    limited by equal advancement of
        interests 288
    reflexivity of 286
    why it is not fundamental 286
equality of opportunity for welfare 58, 84
equality of resources 58, 83
equality of stakes 80–3
establishment of justice 53–6, 237–9
Estlund, David 93, 104, 108, 121, 253

fair lotteries 108–11
faith, religious 212
Feinberg, Joel 146, 164
Frankfurt, Harry 27, 32
freedom of association 135, 147
    collective interests in 149
    defined 147
    family 148
    friendship 148
    fundamental interests that ground
        147–50
    And sense of self-worth 148

freedom of conscience 138–44
    brainwashing 181–4
    collective interests in 141
    defined 139
    fundamental interests that ground 139–44
    and learning from trial and error 139–41
    public equality and 144
freedom of expression 134–5, 150–4, 165
    collective benefits of 150–1, 176
    fundamental interests in 151–4, 166–7
freedom of private pursuits 144–147 (*see also*
        paternalism and moralism)
    defined 144–5
    fundamental interests that ground 147
freedom of religion 135, 145
Freeman, Samuel 202, 219
fundamental interests in judgment 60–7,
        89–96, 101, 115, 147, 154–5, 166, 182,
        200, 235, 251, 255, 265, 268, 271, 287,
        296
    in the argument for the authority of
        democracy 235, 251, 255
    in argument for democracy 89–96
    in argument for equality in public
        deliberation 200–2
    in argument for equal right to judge
        competence 125
    in argument for liberal rights 141–56
    in the argument for the limits to the
        authority of democracy 265, 268, 271
    in argument for minimum
        competence 128
    in argument for public equality 60–6
    in being at home in the world 61–3, 64–6,
        67, 90–2, 141–2, 147, 148, 152, 177, 201,
        229
    in being recognized and affirmed as an
        equal 63, 64–66, 67, 93, 143, 147, 153,
        177, 201
    in being recognized and affirmed as a
        particular person 148
    in correcting cognitive bias 60–1, 64–6, 67,
        89–90, 142, 147, 149, 152, 176, 200–1
    in learning the truth about interests and
        justice 92–3, 139–41, 147, 149, 151, 176,
        200
    and objectivity of judgments 156
    and persistent minorities 296
    as political interests 64, 94, 155–6

Garret, Geoffrey 82
Gaus, Gerald 206, 210, 220, 221
generic principle of justice 20, 37, 41

Goodin, Robert 129, 146
Gould, Carol 81
Green, Leslie 233, 243
Griffin, Christopher G. 96
Gutmann, Amy 202

Hardimon, Michael 61
Hardin, Russell 112
Hayek, F. H. 258
Hegel, G. W. F. 61, 141, 148
Hobbes, Thomas 112, 157
Horowitz, Donald 228, 299

ideal equality point 38–41
impersonal standpoint 30–2
indigenous peoples 227, 289
instrumentalism 86–8, 117
interests, *see* well-being
intrinsic fairness of democracy 88, 108–11
  (*see also* fair lotteries) 299–300
intrinsic goods 14–19
IQ tests 118

judicial review of legislation, *see* legitimate
  political authority

Kamm, Francis 16
Kant, Immanuel 14, 54, 135
Kohlberg, Lawrence 128
Korsgaard, Christine 299
Kukathas, Chandran 113, 115, 116
Kymlicka, Will 90

Ladenson, Robert 241
Larmore, Charles 216–17
libertarianism 24–5, 112–16
LeBar, Mark 113
legitimate political authority 223, *see also*
  limits to legitimate political authority
consent theory of 237–40
of democracy 243–9
executive, judicial and bureaucratic
  authority in a democratic state 255–9
the grounds of democracy's 249–55
internal and external 249
of judicial review of legislation 258,
  278–86
legislative authority 245
and moral necessity of the state 237–9
and moral importance of disagreement
  among equals 235
normal justification thesis 232–6
and requirement of minimal justice 233–4

requirements of an account of 232, 255
the right to rule 241–3
the right to rule of the democratic assembly
  as the pooled equal rights of citizens to a
  say in legislation 247–8, 250
three concepts of 240–3
Lehrer, Keith 210
Levy, Leonard 163
liberal rights (*see also* freedom of association,
  freedom of conscience, freedom of
  expression and freedom of private
  pursuits)
antiliberal equalities 186–8
conditions under which they may be
  restricted 179–80
costs of (or interests at risk from) 157, 167
  (*see also* blasphemy and pornography)
core of 165–7
desiderata of a conception of 131
difference between democratic rights
  and 282–3
grounded in interests 136, 138
interest based and deontological aspects
  of 132
of the intolerant 176–80, 269–70
and inviolability 136–8
as limits to the authority of
  democracy 271–2
maximum threshold of competence for
  liberal rights is necessary 184–6
minimum threshold of competence for
  liberal rights is necessary 185
mutually reinforcing package of
  rights 153–4, 159
parallelism of grounds for democracy
  and 189, 271, 288
private protective function of 159–61, 166
protecting unconsented to exercises of
  power over others 134
public protective function of 161–2, 167,
  177, 179
as restrictions on reasons for action 134
and self-regarding actions 133
similarity of nature with democratic
  rights 282–3
as spheres of activity 133–6
strong protections grounded in public
  equality 167–72
trust and distrust of persons with liberal
  rights 283
undefeated preeminence of interests
  in 158–65
Lijphart, Arend 228, 298

limits to legitimate political authority
  basic argument for 264–5
  countervailing limits 262, 265–6
  definition 261
  democratic rights as 266–70
  economic minimum as 272–4
  external limits 262
  internal limits 263
  judicial review and 278–86
  liberal rights as 271–2
  main premise in the argument for 266–7
  and persistent minorities, *see* persistent
    minorities
  undercutting limits 262
Locke, John 54, 135, 162, 165, 174, 257,
  277

majority rule 103–4, 290
Manin, Bernard 193
May, Kenneth 290
Meiklejohn, Alexander 263
Mill, John Stuart 117, 119, 135, 140, 143,
  145, 147, 150, 179, 193, 194
Miller, David 27, 219
moralism 145–6
Morris, Christopher 243, 255
multiculturalism 172

Nagel, Thomas 16, 31, 136–8, 143, 212
Narveson, Jan 32
nationality 82
Nozick, Robert 25, 112

ought implies can 36

Pareto optimality 36–42
Parfit, Derek 32
paternalism 145–6
persistent minorities 226–8, 288–99
  different from majority tyranny 289–90
  minimum outcome standard as limit of
    authority of democracy 297–8
  moderate proceduralism 295–9
  a problem from the standpoint of public
    equality 296–8
  a theoretical problem for a theory of
    democracy 291
Pettit, Philip 14
Plato 117
Pogge, Thomas 81
political equality 105, 106–11, 127–8
Pollock, John 262
pornography 178

principle of propriety 20
productivity 42–4
property rights 53–6, 112–13
public deliberation (*see also* cognitive
    conditions for effective citizenship,
    agenda setting, and equal respect)
  arguments for wide conception 208–14,
    218–23, 224–6
  equality in 197–200
  grounded in public equality 200–2
  grounds of equality in 200–2
  importance of public deliberation 192–202
  instrumental value of 192–7
  narrow conception of 191, 202–6
  and principle of reasonableness 202–5
  wide conception of 190, 197–200, 224,
    229
public equality 70
  and democratic authority 164
  and economic minimum 273–4
  and equal respect for judgment 287
  importance of 63–7, 251–2
  and intrinsic fairness of democracy 88–96,
    296
  and judicial review 278–86
  and legitimate authority of
    democracy 236, 249–55
  and libertarianism 112–16
  and liberal rights as trumps 144, 150, 153,
    164, 167–72, 271
  and limits to the legitimate authority of
    democracy 260–74, 296
  and persistent minorities, *see* persistent
    minorities
  and public deliberation 191
  and the rule of law 172–76
  and unequal competence for
    citizenship 116–30 (*see also* competence
    for citizenship)
  and unilateral disobedience 253–5
  violations of 104, 265
publicity 47–68
  argument for publicity 56–68
  comparison with voluntariness 52
  the egalitarian standpoint 69–74
  impossibility of full publicity 68, 73
  interests in 60–6
  in the law 48–51
  the nature of 47–53
  and social justice 51–68
  when it matters 53–6
public justification, *see* reasonableness,
    principle of

public realization of equality 70, 87
  democracy as 78–100
  liberal rights as 167–72

Rainbolt, George 93
Rawls, John 23, 40, 48, 68, 70, 143, 165, 179,
  197, 204, 206, 212, 214, 217, 219, 227,
  230, 239, 286
Raz, Joseph 19, 53, 54, 232–7, 252
reasonableness, principle of 202–5
  the deliberative impasse 218–21
  democratic argument for 223–30
  and equality 224–6, 229
  epistemological arguments for 206–15, *see
    also* epistemic justification
  moral argument for 215–23
  and neutral baseline for justification 220–1
  and overlapping consensus 218–20
  and persistent minorities 226–8
reasonable pluralism 203
reciprocity, criterion of 203, 287
relevant differences 24–5
Richards, David A. J. 163
Richardson, Henry 246, 257
Rousseau, Jean-Jacques 193
rule of law 55, 172–6

Scanlon, Thomas 134, 135, 137, 157
Schumpeter, Joseph 282
Schwarz, John 274

self-interest 19
Sen, Amartya 100
Simmons, A. John 237, 239, 250
Smith, Holly 108
social justice 47
sufficiency 26–30
Sunstein, Cass 193, 195
Supreme Court of the United States 135, 281

Temkin, Larry 33
Ten, C. L. 144
Thompson, Dennis 202
Tushnet, Mark 281
tyranny of the majority 103–4

utilitarianism 22

Van Parijs, Philippe 106
voluntary associations 91

Waldron, Jeremy 17, 87, 281–6
Wall, Steven 234
Walzer, Michael 61
well-being 18–19, 56–7, 61–6, 120, 159, 271
  And interests 106
Wenar, Leif 137, 214
Williams, Bernard 233
Wolff, Robert Paul 245

Zolo, Danilo 258

Lightning Source UK Ltd.
Milton Keynes UK
UKHW022137280519
343484UK00003B/136/P